THIS AMERICA
OF OURS

To Merilee and Bob
With warmest wishes

Doris & Elizabeth

December 2003

THIS AMERICA OF OURS

The Letters of
Gabriela Mistral and
Victoria Ocampo

EDITED AND TRANSLATED BY

ELIZABETH HORAN

AND DORIS MEYER

University of Texas Press

Austin

Letters by Gabriela Mistral from Victoria Ocampo Papers, shelf mark *MS Span 117* (525), published by permission of the Houghton Library, Harvard University.

Correspondence of Victoria Ocampo to Gabriela Mistral published by permission of Fundación SUR.

Translation of Victoria Ocampo's essay "Gabriela Mistral en sus cartas" published by permission of Fundación SUR.

Excerpts from *Cartas a Angélica y otros* and *Correspondencia (1939–1978): Victoria Ocampo/Roger Caillois* published by permission of Editorial Sudamericana.

First edition, 2003

Requests for permission to reproduce material from this work should be sent to Permissions, University of Texas Press, Box 7819, Austin, TX 78713-7819.

∞ The paper used in this book meets the minimum requirements of ANSI/NISO Z39.48-1992 (R1997) (Permanence of Paper).

LIBRARY OF CONGRESS CATALOGING-IN-PUBLICATION DATA

Mistral, Gabriela, 1889–1957.
This America of ours : the letters of Gabriela Mistral and Victoria Ocampo / edited and translated by Elizabeth Horan and Doris Meyer.
p.   cm.
Includes bibliographical references and index.
ISBN 0-292-73455-7 (hardcover : alk. paper) —
ISBN 0-292-70540-9 (pbk. : alk. paper)
1. Mistral, Gabriela, 1889–1957 — Correspondence.   2. Ocampo, Victoria, 1890–1979 — Correspondence.   3. Mistral, Gabriela, 1889–1957 — Translations into English.   4. Ocampo, Victoria, 1890–1979 — Translations into English.
5. Authors, Chilean — 20th century — Correspondence.
6. Authors, Argentine — 20th century — Correspondence.   I. Ocampo, Victoria, 1890–1979.   II. Horan, Elizabeth, 1956–   III. Meyer, Doris.   IV. Title.
PQ8097.G6 Z488   2003
860.9'0062 — dc21
2002156526

Contents

Preface

This first publication of an extended collection of letters between two modern Latin American women documents the unpredictably close friendship between Gabriela Mistral (1889-1957) of Chile and Victoria Ocampo (1890-1979) of Argentina. It would be difficult to imagine two writers more dissimilar in background and upbringing, appearance and habit, not to mention literary careers. Yet because of their accomplishments, they shared an anomalous status as celebrities in their own countries and internationally. They were arguably the two most influential women of twentieth-century Latin America if one considers that their influence derived from their own authority, rather than from marriage to famous men (à la Eva Perón or Frida Kahlo).

Despite their differences, they had more than a little in common. Both Mistral and Ocampo lived their adult lives as single women. While their public worlds were principally male, they lived in predominantly female households. They both claimed pride in their Basque heritage, and they took an unorthodox approach to religion. Both were physically imposing women in societies that prized petiteness. In their letters and visits, they shared their love of the open countryside and seashore. Because they led unconventional lives, they were controversial figures, subject to false rumors and mythologies that plagued them all their lives. And to their mutual surprise and delight, they had the same birthday, April seventh, one year apart. This became a touchstone in their letters; no matter where they were living, they sent affectionate messages to one another on that date.

Stubborn and nonconforming, both women described themselves as having "violent" dispositions, which Ocampo would express in explosive bursts of temper and Mistral by reciting accusations of real and imagined wrongs. Both women, above all, felt passionately about distinct aspects of their American condition, which they perceived from a transnational, Latin American perspective. They both cared deeply about fostering spiritual unity and moral purpose among fellow Americans in the context of the continent's truncated modernity. Yet their

priorities did not always mesh: Mistral's emotional defense of indigenous America seemed excessive to Ocampo, and Ocampo's predilec-
tion for European culture struck Mistral as misguided.

They also shared a penchant for letter writing. Each cultivated
hundreds of correspondents, writing up to a dozen letters a day.[1]
Unique to the texts here is the development of an unusual friendship.
Within weeks of their first meeting, Mistral and Ocampo discovered
one another as women charged with writing, exploring, and defining
the American (read Latin American) condition. That absorption in
and engagement with America, expressed throughout their correspondence, arises from the unsettling political, social, and literary events of
their era.

The publication of these letters reveals two women who contributed in many ways to Latin America's emergence onto the world
stage. They write and enact female perspectives and responses to the
Spanish Civil War and to World War II, to dictatorships at home, and
to the Cold War between the superpowers. The Mistral-Ocampo letters testify to the complex interaction of politics and aesthetics in Latin
America, and to the development of Latin American identity in relation to the rest of the world — concerns essential to documenting
twentieth-century intellectual history.

Earlier scholarship has recognized the importance of their correspondence, but the present work is the first to accurately date, tran-
scribe, and publish it in full.[2] In an effort to reach a wider group of interested readers, we have elected to publish their letters in English
translation. We hope that they will also appear in the original Spanish,
especially considering the unique importance of language itself in their
epistolary discussions. Our work as editors in all its facets has been accomplished at long distance from one another through the interactive
capability of computers and our own frequent e-mail correspondence.
Over prior years, each of us had developed expertise in the work of
Mistral (Horan) and Ocampo (Meyer). Our joining forces in this en-
deavor was prompted by the desire to do literary justice to both writers
and to share our own passion for their contributions to Latin American culture.

Many individuals have helped us bring this project to fruition. We
express our profound thanks to Doris Dana, executor of Mistral's literary estate, for her early cooperation with Doris Meyer in the planning
of this project. Also, our appreciation for many kindnesses goes to
María Renée Cura, a close friend and literary associate of Victoria

Ocampo. We also want to acknowledge special assistance from Russ Davidson, curator of Latin American and Iberian collections at the University of New Mexico. Our thanks to the Women's Studies Summer Research Program and the English Department at Arizona State University for a summer research grant, and to Susan Carlile and Jana Carter for several weeks' assistance with typing and background research. To Theresa May, editor in chief of the University of Texas Press, we convey our special thanks for encouraging this project and understanding the various delays entailed in its development. We are also grateful to Carolyn Wylie and Nancy Warrington for their editorial expertise in the final stages of the writing process.

We owe a special debt to Victoria Ocampo for her foresight in preserving the letters sent to her by Mistral, beginning in 1926, before either woman was internationally famous. The extant letters were collected by Fundación SUR and subsequently microfilmed. Those attempting to use the microfilm need to be forewarned that the collection is very loosely, and in many places inaccurately, labeled with regard to places and dates. The Mistral manuscripts, now part of the Victoria Ocampo Papers at the Houghton Library, Harvard University, are published by permission. Ocampo's letters to Mistral are found in the Library of Congress in the Gabriela Mistral Papers (on microfilm), with copies also in the Columbus Memorial Library of the Organization of American States (OAS). Two additional photocopies of Ocampo letters (V.12 and V.34) are in the collection of Doris Meyer. We are indebted to Fundación SUR, in Buenos Aires, Argentina, for permission to publish the correspondence and other pieces by Ocampo.

This has been an exhilarating literary and personal experience for both of us. Working together and learning more about two exceptionally interesting women and the intricacies of their friendship has brought us great satisfaction. We hope other scholars will similarly seek out women's correspondence in Latin America and bring it to light. Epistolary literature is a vital but much neglected source of information and insight into the lives of women, particularly where access to public discourse has been subject to gender restrictions. Gabriela Mistral and Victoria Ocampo were freer than most Latin American women, but they still used the privacy of their letters to treasure their relatedness to one another, to authorize their own American identities, and to construct a corresponding space in which to nurture a better future for their America.

NOTES

1. Gabriela Mistral's published correspondence (listed in our bibliography) includes exchanges with Amado Nervo (ed. Loveluck), Rubén Darío (*Antología mayor: Cartas*), Alfonso Reyes (*Tan de usted*), Joaquín García Monge (*GM y Joaquín García Monge*), Pedro Prado (*En batalla de sencillez*), Eduardo Barrios (*Epistolario*), Eugenio Labarca (*Antología major: Cartas*), Teresa de la Parra and Lydia Cabrera (*Cartas a Lydia Cabrera*), Manuel Magallanes Moure (*Cartas de amor*), and the Errázuriz Echenique and Tomic Errázuriz families (*Vuestra Gabriela*). Many of GM's earliest publications take the form of meditative epistolary prose, and much of her verse names historical recipients in dedications and in titles. An overview of unpublished correspondence received by GM appears in the *Index to GM Papers on Microfilm*.

   Victoria Ocampo sustained epistolary relationships with many individuals throughout her life, beginning with her letters to Delfina Bunge, from 1906 to 1910, which expressed her antipathy to traditional norms of female behavior in Argentina and her longing for intellectual fulfillment. Among her correspondents during her twenties and thirties, the years when she was finding her own voice and expression, were José Ortega y Gasset, Ricardo Güiraldes, Waldo Frank, Alfonso Reyes, María de Maeztu, Hermann Keyserling, Rabindranath Tagore, and Ernest Ansermet. After *Sur* was established, VO met and corresponded at length with dozens of authors and artists in Europe and the Americas, including Aldous Huxley, Anita Loos, Graham Greene, Virginia Woolf, André Malraux, Albert Camus, and André Gide, among others. Her personal collection of correspondence was acquired by the Houghton Library of Harvard University, where it now resides.

   Publications of VO's correspondence to date include exchanges with Alfonso Reyes (*Cartas echadas*), Roger Caillois (*Correspondencia*), Angélica Ocampo (*Cartas a Angélica y otros*), and Alfonso de Obieta, toward the end of her life. Ocampo's essays in *Sur*, along with her *Testimonios* and *Autobiografía*, contain excerpts of letters to/from Bunge, GM, Waldo Frank, José Ortega y Gasset, Rabindranath Tagore, and others.

2. See Meyer, "The Correspondence of GM and VO"; Jurado, "La amistad entre GM y VO"; and Kaminsky, "Essay, Gender, and Mestizaje." An edition that includes selections from letters GM wrote to VO from Spain appeared when our book was in press; see Vargas Saavedra, *Castilla*.

THIS AMERICA
OF OURS

Introduction

A biographical perspective presents immediate, striking differences between Gabriela Mistral and Victoria Ocampo. Mistral (whose given name was Lucila Godoy Alcayaga)[1] was born into a middle-class family in a provincial town in the Chilean Andes, 400 kilometers north of the capital city. She pushed her way out of poverty and obscurity through publishing poetry and a range of teaching materials for use in schools. Her formal education ended shortly after she turned thirteen. By age fifteen, she was working as a schoolteacher to support herself and her mother, long since abandoned by her father.

Her first publications, which date from this time, appeared in local newspapers: her baroque, melancholic prose poems, like her social commentary, show dissatisfaction with her surroundings and keen interest in art and politics abroad. While teaching at night and working by day as a school secretary, the young writer passed equivalency exams qualifying her for various full-time positions in public schools throughout provincial Chile. The poetry that brought her fame through a national competition in 1914 gave a boost to her pedagogical career, culminating in her controversial appointment to direct a prestigious girls' high school in Santiago. Shortly thereafter, Mistral's writings as a poet and her familiarity with rural education led the postrevolutionary government of Mexico to invite her to work for them in 1922–1924.

Collaborating with writers, artists, and educators in postrevolutionary Mexico awakened Gabriela Mistral's awareness of indigenous American peoples. Over the next decades, that awareness became a personal mantra that allowed her to express — amid the nomadism of her own life — emotional identification with the more threatened lands and peoples of the New World. Following her experience in Mexico, Mistral traveled in Europe and then returned to Chile, where she resigned her position in the Chilean school system in 1925.[2] After agreeing to represent Latin America in Europe, serving on a League of Nations subcommittee (the Paris-based Institute for Intellectual Cooperation), she would return to Chile for only two other short visits before her death.

The years of expatriation, from 1925 on, are precisely the portion of Mistral's life that the letters best document. These years have received relatively little attention from scholars, even though Mistral was then publishing as many as ten newspaper essays per month. She was in these years chronicling many aspects of the experience of Latin Americans in Europe, paying particular attention to the books, people, and landscapes that might interest the growing number of women readers in Latin America, especially those who could now begin to consider such travel themselves.

The rootless, vagabond quality of Mistral's early career accelerated with her move from national to international fame. Constant changes of residence enriched the depth and diversity of Mistral's writings, but they also present editorial challenges in assigning dates to her letters (which she rarely did) or in comprehending the scope of her influence (which she habitually underestimated). Clearly, her work as a lower-ranking consul in Chile's foreign service both accommodated and incited Mistral's urge to travel. It was not the consulship, but her lecture tours and journalism that supported her and her dependents. Monetary need forced Mistral to shift from writing poetry to writing what she termed "propaganda" to supplement what she called the consulate's "semi-amusing salaries." In later life, she recognized this squandering of her talents, as she wrote to Ocampo: "I set out to write prose: two hundred articles and more. By now I'm old and, what's more, I realize that *prose* isn't my thing" (G.66, 29 December 1953).

One of Ocampo's great gifts to Mistral was to spur her return to poetry. Mistral acknowledges this effect from early in the relationship, in a letter written from Madrid: "You left in the house, with those who saw you, a tinge of bewitchment. Tinge and all, Victoria, it lasts. Through you, I've understood the mission of the Beatrices, and I've gone back to give prestige to the Muses, which I allowed to fall, like great Myths, years ago" (G.4, 14 March 1935).

Even as she thanked Ocampo for prompting her to resume writing poetry, Mistral (like many other Latin American writers) found herself immersed in the politically charged atmosphere of Spain prior to and during the civil war. The poetry that Mistral wrote in response to that war, plus a compilation of sixteen years of verses, formed a new volume of poetry, *Tala* (Felling Trees), which she presented to Ocampo for publication (G.9, 4 August 1937). Understanding that the proceeds would benefit Basque children driven from their homes and that Mistral would tour to promote the text, Ocampo agreed to print and distribute the text at her own cost. The publication of *Tala* by Ocampo's publishing house, SUR, the most prestigious one in Latin America at the time, brought Mistral the international recognition instrumental to her receiving the 1945 Nobel Prize.

The contradictions and peculiar silences that characterize Mistral's life and work overall are reflected in these letters. Although many who knew her have described Mistral as proud, her letters urge Ocampo to practice humility and self-abnegation. Mistral's counseling of Ocampo in her amorous relationships, as with the Argentine writer Eduardo Mallea, offers some extreme examples: "If patience is something heroic in you, on account of what it costs you, that arduous thing is owed to him; if humility — this is the great thing — humility is what's most *bleedable* in you, that humility with blood and weeping floods, within you, is also owed to him" (G.18, May 1938).³ Such advice favoring humility hardly corresponds to the later Mistral, whom Ocampo describes (in writing to Caillois, see appendix) as being distracted from human contact by her own heartache and despair.

Still more contradictory is Mistral's reputation, gained early on, as a poet of suppressed erotic longing, supposedly sublimated into love for children and the dispossessed peoples of the world. She was often referred to as "la Divina Gabriela" or "Santa Mistral," curiously akin to the cardboard mythologies surrounding Evita Perón in the 1950s. Francisco Ayala is particularly exacting in his criticism of superficial representations of Mistral as a mother figure:

> Gabriela poured out the abundant tenderness of her words onto the humble heads of unfortunate Indians, helpless children, and all the dispossessed of the world. In practice, I never observed her stopping to take note of any child, except for the day when she officially learned of having obtained the Nobel Prize. That day, yes, she came to my house [in Brazil] carrying a heap of clothing directed to needy children and, as usual, she entered — not paying the slightest attention to my daughter, who was, in the end, a privileged girl — and she told me that she had made an appointment with the journalists in the bar of the Copacabana Hotel, whose terrace was visible from my balcony. She had made an appointment with them for 5:30, and a little before, she went down to wait for them. When they arrived, they found her there, surrounded by the flock of noisy, begging children, with two little urchins pulling on her skirt. On the following day, the press registered the scene, with photos and stories. (Ayala, 91)*

*All translatons, unless otherwise noted, are our own.

The poet's public image aside, in private life she had a nephew who lived with her from infancy, Juan Miguel Godoy, known as "Yin Yin." More of the dark and strange circumstances leading up to his death by suicide at age seventeen emerge in these letters. At a time when world events totally preoccupied Mistral, who agonized over the prospective triumph of Fascism and, to a lesser degree, of Communism, such information is useful, given that so much about Yin Yin remains unknown. Mistral's correspondence rarely mentioned him until he became a difficult adolescent in Brazil. During his life she kept his existence something of a secret. Perhaps she found she could only love deeply what she felt was already lost. Whatever the case, Yin Yin's death precipitated an emotional and physical decline in Gabriela Mistral. Even amid that decline, replete with delirium, religious obsessions, and dementia, her letters demonstrate the same condemnation of war, dictatorship, and social injustice that likewise appeared in her poetry of these years, which includes some of her greatest work.

Still another contradiction emerges between the general perception of Mistral as sturdy and monumental, a living statue, a "caryatid in motion,"[4] and the writer's complaints of poor health. Resounding through these letters are problems with her heart, her eyes, and frequent stomach ailments from tropical travel. Most of the health problems she reports proved unrelated to the medical conditions diagnosed when she finally began receiving regular medical care, toward her life's end. The fact that she smoked quite heavily is noted only once in these letters, and nowhere else in any of her published correspondence. Despite her concerns for her heart, untreated diabetes brought her close to blindness. Wasted by illness, her mind alternating between lucidity and delusion, Mistral persisted in her rounds of writing, travel, and public appearances. Such constant activity amid a range of physical ailments rounds out the portrait of the generous yet impossibly demanding woman that emerges from these letters. Pancreatic cancer was responsible for her death in 1957, at sixty-six years of age.

Victoria Ocampo was the oldest of six girls born in the heart of Buenos Aires into a patrician family of successful businessmen and nation builders. She grew up trilingual as a consequence of her traditional home education provided by French and English governesses and lengthy stays in Europe with her family. She read voraciously in these languages, and her self-image was formed under their influence. By the time she was in her teens, however, Ocampo had already devel-

oped an aversion to the values of her social class vis-à-vis women's status, and she determined to resist its dictates. Against the expectation of
a traditional marriage and children, Victoria Ocampo quickly rejected
the callow husband she had married in 1912 in a misguided effort to
gain freedom from parental constraints. Thereafter she had a secret
love affair for many years; since no public separation from her husband
was possible without wounding her family, she never married again.
Eventually, this relationship ended as well, and Ocampo then had a
number of other affairs, often with men much younger than herself.

In her elegant public profile, Ocampo reflected her class and era.
She was strikingly beautiful well into middle age, which was noted
even by her enemies, who used it to mock her.[5] Photos of Ocampo in
her twenties through her fifties show her dressed in couture clothes in
the latest European fashions. A lover of avant-garde music and the
arts, Ocampo chose a modernist design inspired by Le Corbusier for
the first home she built for herself in Buenos Aires in 1927. The total
effect of her bearing and appearance was the very opposite of Mistral's
impromptu style and disregard for formal attire. As often happens
with women of power, Ocampo's beauty, wealth, and cultural sophisti-
cation sparked resentment among those in Argentina who coveted her
privilege while condemning the oligarchy.[6] In fact, under the military
dictatorship of Juan Domingo Perón, Ocampo was persona non grata
in her own country, the complete antithesis of Evita, who dominated
headlines with her defense of the *descamisados*.

Ocampo's preference for French in her earlier writings was consistent with her background and education, as was also the case with
other literary figures of her generation, such as her close friend Ricardo
Güiraldes (author of the definitive gaucho novel *Don Segundo Sombra*).
She did not begin to use Spanish as a literary language until the 1930s,
in response to both the urgings of friends such as Mistral and Waldo
Frank and her own dissatisfaction with translations others did of her
work.

Ocampo's preferred genre was the personal essay, or *testimonio*,
which eventually resulted in more than ten volumes of collected writings. Unlike Mistral, poetry was not Ocampo's medium, although the
first letter in this volume shares with Mistral a long and very subjective
poem that was published under a pseudonym years later. Ocampo's
profound poetic nature, however, is repeatedly expressed in her prose
essays through a kind of "imaginative understanding" based on intu-

ition, not intellect.[7] In fact, Ocampo's constant concern as a writer is to
find unity between the intellect and the spirit, and to bridge cultural as
well as geographic divides. For this objective, the essay's malleability
and its inherent resistance to boundaries of containment made it the
perfect genre for her wide-reaching interests.[8]

Ocampo's true entry into the public sphere followed in part from
her work with *Sur*, the literary magazine she founded in 1931, and, more
broadly, from the death of her parents, whose conservative sensibilities
she had tried not to offend. After 1935, Ocampo became emotionally
and financially independent. It was likewise at this time, in the early
years of *Sur*'s publication, that Ocampo and Mistral developed the
epistolary friendship that began with brief notes in the late 1920s, before they finally met in person in December 1934. The work of founding and directing *Sur*, first as a magazine and later also as a publishing
house, provided Ocampo with a challenging arena in which to exercise
her considerable linguistic, diplomatic, and aesthetic skills. Undaunted
by skeptics, Ocampo seized the initiative and established correspondences with the leading writers and artists of the time, bringing them
and their work into the pages of *Sur*. In the cases of Ernest Ansermet,
Hermann Keyserling, Drieu la Rochelle, and María de Maeztu — to
name just a few — she tendered invitations to Argentina and provided
lodging and public venues for their lectures. Within a short time of its
founding, *Sur* gained a reputation as the leading magazine in Latin
America for writing by both American and European authors. Her
goal was ambitious and remains unparalleled: at the same time as
Ocampo worked to make *Sur* a cultural bridge between continents, it
became a definitive expression of national literary culture, as John
King's comprehensive study indicates.[9]

Within its international cultural orientation, *Sur* reflected Ocampo's
intense concern for America, south and north. Although her original in-
tent was to deal only with American issues, the magazine soon developed a broader focus reflecting the impressive editorial board drawn by
Ocampo from several continents. She often said that internationalism
and ecumenism were wholly compatible with being Argentine. Yet many
of Ocampo's compatriots and other Latin American intellectuals denied
this fact of history and criticized her as an elitist and foreignizer.

Gathering good writing was perhaps the more glamorous part of
the work Ocampo did for *Sur*, but the magazine was a costly venture.
Seeking to increase profits, she started a publishing house of the same
name in 1933. The books she chose to publish were often by foreign

writers (like D. H. Lawrence, William Faulkner, André Malraux, Virginia Woolf, or C. G. Jung) and required translation; this was a task that Ocampo took on herself or contracted with others who worked with *Sur*, such as Jorge Luis Borges, Eduardo Mallea, and Ricardo Baeza. These publications only heightened the criticism from her xenophobic detractors. The populist orientation of Peronism and its repudiation of the upper classes increased tensions between the *Sur* group and Peronist sympathizers. Ocampo denounced the regime and its tactics: her insistence on *Sur's* support for the democratic ideal of free speech is evident throughout these letters, as is the bureaucratic and judicial harassment that she endured in the early 1950s for her refusal to betray that ideal.

Association with Mistral was consistent with Ocampo's desire to build bridges between Europe and the Americas. The fact that Mistral took her seriously also reinforced Ocampo's sense of the fundamental worth of her own work. Mistral's lifelong devotion to biography and letters made her appreciative of Ocampo's essays and memoirs. Mistral was clearly enthusiastic in responding to the autobiographical foundation of Ocampo's work. In a letter following the publication of Ocampo's *Testimonios I* (1935), Mistral begged Ocampo to continue writing her memoirs:

> Finish them, and don't delay very much, because a book, like an angel, passes from your hands if you don't hold on to it. And then go on from *Childhood* to Youth. We who never had you close by feel a furious appetite, which isn't idle curiosity, for your soul and its years, for ranches where we never lived. There's no other way to have you with us and make life without you somehow less wicked and despoiled. (G.5, 7 April 1936)

Ocampo did not seriously turn to finishing her memoirs until 1952. She was called, instead, to political struggle, such as countering the threat to women's civil rights in Argentina, a cause she championed publicly, starting in 1936 when she helped found the Argentine Women's Union. Hostility to the union's demonstrations and pamphlets was widespread, but the organizers persisted despite limited success. The political rights they had also hoped to gain for women would not come until the Perón years, and in that context, with Eva as the model woman, Ocampo withdrew her support. Mistral backed Ocampo's political efforts: she asked, for example, to be signed up as a member of the union (G.8, July/August 1937). Ocampo later said that her friend was not a feminist at the time, but Mistral sensed that her public support of the cause would be useful and thus expressed her solidarity.[10]

Ocampo would outlive Mistral by some twenty years. In that time, she enjoyed at least a portion of the validation she had been denied as a younger woman in the world of letters. Two years before her death in 1979 she was elected to the Argentine Academy of Letters, the first woman to be accorded this honor.[11]

SHARED MISSION

Whether expressed through poetry or letters, Ocampo clearly provided Mistral with more than an avenue to publication. Mistral, whose fascination with America informed much of her writing, recognized in Ocampo from their earliest encounter the embodiment of *criollo* (Latin American born of European ancestors) awareness. She saw Ocampo as someone who, like herself, was drawn to the concept of America as an identity in formation. Shortly after they met, Mistral wrote her new friend an affectionate letter that established another touchstone of the correspondence, which was that Ocampo, for all her unapologetic Eurocentrism, was deeply Latin American: "It's been a tremendous surprise for me to find you so *criolla*," writes Mistral, "as *criolla* as I am, although more refined. What's more, it's been a real joy" (G.3, 9 January 1935).

By exploring American identity, both women were simultaneously constructing self-identities. And each was defining the other in terms of an American experience otherwise distant or unknown to her.[12] Writing from wartime France in April 1939, Mistral expresses this distance in frankly racial terms:

> Votoya, we almost didn't meet one another in this world. You wouldn't have lost anything by it, except for one more bite, just another, from the American corn. But you have done many good things for me: I needed to know, *to know, to know,* that a totally white person *could be a genuine American.* You can't fully understand what that means to me! (G.26, April 1939)

The idea of America, of "*americanidad*" or Americanness, appears in the first real letters they exchange in the 1930s. Unlike the Americanist concerns of their contemporaries in the United States, Mistral and Ocampo wrote from a self-conscious position of otherness as Latin Americans, at once affirming their hemispheric right to define Americanness on their own terms but also aware that their condition as Americans was not only different from but invisible to most writers to the north.[13]

The search for specifically American themes that characterizes Mistral's mature (post-1930) work likewise pervades Ocampo's writings, as well as the pages of *Sur*. Ocampo had already expressed a concern with American identity in her early essays, which were typically inspired by personal experience and her sense of cultural exile as a woman and an Argentine.[14] This need to articulate American identity (which critics have noted in other, male writers of their generation)[15] appears in Ocampo's "Palabras francesas," an essay written in 1931, the same year *Sur* was founded:

> If I hadn't been American, after all, I probably wouldn't have felt this thirst to explain, to explain us and to explain myself. In Europe when something is produced, you could say it is explained beforehand; each event gives the impression of carrying an identity tag from the time it occurs and is appropriately shelved. Here, on the other hand, each thing, each event is suspicious and suspected of being something without precedent. We have to examine it from top to bottom to try to identify it, and sometimes when we try to apply the explanations that analogous cases would receive in Europe, we find that they don't fit.
>
> Then, here we are, obliged to close our eyes and to advance, gropingly and hazardously, toward ourselves; to try to find out to what extent the old explanations can be applied to new problems. We hesitate, stumble, deceive ourselves, tremble, but continue obstinately along. Even though, for now, the results may be mediocre, who cares? Our suffering isn't. And that's what counts. This suffering must be so strong that someday someone feels the urgency to overcome it by explaining it.[16]

Mistral recognized Ocampo's visceral need to express the American experience as rooted in an awareness of geographic as well as linguistic circumstance. Language was one of their great dividing points, however: Ocampo's fluent French and preference for writing in that language for many years irked Mistral, who chided Ocampo for her "linguistic bigamy." Ocampo protested that Mistral was shortsighted regarding language diversity in the Americas, and that her love of French was an authentic part of her multicultural Argentine upbringing, a cultural *mestizaje* that many upper-class Latin Americans experienced, particularly in her generation, and for which she saw no need to apologize. Eventually they both acknowledged that many of their disagreements could be traced to the disparities in their birth and their domestic circumstances.

This sense of otherness in their own relationship is key to Mistral's recognition that her need for Ocampo exceeds Ocampo's for her; life experience caused her to align herself with the downtrodden in a way Ocampo never could. Writing from France, in April of 1939, Mistral acknowledges this:

> Maybe what I miss in you is nothing but a share of common experience. The experience of poverty, of fighting, in blood and mud, with life. There's no remedy for it in this life's journey. In me there's hardness, fanaticism, *ugliness*, that you can't *be aware of*, being unaware as you are of what it's like to chew bare stones for thirty years with a woman's gums, amid a hard people. (G.26, early April 1939)

Mistral's emphasis on her have-not background as a character-shaping factor found no counterpart in Ocampo. Where Mistral saw ceaseless conflict, Ocampo believed simply that, whatever one's background, words and deeds must be in conformity for a person to merit respect.

Although Mistral clearly took liberties in harping on Ocampo, both women understood that their ability to find common ground was crucial to the larger cultural and historical importance of working on behalf of America. Permeating the letters is the drive to define American identity beyond social or national boundaries. Both women regarded this task as a civilizing mission.[17] In an early letter to Ocampo, Mistral speaks of "the American movement," an interest shared by many writers of their generation (G.3, 9 January 1935), such as their friends Waldo Frank, in his message to the Americas in the 1920s and 1930s,[18] and the Mexican philosopher Alfonso Reyes. Both women engaged in a lifelong correspondence with Reyes, who published several of his most Americanist essays in early issues of *Sur*.[19] One might also recognize the best of José Vasconcelos, another Mexican contemporary. Earlier writers such as José Martí (Cuba) and José Enrique Rodó (Uruguay) also shaped these two women's sense of America as an ideal at once transnational, spiritual, and telluric.

Ocampo and Mistral went beyond these latter writers, however, in arguing for an "*americanidad*" that would surpass the limitations of national identities, usually male-defined. As they had often felt foreign when abroad and in their native lands, their notion of America stressed interrelation and international cooperation. Ocampo stressed this mission as cultural bridge building, with what could be called "culture with a C"; Mistral, on the other hand, interpreted it in literature informed by verbal and material folklore.[20]

From the very moment of their first face-to-face meeting, at the end of 1934, their sense of sharing an American mission was crucial to their friendship. Mistral spoke of Ocampo's immense potential to lead the continent toward a superior form of "*americanidad*," discarding the clichéd symbols of "saddle pads and spurs," whereas Ocampo saw that Mistral's passion for America expressed absolute disinterested love:

> Gabriela had no choice. In order to love what she loved, from "the high reaches" as she would say, she had to believe in her heart. Children demand it that way, and poetry too, even the most unreligious kind. And like children as well as poetry, *our America* needs to be loved in the same way. And if we don't love her, her existence, just like a child's, is threatened and almost extinguished. Because the love to which I refer is disinterested love that creates what it loves and helps it to thrive.[21]

Their letters show that they both felt a protective yet frustrating love of Latin America — an orphan child, ignored by the world at large, and in need of nurturing to realize its potential. Ocampo pointed to this protectiveness again in an essay she wrote years later about their correspondence: ". . . what is interesting about them [GM's letters] is to see how Gabriela took everything American (that is, South) to heart and how she was opposed to any flight of capital when she thought that one person or another, for one reason or another, could enrich or serve, intellectually, *this America of ours*."[22] Their experience as women undoubtedly contributed to this attitude of defensive nurturing. It may also have made them more sensitive to the vulnerable and marginalized condition of Latin America in the world context, and thus more determined to confront it repeatedly in their writings.

THE BOND OF CORRESPONDENCE

Mistral and Ocampo inevitably found self-reflections in writing to and about each other. Mistral saw in Ocampo a world of access to books and languages that her own hardscrabble youth had denied her. Likewise, Ocampo regarded Mistral as a connection to a range of experience and identity from which her birth and education had precluded her. Without Ocampo's publication of *Tala*, we would not have Mistral's most definitively Americanist volume.[23] Without Mistral's 1942 portrait of Ocampo (see appendix), we would miss the subtleties of her

Europeanist proclivities. Without this correspondence, we would not know of their political, diplomatic, and cultural collaborations with one another, which touched many people in Europe and the Americas.

Ocampo offered the Chilean poet personal hospitality and valuable introductions to writers and diplomats in both Argentina and Europe. The loyalty that Mistral expressed to Ocampo, by taking her seriously as a writer and encouraging her to write, was a gift few others offered. Mistral additionally defended Ocampo from random charges of Fascism and Communism. By publishing in *Sur*, Mistral undermined the accusations of Eurocentrism and elitism directed at the magazine.

The two women's affective relationship worked on many levels. Mistral's relation with Ocampo began with infatuation and matured into affectionate respect. Ocampo would discuss her relationships with various men over the course of her life, but Mistral was nearly mute on the topic of sexual preference.[24] For Ocampo, the friendship with Mistral was unique because, as women, they shared such a strong Americanist sentiment.[25] That sentiment grew as they worked together, responding to and shaping the political and cultural events of the time.

This conviction, this sense of urgency becomes especially evident following the onset of the Spanish Civil War. Against the backdrop of a Europe destroyed by World War I, whose limitations were evident and whose hegemony was now vulnerable, the war in Spain signaled an ominous wider threat of totalitarianism. In their response as Latin Americans to the European upheavals of the 1930s and 1940s, specifically their rejection of factionalism and militarism at home and their work to establish havens for war refugees in the New World, both women could be described as liberal humanists, as individuals to whom spiritual energy and social justice ultimately mattered more than intellectual ability. Although they each avoided politics per se, they were both overwhelmingly political by the very act of using female voices to challenge the traditional male-centered canon of national discourse in Latin America.

Mistral's tendency to mythologize Ocampo (comparing her, for example, to Diana, Minerva, and the Corn Goddess) probably strained the friendship, once the crisis of war in Europe had passed. Hyperbole or projections of exoticism were all too familiar to Ocampo, who encountered them in her attempts to seek a closer friendship with Virginia Woolf. Although Woolf was a writer with whom Ocampo shared a common commitment to women's rights and the life of the mind, the

English writer couldn't get past her own invention of Ocampo as a creature from "the land of great butterflies."[26]

The letters show us that Mistral didn't always set her friend on a pedestal. When it came to Ocampo's affairs with European men, Mistral expressed wonder, annoyance, and mockery reinforced by a certainty that Ocampo's destiny lay in America, not in Europe. It's possible that the poet's annoyance with Ocampo's escapades had some basis in jealous projections of the sort that appear throughout Mistral's earlier poetry. Mistral's repeated assertions of how much she and Eduardo Mallea had in common can be seen in this light (see G.18, May – September 1938). Rivalry and triangulated desire, rather than consummation, ever characterized Gabriela Mistral's expression of sexual drama.

For both women, the act of letter writing evolved in the context of immersion in books and reading. Mistral's eyesight was already troubling her by middle age, so that Ocampo became the more voracious reader. Both women's insistence on sharing a passion for literature through writing letters was also an act of love. Ocampo aptly pointed this out: "To communicate in writing one with another. To care for and love one another. This is the definition that the Royal Spanish Academy gives to the word 'correspond.' And that's the double meaning the word has always had for me. To write letters is this or it's nothing."[27] As Mistral observed in her notes to *Tala*, letter writing stands between prose and verse, even as it is caught up in purely temporal matters. Spontaneity is a good part of its charm, as it builds connections and compensates for years of exile:

> Letters that travel far and are written every three or five years tend to set what's very temporal — the week, the year — and what's very trifling — the birthday, the new year, a change of house — to the wind. And when, moreover, a letter is written on the warm embers of poetry, with a rhythm somewhat cut short and some rhymes intruding, with both rhythm and rhyme lingering in the air, the letter turns into a playful thing, pulled here and there by the verse and the prose that dispute it.[28]

PUBLIC AND PRIVATE PERSONAE

Even as Mistral and Ocampo shared the written word as their primary medium, they were public performers who appreciated the impact of theater and gave readings with a full sense of their status as celebrities. They also worked with the developing media of radio and film. When they wrote one another, it was with implicit understanding of how their public personae regularly exceeded the bounds of feminine decorum. Still, the two women experienced fame in distinct ways. Ocampo's stage roles and speeches were angled toward select audiences, but after their performance she was able to retreat into privacy. Mistral's educator image, on the other hand, put her in the center of open-air homages. Her status as a traveler and guest afforded scant privacy.

Ocampo seems to have dealt easily with public appearances. She enjoyed her recitation performances of "Perséphone," with a text by André Gide, composed and conducted by Igor Stravinsky in Buenos Aires, Rio, and Florence. This and other public recitations only partially satisfied a thwarted youthful desire to make a life in the theater. Ocampo followed the latest plays and films with great enthusiasm, but when it came to giving interviews, she was distrustful of reporters, who frequently cast her in the stereotypical role of a wealthy dilettante or a cultural elitist. Mistral, by contrast, knew fame from her twenties and grew increasingly ambivalent toward it. By 1938, for instance, her letters to Ocampo use a code word, "organdy," apparently to refer to the stiff, schoolteacher-organized homages to which she was endlessly subjected when she traveled in Latin America (see, for example, G.15, 18 April 1938). Further, the Chilean writer was rebuffed when she tried to move beyond the niches allotted to her as an educational missionary or icon of quasi-maternal suffering. In describing a failed attempt to give a public reading at the University of Buenos Aires, for instance, she says that professors are hostile to her as a poet, a foreigner, and a schoolteacher:

> They believe, bless them, that poetry *isn't culture* and has nothing to do with education because . . . education — the education that they provide — thoroughly hates creativity, in any form. But we die, we poor poets, and then they get hold of us to gnaw on our bones in their literature classes, and from that gnawing they live, year in, year out, fabricating classes that let them eat. (G.16, April 1938)

It is in letters such as these, rather than in the public display of interviews or newspaper reports, that Mistral's and Ocampo's self-awareness as public figures emerges. Each used the letter as an opportunity to express confidences that celebrity otherwise denied them. Mistral is the more effusive, to be sure: she apologizes more than once for monopolizing the conversation when they've met in person, and explains that there are few people to whom she can talk as freely as she can with

Ocampo. For her part, Ocampo prefers to detail literary projects and the progress of *Sur*. The letters also offer her a chance to document, to the limits that censorship allowed, the escalating difficulties of life under Peronism, from 1946 to 1954. During this same period, Ocampo seems to hold back personal confidences in letters to Mistral, perhaps because her letters could fall into unwanted hands or perhaps because of Mistral's own obsessions. Mistral writes long letters regularly, but she begins repeating herself after 1950, and Ocampo seems to lose patience with her. They often refer to face-to-face contact as a necessary defense against oppression and infirmity.

The conditions of celebrity that both writers knew relate to Jean Franco's observations about women's emergence into public space in Hispanic culture. Writing about "self-destructing heroines" in *Critical Passions*, Franco points to two roles available to women in the de facto male public space of Latin America: the maternal figure, whose entry into the plaza is tied to suffering and sacrifice, and the performer/libertine, whose sexuality is a central aspect of her taking the stage.[29] Mistral encountered that legacy in her quasi-maternal status as a public schoolteacher and in her tragic relationship with Yin Yin. Ocampo's sexual freedom, an open secret during her middle years, played into a public image that she neither explained nor acknowledged, thereby attracting more attention to her privilege and beauty.

Mistral's origins forever linked her with the rural middle class, a group associated with the impoverished countryside and with those seeking a better life by moving to the outskirts of the larger cities. In her complex racial identification as *una mestiza de Vasco* (a mixed blood of Basque descent), she overtly associates herself with suffering and loss, and with the descendants of those who settled Chile in the eighteenth century. It is no accident that Mistral lays fullest claim to the Basque side of her heritage during the darkest moments of the Spanish Civil War, or that her expressed allegiance to a vanishing indigenous identity grows more vehement with age, articulated in the poet's sense of being a living ghost and the last of her line. These intertwined aspects of identity and suffering may seem far from the Gabriela Mistral that liberal bureaucrats in Chile and Mexico fitted out for public consumption. Their celebrated *maestra de América*, the embodiment of education as a ticket to upward social mobility, was nonetheless denied access to a forum in Latin American higher education: only in the United States and Puerto Rico did she teach university-level classes.

Mistral's discomfort with the public plaza can be traced in part to

gender discrimination in Latin America, but it also derives from the
material conditions of her life. Unlike Ocampo, Mistral had no physical retreats, no stable residence, no trusted circle of nearby friends. Her
livelihood as a consul, journalist, and lecturer guaranteed her nomadism. The sundry stationery and multiple return addresses of her
letters reveal provisional and precarious dwellings: anonymous *pen-
siones*, rented apartments, borrowed houses. The 1945 Nobel Prize in
literature made Mistral's life marginally more secure, but by this point
she was physically and emotionally battered by ill health and the death
of Yin Yin, and she continued to move.

Ocampo's celebrity, founded on her family's identification with the
Argentine upper classes and her friendships with a range of world-fa-
mous intellectuals, was played out in more exclusive venues on both
continents. Her financial well-being was never in question, even when
Sur suffered grave losses. Except for the three-year period when the
government restricted her freedom to travel abroad, Ocampo traveled
almost annually to Europe and the United States, staying for extended
periods. Neither the comfort of her two homes in Argentina — one in
the suburbs of Buenos Aires, the other in the seaside resort of Mar del
Plata — nor a coterie of loyal friends could protect Ocampo, however,
when she became a target of police surveillance and harassment, and
then a political prisoner for a month in 1953. Her experience in prison,
in close contact with women of all walks of life, had an enormous impact on Ocampo, who thereafter was even more committed to speaking out on women's rights and social justice. Among her many friends
on three continents, Ocampo's imprisonment was a *cause célèbre* that
elicited many public protests to the Perón regime.

When Ocampo was freed from jail but still restricted to remaining
in Argentina, she gently noted the irony of Mistral's repeated criticism
"that I should stay in my own country and work on its behalf. You
wouldn't complain about me now. I've hardly lived outside my land
these last few years" (V.16, 29 September 1953). In having chosen to
make her home in Argentina, Ocampo had lived nearly all of her adult
life in Latin America, whereas Mistral, the great symbol of Spanish
American identity, effectively lived more than half of hers in Europe
and the United States, establishing a total of at least ten consulates
over the course of their correspondence.[30] Mistral was semi-solitary in
her travel, but Ocampo generally traveled with her maid, her sister
Angélica, or a close friend. Mistral loved to stay up all night talking and

smoking; Ocampo hated smoke and woke early so she could write in bed before rising.

Ironically, given her impatience with Mistral's Indianism, in the later years of her life Ocampo discovered and proudly claimed indigenous blood in her own background. Her mother was a descendant of Domingo de Irala, a Spanish conquistador and governor of the River Plate colonies; it seems that Irala had a Guaraní Indian concubine whose children he legally recognized. In her acceptance speech to the Argentine Academy of Letters in 1977, Ocampo recognized the importance of both Gabriela Mistral and Agueda, her Guaraní ancestor, in her own life. It was highly appropriate, she said, that she pay tribute to these two women who had contributed, one by blood and the other by nurturing example, to the formation of her own identity.

CHRONOLOGY, EDITING, AND TRANSLATING

The correspondence begins in January of 1926, with each woman expressing interest in the other through a characteristic act of courtesy. Mistral, leaving for Europe, writes to thank Ocampo for a gift of flowers that Ocampo evidently sent to Mistral's hotel in Buenos Aires. (Ocampo had probably initiated this contact at the recommendation of mutual friends in Spain.) Following nearly nine years of frustrated attempts, the two women finally met in December of 1934, at Mistral's residence in Madrid, in the company of María de Maeztu.[31]

Mistral immediately assaulted Ocampo with questions: Why was she born in the least American city in Latin America? Why was she so Frenchified? Why had she ignored Mistral's friend, the middle-class Argentine writer Alfonsina Storni? Ocampo defended herself as best she could: she had not chosen the place of her birth or the European education her parents had given her, and she'd never had occasion to meet Storni.

By the time of that first meeting, Mistral and Ocampo were forty-five and forty-four years old respectively. Each had moved past a mentoring relationship with an older Spanish man who had sponsored the publication of their first books in the 1920s: Federico de Onís, on Mistral's part, and José Ortega y Gasset, on Ocampo's. As of 1934, however, Mistral and Ocampo were no longer neophyte writers. Their involvement with the world of letters was bringing them into spheres of national and international influence newly open to women: in organizations such as the PEN Club for both of them, the Argentine Women's

Union for Ocampo, and a consular post in Spain, along with membership in the Institute for Intellectual Cooperation, for Mistral.[32]

Eighty-four letters by Gabriela Mistral and thirty-six letters by
Victoria Ocampo survive. There were undoubtedly more letters from
Ocampo, but Mistral either did not keep them or they were lost in her
many moves.[33] Difficulty with dates and handwriting forestalled previous attempts to work on this correspondence. Only sixteen of the
eighty-four Mistral manuscripts were typed (with corrections added in
the poet's hand); all of the letters that Gabriela Mistral sent to Victoria
Ocampo during the last six years of her life, from 1950 onward, were
pencil written and, consequently, very faded. Though Mistral claimed
to use pencil because it hurt her eyes less, Ocampo took Mistral's pencil habit as an indication of her disregard for posterity. Mistral rarely
wrote the date in her letters, but Ocampo, for her part, scrupulously
dated her letters. Thanks to Ocampo's care with preserving these materials, we can match the two sides of the surviving correspondence with
a good degree of accuracy. Frequent references to current events, consultation of other published editions of correspondence, and other biographical studies have helped us further locate the letters in time, and
arrange them in this text.

The condition and quality of the letters bear out the temperamental and circumstantial differences between the two women. Where
Mistral's letters can easily run to thousands of words on any available
stationery, Ocampo preferred brevity and personalized, engraved stationery. Ocampo wrote quite legibly in pen or with a typewriter. She
probably used French to compose the earliest, now lost letters of the
correspondence, as this was her custom with many friends at the time.
Although her letters are less personally revealing than Mistral's,
Ocampo does not hide her emotions, especially in describing friendships near and distant and in detailing the injustices that she suffered
and to which she was witness. On Mistral's part, the letters written
prior to the deepening of the friendship during Mistral's visit to Argentina in 1938 are carefully drafted and solicitous of Ocampo as a
prospective colleague. Subsequent letters from Mistral's travels, by
contrast, take the form of reports brimming with lively observations
and charges to her correspondent. Finally, the letters from the end of
Mistral's life iterate pleas for visits and explanations that Ocampo
could not supply: with her passport withheld, her movement restricted, and her mail routinely opened, Ocampo was prevented from

traveling. The certainty that her mail was intercepted further kept Ocampo from writing freely to her friend during the very years when Mistral most needed her.

The vagaries of lives lived in turbulent times brought the two writers together only six times in all. Following their first meeting in 1934, Mistral's 1938 visit to Argentina marks the second and most intense time that the two spent together. The week they shared at Ocampo's home in Mar del Plata remained deeply impressed on both women's memories. The span of Mistral's residence in Argentina (from late March through May of 1938) was impacted by events in Europe, such as the fall of the Spanish Republic and the onset of World War II, and related politically tumultuous events in Latin America. The next meeting between the two women occurred in late February of 1939, as Ocampo paid Mistral the surprise tribute of meeting her ship upon her arrival in France and traveling with her to Nice to help her establish the Chilean consulate there. The gesture showed compassion for Mistral's condition as a homeless traveler. Following Mistral's receipt of the Nobel Prize in late 1945, Ocampo and Mistral experienced a fourth fleeting but intense encounter in Washington, in 1946. There was an equally brief, apparently difficult meeting in Rome in late 1951. As Ocampo indicates in "Victoria Ocampo on Her Friendship with Gabriela Mistral," they were together one last time, when Mistral was near death in New York.

The notable silences and omissions in the correspondence are revealing in themselves. The lost letters from Ocampo prior to late 1942 can, to an extent, be imaginatively reconstructed through a close reading of Mistral's replies. In some cases, such as the long letter Mistral writes about Ocampo's floundering affair with Eduardo Mallea (G.18, May/September 1938), we can follow point by point the issues Ocampo must have enumerated in an earlier letter. A hiatus seemingly occurs in the correspondence during 1948–1950, while Mistral was living in Mexico. We know that Mistral was wont to stop and then resume correspondence without explanation in these years, as with her letters to Alfonso Reyes, interrupted between 1950 and 1953.[34] For Ocampo, the years of their hiatus were extraordinarily busy, with multiple trips to postwar Europe and a full literary agenda for *Sur* at home.

Because so much of what Ocampo must have written is missing, we have elected to include, following the correspondence, a group of writings — primarily by Ocampo, but also a few by Mistral — to help round out Ocampo's voice in the relationship with Mistral and to fill in details of those years. These include portions of the Ocampo-Caillois correspondence where the subject is Mistral.[35]

Assigning reliable dates to these letters reveals the need to place Gabriela Mistral's poetry in sociohistorical context, and thus to move past the view that she wrote poetry in an attempt to compensate for her personal suffering. Her war-related writings indicate Mistral's deep absorption in war and politics. She brought the war home, personalizing the political, as the troubled environment of her household during World War II probably reflected the conflicts in Europe and the Americas. Mistral's identification of herself as Latin American and her disparagement of France accelerates during the war, for example. Writing to Ocampo of "rotten France" (G.34, 6 January [1942]), she is preoccupied by the gains of Fascism in Europe and the potential for similar gains in the New World. The poet's letters from Brazil show her assaulted by ill health and with a heightened awareness of battling nations and ideologies. These factors surely impacted her household in general, and her French-speaking nephew in particular.

Scholars agree that Yin Yin's death in August 1943 presented an irreparable blow to the poet's sanity. Separating reality from fantasy in her letters becomes increasingly difficult after August 1943. As Luis Vargas Saavedra conservatively estimates, "It isn't possible to believe any affirmation of a personal sort that G.M. might give after 1950; and perhaps after 1946."[36] During these same years, and especially after 1950, the Ocampo side of the correspondence became more agitated as Perón established his power in Argentina. Crosses were painted on the gate of Ocampo's house, and in mid-1953 she was arbitrarily arrested and imprisoned. One of Gabriela Mistral's last public acts was to issue a press statement, sent in copies to Ocampo's friends throughout Europe, Latin America, and India, calling for Ocampo's release. Mistral's identification with the working classes that constituted Perón's basis of support might have supplied the Argentine government with the necessary pretext to release Ocampo. Ocampo herself believed that it was Jawaharlal Nehru's appeal that made the difference.

Mistral's intervention on Ocampo's behalf was an important moment in a friendship that had cooled. Mistral's obsession with Yin Yin's death and ghost, and her repetitive insistence that Ocampo come to the United States, were wearing on Ocampo, who was distracted by her own problems. But for all the signs of forgetfulness and confusion in the letters that Mistral wrote from New York in the last three years of her life, there are many lucid moments as well. At these moments, the two women's common interest in Latin America and its relation to the world, plus their recalled gratitude toward one another for past generosity, drew them together.

The Mistral-Ocampo correspondence presents real challenges for translation because their very Americanness is expressed through their particularistic use of language. Ocampo aptly said that Mistral's missives were "spoken letters," that she wrote without composing, just as she spoke. Comparing Gabriela Mistral's and Virginia Woolf's use of language, Ocampo could also have been defining herself:

> Let's keep in mind that both women spoke in their own distinctive way, with complete spontaneity and naturalness. Being two writers and two totally different, almost opposite personalities, their command of the language enabled them to use it however they pleased. I mean to say that they used words like they used a comb. Sometimes the comb was made of bone, other times of tortoiseshell, but above all it was what it had to be: a comb.[37]

Prior even to the act of translation for this volume was the effort of transcribing the correspondence. The procedure involved, in Mistral's case, a first stage of hand-transcribing the texts (many of them extremely faded), then, for both authors, typing and comparing them with the originals. We followed this up with research into dates, then translation into English. Although we checked one another's work, Elizabeth Horan worked primarily on the Mistral texts, and Doris Meyer dealt with the Ocampo materials.

While trying to make the writers accessible in English, we also conserved linguistic elements critical to their self-expression, including words and phrases used in a foreign language, which we have left as they were in the original letters. Some variable formats in the placement of salutations, signatures, and paragraphing have been regularized, and we have numbered each letter in sequence (i.e., G.1, G.2, etc.). The writers' underlinings and marginal comments, many of which are consistent with their spontaneous, colloquial tone, are conserved in the translated texts. (Italic type indicates underlining; underscored italic type indicates double underlining.) We have used brackets to indicate a range of material (most often dates and some punctuation) that we have supplied in the interest of clarity, based on internal and external evidence. Our endnotes following each section and the biographical

dictionary are designed to further enhance historical and literary references.

We have divided the letters into three periods corresponding to
major shifts in the friendship and in geopolitical events. During the
first period, from 1926 to September of 1939, only the twenty-nine letters of Mistral to Ocampo are known to exist, although Mistral alludes
to nine now missing letters from Ocampo. In these years, both she and
Ocampo traveled back and forth between Latin America and Europe.
The Mistral letters (written from Paris, Madrid, Lisbon, Rio, Mar del
Plata, Buenos Aires, Santiago, Viña del Mar, Lima, New York, Paris,
and Nice) reveal the two women's concern with the repercussions of
the Spanish Civil War and the potential for Fascism to take hold in
Latin America.

During the second period, from 1940 to 1952, Mistral's fourteen letters find her moving from Brazil to California and Italy after the war.
In these same years, Ocampo's texts to Mistral begin (in December
1942) as she visits the United States and Europe while keeping her residence in Argentina, where militarism is on the rise and Perón seizes
power. In addition to referencing events at home and in Europe, the
letters show a preoccupation with the tragic suicide of Mistral's
nephew. During these same years, both women become aware of the
need to educate the United States, in its role as an emerging world
power, about Latin America. Mistral's letters from California and Italy
after receiving the Nobel Prize include prescient observations about
postwar Europe. Ocampo similarly writes of deteriorating conditions
at home.

The final years of their friendship are represented in the last section, 1953 to 1956, when Mistral took up residence in New York, her
health in evident decline. These same years represent Ocampo's struggle with the Perón regime in Argentina and her efforts to resist with
dignity and to keep *Sur* afloat. Their last letters testify to the Chilean
poet's increasing distance from friends and, in Ocampo's case, to the relief of the post-Perón years and renewed travels abroad. Over the
decades, the nature of their correspondence had changed, as their lives
had, but they still shared sentiments of concern, if not frustration, over
the shortcomings of their America. Against time and distance, their
letters kept alive the bond that they felt as Latin American women
who had persevered in their commitment to a beloved but capricious
homeland.

NOTES

1. The writer regularly used the pseudonym "Gabriela Mistral" by 1908. Some of her earlier publications appeared under alternative pseudonyms such as "Alguien" or "Alma," and she occasionally published prose under her civil name of Lucila Godoy. Most women who wrote for publication in early-twentieth-century Chile used pseudonyms, but unlike the names chosen by her female contemporaries, the choice of "Gabriela Mistral" invoked male, European intellectuals (Gabriel D'Annunzio and Frederic Mistral) and supernatural forces (the Archangel Gabriel and the mistral wind that blows from North Africa to Provence). Also unlike self-consciously poetic pseudonyms that upper-class, coterie writers such as "Iris" or "Shade" chose for themselves, "Gabriela Mistral" could and did function as the civil name of this writer (Horan, "GM's Alternative Identities"; Horan, *GM, an Artist and Her People*; and Zemborain, "Resonancias").

2. Related to GM's resignation of her post in 1925 was the changed status of teaching as a profession, evident in 1925 legislation requiring teachers to possess a university degree. GM's lack of a university degree was part of a wider, complex relationship with the educational bureaucracies of Chile (Horan, *GM, an Artist and Her People*, Ch. 3) and of Mexico (Schneider, "GM en México").

3. Unlike GM's correspondence with distinguished men, the exchange with VO includes GM's advice about love and ribald jokes (G.16, 24 April 1938; G.18, May 1938).

4. Rodig, "Presencia," 285.

5. Ocampo reports that when she asked a Buenos Aires police inspector to leave her in peace and respect the rights of the aged, his response was to laugh in her face and tell her that she didn't look aged (Statement, following V.15, 17 June 1953).

6. See Meyer, "The Multiple Myths of Victoria Ocampo."

7. "Imaginative understanding" was key to Ocampo's approach to writing (Meyer, *Against the Wind and the Tide*, Ch. 6).

8. See Meyer, "Victoria Ocampo, Argentine Identity, and the Landscape of the Essay."

9. "However the magazine is judged, *Sur* is one of the most important achievements in Latin America. In this way, its founder Victoria Ocampo shall be said, in Waldo Frank's words, to have 'prophesied for her country . . .'" (King, *Sur*, 202). For more information about those who contributed to *Sur* and the magazine's intellectual and political history, see Matamoros, *Genio y figura*, 201–308.

10. From personal conversation between Ocampo and Meyer in January 1976. Mistral first read Virginia Woolf's *A Room of One's Own* when it was published by SUR under Ocampo's initiative (G.6, 21 August 1936).

11. The most informative biographies of VO are Meyer, *Against the Wind and the*

Tide (1979); Vásquez, *Victoria Ocampo* (1991); and Ayerza de Castilho and Felgini, *Victoria Ocampo* (1992).

12. See Meyer, "Reciprocal Reflections," 102–108. "To recuperate the full history of female literary expression in Spanish America we must examine the ways in which women, particularly in the earlier periods, turned to writing to inscribe their own configurations of truth in a society that traditionally devalued the female intellect" (102). This study focuses on how women (GM and VO as prime examples) used the essay genre and literary portraiture to find their own voices and "author-ity."

13. This concern with Americanness has its counterpart among twentieth-century U.S. writers known to VO and to GM, such as Van Wyck Brooks, Lewis Mumford, and Waldo Frank (all members of the Seven Arts circle, after the magazine by the same name). They called for spiritual renewal through literature to counteract the impoverishment of American life caused by technological and commercial modernity (Steinman, *Made in America*, 1–30).

14. Meyer, "Early (Feminist) Essays of VO."

15. Stabb, *In Quest of Identity*.

16. Ocampo, "Palabras francesas," 40–41.

17. GM's and VO's friends Waldo Frank, Alfonso Reyes, and Eduardo Mallea all shared this concern in different ways. It should be noted that women were not included in Stabb's well-received book on the Latin American essay.

18. *Waldo Frank en América Hispana* (1930) gives the context of and contemporary reactions to his message, both in his works and during his trip to Latin America in 1929.

19. Americanist essays by Alfonso Reyes published in *Sur* include "Un paso de América" (1931), "Notas sobre la inteligencia de América" (1936), and "Utopías americanas" (1938).

20. Each emphasis had its political dangers: championing ethics and aesthetics over political ideology brought Ocampo ingenuously close to Fascist figures such as Mussolini and the collaborator Pierre Drieu la Rochelle. For her part, Mistral's frequent allusions to relations between race and character (quoted in C. Alegría and F. Alegría, and analyzed in greater detail by Fiol-Matta) seem rather dated today. Among them are various gratuitous references to Jews.

21. Ocampo, "GM en sus cartas," 59.

22. Ocampo, "GM en sus cartas," 70.

23. The Americanism of *Tala* is a complex subject. It is most openly expressed in what GM termed (in the notes to *Tala*) the "minor tone" epic "Dos Himnos," as well as in the elegiac verses "Nocturnos" that GM dedicated to writers who shared her intellectual commitment to expressing American unity: Waldo Frank, Alfonso Reyes, and VO. Spanish Americanism pervades GM's evocations of women's relation to war in Mexico and Spain, and her celebrations of southern France are couched in terms of an archaic and elemental ruralism nearly interchangeable with rural Latin America.

24. In *Desolación* (1922) and earlier works, GM critiques marriage as hypocritical and associates heterosexuality with violence; her manuscript drafts reveal a process of revising the expression of sexual desire from first- to third-person accounts (Horan, "GM's Alternative Identities"). Fiol-Matta argues that GM's self-censorship included a range of such mechanisms ("GM: Maestra" and *A Queer Mother for the Nation*).

25. Among the women with whom Ocampo corresponded more or less regularly for extended periods are María de Maeztu and Victoria Kent (Spanish); Vita Sackville-West and Virginia Woolf (British); Anna de Noailles and Adrienne Monnier (French); María Rosa Oliver, Fryda Schultz de Mantovani, and Delfina Bunge (Argentine). The collection of Ocampo's letters to her sister (*Cartas a Angélica*) is the only one of her female epistolary relationships to be published in its entirety (apparently) with extensive documentation.

26. Letter from Woolf to Ocampo, 22 January 1935, reprinted in Meyer, *Against the Wind and the Tide*, 123.

27. Ocampo, "GM en sus cartas," 60. Also see Ocampo, "El capítulo de la correspondencia," in which she expounds on her preference for letter writing.

28. Mistral, "Recados," in *Tala*, 163.

29. Jean Franco, "Self-Destructing Heroines" in *Critical Passions*.

30. A review of GM's correspondence shows that she established consulates in Madrid (1933), Barcelona (1934), Lisbon and/or Oporto (1935), Nice (1939), Niteroi (1940), Petrópolis (1941), Los Angeles (1946), Santa Barbara (1947), Naples (1951), and New York (1952).

31. VO's description of the first meeting between herself and GM (which occurred in December of 1934) appears in Ocampo, "South America: Merecemos la ignorancia de Europa?" Writing shortly afterward, in April of 1935, VO states, "I met GM for the first time last December . . . it was a momentous event for me. Everything is from America in her: the quality of her sensibility, her riches, her strength, that Spanish very much her own, which is pure Spanish, but whose extraordinary taste comes from having dwelled in a strictly American flesh and soul. On meeting GM again in Madrid (since our first encounter was a re-meeting) [they had become acquainted earlier through their letters], she once again seemed to settle me in American soil '*at his* [sic] *best*' [italics and English in original]. An American soil in which I had a thousand reasons to take great pride.

   "And — I repeat — meeting a GM, an Alfonso Reyes in Europe isn't like meeting Chile or Mexico: it's like meeting one's own homeland. Latin America '*at her best*.' One understands, then, how, when one reaches the highest levels, all of this America is one and indivisible" (VO, *Domingos en Hyde Park*, 46–47). In this statement of VO's, as in GM's later letters describing how she saw America in Ocampo as a compelling ideal involving the spirit and intellect (G.3, G.26), Latin America is not bound by national borders.

32. These letters reveal that GM held her consular post partly through the inter-

vention of the Argentine branch of the PEN Club and a range of well-
known European intellectuals.

33. GM's correspondence with VO mentions twelve now missing letters from
    VO prior to 1943, plus at least two missing photos and four missing tele-
    grams from VO.

34. GM's correspondence with Alfonso Reyes includes multiple references to
    visits with Waldo Frank and Victoria Kent during this time, making the gap
    in the GM-VO correspondence all the more striking: see *Tan de usted.*

35. Roger Caillois figures in the Mistral-Ocampo relationship because his corre-
    spondence with Ocampo shows that the two women kept in touch even
    when letters were not exchanged or have not survived. In 1944, while Mistral
    was grieving over the death of her nephew, Caillois visited the poet in Brazil
    at Ocampo's urging. Mistral subsequently visited Caillois in Paris in early
    1946, and Caillois visited Mistral in California the following year.

36. Vargas Saavedra, *Otro suicida,* 27.

37. Ocampo, "GM en sus cartas," 64–65.

PART ONE

LETTERS 1926–1939

BUENOS AIRES, PARIS, BARCELONA, MADRID, LISBON, RIO
DE JANEIRO, MAR DEL PLATA, SANTIAGO DE CHILE, GUA-
YAQUIL, LIMA, HAVANA, WASHINGTON, D.C., NEW YORK,
AND NICE, FRANCE.

*Gabriela Mistral during her
1938 tour of Latin America.*
Courtesy Archivo del Escritor,
Biblioteca Nacional de Chile.
Collection of Elizabeth Horan.

*Waldo Frank, María Rosa
Oliver, Eduardo Mallea,
and Victoria Ocampo (?)
at Villa Victoria, 1934.*
Collection of Doris Meyer.

ꙮ

G.1 [Letterhead: none. 1 p., pen, hand of GM.]

20 JANUARY [19]25[1]

Victoria Ocampo,

Thank you for your pretty flowers. I leave [for] Europe early tomorrow morning. I've asked various people about you. I would have been honored and very happy to get to know you. Now isn't the time. In you I salute an extraordinary sensibility within our race, and I declare myself your servant.

Gabrielamistral[2]

1. GM probably wrote this letter when passing through Buenos Aires en route to Europe in January 1926. The date GM indicated, [19]25, would be a common mistake in dates written during January. The note is unlikely to have been sent in 1925, as GM was returning to Chile at that time.
2. "Gabrielamistral" run together as a single word is typical of the writer's pre-1930 signature. In G.2 she underlines it.

ꙮ

G.2 [Letterhead: Société des Nations—League of Nations. Envelope postmarked: 22 March 1929, Paris "Ste. ANNE," and addressed, hand of GM: "Diplomatique" to Mme. Victoria Ocampo, 40, rue d'Artois, Paris. 3 pp., pen, hand of GM.]

[PARIS, FRANCE.] 22 MARCH [1929]

Admired Victoria Ocampo:

I send you greetings. Only yesterday I learned that you're here. And it's very difficult for me to leave without seeing you. I'm leaving Monday.[1] Could you favor *us* with a visit to the Institute for Intellectual Cooperation, 2 rue Montpensier?[2] Mr. Levingson has been advised in the event that you grant us this honor and courtesy.

I'm buried in paperwork and don't have a bit of free time. I've loved and admired you for years now. Receive these words without smiling. Affection is always a beautiful thing, whomever it comes from.

This year in Madrid, M[aría de] Maeztu and I often remembered you.[3]

Yours truly,
Gabrielamistral
Today, 22 March.

1. When GM wrote this letter, she would have been preparing to leave for southern France (Bedarrides, Provence) or northern Italy (Cavi, near Genoa), where she often traveled between 1927 and 1933.

2. The Institute for Intellectual Cooperation was a subcommittee of the League of Nations, composed of leading intellectuals from throughout the world, with the largest representation from Western Europe and the United States. The Institute was disbanded with the rest of the League in 1939. Following World War II, the Institute was replaced by UNESCO (United Nations Educational, Scientific, and Cultural Organization) within the United Nations. GM worked within the Institute from 1926 to 1939, promoting and overseeing the publication of Latin American literature in Europe and serving as a delegate at multiple conferences.

3. The Spanish educator María de Maeztu arranged VO and GM's first meeting, which took place at GM's house in Madrid in December of 1934. GM had met María de Maeztu in 1924 during her first visit to Spain, and subsequently stayed with her at the Residencia de Señoritas while attending a women's conference in Madrid in the autumn of 1928. VO and Maeztu first met in 1926 in Buenos Aires, where Maeztu had been invited by the Spanish Cultural Institute to deliver a series of lectures. Following the Spanish Civil War, María de Maeztu came to stay with VO in Buenos Aires (VO, "María de Maeztu," in Meyer, *Against the Wind and the Tide*, 212-216).

ʂℓʑ

G.3 [Letterhead: none. 8 pp., pen, hand of GM.]

[BARCELONA.] 9 JANUARY [1935][1]

Dear Victoria Ocampo;

These have been days of setting things up in Cataluña;[2] you've always been on my mind, but I haven't been able to write you.

I repeat, because it's not too much, what was said to you with force and affection or with the force of affection: some of us concerned with the fact of America as a *unified whole* need you, and we tend to feel that you pass us by. How do you pass us by and in what ways? It's a little ingenuous to spell out and specify; you begin passing us by in language, you continue passing us by in a kind of being more European than . . . Europeans, you wind up passing us by in preferring exotic topics when you write.

It's been a tremendous surprise for me to find you so *criolla*,[3] as *criolla* as I am, although more refined. What's more, it's been a real joy. And needless to tell you, a hope of mine. From age twenty to forty we wear cosmetics, at forty everything that isn't our bone and marrow falls away. I await in you, then, the years to come, and I do so with patience and certainty. When you live with the full volume of your blood and not with a portion of it, you will return or you will go toward Spanish, all by yourself. Until then, you should let some eager people like us send you books, old and new, written in a language that you can't help but love and that will give you absolute pleasure. Let's see what you make of Gracián, whose "El héroe y el discreto" [A pocket mirror for heroes][4] I'm going to look for, for you. [GM note added, bottom of p. 3]: I left two books for you in Madrid.

My letter is taking on a tinge of imperiousness that I find disagreeable. Try to overlook it.

Your case wouldn't matter much to me if I had the dishonesty of the literary types, male and female, who deny you the category of "writer." But ever since I read your first book ("De F[rancesca] a B[eatrice]") [From Francesca to Beatrice],[5] I knew that you threw yourself into literary writing, body and all. If along with those same invidious people I believed that your sphere of influence did not extend beyond a group of snobbish gentlemen, I wouldn't waste my time writing to you. The caste of snobs matters less to me than the guild of stamp collectors. But I know, principally by way of *Sur*, that you reach and influence our South American youth. The magazine would not turn without you turning, from the very depths of your being.

I vaguely understand that you fear falling and causing *Sur* to slip into that creole nationalism of saddle pads and spurs and mate or tango, into which others fell and became mired. You who have the possibilities in your mind and your soul should create a superior *criollismo*, an Americanness both smooth and fine, like that of your beautiful personal manner, and identify and weed out all that our manner might lack; take care, with the most zealous carefulness, of your Spanish and that of the people who follow or surround you. Perhaps this is your duty in this world: to transpose Argentineness along more qualitative lines. Americanness isn't resolved by a repertoire of dances and colorful fabric, or by a few foolish and insolent postures of defiance toward Europe. That portion of Americanness is dealt from the left hands of jokers and fools. There are a thousand possible directions and paths to follow, and with your subtle aim, you can choose the least expected ones.

We ask nothing of you, only a *presence*, as complete as possible, within the American movement. As I told you, I really fear that this *presence* might not be possible if you remain rooted in the French language, and I fear that you deceive yourself in believing that by merely dealing with American *topics*, you fulfill your obligation to us.

Pardon my impertinent demand. Some of those of your race,[6] whom you must love, Sarmiento,[7] for example, would tell you more or less what this schoolteacher is telling you.

I will continue in another letter, Victoria. The topic is huge and everything that you know matters to me.

Believe in my longtime, affectionate admiration. I'm at your command, and I hope that you accept my Spanish greeting, a greeting that is joyous because knowing you has been a gift of joy for me.

Regards to María [de Maeztu]. Palma [Guillén] sends her affection.[8] Give me your address in Argentina.

9 January. Gabriela.

The portrait was mailed. Send me yours.

1. VO's encounter with GM in late 1934 was part of a European trip that included VO's meeting Mussolini in Italy and Virginia Woolf in England.
2. To judge from GM's subsequent letters and interviews, GM much enjoyed Barcelona, where she had stayed in early 1933 (Figueroa, *La divina Gabriela*, 32; also G.9, G.10). GM's residence in Madrid (1933-1935) has been the subject of numerous studies (Gazarian-Gautier; Délano; Gascón-Vera; Vargas Saavedra, *Castilla* and *Tan de usted*, 88-90). Writing to the Mexican writer and diplomat Alfonso Reyes at this time, GM registers affection for Cataluña, antipathy for Castile, and ambivalence toward Argentina: "Except for a long stay in Cataluña, this Spain has given me the most inclusive, the most complete sense of foreignness . . . A great *patria*, Argentina, but *patria* of what race and of what destiny? At best, it's an anti-American one . . ." (*Tan de usted*, 102). In this letter, as in her correspondence with VO, GM struggled with national identity within the wider question of what it means to be at once Latin American and European. Argentina, for GM, is situated between Europe and Latin America, and always tending toward the former.
3. The words *criollo* and *criolla* recur throughout GM's letters to VO. GM used the word to signify persons of European or mixed European and native ancestry, born and educated in Spanish-speaking Latin America. More broadly, GM regards herself as sharing this identity with VO, even as GM also identified with indigenous Americans.

4. Baltasar Gracián's work was part of a tradition of southern European Medieval and Renaissance literature that was important to GM, evident in various remarks on Spanish, Provençal, and Italian writers (G.5, G.10, G.18, G.33, G.40). Gracián's book, like Machiavelli's *The Prince*, belongs to the genre of self-improvement handbooks, a literary form that interested GM throughout her life, and to which she contributed from her earliest publications. Seven years later, GM insists on her recommendation of Gracián to VO (G.33).

5. VO's first book, *De Francesca a Beatrice*, a personal commentary on Dante's *Divine Comedy*, was published by José Ortega y Gasset's Revista de Occidente Press in 1924.

6. *"raza"*: GM's use of this term varies; here, she seems to mean people sharing the same cultural history.

7. Domingo Sarmiento was an intimate friend of VO's father's family. VO took pride in this association (*Testimonios VI*, 24-26, reprinted in Meyer, *Against the Wind and the Tide*, 196-198). GM's focus was on Sarmiento's educational activities during his exile in Chile ("Sarmiento en Aconcagua," which she wrote in October 1930).

8. Palma Guillén and GM became friends when they worked for José Vasconcelos in Mexico from 1922 to 1924. Guillén was the first woman from a Latin American country to serve at the ministerial level. Life in the diplomatic service enabled the two to visit and travel together throughout GM's years in Europe (1926-1940). They co-parented GM's nephew, Juan Miguel Godoy (Yin Yin), from his infancy, and he stayed with Palma Guillén when GM was on lecture tours in 1930-1931 and 1937-1938. Learning of the death of Juan Miguel Godoy in 1943, Palma Guillén rushed to GM's assistance (*Otro suicida*, ed. Vargas Saavedra, 42-43). Only a handful of letters from Palma Guillén have been published (*Otro suicida*, ed. Vargas Saavedra; Arce and von demme Bussche, eds., *Proyecto*). The Guillén-GM correspondence, if ever available, could answer many questions about the Chilean poet's life.

ΩΩ

G.4 [Letterhead: none. 5 pp., pen, hand of GM.]

CIUDAD LINEAL, MADRID. 14 MARCH 1935

Dear, admired Victoria Ocampo:

I had to write you on receiving your portrait, which, because of light and machinery, unhappily differs from your physical form.[1] Light and machinery are, put more precisely, almost like people, so unfaithful are they. Even so, weak and faithless, it has accompanied me and accompanies me in Ciudad Lineal, where I'm living now, in a bare room in which I work with a certain comfort precisely because of this aridity of wall and space. You and Don Miguel de Unamuno offer counsel and support.[2] It would be somewhat tasteless to explain that *support* to you, what part you have in it. You affirm and maintain the Americanness that I so often denied you, an Americanness more physical than literary. But since the body exists terribly, Victoria, the other varieties of Americanness will come carried along, hissed at or swelled up by it sooner or later. I believe that you are already contained, like water behind a dam, by doubts, by anxieties, by I-don't-know-what *fierce loyalty*, all awoken in recent years (3, 5?) in your greatest depths, that is, in your innermost nature. This photo that unfortunately *does not gaze* will go with me and will work diligently on me, which is how *matchless* things work in my being, from within, seismically, like Chilean geology. (This is badly put, but leave it at that.)

Your book came, for which I thank you very much.[3] And now, I'm only missing those pages of *Infancia* (Childhood) from my Victoria, who isn't exactly the same Victoria as others. I believe I recall María [de Maeztu] spoke to me of this publication as an imminent thing. I'll not talk to you about the beautiful and noble *Testimonios* so as not to make you read the same thing twice over, here and in my article.

Palma Guillén went off to Colombia as her country's embassy attaché.[4] She's there right now, suffering a turbid, violent, and medieval rain of insidiousness from the clergy, who have had the good graces to declare her a Communist, an atheist, an advocate of divorce, and other nasty comments in *Holy Colombia*. [GM note in bottom corner, left-hand margin, p. 3]: Palma is Catholic and never engaged in politics. Oh, Victoria, how our America resembles, in its two faces, its precious guanaco of the mountain ranges: smooth to the touch, the color of toast, with a skittish air that tends to become wild and spits on the familiar and the foreign alike . . . There she [Palma] went, with a pretty image of you. You were, for her, exquisitely attentive and cordial. She is among the best of our women, and her head, the most careful and organized of the women of Mexico. Your paths will cross again: take care of her and get to know her.

I've seen María only once, and very quickly. She and I have our lives full to overflowing. And I fear that both of us, side by side, are full of inconsequential things or the ashes of hard, sad dust, which give neither strength nor joy.

You left in the house, with those who saw you, a tinge of bewitchment. Tinge and all, Victoria, it lasts. Through you, I've understood
this mission of the Beatrices, and I've gone back to give prestige to the
Muses, which I allowed to fall, like great Myths, years ago. You have a
mission (the word is trite, put whatever word you want), a clear and evident job, which you know about, but also others. Be careful of the
transparency (the clarity) of the message that you bring to spread and
to spread with fitting insistence. Be careful of the instrument (a seismograph they call it?) so that they don't cut or alter its operation without you. And be careful of those who are being careful.

This letter will cost you effort because of its unconventional handwriting. I won't be hurt if you don't finish it. You are one of those rare
people (the ones who are naturally great) who cure others of their vanity, even the slightest kind, because you cast them away to such heights
that only little stones, trifles, and pruderies are left behind. You bathe
others with your broad, direct gaze, and you leave them in bettered
conditions, so that they can speak with you in this state of decency.
This, among other things that you do and that you surely don't know
that you do.

This address is good only until September: 5 Sánchez Díaz, Ciudad Lineal, Madrid.

May God watch over you, Victoria, the American, and may I meet
you again somewhere, but with more leisure for you and for me.

Gabriela

1. GM and VO exchanged photos of one another by 1935. GM exchanged
   photographs with most of her literary correspondents before and during this era.

2. GM apparently displayed a photo of Unamuno alongside that of VO.
   GM recounts her 1927 meeting with Unamuno in the south of France
   ("Cinco años de destierro de Don Miguel Unamuno"), and Unamuno
   later joined the group that successfully petitioned for GM's appointment to the Chilean foreign service (Gazarian-Gautier, *Teacher*, 57). Although GM's respect for Unamuno is evident from several references to
   him (G.10, G.27) and from their correspondence (Vargas Saavedra,
   Castilla, 141, 149, 153, 154), Mistral and Unamuno deeply disagreed about
   the fate of native Americans. Unamuno argued for favoring whites,
   while Mistral asserted the importance of modernizing native peoples
   into progress through education.

3. "Your book . . .": GM's insistence that VO write more about her early
   years is a recurring theme (G.5, G.26, G.36).

4. Palma Guillén received a cable appointing her minister (part of the am-
bassadorial staff) for Mexico to Colombia on 6 January 1935.

ςΟΟ϶

G.5 [Letterhead: Embossed three-by-five-inch note card with "G.M."
printed in upper left-hand corner, and "Av. Antonio Augusto Aguiar, 191,
Lisboa," printed in upper right-hand corner. 16 pp., pen, hand of GM.]

LISBON, PORTUGAL. 7 APRIL [1936]

[GM note, left-hand margin, p. 1]: This article is *not* for use in *Sur* and isn't
sent for *Sur*. G.[1]

Dear, remembered V. O.:

Truly as "dear" as "remembered," even though you don't write. I have had
in these months a change of countries and a long, cloying, clinging in-
testinal illness that, on account of a ferocious diet, drains my energy. I
have abandoned *long* letters and sent only brief ones in these six
months in Portugal, so sweet for getting cured, for convalescing, and
for growing old, too. Here's where I'd like you to be so we could converse, without passports and . . . without Castilian raging, on the topics
that you bring to the foreground and that are American ones, *very much
ours*, as are you, our Victoria, finally clear to me, as definite and trim as
one of our pineapples or apples, after much turning it around, checking
it out, and *telling it off* (scolding it) as well.

I left Spain: it seemed that it couldn't be. But a messy combination
of *patriotic* Spaniards (*shopkeepers*, that is) from Santiago, and some
three colleagues keen on the job in Madrid, facilitated the operation of
cutting me loose from Castile, where I was already moving from exasperated to despairing . . . Our Hispanophiles, Columbus Day types,
wouldn't understand it, but that's how it was. The Spanish climate,
aridity, working conditions, the air heavy with Furies (the Furies that
have since broken out and the Furies that will follow) made that atmosphere overwhelming to me.[2] Even so, it sparkles and it formed my
precious St. [Teresa] and the other ones whom you also love, St. John
[of the Cross], whom I like more and more each day, and the smooth-
sharp Luises [of León and of Granada].[3] Wild ones, that's how we
are . . . And there's no helping it: we come from those slimy depths and
from that scrubby highland.

We've been thinking and speaking of you often with V[ictoria] Kent. She's a friend of recent months with whom I get along marvelously, as much as I was run-in and stand-offish with the other ones. I greatly admire and cherish her, and because of you, we began getting together and loosening our talk in lovely confidence. That sizable article will tell you more about this friendship.[4]

Here I am in these angelic Portugals. They are almost South America. It rains too much, but since it's not cold, I don't suffer.

I learned that Palma Guillén received *Testimonios* directly from you. She told me nice things about you and the book in a letter that I was going to send you, my Vict., and that I misplaced. There you have another Frenchified American, much to her good, as with you. She's managed it in such a way as to turn out, in the end, always and tremendously Mexican. The same will happen to you, and I'll celebrate it . . .

I still owe you the commentary on "*Test[imonios]*."[5] It's become more than that for me: the commentary is about you. It's drafted, and I haven't corrected it because ever since I could get to anything (on account of being ill, I wasn't good for anything) I've been busy with some of those things called "propaganda articles." They've got me on recess here, the office on vacation, and I have to pay those semi-amusing salaries with something. Because that famous law finally emerged,[6] much knocked about, but it emerged, thanks to God and many interventions, among which I'm particularly aware of that of your Argentine PEN Club. This dispatch of budgetary heroics was the *secret* cause of the press campaign that I endured in my country.[7] Writers don't want their absent brothers and sisters to eat, and the thing drove about five of them crazy and they joined in the gothic-colonial furor . . . It's good to know that one will eat tomorrow; this gives a feeling of peace for recovering and helps one get to sleep at night. I'll get out from under another six articles about Chilean things, and I'll have yours copied. My head with daily migraines has given me a horror of the typewriter.

I beg you to have *Sur* sent to me. In Madrid, I'd find it in the bookstores; here, I don't have it.

With regard to that article about V[ictoria] K[ent], I want to ask you a favor: have it published in some Argentine publication where there's space for lengthy contributions. It interests me in an extra-literary way (it's very loose, poor thing) on account of our women's orientation toward social work and so that they might know what a sensible woman she is among the feminists to the 101st degree! I've lost touch with your newspapers. They fired me from *La Nación* like a servant in the past century, not even telling me "Scram!" Guillermo de Torre, a fine man, let me understand that I'd done poorly in going off to *Crítica*. And I — who'd believe it — didn't know *Crítica* even though I was writing in it . . . I needed money in those years in Spain, which were hard ones. They offered me the opportunity to contribute, and I accepted it. I first saw the periodical *two months ago*, and now I've understood getting kicked out of *La Nación*. Still, I was less than guilty for not knowing certain hatreds between one newspaper and another. I don't know anything about Argentina, my Victoria.

I beg you not to take these words as a *subterranean* request, Indian-style, to be reinstated [at *La Nación*]. I don't return when I leave, even less when they toss me out. I had to tell you this because the process struck me as strange in a people from a nonviolent country, and among well-mannered persons. You might give that article of mine, when you have the time, to some magazine where it could do its work, which is *for women to read it*.

What are you writing now? Or do the preparations for that PEN Club Congress have you rushing around? I read in a Chilean newspaper that two official delegates from Chile are going there, a lady (I don't know her) and Mariano Latorre, the novelist. I doubt that I can go, my Victoria, although I'd find it a rare and profound joy to see and hear you. If I went to Buenos Aires, I'd have to go through Chile, and my land is in a seething mass of hatreds into which I do not wish to fall. I'd say imprudent things — because each day I'm less capable of keeping quiet — and they'd run me out on a rail. Keep this reason for my absence to yourself. In a few more months I'll thank PEN, and I'll excuse myself in some way. I don't believe anyway that I'd get from the trip the pleasure and delight of being in your company. You've a lot of life around you. When I measure my little strength, I lose the hope of knowing provincial, rural Argentina, which is the one I most love. I walk an hour, and it no longer gives me any energy: it's the fruit juice diet that doesn't nourish my big body . . .

It seems that I'm here for some months, which I'll try to stretch into a year. Perhaps they'll send me to Brazil after that. I'd rather stay in this tender land that pampers the eyes and the spirit. There or here, I want and hope to see you again.

In the conflict with the Spaniards, M[aría] de Maeztu acted very

nobly toward me, quite beautifully. Her qualities are noble; the circumstances are harmful to her. I fear that she's going to suffer a good deal
again with the new situation (much better, in any case, than the past).
Why don't you bring her to your university for a year or two? Whether
she knows it or not, her Spain is sick and broken, with its brutal con-
trasts pushing it around and breaking it into pieces.[8] Take a look yourself, my Victoria, and think about the problem, which is moral and, indirectly, physical.

May they give you — may you give yourself — some long stretches
of peace in order to write. No woman and few men in America today
write as you do. Don't let your life be infested by what they call *the social
scene* — as if it consisted of those ladies who serve tea with almond
dainties. Preserve your precious soul for your writing and for the delight of those who are yours. Protect yourself with the force of courage:
the childhood book, when will it be coming out? Or has it come out?
Portugal keeps quite apart from Spain and I don't know anything.
María told me that you're about to finish the pages that you were kind
enough to read to us. Finish them, and don't delay very much, because
a book, like an angel, passes from your hands if you don't hold on to it.
And then go on from *Childhood* to Youth. We who never had you close
by feel a furious appetite, which isn't idle curiosity, for your soul and its
years, for ranches where we never lived. There's no other way to have
you with us and make life without you somehow less wicked and de-
spoiled.

Sooner or later some words of mine will go out to you — not as
lengthy as these — reminding you to write and to defend yourself
from the *enemy* that theology named as the first among the enemies of
the soul: the World, the World, my great and beloved Victoria, the
thick, dry World.

Today, my birthday,[9] I've sat down to speak with you and with
Palma Guillén and with a colleague from P[uerto] Rico.[10] You are perhaps the souls who most matter to me on that side, and this one, of the
great water. In order to tell you that I think of you tenderly, that I'm
better, and may God watch over you for me.

Gabriela

1. GM's correspondence often found its way into publication, with and
   without her authorization. At the time of this letter, GM was especially
   sensitive to the unauthorized publication of her private letters, after a
   private letter in which she wrote critically of Spain was published with-

out her consent. Sent to Chilean friends Armando Donoso and María Monvel, the letter was taken, perhaps, by third parties. On 2 October 1935, it appeared in the Santiago-based magazine *Familia* (Rubio, *GM ante la crítica*, 256; Vargas Saavedra et al., *En batalla*, 159). The subsequent controversy prompted GM's rapid transfer to Portugal in October–November 1935. Memory of the letter's publication lingered with GM all her life, yet she continued to send "private" letters expecting that they might be printed, as is evident in her correspondence with Joaquín García Monge.

2. GM understood that war in Spain would not be a short-term conflict. She uses here the classical term for the Furies, "Las Euménides," to stress war's irrational brutality and tragic waste.

3. During her first travels in Spain, in 1925, GM wrote an imaginary dialogue-travelogue with Teresa of Avila, described as "the wanderer, the founder, the woman crazy with love for Christ" ("Castilla"). GM identified with Teresa's vagabond life, use of autobiography, lack of formal education, and immersion in founding institutions for women. Writings by the Spanish authors she describes (John of the Cross, Luis of León, Luis of Granada) were in her library at the end of her life (*The Gabriela Mistral Collection Barnard College Library*).

4. The essay "Victoria Kent" that GM had just sent to VO was immediately printed in *Sur* (May 1936), with GM's permission. Victoria Kent is another of GM and VO's mutual friends who appears throughout this correspondence. Like them, she was unmarried and deeply involved in public service, especially to women.

5. VO's *Testimonios I* was published in Madrid in 1935. This is GM's first reference to an essay about VO that she drafted in various forms over several years. A version was published in 1942 (see "Victoria Ocampo" in appendix).

6. A special act of the Chilean legislature, passed on 17 September 1935 and signed by President Alessandri, made her a consul (Second Class), with the right to choose her own residence.

7. "Press campaign" refers to the controversy in Santiago following the publication of a letter in which she criticized Spain's social division; see note 1 to this letter.

8. GM's criticism of Spain's social divisions turned out to be prophetic. Those divisions, abetted by Fascist alliances with Germany and Italy, pushed Spain into civil war just three months after GM wrote this letter.

9. GM and VO discovered that they shared the same birthday during GM's visit to Mar del Plata in 1938 (See G.36).

10. "A colleague from P[uerto] Rico" refers to Margot Arce de Vázquez (G.15), who subsequently wrote one of the earliest reliable critical and biographical studies of Mistral's work.

ɷɷ

G.6 [Letterhead: Embossed three-by-five-inch card with "G.M." printed in upper left-hand corner, and "Av. Antonio Augusto Aguiar, 191. Lisbon," printed in upper right-hand corner. 5 pp., typed, pen corrections, hand of GM.]

LISBON, PORTUGAL. 21 AUGUST [1936]

Dearest V.O.:

Your lovely letter came, in which you told me about your inclination toward the theater.[1] I know that Christmas seasons are always happy, and I was happy about it since it was a successful performance. But I was afraid and I continue to fear that the genre might entrap you, and if this happens, I know that the theater as a profession — even lived at the greatest possible height, at that of Eleonora Duse — would never make you happy.

After the news came in your letter I've read two reviews of your premiere, both of them full of praise. What a pity, a pity not to have seen it; I should have seen it.

No, I knew nothing of your mourning and I learned of it very late, when it's stupid, now, to go digging into that kind of sadness.[2] It's such a serious thing when one of our own dies on us — and not us — that no other thing comes close to this circumstance. Since we don't see our own death, or suffer it either — although some believe that we do — the only death that truly falls on us is that of a father, mother, siblings, and children. I don't know if you've amassed such pessimism from life to be able to see absolutely and to take absolute joy in the liberation of a being. It's liberation, in any case, whether from chronic illness, a great shame, or from old age, an even worse shame. May God watch over and keep, wherever that might be, but close to Him, that creature, who must have been very kind, very lovable, to be your kin, your progenitor, admirable Victoria.

My head is spinning as I write you. In three newspapers and in two different versions I just read about the death of Ramiro de Maeztu, executed by firing squad in Madrid. I liked him, despite his absurd ideas, I liked him: he was a great believer; he was furthermore a man of organic ideology, which is very important. He was a man with heart, crazed by the loss of his friends and of a lamentably monarchical Spain, which he nonetheless saw in a beautiful way that dazzled his eyes, his poor eyes of a Basque boy, a mystical boy. It seems horrible to me that they killed him, whatever it is that he might have done, which were childish things, to be sure. For God's sake! The Spaniards are waging their civil war the same as the conquest of America,[3] and the worst of it is that now they're beginning to be proud of the "epic," according to what I saw yesterday in a conversation in the Embassy Council in Portugal. Just like they live full of pride in the other "heroic action" in America.

Needless to say, my heart goes out to the people of Madrid, for the sake of ideas and of that so well-named mass of air called justice. But today's newspaper brings news that could singe flesh. I hope it's not true, about the shootings, the executions of Benavente, the Quinteros, Zuloaga, etc.[4] These aren't confirmed, not like the other one.

Dear Victoria, I feel a certain remorse for not having listened to my instinct some days ago, when I wanted to write to Ramiro telling him to come here, and to my house, if he was in danger.[5] I held back because of a very stupid prejudice. Now it's a matter of accepting today's blow to the heart, *which is to call [his sister] María.*

My Victoria, there is no mail between here and Madrid. Yesterday, in that Council, they told me that they manage to do it by sending the letters to Barcelona, where they are re-sent. But this is for communicating with people on the left; this doesn't work for a letter directed to María. María won't get anything that doesn't run the risk of being observed or waylaid. I'll try, in the coded cablegrams that our legation here sends to the embassy in Madrid, to see if they can put in a message from me for María. I really doubt that our embassy would transmit it, to avoid suspicion. Couldn't you possibly try, Victoria, to have this message arrive from where you are [in Buenos Aires]? It would say that she could come to Portugal, to be with me, via Galicia at the present moment, *by what way in days to come, I don't know.*

It's no fantasy to think that María is in danger. Many, but really many, women on the left hate her. Given the chance, they'll do her injury; I don't know if it would be rash to tell you, but one cannot discount *the most serious sort.* I think that maybe she's gone to Biarritz, since the roads to France are open. But to do this, the same as going to Portugal, she must run the risk of declaring herself *dissatisfied,* as a person who wants to escape. This is the trickiest difficulty. You, my noble Victoria, give some thought to the problem. I could talk about this with [Enrique and Teresa] Díez Canedo, who are friends.[6] Nonetheless, I'm seeing here, day by day, that partisanship has gone to such a point that it doesn't allow for *conversation with Spaniards, A to Z, about their enemies.*

It's been twenty days since I've had news of a Catalan friend [Luis Nicolau d'Olwer?] whom I greatly love and esteem, who has become ill in the middle of the revolution, a person from the left wing, but from the pinkish leftists,[7] not a bull's-blood red. Now I know he's alive, recovering from a very grave condition, but he tells me in a very serene, very calm letter "that there are things worse than dying and they're what I've seen."

At the least, I want to know if María is in Madrid and if she thinks of the possibility of leaving or *if she sees extreme danger ahead, for herself.* And the women in Spain, the crazy Falangists and the Communists, are already fighting, carbines at their shoulders. I would like the women on the left to win, but I will never understand women being brought to guerrilla warfare, that filthy thing, even if it were to save the Baby Jesus from running into . . . danger. For God's sake, those battalions of women set my crazy head to spinning. They can go off to cook for the soldiers, to sew their clothing, to bring them their children so that they can see them, to heal them, to sow wheat in Castile so that there's no hunger, to irrigate, to work in the factories, to do a thousand things; but because the spectacular thing is trousers and a carbine, there they go, the big sensationalists.

You must be very busy right now with your visitors from the PEN Club. I beg you to make a bit of time, to take a moment to think about this, my well-loved Victoria, about what can be done about all this. Who knows what may have happened in Spain between today and the day my letter finds you in Buenos Aires. (In passing, another request. If Duhamel's wife, Blanche Albane, has gone to Buenos Aires, she's someone you'd do well to get to know; do me the good favor of sending her some flowers, from me. Perhaps Duhamel has gone alone, or with one of his children.[)]

Braga came through and stayed awhile.[8] I sent my regrets, telling him I couldn't come by. He told me that they had named him to that Committee on Letters, in the League [of Nations]. I'll see if it's true, and then ask you to give me some advice about what can be done there, for Argentina.

Palma Guillén is being transferred to the [Mexican] Legation in Denmark. I'm satisfied with that; we will be living far apart, but always able to get in touch with one another in case of hardship, hers or mine.

Many thanks, generous Victoria, for the placement you gave to that article about V[ictoria] Kent. No, it wasn't sent for *Sur*. I realize that you want to publish there articles *by women about women*. So now things will change. Two "*recados*" (really articles) have gone out — they should be *forged into one* — about that Venezuelan, whom I loved so much and who died, Teresa de la Parra, whom I spoke to you about in Madrid, giving you a childhood story of hers to read that I much admire.[9] If you are interested in that long memoir of hers, publish it; I have not sent it for publication to Argentina.

The SUR collection came, and it struck me as magnificent, just magnificent, worthy of you. The first time that a feminist argument has really *hit home for me* is in this work by V[irginia] Woolf.[10] I have a lot to tell you in this regard. Next time. I thank you, *as a personal service*, for having it translated and for having it sent to me.

And no more, in order not to tire you out for now, my Victoria.

A faithful embrace from your reader and friend who is with you, always, talking to you, in her way.

Gabriela

21 of August.

1. A now lost letter from VO to GM probably recounted VO's perform-ance of "Perséphone," with Stravinsky conducting, in the Teatro Colón in Buenos Aires (Meyer, *Against the Wind and the Tide*, 96).

2. Victoria Ocampo's mother, Ramona Aguirre, died in Argentina in De-cember of 1935.

3. The Spanish Civil War began on 16 July 1936 and lasted until 1939, when Francisco Franco became a military dictator who ruled Spain until his death in 1975.

4. "Benavente, the Quinteros, Zuloaga": Writers and artists, well-known satirists of the Spanish middle-class, associated with leftists in Spain. Rumors of their deaths in the first months of the Spanish Civil War proved untrue.

5. GM similarly writes to Alfonso Reyes (*Tan de usted*, 122, a letter that should be dated 5 September 1936) of her foreboding that Ramiro de Maeztu was in danger and of her sense of being haunted by his ghost.

6. Enrique and Teresa Díez Canedo organized a PEN Club dinner honor-ing GM during her visit to Spain, in December 1924, a courtesy that mattered a great deal to GM, who on that occasion met a number of Spanish intellectuals. Many attendees at the dinner, along with col-leagues from the Institute for Intellectual Cooperation, subsequently supported her appointment to Chile's Foreign Service in 1933. In 1932, GM wrote an appreciative essay about Díez Canedo ("Enrique Díez

Canedo"), and their friendship continued for decades (*Tan de usted*). GM was instrumental in helping the Díez Canedo family, supporters of the Spanish Republic, escape to Mexico.

7. In hand, on the typescript of p. 3, GM has drawn a line from *"izquierdas"* (leftists) to the lines above, drawing a triangle around the "A," probably a reference to Spanish anarchists.

8. Dominique Braga came to live in Petrópolis, Brazil, from 1942 to 1945, close to GM (Gazarian-Gautier, *Teacher*, Ch. 4; G.32).

9. GM wrote two *"recados"* about her friend Teresa de la Parra ("Gente americana: Teresa de la Parra" [1929], and "Teresa de la Parra" [1936]). GM's correspondence with de la Parra and her partner, Lydia Cabrera, dates from the 1930s (*Cartas a Lydia Cabrera*, ed. Hiriart). The "child-hood story" by de la Parra was the novel *Las memorias de Mamá Blanca* (Mama Blanca's memoirs).

10. Virginia Woolf's *A Room of One's Own* was published by SUR, in a translation by Jorge Luis Borges (although Borges liked to say that his mother really did the translation; see Woodall, *Borges*).

ΩΩ

G.7 [Letterhead: none. 2 pp., pen, hand of GM.]

[PORTUGAL.] 24 JANUARY [1937]

Dear Victoria:

Maruja Mallo will be arriving there.[1] I hope the rest of the teachers were able to travel by the same boat and be rescued for the good of their country's future.

I know that you will comfort the distressed soul that she bears, underneath her smile.

How good it is that your Argentina is big enough for its own people and for those who need it in these bad times. Mexico, thank God, is going to take ten, no less than ten teachers in a little while. I haven't gotten anything out of my land, yet, but getting this from Mexico, managed from Portugal through a friendly minister, soothes my American conscience.

I hope very much — more and more — to speak with my Victoria. I've traveled more than two months abroad, in France, in Germany, and Denmark.[2]

When I stop to rest — I just returned — I have to send you that article about you.

I heard Duhamel and his wife remember you, in Paris.[3] I very much liked some scenes they were sketching in which you appeared.

God keep you and remember me from time to time.

I admire you, I love you, and I follow you,

Gabriela

1. On the same day as this note, GM wrote a letter of introduction for Mallo directed to Alfonso Reyes (*Tan de usted*, 109-111), who was located in Buenos Aires as part of the Mexican Legation to Argentina.
2. GM traveled with Palma Guillén in the winter of 1936-1937.
3. GM traveled to Paris for a 25 November 1936 meeting of the Institute for Intellectual Cooperation, where she would have spoken with Georges Duhamel and Blanche Albane about VO.

ᘏ

G.8 [Letterhead: none. 6 pp., pen, hand of GM.]

[LISBON, PORTUGAL. JULY OR EARLY AUGUST 1937][1]

Dear Victoria:

I think of you often and *I live with you, a little*, although I don't write you. A month ago I had a long conversation with [José] Bergamín about that nasty letter.[2] I told him as much as possible, and I found him very gentlemanly and thus upset on that account. Now he has clarified or set the document straight. I promised to write a letter *to you* about the terrible matter. And I've written it, but it hasn't gone out to you yet because I'm currently without someone to type for me. I return to Paris the seventeenth, and if they still haven't copied it for me here, the secretary of Eugene Imaz will do it there.[3] I have a respect bordering on veneration for J[osé] B[ergamín]. He's a profound creature, crazed by the tragedy of those around him and, it must be said, by the shameful deafness of our Latin America and hateful Europe, at this moment, toward the tragedy in Spain. *This letter of mine is private:* you can publish the other one. I will send it to *Crítica*, although I'm not sure that they'll give it space there ...

My article about you (that I'm bringing with me) seems as if it will never end. I traveled with Amparo G[onzález] Tuñón, from Lisbon to Cherbourg. We talked about you night and day, and much to my benefit. The truth is that you won me over easily in two conversations, but

this admiring friendliness was a little . . . superstitious. I knew very little of you as a real person. Amparo's news has touched me deeply. I
knew nothing of the ugly campaign of those zealots against your
League or Society of Argentine Women [GM refers to the Argentine
Women's Union].[4] I authorized her — and I repeat it, here — to request *my membership in that society*. It seems to me that this is the moment to be with you, not just like *this*, tacitly, but in an express, public
way. Some stupid gossip about your subterranean but effectively Fascist tendency came to me from Buenos Aires. I didn't believe it, but like
all gossip, it gave me a sinking feeling . . . *Per cause* [for good reason].
Fascism will befall America, vertically, if it wins in Spain. And it looks
like it's winning, Victoria. So it's a matter of beginning, right now, some
work to head off the white plague (Fascism) invented by the whites
who are making a disgrace of their famous Europe; that sore, that *white*
leprosy doesn't come from the Orient this time, that leprosy is really
Caucasian, fully Latin and German, to make matters worse. The danger for us, my Victoria, is truly mortal.

They know, dear Victoria, that my mouth isn't free, nor is my hand
free to write. I will do something nonetheless. In any event, not even a
tenth part of what you can do, with your more organized culture, with
your life in America, and with your full strength. I have never fully recovered from my illness, and this has a terrible impact on the body. My
diet is turning me into a kind of old woman or a one-year-old. I thank
you, with the deepest thanks, for your work in organizing our women.
God give you energy — and give you inspiration. He alone can gen-
uinely give this.

They have also told me that our María de Maeztu is with you and
that she is acting Fascist. I hope that this is censured, as it was with
[Gregorio] Marañón. Send her my fondest. Tell her, for me, that I've
asked every Spaniard who has passed through Lisbon about Ramiro's
death, that I did the same in Paris, and that although I don't see it
clearly, *I still hold out a certain crazy hope*. I loved him, aside from his
ideas, his ideas that seemed naïve, and that have suddenly become
Spain's death-knot. María should stay there a long time. The worst
that could happen to her is to come to Madrid to see the beginning of
the Franco era. On the radio in Lisbon I've heard the worst threats toward the *Junta para Ampliación de Estudios*.[5] It's necessary to allow the
debut of Fascism in Spain. It will not last, it cannot last, and it would
be lamentable were she to join that regime of violence and somber hatred toward the Spanish intelligentsia. I hope that she doesn't take me

for a Communist. There are, *as yet*, some two or three things that separate me from that party. They seem like trifles, but each one goes to the
center of the Earth . . . One is its 100 percent atheism, stupid and
closed off. But I don't see where Fascism could be the lesser of two
evils, I don't see it.

Yes, Victoria, you are now more alive to me, after the collection of
anecdotes that [Amparo González] Tuñón told me. Keep being yourself, for the good of us all. I'm going to Brazil (tell Guillermo [de
Torre] to read my letter). I didn't accept going to Argentina, and it
turns out that I'm going to a Fascist country again. I always feel a vague
animosity toward that country of yours, for its neglect of the most
wretched America, the abandonment of our global problems, the "what
does it matter to me" of a happy country.

I was hoping to see you in the Congress of the P[EN] C[lubs] in
Paris. You didn't come and it was a great pity. Many were wanting you
and we all remembered you, together.

With admiration and the true love of your

Gabriela

Affectionate regards from Palma Guillén.

1. Although this letter is not dated by GM and no envelope survives, a date
   can be assigned by the internal references to the conference "The Future
   Destiny of Arts and Letters," held in Paris from 20 to 23 July of 1937
   (Gazarian-Gautier, *Teacher*, 58-59). GM was a featured speaker at this
   conference, which was sponsored by the Institute for Intellectual Cooperation.
2. In April 1937, Bergamín wrote a letter to VO harshly criticizing her for
   receiving Gregorio Marañón, a self-exile from Spain, in Argentina.
   Bergamín accused her of intellectual "coquetry" and of being an "enemy
   of the Spanish people" (67). VO replied to him in May, chastising
   Bergamín for being un-Christian toward Marañón and demeaning of
   her as a woman. "In my woman's way I have read your letter and in my
   woman's way I answer it" (74). She made her support for the Republican
   cause very clear (Ocampo, "Cartas abiertas").

   José Bergamín and GM corresponded as well; see Vargas Saavedra,
   Castilla, 138–140, in which GM declines to publish in his magazine *Cruz y
   Raya*, "a magazine whose editorial board and regular contributors don't
   include any women whatsoever" (138).
3. In mid-June 1937, GM traveled from Lisbon to Paris to attend the Committee of Arts and Letters, the PEN Club meeting, and the Women
   Teachers' Congress (*Tan de usted*).
4. In March 1936, VO was among the principal founders of the Unión de

Mujeres Argentinas (Argentine Women's Union), which sought the legal equity of Argentine women.

5. The Junta para Ampliación de Estudios, a center for university studies formed in Madrid, 1907–1936, was initially scientific in orientation. The center branched out to include the Residencia de Estudiantes, a center for interdisciplinary dialogue frequented by many of Spain's most creative intellectuals.

ဿ

G.9 [Letterhead: none. 2 pp., pen, hand of GM.]

[PARIS.] 4 AUGUST [1937]

Dear Victoria Ocampo:

Pardon these rapid, much-burdened lines. I write you pending the trip to Brazil, full of anxieties.

A book of mine — twelve years of verses — is finished and ready. I have given it to the Basque refugee children in the Residencia of Pedralbes, Barcelona, where I lived for a few months.[1] Since the poor Catalans scarcely have paper and they want at all costs to make an edition, it seems that the book will have two or three, for several reasons.[2] One would be the Catalan one that the Humanities Department will do on their own account. The State of Pachuca, Mexico, will do another one for Mexico and the United States *only*. And the third should be one by Calpe in Buenos Aires. But Guillén thinks that it wouldn't make very much for the children, and in this case it's really a question of getting money out of a book as the goal. She wanted me to propose to you that you, alone or with her, for the Spanish children, do this third edition aimed at Argentina, which perhaps could be some 2,000 copies. SUR would do it, although Calpe would *distribute* it, so that you could watch over it and keep the money from evaporating . . .

And so, abruptly, I propose it to you, before leaving Paris. I'm taking a ship to Rio de Janeiro. The originals remain in the hands of Palma Guillén (Legation of Mexico in Copenhagen). Please do me the favor of answering her. Since you know me, you'll pardon this direct request, which seems pretentious. In its abusiveness there's nothing but the desire to do something useful for those creatures with half of our blood. According to Vict[oria] Kent, about 200,000 children (no less!) have left Spain. It would be best, good God, that they remain there with their own. Our America, blinded by political fanaticism, has crossed its arms. Except Mexico, which has accepted 6,000 and is going to receive more.[3] My Basque Chile, Hispanophile Peru, and the rest of our people have pretended not to know what's going on. And those children go to England and to Russia, as if a continent half theirs and with their flesh and blood didn't exist!

I beg you to remember your Gabriela: a negative response from you would not offend me.[4]

Yesterday with [Jacques] Maritain, who loves you and thinks of you, we spoke of you a great deal.[5]

I, I always have you with me.

4 August. Gabriela

1. January and February 1933 are the most probable months of GM's residence in Barcelona.

2. In his autobiography, *Confieso que he vivido,* Neruda confirms the shortage of paper in wartime Cataluña, describing how Republican soldiers contributed their clothing so that his book *España en mi corazón* could be published. None of the other editions of *Tala* that GM describes in this letter to VO were published.

3. Mexico accepted more war orphans and Republican refugees from Spain than any other country. Many of these had sought refuge in France and French North Africa following the fall of the Spanish Republic in April 1939, but Germany's occupation of France subsequently forced the refugees to move again, and many Spanish Republicans perished in forced labor camps during World War II.

4. Although GM asks VO to publish *Tala* on behalf of the war orphans from the Basque country of Spain, GM was apparently confident that VO would agree. Writing to Alfonso Reyes in August 1937, GM indicated, "Finally you'll have this book of mine, before I have it, from the hand of our Victoria" (*Tan de usted,* 113).

5. GM visited both Jacques and Raissa Maritain in Paris. Shortly after this meeting Jacques Maritain published "Sobre la guerra santa" in *Sur,* arguing that the civil war in Spain should not be seen as a clerical crusade; the Church had no right to support either side in a battle for economic and political power. Maritain's philosophy much influenced GM subsequently, and his friendship was also important to her from this time onward (G.10, G.22, G.34, G.37, G.55). Maritain's thought shaped the perspectives of Tomic, Frei, and other founders of Chile's Christian Democratic Party (Frei, *Memorias;* GM, *Vuestra Gabriela*). A final encounter between Maritain and GM took place shortly before her death in New York; Maritain was living nearby, in Princeton, N.J. (Gazarian-Gautier, *Teacher,* 104).

〇〇〇

G.10 [Letterhead: none. GM printed the following address at the end of
the letter: "Hotel Souza, Dantas, Rua Laranjeira." 7 numbered pp., pen,
hand of GM.]

[RIO DE JANEIRO, BRAZIL.] 31 AUGUST [1937]

Dear Victoria:

Many, many thanks for your letter. I found it here at my arrival; ten
days have passed, but I've had no peace. You already know how hectic
and fatiguing our American hospitality is wherever you go, even among
the Yankees.

Your letter brought me the honor of your good thoughts; but in it I
found, at the same time, some bittersweet paragraphs that you'll clarify
for me when we see each other. You say that in my letter there are
things that you recognize as being from Gabr[iela], and others that
aren't from her. Who are they from, then? My dry, hard face always
freed me from bossy people and advisors. That letter is mine, wholly
mine. Give me, on its account, what I deserve, but don't think it's the
work of others.

I don't know if I mentioned it: I went off to find [José] Bergamín
— whom I never met — *exclusively to deal with your matter*, to tell him
about my astonishment at what had been done and to give him my
opinion about you, since I believed that he was absolutely uninformed
about you. If, on leaving Lisbon, I hadn't received those two letters that
you sent me, I wouldn't have sought out or met J[osé] B[ergamín]. I
even fear that some of the people around him, if not him, have seen me
as a flatterer of the Minerva or Juno that you are, in the flesh and in literary portraits.

It happened to me like in the fables: the hero won me, he trapped
me without trying. And it's because Spain has remained, after Unamuno's death, quite bereft of a certain accent, and of a certain mystical
or supernatural marrow, and I found in my long conversations with
B[ergamín], a restitution, a recuperation, partial or what-have-you, of
that admirable old man whom I loved more than he knew and whom I
miss terribly as I try to live, *nothing less than try to live!*[1]

B[ergamín] sent me the correction to his first letter. No, he brought
it to me; but it was read to me in the middle of a tremendous racket. It
left me with the impression that it was *half-bitter and half-good*. Is that
how it was? Then the sediment, the *dregs* of the conflict came; that ter-

rible letter from Mallea and the worse one from B[ergamín] to him [Mallea].[2] There's no way out of the matter now. Mallea, a man of intellectual bent, dealt with the matter that way, in *the weighing of words*. And with J. B., he has to be read from above or underneath his writing.

No, Vict[oria], contrary to what you believe, it doesn't have to do, in my case, with political fervor, with being wounded by *a cause*. It's that I don't want, not for anything in the world, for J. B. to persist in not understanding you, *so that you might lose that man*. I mean lose your soul's relation to the leading Spaniard of this point in time. Despite his unfortunate violence and his *written* language, which is the language of Quevedo when he's angry, that man is of a high spiritual quality and the most Spanish of all the writers of his time. To know him one needs to draw him away from conversation about the war for a while and move him toward religious conversation. The man is a pure marvel then. And I, Vict., this old Gabriela of yours, I *become more pious*, in my own way, but very quickly I find myself moving, *whether rising or falling, I don't know*, toward my irremediable lot of burning faith. A faith — calm down — still heretical enough not to require dogmas or convert anyone, but *an obsessive faith* that envelopes me and floods my days. It must be the solitude in which I've lived, in Portugal. Or maybe it's not that, because this faith, for the first time in my life, is *joyful*, it gives me a keen, childish pleasure, a foolish pleasure that I didn't know before and that I don't want to leave me again.

Let's go on to something else: it disturbs me that *Crítica*, which is my newspaper, didn't publish my letter. But if it is, truly, as you think, *or it seems to be*, a mixture of mine and someone else's, you must have preferred that it not appear in print.

No, that business of my visit with your sister has been poorly told. Someone told me, maybe Amparo Montt, that she wanted to see me. I said that they should tell me when and where. They didn't tell me, and I didn't go. Nor did I believe, because I never believe it, that she had great interest in seeing me, myself. I get along well with few women. But, above all, *women who feel good with me* are very few. And they have created in me, in the end, a certain nonfeminist complex. I don't seek them out. It's true that in this case it had to do with a sister of yours; I should have thought about it and looked for her address. I'm writing her today — to ask her to excuse my clumsiness and to promise to meet her later, somewhere. Now I know *calming* things about her. A woman from the fashionable world frightens me and makes me fearful, too.

I'm happy that M[aría] de M[aeztu] is returning to Colombia. But I'm happy that she was successful in Buenos Aires, against the wind and the tide. You and your merits have validated her against the sea swell. It's a shame, dear Victoria, *a complete shame* that we live in times when excellence doesn't matter a bit; what only matters are some insolent badges that people wear on their chest or in their flesh, of this Kabala or that, of the tribe or subtribe, A to Z. María has a contract to go to the United States for six months or one year, then she will be able to cross into her Spain. Not into a peaceful Spain, to be sure, but surely into one with an open border. She must go there to save many fundamental things in the area of education — *if anyone can save them.* There, another Montes and a few others will be able to do something. One sees that there's about to be such a crumbling of precious, crucial institutions, which is scary or sad, enormously sad, and concerns me and fills me with anxiety.

Vict., you know that in *the papers* I am called a raging anti-Spaniard. It's because I spoke out about Hispano-Americanism some four or five years ago.[3] The Spaniards interest me in regard to their being masters of certain spiritual essences that I don't find elsewhere in Europe, the core inspiration of my mystics, of this group of five or six men and women that have *shaped my soul.* I look at the Basque as mine with relation to blood; at the Catalan as mine by way of co-existence. The rest I see with absolute disinterest, personally, *racially.* But in the nameless and measureless misfortune that they are living, I have followed them and held them *breast to breast.* Peixoto was telling me — and he has some reason — that what the Spanish are going through can be seen in me, printed across my face. Many sleepless nights have I given them, in the middle of the deepest conversation, and they pass before me and carry me away with them like the "Holy Campaign" of their folklore, and I stop seeing those who are with me, and I don't know how to keep on talking.[4] They know the story [of the war], in a certain way. I have lived it from Portugal. It will take days and nights to tell you about it ...

Noble and good Victoria: it's true that *whole novels* are being circulated about you. From Mme. Duhamel, I heard about an almost Communist Victoria, sister of La Pasionaria — who's Basque, don't forget. And here, at a table in the PEN Club, I heard about a V.O. proud of her power and disdainful of the Brazilians. And in Paris, I heard you called a Turin-style Fascist, and *surely you wouldn't believe me foolish enough to believe any of the three legends.* I try to understand you and I understand you two-thirds of the way. I'm missing another third, Vict., and that one you owe me, in slow and patient explanation.

It's possible, Vict., that I'll go to Arg[entina] if I go to Chile. The signs, up to now, are that I'll go. That is to say, there's a letter from the wife of my boss in the Foreign Ministry, in which she tells me I should go.[5] If *they order* me to go, I will, at the risk of many things. I am — very much wounded by my people; but I've pardoned the Spaniards who insulted me, not like they have you, but very, very much more, and it will not be unlikely that *some day* I may pardon my Chileans. To date this hasn't happened, Victoria; I'm a resentful Indian and a pigheaded Basque, the two things, my God, together!

But you are leaving for Europe, and I run the danger of not seeing you. Tell me: is it possible to ask you to stay in Rio a few days? It's the surest way of my speaking with you. When will you pass this way? I'm not thinking of staying in Brazil less than two months. The truth is that I would like to stay about six months. This country fascinates me, and I want to know the provinces. But I don't know anything about anything. They've received me very well, without convincing me that, in the long run, I won't wind up with a policeman on the corner and with two or three spies in the hotel, like in my Portugal — beloved in spite of those things. Who knows anything for sure in these extraordinary times. For right now, tell me when you will pass this way. I'm not at all happy about going to Argentina and not finding you there. It isn't that I intend to cause you any trouble over my personal needs, as I am wont to do, no, nothing of that sort. It's just that your being there would give me a sense of tranquillity, and conversing with you for a few days would compensate me for tiredness and nuisance. Too much!

I'm already on page seven and haven't spoken to you about my book and its Argentine edition. I sent a *very detailed* letter to G[uiller]mo de Torre, and I hope that he has read it *all* by now. It's enough that I sent G[uiller]mo a second letter asking for a quick reply. I'm expecting it any day now.

See [Jacques] Maritain in Paris, Vict., and talk with him at length. He seems almost a saint, to me, and at any rate, a soul capable of saving, an extraordinary guide. *He and his wife love you very much.* They've realized it and they don't deform it with silly admiration or hatred. What a relief and a pleasure to know that, ceaselessly, humanity produces these beings, and that they are within our reach for great crises.

You, with your aversion to atheism, remember on your bad days that that man is there, in France, and that your soul is *very important to him*.

I beg you to write down my address and not to write to me someplace else.

Hugging you with total loyalty and warmest appreciation,

your Gabriela

1. Although GM rejected modern Spain, she supported the values of the late medieval mystics and the early Golden Age (G.5, G.15, G.33).
2. "That terrible letter from Mallea and the worse one from B[ergamín] to him" apparently refers to a polemic between Mallea and Bergamín that was related to Bergamín's criticism of VO.
3. While GM's sense of Latin American identity arguably dates from her residence in Mexico in 1922–1924, the dates mentioned in this letter, and materials published in *Tan de usted*, confirm that GM's sense of that identity substantially grows in 1930 as a consequence of classes in Latin American literature and pre-Columbian civilizations that she taught at Barnard College, Vassar College, and Middlebury College in the United States.
4. GM's note on "Santa Campaña" that appears in *Tala*, regarding her poem "La cabalgata," is relevant here: "The Holy Campaign, but the one of the heroes."
5. GM refers to career diplomat Carlos Errázuriz and his wife, Carmela Echenique de Errázuriz. Their daughter Olaya subsequently married Radomiro Tomic, a lawyer and founder of Chile's Christian Democratic Party, who helped GM with her business concerns in Chile toward the end of her life. *Vuestra Gabriela* reprints a selection of GM's letters to these colleagues.

☙❧

G.11 [Letterhead: engraved stationery inscribed "Villa Victoria, Mar del Plata," followed by an icon of a telephone and the number 504. 1 p., pen, hand of GM.]

[MAR DEL PLATA. EARLY APRIL 1938][1]

Dear Victoria,

I very much fear that your cough last night can be blamed on my smoking and the fatigue we gave you.[2] (Fatigue can become a thousand things.) I humbly ask you to take that remedy of mine: there's none better.

Don't get out of bed, or stay in your room, even if we don't see you all day. The flu is more jealous than the most jealous ones....

So that you can rest, I'm not going to see you.

Yours
Gabriela

Regards from Connie.[3]

1. GM spent eight days (G.14) at "Villa Victoria," coinciding with their April seventh birthday. Samatán's comprehensive account of GM's days in Argentina suggests that the visit to Mar del Plata was the final leg of a tour: "GM arrived in Santa Fe in the last days of March of 1938, invited by the National University of Litoral.... From Buenos Aires she had already been moved to Mar del Plata, as a guest of VO" (Samatán, *GM, campesina*, 132).

2. GM was a heavy, lifelong smoker of cigarettes, but by a seeming agreement between herself and the press, she was rarely photographed holding cigarettes.

3. "Regards from Connie" is written along the left-hand margin. Consuelo Saleva accompanied GM through her South American–U.S. tour of 1937–1938, in wartime France in 1939, during several years in Brazil, and for shorter periods of time in both California and Mexico.

ΩΩ

G.12 [Letterhead: engraved stationery inscribed "Villa Victoria, Mar del Plata," followed by an icon of a telephone and the number 504. 2 pp., pen, hand of GM.]

[MAR DEL PLATA, ARGENTINA. EARLY APRIL 1938]

Dear Victoria:

I slept, not soundly all in a block, but I slept. And I awoke without knowing where I was, until the face of Victoria came to me, and the peaches and the figs arrived ...

I am grateful that you love me a little. I need it. Perhaps, along with sleep, it's the only thing that I need.

If you are the same as yesterday, then you're not as well as yesterday. You should have woken up much better. Maybe I tired you yesterday. Don't let me talk so much, and even less about Spain!

I'm going to see your trees and write some letters.

I want to read that thing by the Chileans whom Neruda is captaining.[1]

God keep you.
Gabr.

1. In October 1937, Neruda left France for Chile, bringing with him the copies of his pro-Republican volume *España en mi corazón*. On his return to Chile, Neruda was immersed in political activity, including promoting the presidential campaign of Popular Front candidate Pedro Aguirre Cerda, a good friend of GM's.

ɷɷ

G.13 [Letterhead: engraved stationery inscribed "Villa Victoria, Mar del Plata," followed by an icon of a telephone and the number 504. 2 pp., pen, hand of GM.]

[MAR DEL PLATA, ARGENTINA. EARLY APRIL 1938]

Dear Vict.:

The second set of proofs arrived.[1] But a major part is missing. Will they come later or *have they forgotten them?*

Missing, in the "Nocturnos," is the one dedicated to you, which shouldn't go anywhere else but in the section of the "Nocturnos."[2] Wasn't it already incorporated into the book? It's the last "Nocturno" in the Section.

I'm going to the city. I may be late. I'll see you at 4:30 or 5.

I hug you without pins . . .

Gabr. [Written along left-hand margin]

1. "Proofs" refers to galley sheets for *Tala*, to be published by SUR. María Rosa Oliver helped GM correct the galley sheets for *Tala* while the two of them stayed at VO's house in Mar del Plata (Letter, María Rosa Oliver to GM, 19 March 1947; Houghton Library Collection, Harvard University).

2. The section "Nocturnos" opens *Tala*. Among the poems in this section, the second to last is "Nocturno de descendimiento," dedicated to VO, which closes, "Year of the Spanish War." Nocturnes were a poetic form cultivated by GM and other poets influenced by *modernismo* (Rojo, *Dirán*, Ch. 4).

ʊʓ

G.14 [Letterhead: none. 3 pp., pen, hand of GM.]

[BUENOS AIRES. 16 APRIL 1938] HOLY SATURDAY

Dear Victoria:

A hybrid day, yesterday that is, on one hand pure *saudades*[1] for you, and on the other, Sarita Bollo. (She left last night.)

Broad and emotional nostalgia for Connie and for me, for those eight *happy* days (it makes me fearful to set down the adjective . . .).

Yesterday Angélica and [Eduardo] Mallea called,[2] Mallea in order to say that he would be leaving Buenos Aires for the day, but that he would be at the conference at the Hebrew Institute.[3] (Sarita Bollo spoke with him by telephone.)

Vict., we were hoping that you would do what you promised and write an hour at least, in the morning, if that's what's most agreeable for you. But you shouldn't let a day pass without taking a look at our Emily Brontë and moving further along with the biography.[4] Tell yourself this when you write, dear Victoria, so pained at not seeing and hearing; promise and fulfill the promise and don't forget us so much.

Horrible the news today about poor Cataluña.[5]

Tell María Rosa [Oliver] that Chile has closed the consulate in Rosario and all along the coast, apparently owing to lack of work for the consuls now that passports are not being issued: Argentina is lost, then.[6]

I'm correcting the talk for the Hebrew Institute, and then I'm going out because the day is beautiful. Again I tell you that you are all much missed and that one has the feeling of an arm amputated or the loss of one of the theological powers. It's hard to lose you, Vict., although I may only have won you over by a third. I don't know if Connie is saying this or me. The plural is very comfortable —

God watch over you for me

Your big, pious woman
Gabriela
Holy Saturday

1. Nostalgia: The multiple meanings that GM assigns to this Portuguese word are printed in her notes to *Tala*.
2. Angélica Ocampo was VO's next younger sister, with whom she was

very close throughout her life. They called and visited each other regularly when they were in Argentina and communicated by mail frequently when either one was abroad (*Cartas a Angélica y otros*, 1997).

3. GM's speech, "Mi experiencia con la Biblia" was delivered to the Instituto Hebraico in Buenos Aires on 18 April 1938.

4. VO wrote a biographical essay on Emily Brontë, published in 1938 (reprinted in *Testimonios II*, 1941). GM also wrote of Emily Brontë in one of her longest essays about any woman writer. Her "Emilia Brontë: La familia del Reverendo Brontë" (1930) has strong autobiographical overtones.

5. Nationalist troops aided by the Fascist forces of Germany and Italy drove through to the Mediterranean, isolating the Spanish Republican government in Valencia and surrounding Barcelona. This led to the downfall of the Spanish Republic and the triumph of Francisco Franco, who ruled Spain for the next forty years.

6. As war developed in Europe, Argentina and other Latin American nations restricted the issuance of passports. Up to this point, GM seems to have considered the possibility of a consular post in Rosario, Argentina.

ഗ

G.15 [Letterhead: none. 9 pp., pen, hand of GM.]

[CALLE ELIZALDE, BUENOS AIRES. CIRCA 18 APRIL 1938]

Dear, savage Vict.:

I don't know if you're going to come by [the house on] Elizalde [Street], in your Valkyrie-cavalcade fashion,[1] and if I'll have time or not to say something to you and see you, since there will be visits in addition to the cavalcade. And I have to tell you some things:

Until the day I die I'll be bogged down in organdy, the organdy of all the women schoolteachers who take hold of me or write me as something belonging to them.[2] (I must have some deep-hidden organdy, no doubt.)

The thing on the radio was horrible; Coni is hardened by now: she didn't suffer a bit. The most organdy of all was, you'll be amazed, that man with the imbecile presentation, although he didn't recite poetry.

But there were two precious children (orphans from an asylum) who resembled Yin Yin and who didn't speak at all.[3] I always come across an angel in the mountain of student organdy. But it wounds me horribly to see orphaned children. Ay, Victoria, since I'm the same sort as Mallea, I'm likely to think the blackest things: if I die and then Palma and Margot Arce have married, and if Yin Yin, in all this, isn't yet fourteen years old — old enough to go to work — I hope you'll free him for me, from falling into the sterile, white nightmare of religious and lay orphanages. Take him close to you, or almost, for me.[4] I nearly lose my mind when I think about it.

You're wrong to blame organdy on Cinderella and her kind. On the holidays that I've been here, everything has been chemically pure organdy. I give up, like a tired animal. I wore myself out and I killed myself some time ago. My laughter kept me from seeing you.

I promise you, by way of discharging my responsibilities, an article for *Sur* about organdy. Maybe it's worth the trouble. As a result of your angry letter, I said terrible things about "Children's poetry" in Mercedes,[5] beginning with my own work in *Desolación*.[6] And the young teachers took it very seriously and wound up getting hold of the school superintendent to say that something had to be done and that what they heard *was totally true* and should not be forgotten.

Now Dujovne: some days ago he asked if he could speak to me alone, before going to the Hebrew Institute. He spoke to me about *Sur*, about Argentina's *editorial moment* (yesterday Mallea said the same thing to me), about the total lack of business sense of the staff (working with *Sur*) and the proposal of that gentleman — Zaleski?

I told him that the commercialization of the magazine brought with it, unfortunately, the danger of shifting your intellectual direction toward the stockholders, etc. He answered me that he could have this Jewish gentleman acquire stock up to the point that there would be no monopoly interest in *Sur*. (I saw him, Dujovne, as being somewhat implicated here, but I don't know how.) He asked me to go to you, to make a case. I told him that it's very disagreeable to me, to appear as a person who's been commissioned.

Yesterday was the famous meeting between the grandchildren of the chieftains.[7] Nothing came of it, no good or bad for anyone. I have the impression that I spoke with no result, that I heard as little as I could possibly hear in *three hours* (I don't mean in terms of *quality*, but *quantity*, in the material), that the idea of meeting with Mallea was really too much. In his book I gather the buds of his soul and life; I'm going to write an article returning what Mallea has given me there: coming together was *more than enough*. Besides that, I have the impression that the two of you are shameless (stubborn, obstinate, horrible, ugly, stupid, and proud) ah, above all *proud*, my God! The two of you can go to hell, to *your* hell, to your oblivion, to your bare stone, to your flat pampa of solitude and the aftertaste of *insipidness* of which Saint Teresa spoke. I'm not going to waste another word on you or on him, and don't ask me again about what I know of the famous meeting.

Mallea told me that he would always do as he has done, in *Sur*: the irregular (without order); that he can't accept stock or anything at all; and that *Sur*, without you, doesn't seem like anything to him, it doesn't matter and has no reason for being, for him or anyone.

Dujovne came last night, looking for me, to bring me to his house. He announced that he would go to see you to speak to you about his friend and *Sur* (an urgent matter). Mallea also told me that it needs to be resolved quite soon. The thing with the Jew didn't strike him as a bad idea.

M[aría] de M[aeztu] told me four days ago that she would try to sell shares in *Sur* among friends. (Your friends? I hope so. Because woe to her friends, followers of Franco!)

I have really missed you, Vict., every day and also every hour.

Don't get upset about this letter with its pretty insults. You have whatever liberties you may want to take with me.

Later I'll answer you about professional morality.

A thousand thanks for your letter, today, about the little girl Votoya and about Emily [Brontë].[8]

A hug from Gabr.

1. GM uses the term "Valkyrie" to praise strong, independent women, as in her poem "A Lolita Arriaga en Castilla," in *Tala*, about the Spanish Civil War.
2. GM uses "organdy" as a kind of code (G.15, G.24, G.25) to describe the formal public receptions given for her involving starchy, stiffly dressed schoolteachers, over the course of this year-long lecture tour. GM's lack of a fixed residence or a place to which she could retreat for privacy made her particularly vulnerable to the crowds that sought her out, throughout Latin America.
3. Juan Miguel Godoy (Yin Yin) came to live with GM from about October 1926 onward. Vargas Saavedra estimates that Juan Miguel was born in March or April of 1925 (*Otro suicida*, 24).
4. GM's trust in VO is evident in her asking VO to take Yin Yin if something happened to her and Palma and Margot Arce.
5. Mercedes is a city in Argentina, one hundred kilometers west of Buenos Aires.

6. Although GM wrote several substantial essays on "children's poetry," her best-known is the extraordinary piece on lullabies, entitled "Colofón con cara de excusa," which appears in the 1945 edition of *Ternura* (and not in earlier editions). The work condensed several decades' worth of writing and speaking about poetry for children and mothers (Horan, *GM: An Artist and Her People*, Ch. 4; Horan and Brenes García, "Canciones de cuna"; Rojo, *Dirán*, Ch. 3; Fiol-Matta).

7. GM was probably referring to a contentious meeting between VO and Mallea, both descendants of Argentine founding families.

8. "Votoya" was a nickname (abbreviated form of "Victoria") that the children around VO's house in Mar del Plata used for her. GM, after visiting VO there, frequently used this affectionate term in her letters.

ΩΩ

G.16 [Letterhead: none. 6 pp., pen, hand of GM.]

[CALLE ELIZALDE, BUENOS AIRES.] 24 [APRIL 1938]

Dear Victoria:

Today I've stayed in bed because I'm not feeling very well. Not very badly, either.

I'm sending you, by certified mail, the magazine that Uruguay's Education Department publishes.[1] It has the three conversations by the poetesses about "How they write." That might amuse you. The one by Alfonsina [Storni] is good![2]

Connie has found an unpublished article of mine about a matter that interests me very much, which might be important to you, about the linguistic separation of our America: the fact that Brazilian and Spanish-American literatures live side by side, ignoring one another.[3] I'm going to take a look at it and send it to you.

Here your walls, your furniture, and your objects are watching me live, as if they were you, remembering you and keeping you constantly present.

Yesterday I remembered seeing in Paris a white llama (a very handsome one, a *founding father* of Peruvian llamas) and that Palma told me it resembled you. And it's true.

The brief history of what happened at the college is this: I left early and found myself in the embassy with a letter of alarm about my presentation at the college. I tore it up, only halfway believing what it said. In the afternoon, two boys came by asking to see me. Various people were there; the two boys didn't want to come in, and they spoke to me in the corridor because their business was *urgent*. They told me, *word for word*, that they were coming to ask me to have my presentation *sponsored* by such and such a magazine (a chapbook) of such and such an organization of students, and that I be introduced accordingly, by the student. Then I understood what was going on with the letter. And I excused myself truthfully: Connie wants me to cancel two or three of the presentations that were already agreed to or almost agreed to, and this was the occasion to *suppress* this one, which ultimately had to do with my poetry. Then the boys became upset and went into the main room to argue. Connie didn't know anything about the letter. She has no Indian depth and *understands nothing*. Another professor who was there, after hearing her [Connie] argue two hours with me in front of the students, explained after they left what was going on with Mr. [Coriolano] Alberini, whom he knew personally.

I believe, Victoria, I believe that in refusing I've done a good thing, *not just for myself, but for you, who asked that favor from this gentleman*. Carlitos Reyles understands nothing of "faces and ways and appearances," and he didn't see these things on Mr. Alberini's part, when he asked him *the favor*! Alberini ended up remembering it like the sort of person to whom one goes to ask for money. Then it seemed to him that he had done poorly in assigning the university position to a *living* poet, who was a country schoolteacher but whose subsequent pages of services he didn't know, just like Argentines in general don't know anything relating to the smaller countries in America. Then he sought out his students and sent them to me. There's no such shortage of professors to give introductions. There's no reason for anyone to introduce me. But he was refusing so that *the college* would *prohibit* the presentation. You might hear otherwise, but that's the truth.

Let's keep this for later, as the Mexicans say.[4]

You, who are generous and a lady, in this as in everything, need not stir up these . . . pedagogical waters. Next time, don't ask them to offer a university position to a foreign poet. They believe, bless them, that poetry *isn't culture* and has nothing to do with education because . . . education — the education that they provide — thoroughly hates creativity, in any form. But we die, we poor poets, and then they get hold of us to gnaw on our bones in their literature classes, and from that gnawing they live, year in, year out, fabricating classes that let them eat. In some places, even in our America, this handsome pedagogical custom is already corrected and rectified; in other places, it continues undisturbed and the visiting traveler has to . . . respect it. But the ugly part of the story is getting the boys, the students, involved in it.

I've spoken with María about what went on with Ramiro. It's already begun, and we will pursue it.

Be careful about university positions for her, so that the Alberinis don't leave her high and dry.

The Chilean ambassador told me to ask you to have lunch with him one of these days. I told him that you're often abroad. And my Victoria will miss out on the thighs of my dirty old man, and all the rest . . . How bad I am, my God!

Tomorrow I will go off to *Sur*. And I'll give you news. De Torre says that everything will go well.

Please tell Mr. Mallea when you talk to him on the telephone that I'm very grateful to him, very, for the many things he's done for me. I will write him before I leave.

I asked Chile for permission to travel by boat; they sent me papers to travel by airplane.

Pardon the bother, beloved and respected Victoria. A hug for you from

Gabriela
24.

1. This refers to the January 1938 summer session of the University of Uruguay in Montevideo, when GM, Alfonsina Storni, and Juana de Ibarbourou each gave a lecture. GM's text (or part of it) has been reprinted as "Como escribo."

2. GM's friendship with Storni dated from 1920, when Storni was among GM's correspondents during GM's residence in Punta Arenas, in Chilean Patagonia. GM was at that time considering moving to Argentina (see Scarpa, *Desterrada*, 2:329). GM's widely reprinted "Poema del hijo," written in Punta Arenas (according to Laura Rodig), is dedicated to Storni. Based on their meeting in Buenos Aires in 1926, GM wrote a short, impressionistic essay on Alfonsina Storni ("Algunos semblantes: Alfonsina Storni") and another short essay in 1953, "Alfonsina Storni," that notes their shared backgrounds as autodidacts. Uncharacteristically, GM seems to have written and published nothing to mark Storni's suicide later in 1938.

3. GM's essay "Sobre el divorcio lingüístico de nuestra América" was published in *Sur* 46 (July 1938).

4. GM foresaw difficulties in her traveling and giving public presentations

in both Argentina and Chile. In an August 1937 letter to Alfonso Reyes, she explained: "I don't know if I'm going to Buenos Aires. It's possible. But going there is to suffer the trip and I'm afraid of my people and of my anger, of both" (*Tan de usted*, 112).

ιɔɔ

G.17 [Letterhead: none. 1 p., pen, hand of GM.]

[BUENOS AIRES, ARGENTINA. APRIL OR MAY 1938]

Vict., dear:

I sent to you a Yankee feminist: Matilde Fenberg (Jewish, apparently), whom I saw say worthwhile things in a meeting. I ask you to greet her as she may go to visit you. — Fondest regards to María. Tell her, strength and joy. No one really has them in these black days if one is Spanish.[1] And she is very much so.

G.

M[atilde] F[enberg] is going to the Alvear Palace Hotel [Buenos Aires].

> 1. By 15 April 1938, the Nationalist assault on Republican Spain on the eastern Mediterranean coast divided the Republic in two.

ιɔɔ

G.18 [Letterhead: none. 22 pp., pencil, hand of GM.]

[ARGENTINA. MAY 1938][1]

Dear, very dear, so precious Victoria:

I thank you very much for your letter today, more than you could know. Almost tomorrow and I'll be leaving, and it's very unlikely that I'll see you again. If I return to Europe, I'll be in places where I won't be able to call you because it won't be business related; if to the United States, it will be the same thing. And I was leaving in a sorrowful mood or manner (also Mallea, here) toward you. You had given me lots of confidence and none at all, Vict. You're like family, and this without intimacy. Mallea kept floating in the air as the cause of your anxiety and like the knot that doesn't ever let you have joy or break out, open and happy, in full-fledged laughter. I'm not a meddler, Vict., and I usually live with people without asking them to confide in me in a certain way and also being distant, avoiding it when they want to put things in my hands. But precisely the opposite occurs with those *whose salvation* matters to me. (Go ahead and laugh if you want, at the word . . .). Your salvation, Vict., matters a lot, but in this case it's liable to be additionally interwoven with the salvation of another. I was going to leave, putting you behind me like that horrible thing that's called "an important literary relationship." I exaggerate, by an octave, as always. Apart from your work, I've been interested in your soul, but you've given me no indication of arriving at the heart of your problem or of even barely touching it with a pen . . . Now, yes, I can do so, and I take the opportunity, excessively, maybe grossly (in the sense of abundance), because I'm leaving and it's quite probable that I won't see you again in this world.

I'm going to follow the order of your letter and answer you, point by point, before telling you what's truly important for me to tell you.

1. You say that living without you is probably as painful to Mallea as living with you.

In the core of your being, where the truth springs up in a steady stream, you know (I lower by an octave, there) that that isn't true. In suffering with what is esteemed and loved, suffering it from down there, badly, what is most painful, worse, what is most humbling, even, is to live, *to live*, and the rest, a neutral life that's easy for others, is Death, one swallow after another, and what the saints call a bad death. You know (there, where one is aware, in that depth of one's being) that Mallea — and you, you! — that the two of you are better, you exist, you are, together, close, say what you may, including insults. Don't talk to me using language and expressions from outside, which the thinking senses give you. That's *nobody's* true speech.

2. Mallea is farsighted when it comes to good fortune, and he can't touch or feel it except in the form of a memory, *regret* and *nostalgia* [these two words in English in original]. You also can know it that way, but what's more, you can live the present, which *exists* for you.

The sick person and all imaginative people have this vice of *oblique*, indirect good fortune.

I don't believe that he'd be capable of looking at good fortune and drinking it in, with his face in the bubbling fountain. And if he can't, you have to strive after it with him — strive for it, live it, suffer it with <u>Passion</u>[2] — until he learns that good fortune and accepts and lives it.

You know better than I that the only one who'll do this is a mother or a woman who loves a man, to whom *his salvation* matters. (Come and eat this word again, my lioness, but chew it well.) No one bothered that I learn that, and I have had to strive for it on my own and belatedly, and in this as in everything, to live by my own forces alone. Because I know that agony gives me strength, it's important to me that it be taught to others.

3. That I can achieve, with Mallea, what you no longer can! You're not speaking to a vain, silly woman (the two are one and the same). If you believe something like that, at least remember that I'm going away and that, like you — with more certainty in your case — I won't be seeing him again in this world. You are the only woman who can do it, you, not even his mother. But what's more, you *must* do it, or you're going to eat the bitter fruit of remorse all your life. Make up your mind, and quickly, throwing aside the loose threads, the little nothings that cloud your view and are just that, foolish.

4. Coming between the two of you, you say, is what's harsh, rough in you, and what's dark, stubborn, underground, in him. When you — when anyone buys a piece of ground, they also buy, without thinking about it, the subsoil. The farmers never think about it or concern themselves with it, but they have it, there it is. And there are no lands without subsoil and even *without* abysses. You have them, too, despite your precious frankness that I adore in you and this nature of yours, of air, of sun, of marine gusts and enormous openness. You have them, undergrounds and abysses. Only you don't live there, and maybe, as one does when walking along a mountainside, you turn your face to the side when you come across them.

I'm speaking, almost, of an unknown person — I haven't finished his book yet — and it's a little grotesque for me to embark on this adventure of defending him. One is born this way, with half of one's body in a cave, my Vict.; one arrives this way and it seems that one dies this way. Take a look: I seem so frank, my whole body visible and open, like you. But I am Mallea, too: ten subsoils and the depths of the black-and-blue sea that use me or see me. Neither Mallea nor I believe that we're loved, and we're quite vain about being this way: I wish that we weren't, for our own good and the good of others. Last night I spent two hours without writing letters or reading, completely submerged, body and all, in a tremendous cave, my own, the same as always, since I was seven years old. Coni came in late and I said nothing to her. What for? To what end? She's very much a child, and what's more, she's North American. But not you, and with Mallea you have the duty to accept that he lives on the normal plane — the road, the paving by the house — interspersed with his abysses, of tropical or Indian quivering, it's all the same, perhaps with vertigo, and with darkness in any case. I would hope (I'm full of hope . . .) that he might've separated the two planes by now, and that he could live the forbidden and the somber one alone . . . giving you, as much as possible, his pure body and his normal and solar soul. Some day, I know it, a tremendous appetite will make you want him to give you the other one as well, and from then on you won't want, not for anything in the world, to stay with just the Mallea who's easy, flat, and pedestrian to live with . . . That moment would be so beautiful, our Vict. (his and mine).

5. Your arguments have wound up lasting — weeks later — a year. Horror and worse horror: one caused by stupidity, an infinite stupidity. There are no imbecilities like the ones that the most intelligent people cook up. It should shame _the two of you_, a vast, ample shame, a burning shame.

Suppose that one or the other of you were to die in this interval of silence and of separation. Wouldn't the surviving one chew his or her fists in anger and sorrow, saying, a thousand times, _idiot_ and what an _idiot?_[3] And something like dying will happen to you. You're going off, sailing off to beautiful Europe, without cutting this knot first, leaving the stupid conflict intact. And it can happen — may your Guardian Angel not want it and prevent it — that you'll _gamble it all._ That happens. One plays, one doesn't play, so one thinks, one plays with the dice, _putting_ one's destiny out on the table of the air. Full of bile and fury and . . . with remorse — which seems like fire some times — and one plays . . . Then, as the priests say, and rightly, what follows is only the grinding of teeth and hell, plain and absolute.

Slim chance, worth the risk of going like that — with those degrees of frantic pain.

You may or may not know it, but you're in pain, acute, strong pain. It courses through you and we hear it, even strangers hear it. And I don't want you to live this way, because I care about you, and Mallea — the other example of self-negation — must feel the same way; I saw some words from him that carry a similar pulse of frenzy.

Listen, Vict. You waste a lot of patience with fools and rogues; more than you believe. And this patience, which is false, plus a hundred [illegible] like it, you should be capable of giving to Mallea. For the plain and simple reason that he is who he is and that you care for him. An unhappy and flea-ridden woman understands that, why don't you understand it? The best part of ourselves — the broadest and loftiest, I repeat, the best — should go to what one loves. If patience is something heroic in you, on account of what it costs you, that arduous thing is owed to him; if humility — this is the great thing — humility is what's most *bleedable* in you, that humility with blood and weeping floods, within you, is also owed to him.

There's a little white stone, not from the beach but from the soil, from the poor soil, to which you have given scant attention and that perhaps you don't like, as Niestche [*sic*] said, which perhaps they haven't let you see well, which is stupid and divine and is called humility. I, too — pardon the comparison — I, too, discovered it late, but for a little while now I've been traveling with it, carrying it in a little bit of a disk that has to grow in me — like the Japanese mushroom, that ugly thing, which cures. . . .

It offers very curious things, the poor face of the soil: in the long run it offers a fulfilling sweetness, a separate happiness, a joy unleashed by the tears of coming from where it comes and of being so strange, so secret, this — delight, so very . . . — pardon the word — supernatural.

You are living a kind of Satanism: you're capable of that humility with the servants in your house, with children, with animals, and yet you don't want to live it with this man, precisely because it's him, for being himself. You'll see that it pains me to understand this about you, but you'll also see how clearly and well I understand it. It would be better if I didn't comprehend it, as happens to me with so many things! — At this point I went to lunch, and you know what was said.

I've thought over some convictions, and you've left me in doubt about some points. But I'm going to continue answering the letter.

6. You say that you don't want dealings with him to continue slowly roasting you like Guatimogin [Cuauhtemoc]. But what's absurd is that without him you're burning yourself up, and I don't believe it's a slow burn. In these matters, I put it brutally because it's better, the only solution is to stop loving, but since it isn't the case that you've stopped loving him even a pinch less, and perhaps you love him even more than before, the only *remedy* (and how the word will strike you!) is to accept reality. And this is total sacrifice — fear it or laugh at it — the same as Indian women and poor little Oriental women.

If Mallea is that very difficult man, that *algebra* from another planet, that theology which is more Alexandrine than Roman, that spiny sea urchin and shimmering mother of pearl and that snail, hidden away or big as a bull, and that secret doctrine, then there's nothing to be done except . . . devote your life to him, sparing no effort, until you conquer him, in the ineffable conquering that would be his giving in, ultimately surrendering himself for his own good; finally trusting and not fearing anything anymore. Adopting a stable manner of being and no longer clouding his sight with fickleness! Knowing himself loved, if he hasn't already realized that, foolish man! And with this, finding happiness from head to toe, happy with all his might, fearlessly happy, happy without a barometer and without a calendar in hand. The rest would follow from this. It strikes me that this might be the answer to everything: the fact that you aren't happy and can't be is partly due to him but also — don't deny it — due to your pride. Because when it comes to affection, you experience something like what happens in your writing: you're a woman of passion who doesn't want to let it out, either because you think passion shouldn't be expressed on paper or because you prefer famous *ideas* to passions. It could be that Mallea recognizes in you the snare that your readers have encountered: that you cheat them of the best of yourself and then some. What for? I don't know. It can't be stinginess; you are as generous as the uncontrolled Amazon River. Is it fear? And why do you believe that the Great Dealer gave you, precisely, passion? To put it away in canning jars? Or to perform with it the likewise satanic operation of transforming it into coldness and into "an ordered revolving of eternal stars,"[4] when in fact you're not a firmament but just a creature.

And you're going to grow old, if this is the case, and since passion doesn't dry up in women before the bone marrow dries up, you, in years to come, with the burning oven in your hands, will give it to some macaw that they'll bring you from Ceylon or to some microscopic monkey from Brazil or to . . . theory number 2,000 of an English suffragette concerning human happiness.

7. "*Moi, Pur sang*" [As for me, pure blood]. And I knew it ever since I saw you in Madrid, and now, every time that I've heard or seen you. You are such an exemplary type, the crowning example of your caste and such a stellar person, that for this very reason your egregious suicide is angering (much health and desperation on top of it), your wasting yourself is enraging, the full-scale burning of your noblest oil only

to serve what, on the face of it, you didn't want to call arrogant pride and you settled for calling *dignity*. Here I repeat to you that a vocabulary of this sort (imbecilic whether it's dignity, self-love, or scruples) is a language to use in speaking with outsiders, with all of those who come to your doorway, but that no one with any knowledge of life uses with those who are close to them, with their own, with the same breath and the same pulse in their wrists, so to speak. You use this language with Mallea. Still! And if he's heard you say it, then he's right to have broken it into bits that you must now join together like the little metal rods of a Swiss watch, until it runs again.

8. And you've also said that *if you weren't yourself,* you would have had patience *always* and sweetness *always.* And why don't you have them? And what does it matter to you, this business of not being yourself? Or is it that you can't stop being yourself? My Vict., all women at some point could perform this monstrous turnaround, this almost deadly, gut-deep upheaval. When they wanted to. *But as crazy women.* One loves God, a man, a child, a vice, in this way, and one shouldn't love in any other way. *The rest doesn't count.* The rest, which doesn't suffice, which doesn't reach this scalding point, can go to the garbage heap or serve to scour basins: halfhearted affection, halfhearted pity, halfhearted sacrifice, life dished out in cubes or by the teaspoon, like my [blood pressure medicine].[5]

9. You're bored or weighed down, you say, by "good people." I'm not one of them and I don't know what you're referring to. It's not by way of being good that one does the above-noted; as you know very well, there's no merit in loving, there's no virtue in it, no plan, how could there be, good God! One doesn't *make* it, just as one doesn't make summer or cold weather. It only comes by way of taking no shortcuts with dams of limestone and machinery and perverse will and education and I don't know what other nonsense, plus life's high tide, loving on a large scale, the swelling of powers, rising to one's destiny as at one's noon. You need do no more than not stand in your own way, not ruin this seasoning of the soul that you should complete and from which, in a chain of consequences, the rest will follow. I really fear, Vict., that despite your being the patron of the natural that I've imagined with respect to all women, and being the tiger that a wise man says you are and the ceiba tree that a foolish woman has called you, with all this, you, whether on account of venom, poison, or intellectual drug, you may be the one who diminishes your treasure or closes internal reser-

voirs, or perhaps you're not *yet* capable of sloughing off, like a snake's old skin, the rotten parts of that class upbringing, that education you were given (when it comes to upbringing, I've always believed that even a good one was really bad).

10. It's beautiful that you confess that your conscience is uneasy. *Y per cause* [And for good reason]! And you won't rest easy, either, not until you save the soul from which you may hang and depend. Even if it only means saving him from himself, and with more reason if he has no enemies except for those within himself. Why should you want anything other than to make a man happy, a man to whom you gave happiness and *who taught you to receive happiness from his hand?*[6] All the rest will mature in him, for you, because of him, with him, by way of him. Look: I believe that this *interruption* of ten to twelve months has been sterile for you, including your writing, conversation, everything.

11. It's natural that he wouldn't agree to take *Sur* and lose you.[7] You want to exact a Mongolian torture: to walk in your footsteps, breathe in your air, and touch you within your walls.

12. And now comes the most senseless part of the whole letter. It turns out that I could do Mallea some good, and I could do this . . . with my poetry and with my conversation! The ingenuousness, the dotage by which you know me, don't take me that far.[8] My Victoria, I'm not a vain woman. I know what my possibilities are, what I'm capable of, what I can give, what I can achieve in human beings. Mallea is a profound soul; it's not a matter of my not achieving anything — I can't even attempt it — to convince him, with regard to *Sur*: he knows that he should leave if you flee the business, tossing it into his hands. With regard to spiritual resources that I might give him, I need them, I lack them myself. A small group of beings lives off me. They are children or old women. I'm of no use for more than that.

Save him yourself, my Vict., a man of that value and category who's worth all of it. Continue what you began! My God, you have enough to feed the soul of peoples, you are tremendously rich! You can do whatever you might want with whatever place — physical or moral — where you alight or land. But settle in, stay, don't travel, don't be capricious, don't wear yourself out, don't deny yourself, don't give up.

Pardon your Gabr. for bringing you harshness and sourness. The others don't give it to you. I have to give it to you. It's a sad charge.

G.

1. The date is conjectured from references to Eduardo Mallea and to VO's imminent departure for Europe (in the second half of 1938) and to the fact that GM writes without knowing what her next consular assignment or future might be. Her fate would be decided following the September 1938 presidential elections in Chile. In Argentina, Eduardo Mallea was replaced by José Bianco as editor in chief of *Sur* in August 1938 (King, *Sur*, 58).
2. GM here underlines "passion," twice and uses an initial capital letter to insist on its full range of meaning and to refer to Mallea's well-known book *Historia de una pasión argentina* (1937).
3. In "the surviving one chews his fists in anger or sorrow," GM seems to be citing Dante, a favorite poet of both GM and VO. In *Inferno* XXXIII, 58, the imprisoned Count Ugolino, incapable of sorrow while alive, but perpetually crying from rage after his death, chews his fists in anger, realizing that his enemy the Archbishop Ruggieri will survive him.
4. In "ordered revolving of eternal stars," GM simultaneously refers to Dante, *Paradiso* XXXIII, 145 (*"l'amor che move il sole e l'altre stele"* [the love that moves the sun and other stars]) and to VO's book on Dante.
5. Original is scarcely legible, but seems to read "Taka" or "Tata," followed by "Diastolaos." Diastolic, referring to blood pressure, together with "teaspoon," could be the name of an unidentified medication GM might have been taking.
6. GM's question here is the culminating point of the case she has been making throughout the letter. Its self-sacrificing implications, however, were alien to VO's independent, increasingly feminist spirit at the time.
7. It appears that VO was ready to withdraw from day-to-day involvement with *Sur*, though the circumstances are not clear.
8. "Dotage" (*chochez*) is a word GM used to describe herself in one of her earliest extant printed letters, which she wrote as a twenty-five-year-old schoolteacher to Rubén Darío (reprinted in *Antología mayor: Cartas*, ed. Vargas Saavedra, and Arce and von demme Bussche, eds., *Proyecto*).

G.19 [Letterhead: República de Chile, Ministerio de Relaciones Exteriores. 3 pp., pen, hand of GM.]

[SANTIAGO, CHILE.] 25 MAY [1938][1]

Dear Vict.

I haven't written, but you, less. And the Indian woman moves in the hustle-bustle of May twenty-fifth, along Florida [Avenue in Buenos Aires], while Diana in San Isidro doesn't hunt deer and looks only at the little table, that Lilliputian one.

I'm answering your telegram today. But, moreover, today is your saint's day and I want to begin the day with you and to live it with you.

Six days ago I went to see [Chilean ex-President Arturo] Alessandri. I spoke to him at length about publishing matters, a blow-by-blow account, assertively and courteously, making him see what pirating [books] means with regard to our reputation abroad.[2] He was very genteel, and he promised me that he would personally take charge of the matter. Coni will give you details about this and other things. She likewise went to see her blood relative . . .

My Vict, last night (24), just last night, I read the Writers' Alliance pamphlet.[3] Seven days ago, Neruda promised to send it to me. But he didn't bother to do it. And last night Alberto Romero brought it to me. Romero and Neruda and Delia [del Carril] left at 11:00. At 12:00 I laid my eyes on it. Later I looked in vain for the document in every bookstore to which I've gone. I couldn't write my article without reading this, according to what my colleagues say. Tonight or tomorrow, the twenty-sixth (I'm going to Elqui, the twenty-seventh), I'll write my article about you, about your black legend. Coni will send it to you by airmail. Last night I spoke for one and a half hours to Romero (Vice Pres. of the Soc. of Writers) about you. I mention you almost daily, verbally, to people. Your black legend (especially the anti-Chilean aspect) is so firmly entrenched that it's absolutely necessary that my article be published here. We'll see what *El Mercurio* does. Only yesterday did I go over there, to my newspaper. They're resentful about my eight months without sending contributions. But there are other strings left to pull.

I don't know how to tell you rapidly and well, Victoria, how feverish and potentially explosive the land is that I tread in Santiago. They've done as much as possible, on both sides, to launch me into politics. I only want to leave, because it's very difficult to live walking along a tightrope.

The misery of the common people has made me want to shout aloud.[4] I haven't stifled it, Vict. The nakedness of the children, the abandonment of the Indian and the "dark-skins" in the South has turned my stomach inside out.

[Pedro] Aguirre Cerda, my friend, the candidate of the ones on the left, seems as if he won't make it to the fight.[5] And the ugly, brutal [Carlos] Ibáñez fills the horizon . . . from the extreme left to the Nazis![6] What's most likely is that Ross may win, but this could bring us a revolution.[7]

The people — the common people — have enthralled me, Vict. You'll see it in those three poems about the South.[8] And the land, my dear, the stupendous land of Osorno and Valdivia. You should take a look at this, the soil, the Chilean base, the volcanoes blinding with radiance, and the lakes, half-Buddhist, and that austral epic, which has nourished me with its strength.

Vict., if you want to have my article translated into French and distributed, dispose of it freely. And if there's anything else to do, tell me, tell me.

The books haven't arrived yet. Now I won't have them until my return from Elqui. It's too bad. The Andes have been closed.[9] But I fear that the books are lost and I'm angry in advance. It's bad to have so few words from you. It's sad, Votoya.

It made a tremendous impression on me, to find my sister at the station, destroyed, run ragged. Hugging her, I felt her poor, inert body. Likewise, there, it made me want to cry aloud. The place where I'll cry like that will be at my mother's tomb. I have a yearning, Votoya, to break into loud weeping, to split this knot that I've been carrying with me in mid-breast, to loosen into flight, to expel a frightful animal aching that I've been carrying for years now, to howl at death like a dog all night long, in the countryside or in the mountains, in solitude, until I pass out, senseless. (Mallea, in skirts, here I go.) But it doesn't dissolve, it doesn't let go, it doesn't split open.

From Bariloche I sent you a corrected copy of *Tala*. Did you get it? I counted some ten major errors: there are three *entire* lines dropped, in three poems. And your Noct[urno] of Desc[ent] simply isn't understandable. In *Sur*, it came out well.[10] This Noct[urno] was taken here from your magazine and published . . . without the dedication. Loads, loads of resentment.

People believe, because of the delay in the book's arrival, that I don't want the book sold here, out of disdain for the country!

Then, they've noted the matter of the price in Chile. In order *to give them an answer*, I gave a *free* poetry reading in the Caupolican [Theater] (5,000 people) and a prologue, about poetry and the people — the masses. Partisan people didn't distribute the tickets to workers from the left wing. Ay, I could tell you a thousand things more. But people have come, now. (I remembered you at that other poetry reading.) A hug from

Gabriel

[Separately, in a note along top margin, p. 1:] I will tell you separately about the two conversations with Delia and Neruda.

1. This letter was written during GM's stay in Santiago in the house of Carmela Echenique and Carlos Errázuriz.
2. In the references to "pirating," GM manifests her distress with the problems of the book trade in Latin America. She points to the practice of pirating in her first note to *Tala*: "I ask the following publishers, the Catalan publisher Bauzá and Claudio Garúa publishers, from Uruguay, who've pirated my author's rights for *Desolación* and *Ternura*, not to steal from the Basque children, in the name of those orphans: they're the authors of that evil act" ("Razón de este libro," *Tala*, 154).
3. The Writers' Alliance pamphlet was published in *Sur* 8, no. 41 (February 1938): 79–85, under the title "Una declaración de la 'Alianza de Intelectuales de Chile para la Defensa de la Cultura' y su respuesta" (A declaration of the 'Chilean Intellectuals' Alliance for the Defense of Culture' and its response).
4. GM uses nearly identical language in 1939, writing to Marta Samatán to describe her visit to Chile and other Latin American countries: "I saw such misery there, that my flesh aches to remember it. It makes you want to sob aloud. The rest of the Pacific is worse, it's a wound, Marta. Hunger, filth, and dictatorship" (qtd. in Samatán, *GM, campesina*, 124). Chile was one of the Latin American countries hardest hit by the worldwide economic depression of the 1930s.
5. Aguirre Cerda and his wife, Juana de Aguirre, befriended GM during her twenties. While Aguirre Cerda ascended within the national government, he aided GM's ascent in the public school system. GM's visit to Chile was probably timed, in part, to assist Aguirre Cerda's presidential campaign. He emerged in 1936 as the candidate of the Frente Popular (Popular Front), a coalition of the reformist, middle-class Radical Party with Socialists and Communists.
6. Aguirre Cerda and the Popular Front received unlikely last-minute support in 1938 from the leader of the Movimiento Nacional Socialista de Chile, ex-President Carlos Ibáñez del Campo, who withdrew from the election following a failed coup attempt (Loveman, 247).
7. "As the presidential election of 1938 approached, the Right chose as its standard bearer Alessandri's ex-treasury minister, Gustavo Ross Santa María . . . he represented the propertied classes . . ." (Loveman, 244).
8. GM wrote "Lago Llanquihue," "Volcán Osorno," and "Salto de Laja" during her May 1938 travels through the south of Chile. They were subsequently published in the anthology *Panorama pintada de Chile* and then reprinted in *Poema de Chile*.
9. Mail between Argentina and Chile traveled via the mountain pass above Mendoza, which closed in heavy snow or strong winds.

10. "Nocturno del descendimiento" appeared in *Sur* 8, no. 42 (March 1938): 20–26, along with three other poems by GM. In *Tala*, the poem bore a dedication to VO and was printed in the section entitled "Muerte de mi madre," alongside poems bearing dedications to Waldo Frank and Alfonso Reyes, mutual friends of VO and GM.

ʂʘʓ

G.20 [Letterhead: none. 7 pp., pencil, hand of GM.]

[SANTIAGO, CHILE. 26 OR 27 MAY 1938]

Dear Votoya and María Rosa:[1]

I don't have either pen or ink at hand. I went to bed, late, on returning from an all-day automobile excursion, and I've just finished reading a letter from Votoya (Vict.) and another from Mallea. Early tomorrow I leave for the Valley of Elqui and I want to leave this news of mine for you before going off, deep into the mountains. I revive my old habit — of writing a collective letter to two, three, or four people. For two reasons: first, because I always see the two of you together. Second, because *this time* I can't manage to write to you separately about lengthy concerns. I beg you not to hold it against me. And, Votoya, I remind you about my condition as a person who's lost her judgment and whose craziness isn't completely visible. . . .

I told you in my previous airmail letter to you, Votoya, that I spoke with [President Arturo] Alessandri about crooked dealings in the publishing business. I see, in the pamphlet by you-know-who, that they give a formidable list of authors who are paid and with which they now silence the mouth of anyone who sometimes or often speaks out — my mouth, several times. If I didn't read it wrong, there's no list of the rest of *the lovely ones* (the editors). I've spoken about the ugly business to many people and to three journalists who were reporting about me. None of them mentioned a word of it in their accounts. I've chased after the pamphlet, and it finally came, sent by Ercilla, without a word. On the train tomorrow, if my sister doesn't upset me, I'll begin my article. The matter as I see it today isn't just the publishing lawsuit, but the legend of Votoya here. It's black, this legend, only around the edges. Here, there's vehement interest in V.O. among young men, old ones, old women, etc. Something that I hadn't imagined. Some four days ago, I went to have tea at the house of the Menéndez Behetys — old friends from Patagonia. There were more than twenty people at the tea. We went out to a hall, next to the fireplace (how beautiful it is, the wildness of it!), and there a writer for *El Mercurio*, a Spanish woman living in Chile for some years, Doña Juana [Quisidos],² a woman with a talent [for graphology], if somewhat formal, developed her theory about V. based on her handwriting, which I don't know who had brought her. She believes that she *irritated* Votoya (the Ricardito one) with her *graphological* portrait,³ which, she says, V. is familiar with, and in which she has discovered that V., French and English and all, belongs to the pampas! I told her that V. and I both learned this some time ago, but that the meaning of *belongs to the pampas* should be taken in a much larger sense, and very affectionately, and that some of that is set forth in my "Recado" about Votoya. Juanita is formidable and, without an invitation, she went on to give the audience a *portrait* of Mallea. (Coni will give you more details.) The whole thing lasted two hours or more. It was already mythological, that is, along the lines of gods translated into folklore with the force of passion, yearning curiosity, and delight. Good God! I explained what I could about Votoya, and Coni did the underlining. I have never seen a similar discussion in Chile regarding a Chilean woman!

Yesterday Doña Inés Echeverría was here,⁴ the writer (an anti-Amanda [Labarca Hubertson])⁵ who spoke of Votoya not in terms of mythology, but learnedly and delightfully to the point. And without a drop of envy, thank God.

Today I went on a long trip to see a horrible residential school that bears my ill-fated name, and I went with the lady of the house and with H. Díaz Arrieta (Alone), critic for *La Nación*, a gentleman despite his being with the publishers.⁶ Neruda was much spoken of, and I named Votoya various times. He kept quiet the whole time. He's the enemy of Neruda who does him the most damage, here, with his criticism. Some days ago I spoke to the pres. of the Soc. of Writers (it's not the famous *Alianza*) about the publishing business and about V., at great length and with much emotion. That day, V. was very alive to me, very much so, and before me in a somewhat phantasmagoric form — odd, I don't know what the reason was. Alberto Romero didn't attack her; he spoke only about the publication, *in special type*, of the Olympian Ortega's *letter*. I explained again.

I will send you — the three of you [she includes Mallea here] — a poem that addresses the point. It's called "*Jandira*" and it's by the Brazilian Murilo Mendes.[7] Marvelous. It's Votoya, but with children. She does widespread damage and has been alive since Genesis, because she's Eve, a Platonic Eve (the archetype), and she influences the whole world in an amazing way and she is ineffable and frightful and beloved and detestable, at the same time. I translated it without knowing that it was Vict.; I translated it in Rio, some months ago. V. now plays Jandira in Santiago.

I've worn out my hand and eyes. I'm going to sleep and will continue tomorrow at 6:00. Sleep well, my dears.

[no signature]

1. GM uncharacteristically addresses VO simultaneously with María Rosa Oliver in this letter.
2. The surname of this writer for *El Mercurio*, Chile's leading newspaper, is not legible in the original letter.
3. Both VO and GM believed in graphology, or handwriting analysis (Meyer, *Against the Wind and the Tide*, 44–45).
4. GM and Inés Echeverría had been friends since 1914. Some of their early correspondence is printed in the *Boletín del Museo-Biblioteca en Vicuña y Epistolario de GM 1912-1918*.
5. Labarca was initially friendly with GM in 1915, following Labarca's return to Chile from the United States, where she had been studying on scholarship. The two women had a falling out later in 1915, when Labarca seems to have solicited GM's entry in a poetry contest that GM did not win, despite the fact that two of three judges voted in favor of GM's verses (*Boletín* 5:30–39). The relationship worsened in the controversy surrounding GM's 1921 appointment to direct the prestigious Liceo #6 in Santiago, since Labarca, a militant member of the Radical Party, supported the rival candidate, Josefina Dey de Castillo, the wife of a prominent Mason and Radical Party member. Labarca Hubertson, like Dey de Castillo, had the formal training in education, the middle-class urban origins, and the family connections that GM lacked. Labarca was clearly GM's chief rival in Chile, a fact that GM's letters note for decades afterward, to the end of her life.
6. Alone, the pen name of Hernán Díaz Arrieta, wrote literary criticism for *La Nación* and *El Mercurio*. He belonged to the same generation as GM and VO. His friendship with GM, which dated from 1922, lasted until her death (G.59, G.70, G.74, G.76). The memoirs and essays that he wrote are valuable social documents of Chile's complex twentieth-century cultural scene.
7. A complete Spanish translation of the poem "Jandira" appears in Murilo Mendes, *Poemas escogidos*.

ငဥငဲ

G.21 [Letterhead: República de Chile, Ministerio de Relaciones Exteriores.
1 p., pen, hand of GM.]

[SANTIAGO, CHILE. JUNE 1938][1]

Dear Vict.:

Last night the lovely Laureano Rodrigo, manager of Ercilla [publishing house], came to the house, . . . He came to speak to me about *Desolación*, but we talked about nothing but Chilean editions, from 9:00 to 1:00 in the morning. I want to send you some information *in the rough*, Votoya, because I'm going to forget it. Rodrigo says that he has written you five letters proposing to defend SUR's rights here, to list SUR's books in the National Library, etc., and that he has never received a reply from you. He swears that he never attacked you, because he's an Argentine and a nobleman(!), the child of a Spaniard! Take note of this colossal news: that all or almost *all* the books stolen from SUR are done by *Letras* and that *Letras* is a trio made up of Amanda Labarca, her husband, and a Sr. Urzúa, a third party. He knew nothing. And I imagine that My President won't follow through with his word to me, which would hurt the little business of his ex-girlfriend.

Rodrigo says — he began with saying — that he had been the biggest pirate of books ever seen, but that now he's the only one who pays authors' rights; according to him, 30,000 francs go to France alone, each month. He says he hasn't done you any injury, apart from getting in ahead of you to get *L'Espoir* from Malraux, when you were going to publish it. He insisted on this a lot, really, the hapless man — he doesn't understand how you didn't see his plan, from the beginning of his deed: to pirate, left and right, in order to create an American publishing business.[2] He came, bringing me real propaganda about my being an Indianist, an American racist, a folklorist, etc. So poor Mistral had to set herself up as a promoter of Europeans. . . .

He says he has a corps of lawyers to defend himself from the other publishers, primarily *Letras*. The wolves, devouring one another!

Now this news from Don Carlos Errázuriz. (Keep it to yourself.) Ross, the one in charge — sure to become Pres. — will kill off Ercilla [publishers] because it's a *political* enterprise (the latter is the pure truth). It's pro-Ibáñez and promotes Communism . . .

Votoya, in Vicuña I left off on page 14 of your defense; there's still some lacking. Here, I continue under the deluge of people. This will last until I get out of here. It's a real horror.

The beginning of a letter for you is going off, done some twenty days ago.

I live, *encore!* anxious to hear more from you. We live.

Gabriela

[GM note, added in top margin, p. 1]: P.S. The 600 pesos are a payment on my book account (*Tala*). Coni needs the final bill. She is writing to [Carlitos] Reyles today.

1. This letter was written immediately following GM's trip to Vicuña and the Valley of Elqui, from the house of Don Carlos Errázuriz in Santiago (*Vuestra Gabriela*, 40–41).
2. The difficulties of SUR in the book business in the Spanish-speaking world can be traced to the combination of piracy and restrictive import licenses. These economic factors were compounded by the overt efforts of writers such as Neruda who systematically organized against Ocampo's projects in the book business; see King, *Sur*, 141.

ᖬᕪᕪ

G.22 [Letterhead: Hotel O'Higgins, Viña del Mar — Valparaíso, Chile.
Por avión. Via "Condor — Lufthansa." 3 pp., pen, hand of GM.]

[VIÑA DEL MAR, CHILE. EARLY JULY 1938]

Lovely Votoya,

It pains me not to receive "tú" or "vos" from you. That totally unravels my confidence.

Did you receive that public letter from Ercilla [publishers]? Publish it, if you want to. You already know which is the most putrid stitch in the wound. I still don't understand clearly the thing with Zig-Zag [publishers]. "To hear me out" they sent an office worker to me, who didn't know to give me the clear information that Ercilla gives.

I spoke with Don Ismael Edwards, who owns 70 percent of the stock in Ercilla. He repeated to me, with all due respect to you, that he — even he — had not received an answer to his letter to you in which he offered you his lawyers to represent your SUR editions here. He has complaints against *Letras* and eight others for eight books (editions that Ercilla paid for, which *Letras* took without paying and published in the same week). If you, Votoya, want another lawyer, I offer you Pedro Aguirre Cerda (he's the candidate for the presidency who's going to be defeated).[1] He's an honest, upright man. I can ask him to defend SUR as a favor to me. You decide. If you don't want a leftist lawyer, I offer you my pious ones that I have *now*. They are three lawyers from the Conservative Youth.[2] They're Maritain's, and each of them high-quality people, spotless.

Our dearest Votoya: I'm in Viña [del Mar].[3] Our boat leaves the day after tomorrow. Directly to Peru. I feel *terror* at what they tell me about Peru: 2,000 political prisoners from the APRA party![4] From there to Havana. From there to Florida and Georgia. The Sub-Secretary has *promised* me Nice. But the Chilean press, from the pious to the red, has said, *shouting*, that I should return to Chile. Señora Labarca has found herself with an ailing liver, I suppose. I've lived in the middle of a crowd . . . an adoring one. If I return, she'll know what a viper is, when a doctor grabs it with steel tongs.

It seems to me that you're beginning to do your duty toward America. It was high time. Finish V. Woolf, with an eye toward a book on her.[5] Set yourself to that, right away. (Don't bother with me except for when I die and you see the worms working at my poor bones. Not before, there's no reason!)

I'm going to finish that long piece about publishing while I'm in Lima. And I'm going to write a long sketch about you before you get confused in my miserable memory.

I went to say good-bye to the president of the Society of Writers and I asked him, again, to treat you decently, for us, for the country. And every day I've spoken about you in my *meeting* with people [English in original].

Votoya, I don't have *Sur* No. 43. Or number 45 either. My address in Lima is the Chilean Embassy.

I spoke about you to all the assembled personnel in the private conference that the Foreign Ministry requested of me. I told them (I had to provide information about my commission) all that you had done for me.

I love you more than ever. It's very important to me that you use your soul for our good: that you write, good God, a little every day; that you don't doze off or become calloused. And that you don't take literature as an exercise, my God, to set yourself straight, but that you open that reservoir of water, from top to bottom.

May God watch over you: you'll face Him someday. I know it!

Now Coni follows:

[Added in English, hand of C. Saleva]: Vic darling — I hope you have received the poems and the article I sent you. . . . Yesterday we arrived at Viña and my heavens what a "*recibimiento*" [reception] they had for her! The climate here is marvelous — just like spring! It has reminded me so much of Mar del Plata and of course I have thought of you. We'll be sailing for Peru the fourth of July and that means we'll be going farther and farther away from you. However, I know that that won't make any difference — and that somehow, somewhere, sometime in the future I'll see you again. Good, optimistic Connie! Please let me hear from you and not *once* every two months. Keep up your writing! Best love *Connie*.

[Added in left-hand margin, hand of C. Saleva]: Tell Carlitos [Reyles] to give the 600 *nacionales* to Polola — she'll send them to Yin Yin. Polola will go to SUR for them.

1. Writing a few weeks before the election, GM here predicts that Aguirre Cerda will not win the presidency in 1938, but he did.

2. The "Conservative Youth" broke off and formed their own party, initially called the Falange, renamed the Christian Democrats. Among the three lawyers GM mentions, one would have been Radomiro Tomic, who later handled many of her business and family concerns in Chile; see *Vuestra Gabriela*.

3. GM starts a new page here, and seems to be writing at a different time of day than the previous page.

4. APRA, a political movement beginning in Peru in the 1920s, led by Victor Raúl Haya de la Torre, spread throughout Latin America and took an anti-imperialist stance. GM's acquaintance with Haya dated from her first residence in Mexico.

5. VO went to London and met Virginia Woolf for the first time in November 1934. VO wrote several essays on Woolf, published in *Sur*, and a book, *Virginia Woolf en su diario* (1954).

ಚಾ

G.23 [Letterhead: none. 2 pp., pen, hand of GM.]

11 [JUNE OR JULY 1938][1]

Dear Vict.,

I'm going to read that straightaway.

Last night I was thinking — you'll be furious — that Mallea is right and is *much in the right*, in being quintessentially supersensitive. Without that, he'd be nothing, and you wouldn't even have noticed him. It's well that it is as it is.

I'm going to read Mallea's book (how can the chieftain [illegible]!) and maybe I'll write about him as well, because the man's worth hurting my eyes, scribbling for him.

I also thought, last night, that for Peru I'll provide commentaries to another ten poems, of the ones that I read.[2] With the ten commentaries that I already have, plus those, maybe a little book could be made, like those shameful ones that are put together . . .[3]

Lately, you've been very much a lioness and a leopardess. A jaguar gave me, in Rosario, my Valley of Elqui.[4] I'm carrying it, all rolled up. And you, too: I'll carry you in a little token of jaguar roses, within my heart. To love you is a brave thing.

Gabr. hugs you.

Today . . . 11. I know dates now.

P.S.: If you can, if it's at hand, send me Mallea's book. Yours. I'll return it to you. G.

1. This letter could be dated from 11 June 1938, immediately after GM's return to Santiago from Elqui, or 11 July, as GM was en route to Peru.
2. GM offered commentaries on her poetry in her public readings. Her "Colofón con cara de excusa" opens, for example, with a reference to GM's public presentation in Lima.
3. The notes printed at the end of *Tala* include her commentaries on ten of the poems included in that text. The letter proposes creating a short book of commentaries on poetry by bringing such notes together with other oral commentaries.
4. In a journey along the Argentine coast of the River Plate, GM had traveled from Santa Fe to Rosario, Argentina, where she gave a presentation on 5 April 1938 (Samatán, *GM, campesina*, 137–188), subsequently printed in *Sur* 44.

ɕʘɕ

G.24 [Letterhead: none. 6 pp., pen, hand of GM.]

[IN LIMA, PERU. JULY–AUGUST 1938]

Dear Votoya, so very present.

We've been in Lima for twenty-one days. We'll leave on the seventeenth. We don't know, yet, if to. . . . Guayaquil. Zaldumbide wants me to visit his part of the country, but I can't go up in a small car. I'm tired again, like when I left Uruguay. And Coni sighs, in full organdy, for the atmosphere of the United States . . . In any case, we will stay only eight days in Guayaquil. (They say that it's lovely to see the Guayas *flow by*, the big, slow river[)].

Today, in a bookstore, I chanced upon No. 45 of *Sur*. I suppose that you've already sent it and that maybe you also sent the fifty copies of *Tala*. Nothing has come. And since they tell me here that books are censored, I need Guillermo [de Torre] or Carlitos [Reyles] to tell me this. I'm going to send them an airmail letter. If *Tala* hasn't come, it probably won't, Votoya, and we're leaving. Have them sent to Cuba. From La Serena they advise me that the books arrived there. I left a guarantee for the remittance of the payment for those books.

We've gone to bed after a bad day. I've been reading without eyeglasses, and my head feels as if it's been battered. Coni is going to read me your conference presentation, finally! It seems unbelievable that at this short distance the things that you send me don't arrive. It pains me because now we'll really be far away from one another: you in England and I . . . in one or another pleated fold of this earth, wrinkled like a walnut.

You were saying to me, Votoya, that I wasn't telling you the news from Delia [del Carril], on account of it being bad. I didn't know that you were such close friends. When I was in Buenos Aires, I told you something about Delia, and you didn't know it. I'm sure that if they were to speak to Palma about me after having broken off with me,[1] she would hear, with disgust, what they would tell her. On the other hand, it's simply the case of a woman utterly in love [Delia], changed, all turned around by her passion. And in this context one can no longer speak of good or evil. I don't talk to you about Neruda either because it would be the same as talking about Delia. You understand, with your radical understanding, in the blink of an eye, and once for all. I'm going to stop here and listen to Coni read. I'll continue quite soon.

This letter has been lying unfinished for three days. I'll be speaking to you separately about your wonderful lecture [on Emily Brontë].

They arrived, finally! One hundred copies of *Tala*! Very late for selling them here; I'm bringing them to Guayaquil and from there to Cuba. Many thanks, Votoya.

Coni sent you a telegram about the thing with Sarmiento. It may surprise you, but I haven't had time here even for a walk around Lima, or to see more than one of the three indigenous museums, nor even to see a bookstore. Although I made just one exc[ursion] the day before yesterday, to [illegible]. Believe it, Votoya, Your Gabr.

[New page, written later] Votoya, the conference paper has been a total surprise for us. The style is loose, flowing, *votoyesque*. There's wisdom about beings, about life, about human circumstances that we didn't know you so fully possessed. There's a pleasantness (don't slight this virtue) and on account of this, the length of the narrative *isn't felt*. The naturalness seems classical. And one touches, in you, the love of Emily plus the love of life, of life's secrets. And it's wonderful, this touching you in a creature you love purely and defend — without naked allegation of its object. A certain stiffness has disappeared, like a kind of parchment not well rubbed or well worn, of some of your earlier things. And running throughout, within, is some organic literary quality, of the corporeal bonds of prose, of the joining of periods, that functions admirably. In any case, what's most visible is that wisdom about beings that you have, and your extremely natural articulation of the era. *Eureka* for Spanish, *evohe!*[2] Votoya! It gives me more and more pleasure to love you.

Again, I tell you that I'll follow through with everything, my God, when things calm down even a little bit! You don't know what the Pacific Coast is like! I told you, already, in the cable, the "full organdy!"[3]

Enduring affection from Coni and Gabr.

1. GM seems to refer to an estrangement between Pablo Neruda and VO over political or literary differences.
2. Greek salutation indicating the close presence of a god or goddess. GM frequently compared VO to pagan goddesses; see "Minerva" (G.3), "Muses" (G.4), "Valkyrie" (G.15), and "Corn Goddess" (G.31).
3. Here, as before, "organdy" is a kind of code phrase that GM uses to suggest "pomp and circumstance."

ᘐᘑ

G.25 [Letterhead: none. 3 pp., typed, pen corrections hand of GM, with a note at end from Connie Saleva.]

[NEW YORK OR WASHINGTON, D.C., EN ROUTE TO FRANCE.
EARLY FEBRUARY 1939]

Carissima Votoya,

It seems appropriate to begin with a word in Italian, since Italians are so in vogue with you, thanks to the ineffable suitor.[1] Just what we needed, now, was for you to stir things up for us with a son of beautiful and shameless Italy. (I'll write this whole letter in the language of the Valley of Elqui, with rude words, concrete and hot.) Just what we needed, compared to so many beautiful things seen strolling about America. But, tired and all, falling down and all, I'd show up, wherever you were, to throw a bucket of boiling bleach at you, to get you out of Italy, even from Florence, in a big hurry, as in a protest demonstration.

I've heard you — the defenses, the declarations of cold and snow, the near Nirvana of freedom in which your soul finds itself, etc. But what you don't say is that you've flirted to your heart's content. The best that remains in the Italians, after the scabby crust that the Duce has formed on their skin, the best, which is a pathetic bit of goodness once the false has been expurgated, creating a horizon for them, can be found in a certain person in your Argentina whom you continue to kill from far away, with *Italian stabbing* . . .[2] You won't recover, over there, in Mother Rome, what you have crazily and craftily wasted in the Plate region. You like to make them go crazy, you like the spectacle, even when after a few weeks it becomes boring for you. You turn on your heels, then, and leave, with what your French people call a mountain of images, like a coquette's tattoos that you carry away to look at again among the sand dunes of Mar del Plata, laughing by yourself, cleaning the salt from your lips, salt from the sea and the other kind.

Your letter has been wandering through the South of the United States. It finally reached me in Atlanta, because I left St. Augustine some time ago. I went to N. Orleans, which struck me as the most tasteless city that I've seen, a sub-Marseilles with horrible streets, drives, and clothes.[3] The people sweet, negrified without knowing it. Of France, they've retained nothing but dirtiness. Oh, yes, and Catholicism. And it makes me think, the fact that they have totally lost the language and that the religion has remained. It's something to meditate about, for a while. From there I went to Atlanta, in order to see a prisoner from Puerto Rico — they say, the leader of the nationalists — but it wasn't to do that, although it would have been a great, sweet thing to see the holy man, whom they have in the maximum security prison with hardened criminals, maybe because he's the best man and the only man from that little island.[4] I wanted to see Atlanta, because, if I must return from Europe to here, it could well be to this point, where hot and arid Florida ends and the Yankee kingdom doesn't fully begin yet.

Thank God that you decided to write. You had to ask me about that thing with Spanish children and you picked up your pen, which is always there for foreigners, but not for your own people. Bad girl, big *criolla*, SPOILED petulant, rebellious child. (There isn't a dictionary of the Valle de Elqui yet, but there, these words have a sugar that sweetens them and makes them delicious, giving them a honey that you couldn't get from this letter.) I have to accept something of what's said about your snobbery. You throw away what you know, and above all what is, what's certain and weighty, what's to see and to touch; and you go off — and here there's a pinch of sentimentality — with the vague and the alien, with foggy heartthrobs and with boyfriends made of willow charcoal who come apart in your hands. Because it seems like a year now that I've had no news from you, although Connie has asked you in various tones; I've wound up pleading for your address from the happy mortals who know it. Stay in Europe until it gives you hiccups, until you're full of it and you can't take it anymore. That way, on the next trip, you won't have to see the Arc de Triomphe again and the Pontevecchia and the streets of London, and your wicked hand will grab a card in order to write. I'm not asking for leagues-long letters, which I can't write anymore myself. I'm asking that you, occasionally, send a postcard so that we know that you're well, something of your spirits, and where you are. To know where you are, in order to think about you, Votoya, and not spend our thoughts on sniffing you out, like dogs do, in order to locate you, you great big little rascal, lazy-boned Patagonian ostrich.

I will not have time to write you as much as I want to, or even to send you all the reprehension that I have in my heart for you, the dense rages that I have developed toward you, in these months. Let's go to the matter of the book. In Chile, the Basque community, which is very fearful of the local atmosphere, didn't want me to sell the book in the Plaza: they asked for two hundred copies, promising to sell them. It struck me as possible, because the bookstores and publishers, except for the Catholic ones, haven't put *Tala* in their display cases, on account of the anger they have toward me; and the Basques promised to put it in an unhappy little window of their shop. The book is something like a mangy dog in my beautiful Santiago. Anyone who received it from you, from SUR, keeps it to themselves. Without trusting too much to the Basques, I delegated Doña Carmela Errázuriz, the wife of my boss, to collect the money when the time came. But then came the avalanche of water, the flood, Votoya: the triumph of the F. P. [Popular Front] and the defeat of the . . . family names, in Chile. Since then, Doña Carmela, her husband, and I have exchanged nothing but letters with local gossip. Then came the earthquake. And between these things, there's been the discussion about whether I might go to Central America (Aguirre's idea, after the one about Uruguay), or whether I might go where my boss promised to send me and had me named, to Nice, to the France of naughty, horrible Votoya. It's been a mere week that I've known that they're letting me go there, and I know, to my soul's relief, that they're not going to throw Errázuriz out of the Ministry [the Foreign Service], that they're leaving him in his job. Without him, I'd have the savage followers of Amanda [Labarca Hubertson] on top of me,[5] now in their glory because of the victory of the Popular Front, and they've become emboldened, not like lionesses, but like mountain goats. Until yesterday, with my tickets in hand, I knew that I'd go on the fourth. But last night the newspapers spoke of Roos[evelt's] trip to the Caribbean, which was canceled because of the crisis in your Europe. Pardon the idiotic digression: I have learned nothing about the sale of those books, or the other ones, that I left in La Serena. Now Connie has written, trying to collect once and for all. I have SOLD eighty-six books; their earnings, in the event that I don't leave on the fourth, will go from here to you, and if you go to England, to the other Vic. [Kent] I hadn't thought, again, about this as *an urgent thing*, because I've believed, until seeing in the United States the newsreels in the movies, that the Spanish Republican government, which still has *millions* in the till, wouldn't allow those poor little ones to leave in rags — and half-starved — for France, saving, thus, the money to buy weapons that no one wants to sell them. And, as I told you in Arg[entina], until a very short time ago I intended that our money, Votoya, would go to one of those orphanages that would remain, *in a stable form, within* the Basque country or in Cataluña. Palma, incredibly, never talks to me about that war into which she's put her soul. Until I gave her a strong reprimand last month, and now she's begun telling me the kinds of things that don't appear in the press. Horrible, all that, horrible! In the same post that brought me your letter there were others from Spanish friends, professors, who have left for Provence and Paris. Reading them makes my head spin. I always believe that I'm touching the bottom of the Spanish nightmare, but — deeper dregs always remain. You've seen the big, comfortable ones, the impeccable Ortegas, the Barojas in carpet slippers, the Marañones, midwives to the princess.[6] But there's another portion of emigrants. Just to mention one, there's José Carner, the Catalan, of whom Palma has written, asking you, on his behalf, to publish in SUR. Carner is one of the three great poets of Cataluña. In a love-suicide pact of feverish patriotism, he's only written poetry in Catalan, and you can't know the marvels that have come from him. But Carner is, besides, a magnificent writer of Spanish prose, overshadowed by the Castilian fury toward anything Catalan. He's a living classic, a man who seems to have left Rome and come directly to us, a total Latin, full of Roman-style wisdom and writing in a language that is living Latin. (He could translate Latin classics for SUR.) I hope that you can do something for him. I hope that you can get to know him. *He works with Vic. [Kent] in the embassy in Paris,* where he's an attaché. I would like you to see him, because I know that you would enjoy this man of totally unimprovised nobility, who's a Mediterranean classic, so natural, unassuming, and simple.

If there's no war, Votoya, I'll sail out on the fourth. I'd arrive there on the tenth, by way of Cannes or Nice. If you've left Paris, I'll send the money to Vic[toria Kent]. I'm not doing it today, because they've left me with just the money for my trip. *I'm talking about what I owe you.* The rest, they'll remit from Chile, delayed, because we live where the Devil is always trying to pull a fast one. What they haven't sold in Chile I'll have returned to me, in France, and I'll take care of it.

I beg your pardon for this neglect of our things, Votoya; when I'm on the road, I do nothing but that road, moving about, acting stupid, hearing people, and talking like a phonograph. A walking charlatan, that's what my Chileans are making of me. I've neglected my other affairs in the same way, all except my poetry (or verses), which I continue writing when I find some peace.

I was telling you that the news that I now have from Spanish emigration, by way of the Pyrenees, has changed my plans. It's necessary to help those unfortunate wandering children, whom France rejects and doesn't reject in turn, in its customary way. It wants their fathers as soldiers for the upcoming war, and it makes faces about taking the women and children. Last night I wrote to one of the Republican leaders and I asked him whether they might be thinking of doing something stable and worthy with the millions still available for the families repudiated by France and Spain, but who could be accommodated in France if our *idealistic* Mother [Spain] were paid for their food, shelter, water, etc. If some such thing were to be done, you and Vic[toria Kent] could buy — or have bought — a dormitory for those creatures in one of the settlements. Because Franco, *the Vatican's pet*, has made Spain a wandering Jew, who isn't accepted in America either, *because Franco doesn't want that;* he's created a kind of medieval procession of lepers, parallel to the Hebrew one, but without the money that even the unhappiest Jew carries under this squalid, poor flesh of ours. Votoya, it brings tears to my eyes, although they're too dry for tears to fall.

You'll ask why I'm going to France, since I speak so badly of it. There are but two countries in the world left to me that aren't Fascist, my Votoya: this gringo one [the United States] and that one. I love the French in the only way possible to love them at this moment, after the Spanish War: *with anger,* anger at their avarice, which has risen from their hand to their heart, and from the latter, to the last breath of their soul, a nameless thing. On account of their avarice, *for money and for blood,* they've sacrificed Spain, believing they save themselves, as if there weren't a God looking at them and who's going to make them pay for this wicked BUSINESS, this shame. I'm also going there to be near Palma. She's my only family in this world, since I can't move my sister out of Chile any longer. I found her exhausted, devoured, and dead, with her goodness the only bright thing in her, halfway between a saint and a ghost. My poor little one! And I'm also going because there I can concern myself with the Institute for Intellectual Cooperation, at the very least. That consulate doesn't have work; it exists in name only. I haven't accepted the POLITICAL posts that they've offered me,[7] and I had to indicate something I'd do there. Errázuriz believes that *as long as Ibáñez doesn't come to power,* I'll be left in peace there . . . He never thinks about the European war.[8] Another arrangement was possible for me, which he proposed: to stay in Florida, overseeing a permanent mission of conferences for the Caribbean. I've worn myself out, Votoya; I'm tremendously tired, and I've caught some amoebas and other . . . plants, little animals in Ecuador.

Connie goes with me. As long as Palma continues in Geneva, I would be alone and you already know that I'm not able to do anything, *that I can't manage on my own.* She, the Yankee, is charitable. She's like that with me; she has a profound, tender affection toward you, which you return by not keeping in touch with her all year . . .

We often think about you, Votoya. *We almost live you.* In each lovely place, we say how good it would be to have you there. Facing each explosion of organdy along the Pacific, we laughed at the same thought: of you. We're carrying you so enmeshed in our lives that we don't understand how your soul can be so calloused as to not know and feel this: that two creatures are always walking along and calling on you.

I'll rest, now, in order to tell you things about *Sur.* You did badly in putting the three poems from Chile there. It's necessary that you UN-DERSTAND and believe what I tell you: you should have chosen *one of the three.*

A wide, lovely hug from your
Gabriela.

P.S. Don't concern yourself with speaking and writing about your friend from Elqui. Don't rest. Later. A thousand thanks for having sought out Palma and my Y[in] Y[in]. I want you to love them for me.

[Note added, in hand of C. Saleva, on reverse of final page]: Lovely Vic. — I hope to see you quite soon. What am I going to say to you, for having forgotten us so much, all this time! I love you always, your *Connie.*

1. A reference to the Italian Dr. Frugoni, VO's latest amour.
2. Reference to VO's relationship with Mallea.
3. Despite GM's expression of distaste for New Orleans, she visited again in 1947 and in 1954, and her later letters describe the city with clear pleasure.
4. In an act of solidarity, GM visited Puerto Rican nationalist leader Pedro Albizú Campos (1891–1965), who was jailed in the federal prison in Atlanta, Georgia.
5. Labarca was a paid militant for the Chilean Radical Party.
6. GM compares the lot of the various Spanish intellectuals associated with the "Generation of 1898." Those associated with Catalan or Basque autonomy found themselves fighting, dying, or forced into an exile from

which the Franco government permitted no return, whereas supporters of the monarchy (such as the physician Gregorio Marañón, whom Mistral mocks as "midwife to the princess") were allowed easy and early return. GM corresponded with Marañón before the war; see Vargas Saavedra, *Castilla*, 145–146.

7. At the end of 1938, the Aguirre Cerda administration offered GM the post of Minister Plenipotentiary to Central America, based in San José, Costa Rica. She turned it down.

8. During Nazi rule in Germany, there was a constant threat of an Ibáñez-led coup in Chile. The most serious attempted takeover was put down shortly before the 1938 presidential elections.

ΙΟCΙ

G.26 [Letterhead: none. 7 pp., pen, hand of GM.]

[FRANCE. EARLY APRIL 1939]

Lovely Votoya,

I haven't written you, so that you could rest from my "carrying on" in Cannes. I always feel ashamed of these conversation orgies: *afterward*. And from them, full of repentance, move on to the kingdom . . . of silence.

When I'm with you and with some two other people — I'm not going to name them to you — something grotesque and frantic happens to me: I want to say *everything*, as if I were going to die right away . . . like someone who gropes quickly or says good-bye, in a flood of words.

I was very, very grateful to you — Lady Votoya, for coming to the coast when I arrived. God protect you. It was very sweet to disembark, as they say, from your hand to demonic Europe.[1] I would like that act to become a talisman for me, a supertalisman, in order to resist the black mafia of the duo [Mussolini and Hitler] of bloody-minded devils — more the one from the South than the one from the North, as of yet . . .

How is [your sister] Angélica? I don't know when the two of us women will have a conversation. Likewise I remember, blushing, my garrulousness with her. She is an adorable creature. She's not one of those who are quiet for lack of anything to say, but because she has a wide tent of modesty: of reserve, of our modesties — all those that one ought to have.

It seems that when April comes, I know that spring is certain. You already have it all over you, head, shoulders, toes. And I miss seeing you like that, covered in spring. I don't know if it makes you more fierce or if it melts you halfway — not even Vulcan's forge could do it completely . . . A curious, cold woman who suddenly gives one certain Andean surprises: dumping a load of snow, which, being impetuous, resembles fire . . .

The twenty-first of April is Europe's official day of spring. It's bad that on that day you'll be between the Italian doctor and [Igor] Stravinsky.[2] Even though it'll be in Florence, where there's less pretentiousness than in the rest of Italy — except Rome — to cure [you] of Italian things, with a speech or with a shop window full of organdy —

I always live you, and have been for some time now, Votoya. Whether I write you or not, I continue living you like that (it's not fiction) — with the clays, grasslands, and the little animals of our America. You could be neither noble nor superior; I would live you just the same, because I, too, feel tenderness for our weeds. Do you remember that tremendous shrub — Goebbels-like[3] — at that ranch you took me to, from which you had some branches cut? I see that *geometry of thorns*, that "look at me and don't touch," that machine gun of silence and thorns.[4] That's how you could be, and I would still think the same way about you. Because that "repelling" plant is also truthful, and what most sums you up is your truthfulness; true bones, true rambling legs, true shouts unleashed at Coni or at Fanny: everything truthful in this drippy, limp, and mucilage-filled world. Perhaps other women in Europe could give me your culture and your talent; no one gives me your truth and your vital violence. It's the most open-air American style there is. What a shame, Votoya, that you're a rich woman. I have neither the envy or hatred of riches that attends Communist-types, but I would get along better with a Votoya who was poor. Better and *more*: I would give you years of the few years that I have left and I would ask you for a few of the many that you have left. You'll probably imagine this prospect with horror at how dizzy my loquacity would make you. *Pas peur* [Don't worry]. I believe that those who ought to be reincarnated close to one another, on some star, should spend much time together: as a pledge or security on it, to force the thing somewhat, *so that it won't fail*. I hope I have a less sluggish body in that life so that I can keep up with you. I hope I can learn to see the countryside in silence and that we can take many long walks, side by side, creating the necessary confidence between us, so that you'd shout at me as you darn well please, as you do with Fanny [VO's maid], or you'd curse with me, as you do with Connie. Maybe you're less *certain* about my affection than of these two, and that's why you soften your voice with me, at times.

I always prefer you loosely sprawled out, rough-talking, sharp as that plant, the one with the aureole of spines . . . It's good for you to know it.

I'd like another seven years of life, in order to see you somewhat old, at the brink of old age. This gives one a few curious things that I already have, and that will be somewhat delayed in you. Among them, a bit of foolishness. Because you don't have this hint of foolishness, you don't believe. I'd like to know whether you'll ever *believe*. On the seventh I'll send you some words from Nice (if I don't stay on the road . . .). But what's more, that morning I'm going to pray for you. *For this reason:* from time to time a childish laugh, a four-year-old's laugh, your milk or flour laugh comes to your lips. That laugh isn't foolish, *it's something else*, very lovely. Within you, belief would be the same as that laughter on your face.

Excuse the Salvationist nuisance. These days I've been in a good mood, but yesterday and today I've felt almost happy, I don't dare say how *happy*. The word always makes me afraid. Here [in France] I recently found the edition of *Les Vers Dorés des Pythagoriciens* [The golden verses of the Pythagoreans] with commentary by d'Hierocles.[5] I read it some years ago, but it didn't have this pile of helpful notes by Mario Meunier, the Greek scholar. This version is admirable.

With regard to reincarnation,[6] I'm always somewhat inarticulate, or embarrassed, or considered harmlessly crazy. Coming across it again, there, in the mouth of two big, lucid, marvelous, and what's more, somewhat saintly writers, has made me lift my hunched shoulders and take up again, with pleasure, my incurable heresy. How clean and clear-cut they make reincarnation. Palmita says that reading my Hindus she feels lost in vapors and as if galloping with monsters. Here it's clear, unquestionable, honorable, and straight up and down. This reading has made me happy — the word slipped out. Last night I slept as if I were far from the cares of the world. — Let's see if I sleep like that again, today.

No, I don't deny or become distanced from Christ, nor do I cut myself off from Him, as they say of this great big heresy. Like Yin Yin, I believe in God and in the gods. . . .

Votoya, we almost didn't meet one another in this world. You wouldn't have lost anything by it, except for one more bite, just another, from the American corn. But you have done many good things for me: I needed to know, *to know, to know,* that a totally white person *could be a genuine American.* You can't fully understand what that means to me! Then, I also needed to understand that literature doesn't destroy or cause a woman to decay inside (that is, to create cavities); that it doesn't damage her in her essence; that it doesn't rob her of a certain sacred marrow, exchanging it for some more or less beautiful phrases.[7] The two good things that I mention to you were already a lot. But more remains, which I'll tell you about, bit by bit.

Maybe what I miss in you is nothing but a share of common experience. The experience of poverty, of fighting, in blood and mud, with life. There's no remedy for it in this life's journey. In me there's hardness, fanaticism, *ugliness,* that you can't *be aware of,* being unaware as you are of what it's like to chew bare stones for thirty years with a woman's gums, amid a hard people.

With all that, it nonetheless isn't a lot, being so much. It could've been more.

I imagine, Votoya, that now V[ictoria] K[ent] must be sadder than in Cannes, what with the events in Madrid. It has made me very worried to see her depressed. I love her very deeply, even when I say nothing but banalities to her. She is frightfully sad, underneath her serene face. You can give her companionship in this critical moment of trial. And when I tell you *companionship,* I mean the word in its broadest sense. So-called *strength* isn't a sure thing, not even in strong women like her. It's as if she, so full of faith in life, had seen all the foul-smelling, dark underside of the humanity in which she trusted, and of the famous ideologies. It's as if, all in one go, she learned about the cruelty and the potential for cruelty that life can suddenly reach. I'm waiting for a letter to know what she'll decide, what she'll make up her mind to do. Yesterday, some Colombians who love her a lot — consuls in Geneva — gave me some bad predictions about Colombia, for her. And now I'm trying out another combination, one that I don't entirely trust, yet.

Along with me, Palma sends her best. I feel that the two of you still haven't begun to talk, Votoya. She wants to go to Florence with me, to hear you. We'll see if Signore Basque-Butcher [Mussolini] doesn't ruin the get-together for us. For you, Palmita would be a very appropriate public: she knows Greek topics very much by heart.

I'm going, God willing, on the fifth to Nice, by way of Lyon. Yin Yin will go with me: he has twenty days of vacation. Connie is alone and that's best: she didn't want to stay in my gringa pension. And she's scared of the war. Have you become tired, Votoya?[8] It's your fault, you great big animal, with so much substance and *height*. Now I run my hand through your fine, white hair: forgive me, forgive me. Gabriela.

1. This letter was written after VO met GM's boat from New York. The two women traveled together to Cannes and to Nice in May and June 1939; VO continued on to Florence.
2. VO planned a visit with Stravinsky in Florence in May 1939.
3. Hermann Goebbels, Hitler's Minister of Propaganda, was very fat; GM is here referring to a very large bush.
4. VO quotes these words in *Testimonios VI* (SUR, 1963), 71.
5. The edition described was published in France in 1931.
6. The Pythagoreans were known for their views on reincarnation. GM had a lifelong interest in the subject, evident in her interests in astrology and spiritualism in her youth. She believed, for example, that the ghost of her nephew Yin Yin came to speak to her in her dreams.
7. GM's language referring to women's "certain sacred essence" being exchanged for items of lesser value echoes a concern that she had expressed years before about the "New Woman" looking to the "complicated mess of immediate details," rather than to "eternal concerns" (*Lecturas para mujeres*, xiv; Horan, "Matrilineage").
8. This use of the *voceo*, and the remaining sentences of the letter, mark the first time GM writes to VO using a familiar style of address. All of GM's subsequent letters to VO employ the familiar form.

∞

G.27 [Letterhead: none. 16 pp., pencil, hand of GM.]

[PARIS, FRANCE.] 29 [MAY 1939]

Vic, or rather Votoya,

I'm sending the copies of those letters. The sanest man in this Institute of Babel known as the Society of Nations is Bonnet. [Dominique] Braga is a polite, cold man *with ulterior motives, I believe*. I'm not capable of talking with him for more than a quarter of an hour. They tell me that Reynolds is going to replace Montenach (in the presidency of the Committee for Intellectual Cooperation). He's a count, *very pious*, refined, and insipid.

Your letter, you bad girl, speaks to me about the Institute for Intellectual Cooperation. But what we've read here is your nomination to the Committee for Intellectual Cooperation.[1] The Inst[itute] only *carries out* what the large committee plans. *Ton*[2] Tutankhamonic Valéry's committee is the small one. Palma told me that Reynolds presides over the large committee. Again, give me good information. I am — and always have been, in Europe — in the Valley of Elqui! I haven't sent my address to Geneva yet, and when I was there, I was going around in hiding, because I didn't have official permission.

I don't think that these three organizations have done anything for Latin America, beyond the "Collection of Ibero-American Classics" that we established, Belaúnde, the Peruvian (professor at the Univ. of Lima), and I, despite the bosses' opposition. I obtained the first cash from good old Lagarna: four Argentine books, guaranteed. An evil old man, Don Mariano Mitre y Vedia, Argentina's delegate to the Institute, tried to get the funds denied by our embassy in Paris. Prezzolini, the Italian, Braga's predecessor, and I defended them. Then Chile gave enough for two books, and I then got two more from Venezuela. After that, Votoya, I did nothing more: that was six to eight years ago (I've been in Europe for fourteen). Because I saw that whatever was of interest there didn't serve our America. And because Ibáñez, such a *handsome guy*, left me six years without my retirement pension, I became a peon — writing articles for newspapers. It strikes me as a very bad thing that it's never occurred to them to find other *real*, effective ways of *actually* giving back to South America all or part of the quantity of money that South America has given to the League of Nations. Those monies have only served European culture. You'll be happy, not me. Now, since my country isn't in the League,[3] I don't feel like I have much right to appeal to them for work on our behalf. It's your turn now, Votoya.

Look, it's ugly and foul-smelling, what Aíta[4] has done. If there's something more I can do to clean that up, *tell me about it.* I'm a creature of Votoya's kingdom, but only in that part where you're a *llama* or a *vizcacha* and where I understand you and follow you.

Above all, don't do anything silly, don't give those people the satisfaction of resigning, do you hear? In the end, I'm in a similar situation with the Intellectual Cooperation people in Santiago. To Aíta's advantage, Doña Amanda works like a mole, because she is one; Aíta writes letters and signs them. Our local *criollos* are like that; they do filthy things that have no name. But you, Votoya, are working toward an in-

visible archetype, as Platonic as the others; for America in the year
2000. Are you listening? None of this stepping back and doing what
those guys would like. Has the Buenos Aires Intellectual Cooperation
[group] read and approved those letters? It's necessary to know. Aíta is
only their secretary.

Unamuno, who knew the inner workings of his people, used to say
that the force of envy was stronger than the instinct for preservation in
the Spanish animal. In these things you shouldn't see anything but that
putrid root of the race, with which one has to live, as one lives with a
damaged organ, Votoya. Don't look at the personal aspect, it's collective. You are paying for having many gifts — it's the ransom that's required by the gods. But pay, aside from that, with your disdain, at least
with your *why should I care* about lesser types. And horseflies pester
even oxen.

I'm a *sermon giver* today. You don't like sermonizing or emphasis, because both things are prophetic. But I believe in prophetic speech . . .
still. I believe in Cassandra, I believe in Electra and in the charming
Antigone. Reread them and accept them, even though they aren't
Christian. For me, they're more alive than the Intellectual Cooperation
and its choice group of old men . . .

We never learned if you went to Florence.

Please send my excuses: M[aría] Rosa, Mallea, Anita.

In *your* Europe, after a few days, *my strength has plummeted.*

I think of all of you and I will follow through, for you as for them,
when this passes a bit. Now, at least, I sleep. I rarely go to the office, but
I have to send out American postings and useless official letters.

The European infection continues. Above all, the press, the intellectuals, are responsible. Second or third parties who are the worst
racaille [scum]. I write *Gallicisms* for your pleasure . . .

Yin Yin will arrive soon, and with his pure face and eyes, he'll lift
me out of this living death that is my life, without the American tropics
— which gave me its amoebas, which perhaps are what consume my
physical strength.

> A faithful hug from Connie and from me.
> Gabr.

Today, 29.

Those letters are in your Frenchman's French. They seem to be contra-
Aíta . . . G.

1. In May 1939, VO was designated a member of the Committee on Intellectual Cooperation, of the League of Nations, based in Geneva, Switzerland.

2. GM compares Valéry's eminence and influence to Tutankhamen, the discovery of whose ruins were much in vogue in France in the 1920s. Valéry was a friend of VO's and a member of the Institute for Intellectual Cooperation. Paid by the Chilean government, Valéry wrote the introduction to the edition of GM's poems translated into French, which was published in 1944 and was instrumental in leading members of the Swedish Academy (who did not read Spanish) to accept GM's candidacy for the Nobel Prize.

3. Chile withdrew from the League of Nations on 2 June 1938.

4. Aíta was apparently a Buenos Aires staff member of the League of Nations/Institute for Intellectual Cooperation.

ΩΩ

G.28 [Letterhead: none. 2 pp., pen, hand of GM.]

[NICE, FRANCE.] 10 JULY [1939][1]

Dear Votoya,

Those letters have been much delayed. The translator, Connie's teacher, took on an air of Racine[2] and was late; then, the poor thing had to copy them by typewriter, without accents, and word for word, while living amid a tribe of Jews who want to go to Chile and devote themselves to it. Next time, I believe I'll send the draft to you . . . in Buenos Aires. The translation will come out better there.

It occurs to me that a commission from Int[ellectual] Coop[eration], asking you to give lectures in London and Paris, would really shut the mouths of the ne'er-do-wells there. If you go to London (I don't count on seeing you there, woman), find Prof. Entwistle, in Oxford, who might help you organize those lectures (he's chair of the Spanish Department).

Send a kiss to the "plate matador" for me, the cook's lovely little boy. And my sympathy to Fani because you came back with so much for her to do, and a hug to M[aría] R[osa], and kind regards to Susana Larguía.

1. The year is conjectured by the fact that GM uses "tú" with VO after around April 1939, and that VO was in London in June 1939, on a brief visit. (VO left for Buenos Aires on June 24.)

2. That is, "a tragic air."

ʊʊ

G.29 [Letterhead: Consulado de Chile. 1 p., pen, hand of GM.]

[NICE, FRANCE.] 7 SEPTEMBER [1939]

Votoya, we're caught up in the action now.[1] God help us. In Elqui, my huasos say: — Hold on tight, Catalina, we're about *to gallop* . . .

I believe that I should warn you regarding Marta Brunet,[2] a Chilean writer, presently consul in Buenos Aires or La Plata. She's very much a rural novelist, the one who most convinces me, among the regional novelists in Chile. But as a person, she's false. She's responsible for the publication of my famous letter about Spain just before the war, a felonious act, despite the great regard in which she says she holds me.

Be very careful and act very discretely with her; she seems, what's more, to have become a Communist.

She has a pleasant manner, and I don't detest her, despite how much I suffered on account of her. But it would be very painful to me if she were to play a dirty trick on you, and that's the reason for these lines.

A hug from Connie and one from me, sad and faithful. Gabr.

1. GM writes in a kind of coded language here, as the war anticipated in the previous letters began in earnest with Germany's September 1939 attack on Poland, which led Great Britain, New Zealand, Australia, and France to respond, declaring war on Germany on 3 September 1939.

2. GM held Brunet responsible for the publication of the private letter in which she criticized Spain, prompting GM's reassignment from Spain to Portugal. Brunet was director of the Chilean magazine *Familia* when the letter was published. Despite (or because of) GM's mixed warning and praise, by 1940 Brunet was publishing in the two most prestigious venues in Buenos Aires: *La Nación* and *Sur*. Vargas Saavedra (*Castilla*, 176) believes this letter was written in 1938, but GM at that point had not begun to use the familiar form of address with VO, and Marta Brunet did not become a Chilean consul in Argentina until 1939 (Brunet, *Obras completas*, 864).

PART TWO

LETTERS 1940–1952

BRAZIL, CALIFORNIA, ITALY, MEXICO, AND ARGENTINA

Letter from Gabriela Mistral in France, Sept. 1939.

Gabriela Mistral receiving the Nobel Prize in Literature from King Gustav of Sweden, 1945.
Photo courtesy of Doris Dana.
Collection of Doris Meyer.

Victoria Ocampo in Bariloche, Argentina, 1939.
Collection of Doris Meyer.

ʊʊ

G.30 [Letterhead: Consulado de Chile. 2 pp., typed, pencil corrections, hand of GM.]

[NITEROI, BRAZIL] 19 MAY [1940][1]

Oft-remembered Votoya,

You'll say that I only write you about somebody. That may be the case, but we're always thinking about you, no exaggeration, every day. Your manuscript — what you're writing — has *not* arrived. Get to work, since that's the only salvation in this moment of desperation, of sobbing aloud.[2] The Holy Spirit, whose celebration was yesterday, won't pardon you for slacking off, for deserting your gifts, for your *criolla* laziness.

Look, I'm very worried about Victoria Kent.[3] I doubt that the address that I have for her is still valid. Today, the press is saying that the French government has told emigrants or refugees that they should leave as soon as possible. I imagine how:[4] in Nice I saw things that would shame any human being. It's very well that they seek out and punish traitors, but their own should come forward: they are the most and the least pardonable ones.[5]

Give thought, Votoya, to what you can do for her, for the one who shares your name. The Spaniards always think that they're going to finish off or save the world. I told her, over and over, that she should come here. She paid no attention to me. She was in a *heroic frame of mind*, as she was in Spain, but it is grotesque for her to feel that way in France, where foreigners are pushed by the waist toward the sea, every day, to make them leave. Palma [Guillén] is another story. The Mexicans believe that they are adept at escaping from everything, because they've escaped from the guerrillas . . . she stayed too. God reward you for whatever word of yours you manage to get to Victoria. Maruja Mallo may know someone in Paris *capable of looking for her* in the horrible confusion that's coming, Votoya.

I've had some days of sheer ecstasy in this house, of being overwhelmed with euphoria, with my two vegetal walls of dense mountain on each side. I've wondered to myself, with a burning cry in my throat, what was I doing for fourteen years in Europe! Then, Votoya, came the business with Holland, with Belgium, and with France, and tempers are on edge now, hot and *furious*.[6] The Furies are about, in the air.

Have you read those tacky verses from one of our classic writers, beginning with that thing about "*Virgen del mundo, América inocente?*" Yes, innocents, in the popular sense, not in the theological one, that we are, but only in part; the other part is formed by the fifth column,[7] in each one of our towns, and there's another that barely counts as a part, made up of lucid people who see and shiver, not from fright, *from horror*. A few hundred Yankee-influenced fools have convinced our people that it won't happen here, that the ocean is very wide. But it's coming, clearly, it's coming. Now we're going to see if the outsiders in our lands will fight for us and with us — if they don't jump to the fifth column, which is their natural site.

I read your words in the beginning of the issue of *Sur* dedicated to France.[8] I was moved by the attitude, very much yours, Votoya, that is, very much Minerva. The issue is excellent. But England deserved to be recognized first, because England was the only one that was fighting then,[9] the one that knew from the beginning that it should fight, for it had declared war. If you do an English issue, I'll send you something for it, without fail.

I haven't sent you verses, although there are plenty, because I've corrected nothing, except a poem for Finland that I distributed among all our countries.[10] I didn't send it to you, because it was important to me that it go out to the masses so that the Communists would get what they deserve. When I finish setting up the house — I still haven't unpacked my books — and setting up the office in Niteroi and get out of this burning, dry state of mind, I'll correct it somewhat to send to you. Thanks very much.

Cantiló understands what we are living through, what others are living, what's happening, what the fools don't see. That makes me feel happy, strong. May God protect him.

Susana [Larguía] passed by here. We were with her just one night, that's all. Over there, she could be caught in the war. Here, the *gringos* — the Yankees — say the same thing as people were saying in Nice: that they won't let England become a meal for the savage beasts. Things go so quickly — everything becomes vertical, time and events — that it won't take very long.

Susana spoke to me about a long letter from María Rosa for me. It hasn't come, Votoya. Tell me through M. R. if you receive these lines; it's very important to me that they get to you. And if there's some response from V. Kent, let me know that, too. You're incapable of sending me two lines, quickly.

Have *Sur* sent to me here. My house address is this and you *don't* have to write me at the office: Av. de Tijuca, 1505, Tijuca, Rio de Janeiro.[11] We live on one of the highest hills of the city, on the side of Corcovado.

They've told me that you're sad on account of the failed publishing business. I don't know if it was Susana who told me about how poorly that business went.[12] You and I have strived to defend the Jews and both of us have encountered some types who make people ask: But is it true? It pains me that they've treated you badly and that you've signed over an enterprise of that character and prestige, and at a time for the world in which it was so necessary, more than ever. But don't be upset. The day that you find the person who can properly manage book distribution for you, doing it as it should be done, you'll be able to do it again.

I sent you a message with Alonso and with Torre in which I beg you not to see a veiled petition. I believed that I ought to consult with you before disposing of *Tala* and the other books that I offered you in France. Now I know what's happened. It was a matter of duty and affection, for me, to get your permission.

Write what's yours; loosen yourself up, don't polish too much, dare to be American. Remember Sarmiento, Güiraldes, the others. Forget about culture, *it's already a bad word*. Toss it out and write, forgetting what you know and what's foreign to your blood; write with total disregard for whatever comes from your brains, rather than from your blood. . . .[13]

A hug from Connie and me. She's very displeased with you. She's more than right. Yin Yin also chimes in and sends you a kiss, from his pure little mouth, not Nazi and not Fascist, almost American, it's so clean.

19 May. Your faithful
Gabriela

P.S. — I don't believe I'll move from here unless they throw me out. Nor do I have a desire to travel. [Side margin, last page]: An article of mine about Mallea came out there,[14] with shameful errors. When C[onnie] copies the whole thing (it was in pieces), I'll send it to you.

1. In 1940, GM established the Chilean consulate in Niteroi, Brazil, although she maintained a residence in Rio de Janeiro. The feast of the Holy Spirit, mentioned in this letter's first paragraph, falls on the Sunday following Pentecost. In parts of Brazil, the Feast of the Holy Spirit is celebrated with a week of festivities. Since Easter fell on 24 March in 1940, Pentecost would have been 13 May, hence the date assigned to this letter.

2. The first six months of 1940 offered the prospect of an Axis triumph in Europe following the German-Soviet pact. Soviet Russia invaded Finland on 30 November 1939. Finland and the Soviet Union signed an armistice on 13 March 1940.

3. The Spanish Republican government assigned Victoria Kent to France to assist in establishing child care centers among refugees. She describes her experiences, which included hiding from the Gestapo during her four years in Paris, in her book *Cuatro años en París* (1997).

4. "Imagine how" refers to how the Spanish refugees and emigrants were sent to forced labor camps or deported to the French-Spanish border and killed.

5. GM's horror — based on her eyewitness accounts — at French collaboration with the Nazi occupation also appears in G.34.

6. Germany invaded Holland and Belgium in early May 1940. "Furies" is GM's term for describing murderous rage underlying war in Europe; see G.5.

7. The term "fifth column" originated in the Spanish Civil War with Emilio Mola Vidal, a Nationalist general. As four of his army columns moved on Madrid, the general referred to his militant supporters in the capital, who undermined the Loyalist government from within, as his "fifth column." GM and VO were both aware of Nazi sympathizers as a "fifth column" operating in Brazil, Argentina, and Chile.

8. The October 1939 issue of *Sur* (61) opened with a long essay by VO, "*Vísperas de guerra*" (On the eve of war), describing her travel to Strasbourg; see also GM, Letter to Alfonso Reyes, 20 September 1939 (*Tan de usted*, 122–123).

9. As of May 1940, only England had declared war on Germany.

10. GM notes her poem "Campeón finlandés," which she wrote in praise of the Finnish resistance to the Soviet invasion and later included in *Lagar*.

11. GM also used this address in Rio de Janeiro in writing to Alfonso Reyes in late 1940, expressing similar concern for France and Germany: "without trying to play Cassandra, I saw all this coming and I understood many things when I was in Germany, things that the French, so ingenuously vain, didn't want to come closer to look at . . . perhaps not an hour passes in which the war doesn't dirty my mind, but I saw it coming straight down, like a seagull swooping down on a bit of food" (*Tan de usted*, 129). Her oft-repeated concern that her office mail might be opened or waylaid by third parties was justified both in her personal experience of having her mail opened, read, and published by third parties without her consent, and because during the war Rio was a center for war-related intelligence gathering by many political factions.

12. This reference is unclear. VO's publishing house, SUR, had various periods of financial stress, but it continued to bring out titles throughout the war years.

13. VO marked this paragraph with two lines in the left-hand margin when she was preparing to write "Gabriela Mistral in Her Letters" (see appendix).

14. "Algo sobre Eduardo Mallea" was published in 1940, but the place of publication is not given (*Recados para hoy y mañana*, 252–253).

ဘော

G.31 [Letterhead: Consulado de Chile, Niteroi. 2 pp., typed, double-spaced, pen corrections, hand of GM. Postscript: pen, hand of Connie Saleva.]

[NITEROI, BRAZIL. JULY 1940]

Votoya,

I write you quickly: to give you news. An Argentine professor, Silvio Julio Iglesias, a friend of G[onzález] Lanuza, gave a lecture here about modern Argentine literature.[1] He's the professor in that field at the

Central University of Brazil, a little resentful of *Sur*, according to what
I perceived in a conversation that we had beforehand, because he writes
verses and criticism and it seems that he feels left out of *that coveted
house*. . . . He did quite well. He divided the lecture into genres, and in
speaking about essayists, he cited you first, with lively praise. It's the
first time that your people praise you in front of me, and I liked that
very much and it made Connie happy.

I believe that the Russian friend you sent to me has probably told
you about a long conversation I had with the Venezuelan ambassador
in Rio, about your Emily Brontë biography. He's an educated old man,
a kind of minor Spanish nobleman with a tinge of the hacienda owner,
but not cattleman-crude. He's married to a Brazilian who follows
Hitler, but is intelligent, if you can imagine. He seems more enamored
of you than of his wife, although she's beautiful as well. He said the
same as I did, in I-don't-know-what letter, about your biography, and
about how much life experience is felt in it. When you come to Rio —
sometime you'll come — we'll go see him, because it's worth it.

An issue of *Sur* arrived with two things of yours and that long and
mature article translated from French, dense with culture and *sagesse*.[2]
Need I tell you that it hurts me that you speak about the people of
Paris as if they were your own, Corn Goddess.[3] It's very true, what you
say about European interference in America, that it's going to increase;
keep your eyes on it, and you'll see it grow.

Our Russian friend is off, I still don't know whether to Argentina
and Chile or to the Caribbean. I'm very grateful to you for having made
me see that show. I wouldn't have gone without your advice, because I
live very far from downtown, lovely and naughty Votoya. I've given him
some letters. I went to the mountains to get rid of some flu, and I
couldn't attend to him here, although I've managed to give him some
help in the lands where he's going. He's a fine person.

I've made four significant efforts to see what women and Latin
American writers can do TOGETHER with what's about to happen
to us, three of them in your country. They haven't answered with a single word. Listen, it's the same as always: everyone believes that they'll
escape on their own; everyone looks at the map to see the size of the
group that they're talking about creating . . . The Spanish anarchists
have done us in with their blood. When someone does agree to create a
group, it's someone with some Basque ancestry; watch when this happens, and you'll see.

H[enri] Focillon, whom I admire and have liked for years, said some insightful things about you. The French are late in getting started; they're lost for a while. They have to speak Spanish if they're going to work at the grassroots level, as they would like, now, with our peoples. Usually they don't learn any language very well. It's a good thing that he's at Yale telling the Yankees the truth about many things. And the mission that he's on is well planned.

Here, every night, we pray for England using a precious French Psalter that I'd like you to read.[4]

It makes me happy, I can't tell you how very happy, that you're there, being the godmother of our liberty; but I need to know that apart from this you're writing inspired things like the one about E[mily] B[rontë], which is your only writing where you reveal some of your enormous roots, so covered up by the foreignness that buries them so deep.

I wrote to V[ictoria] Kent by way of Palma [Guillén].[5] Palma tells me that she still hasn't managed to contact any of the Spanish refugees to whom she writes, because of the war, the occupation. Poor people! But Mexico has done this marvelous thing of declaring them Mexicans and notifying the Germans.

I send you a big hug and my desire to talk with you ten days and ten nights, when it occurs to you to come visit. Tender regards from *Connie* — that's how it's written here. . . . Gabriela.

Fondest *saudades* to you — I'll write you soon

Love, Connie

1. GM quotes from Silvio Julio Iglesias' lecture in her essay "Mi estimado compañero José Miguel Ferrer," published in July 1940, Rio de Janeiro (*Recados
   para hoy y mañana,* 142).
2. GM again refers to VO's essay "Vísperas de guerra."
3. "Diosa de Maíz" in GM's hand is added, as a note at the foot of the page, to
   this sentence in which GM returns to the theme of VO's essentially American identity. As Rojo (*Dirán,* Ch. 4) points out, references to pagan "Earth
   Goddesses" abound in GM's work.
4. Writing to Carlos Errázuriz and Carmela Echenique from Niteroi, Brazil, in
   1940, GM similarly mentions using a Psalter to pray for England: "We're
   praying for England every day, here, using a Catholic Psalter that has more
   Jewish prayers so strong that they seem made for this precise moment of the
   world" (*Vuestra Gabriela,* 66). The Battle of Britain lasted from 10 July 1940
   until 12 October 1940, when Hitler postponed the planned invasion of
   Britain.
5. Palma Guillén remained in neutral Switzerland until the end of 1941.

{∞}

G.32 [Letterhead: none. 2 pp., typed, pen corrections, hand of GM.]

[PETRÓPOLIS, BRAZIL.] 22 DECEMBER [1940 OR 1941?][1]

Votoya,

It really bothers me to take your time for this silly little thing; but it's six times now, six, that Dominique Braga has come to this house, calling on me about his concerns, which are . . . Argentine, apparently.

Braga, the head of the Humanities section of the Institute [for Intellectual Cooperation], in Paris — do you remember? — it turns out that he's married and is Brazilian. . . . When the war came, he exchanged his French passport for one from here — he was born in Paris — and he took his wife and went to Brazil. His family is bourgeois, but came down in the world, as they say. Naturally, he hasn't found a way to make a living. He writes for the most liberal newspaper in the country, but his articles about French poetry are common student essays from any high school. A man who's been uprooted loses all notion of reality: he believes that one learns only in Europe, and one learns as much as one forgets. His articles are translated for him, although he speaks perfect Portuguese: young people in Rio de Janeiro know what he is talking about, and plenty more, and now he's really bogged down in his country, stopped up like a marshy wetland or a sand dune, not by malevolence or something like that, but by pure indifference. Either they never knew him here or they don't feel that he's Brazilian.

His French wife doesn't make him feel that life's worth living. Far from that, she makes him feel that he doesn't amount to much, with his jobs and what's happened. The man is suffering, and despite his tiny soul, it's somewhat painful to see him suffer as he speaks.

From the first time to the sixth, he's come to talk to me about you and about what he could do in Argentina. I've told him that maybe the lectures would pay him something, since essays pay very little anywhere. I gave him this answer after thinking and rethinking his case. I know that commonplaces aren't as obvious in a lecture as in a printed text. His spoken French is very good; he's a facile, well-mannered man, good for public relations, etc. He wants to know if he might find *a theater* there that would provide him with a starting point and if this might cover his travel expenses and a bit more. To judge from my news, European ships no longer make this trip and the local and national ships, whether Argentine or Brazilian, *cost little*, although the price of their tickets went up the day before yesterday.

I'm *only* asking you to tell him in a card, clearly and frankly, whether there's interest in his lectures there, and if they can be requested, guaranteeing his primary costs. If you see no such opportunity, please tell him so. He comes here, over and over. On account of an almost ghoulish timidity, it costs him the world to say why he's come. After having heard him out about it, I don't know what answer to give him. It has nothing to do with some terribly poor person or anything like it; it has to do with one out of a thousand or two thousand third-rate writers who've come to this America sure of success, a success *that they won't be able to find anywhere*, and with a man who knows absolutely nothing about how to fit in with his local people, to live among and earn his bread among them. He's a man with no wickedness, no bitterness, who excites no rage or enthusiasm: a common man from Paris.

I'm in bed with my second flu. I just finished answering a message from Braga about a visit that will deal with the same topic and purpose and that's why you're reading this letter. Send him two lines in a card, affirming or denying his plan. Either he goes to Buenos Aires or he'll set himself to locating a way out right here, despite his modesty in asking. The worst thing would be for him to keep on giving his domineering wife the spectacle of his clumsiness in making money in . . . his homeland and to persist in living the life that you can imagine, from what I've said, and what a life that's been over the past six months.

Rosa Chacel spoke on the telephone about a message of yours, for me. She didn't pass along the message. Connie told her not to come until the house was clean and it was possible: the flu has knocked us over, the three of us, plus the two maids and my black gardener. She'll come when this filthy wave has swept past. . . .

Doesn't the war seem a little bit better to you? Oh, but at what cost, and with what prospects for the future!

A tender hug, a grunt, and a good smile.

22 Dec[ember]. Merry Christmas, my good woman, and a year better than the past one. Your

Gabriela

Regards from Connie and Yin Yin.

1. GM became consul in Petrópolis in 1941.

ΩΩ

G.33 [Letterhead: none. 1 p., typed, pencil corrections, hand of GM.]

[BRAZIL. LATE 1940 OR 1941?]

Dearest Votoya,

I jump to answer your letter about your France, without thinking to end my previous one. It's important to me to answer what you say about Spanish. I have neither the look nor the reputation of being a Hispanophile, so you can believe me on this account. . . .

Despite your childhood in French — a pure aberration — and your love for English, which I well understand, I can't comprehend your antipathy toward Spanish. You know that Latin is a fundamental thing in this world. Well, then, Spanish is one of the two Romance languages most tied to Latin. The other is Portuguese, which I believe very tightly embraces the great mother tongue.

Now hear me about this: what most pleases me about you, and what has most bound me to you, whether you know it or not, is a sense of the miraculous land, a sense that I've never seen in anyone in our race. And it's not that you talk a lot about this plant or that animal; it's because in your face and attitude it's evident that you're feeling, *in a deeply rooted manner that abuts the very core of the thing*, something about the land. Well, I can't understand, you being the terrestrial creature that you are, that you don't know that Spanish is, for hearing *and for the sense of sound*, the most plastic language made by man, particularly to express the land, sacrificing the ability to say the angelic for this terrestrial ability. Because the ability to say the angelic is what Spanish lacks, but it is countered by an excess in corporality and its ability to convey the physical.

I don't know if you also disdain Spanish painting. Although you may not like Velázquez for his total lack of dash and extravagance, or of ingenuity, Velázquez is someone whom you have to understand on this planet, before leaving it. I mention him in order to tell you that the Spanish language, as a means for presenting the world, is like Velázquez and Goya together. That's why, if they hadn't ruined your soul's palate at three years old, if they'd left you with a clean, totally naked instinct, *you would have headed straight for expression in Spanish, because, although the idea might repel you today, it's your natural tongue, the language of the most terrestrial creature on this continent of higher and lower sensibilities.*

It's true that classical Spanish scarcely bothered to deal with land-scape, plants, and animals. I mean at the height of the classical period, because in the Spanish era that I most love — or the only one that I love — that is, at the end of the Middle Ages and when the Renais-sance was only just budding, in the time of St. Teresa and St. John of the Cross and the two Luises [of Granada and León], our language — *yes, ours* — strolled the earth as if testing it. I'm sending you, as proof, those passages from [Luis de] Granada about earthly trifles, selected by [Pedro] Salinas.[1] But prior to the time that I note, right before, a certain marvelous atmosphere of medieval Latinity went through Spain, and crossed the entire Mediterranean.[2] South Americans scarcely know the people who wrote in that language of innocence that resembles a flowering peach branch before dawn, when it's just as heavy with dew as with flowers. It's understandable that you don't know those who wrote in the quarter century before the *official Renaissance;* but it's unpardonable that you never read the material that I send you. Most likely, you've never read St. John of the Cross. What an atrocity!

Now another thing. Years ago, in Madrid, where I had the pleasure of meeting you, I gave or sent you the best little book by Gracián, *El héroe y el discreto.*[3] I'm sure you didn't read it. The man wasn't a Spaniard in his language, he was a kind of Florentine from the time of [Dante's] *Vita Nuova;* he was a shrewd and refined man, and *he was a teacher of cul-tured Frenchmen and cultured Germans.* Schopenhauer, and then Nietz-sche, they loved him. Gracián's language — and Gracián's line of un-derstanding — were your destiny, *they were your inheritance. You haven't even looked at it.* And that's because of something quite ugly in you — in me there's an even worse dose of it — and it's your narrow-mindedness as someone who has already chosen, and made up her mind, and sur-rendered. You gave your powers to French, and ever since then you be-came impervious to everything that wasn't that, and English. *If you don't have Spanish, horrors, you'll have to have German.* Today's French — par-don an Indian's meddling in it — visibly bears a flatness or SPIRI-TUAL impoverishment. The antimusical nation, even though it's called the nation of harmony, the nation of the most hateful little dit-ties that can be heard in the world's hearing, *doesn't suffice to feed the soul, which is nurtured, either with metaphysics or great music or simply religion . . . and mythology.*

I can't go on. I'll do it tomorrow. My eyes are bad. Your

Lucila.[4]

1. GM refers to Pedro Salinas' edition of Luis de Granada (1504–1588), *Maravilla del mundo* (1940). GM's admiration for Pedro Salinas is evident in her "Página para Pedro Salinas" (*Gabriela piensa en*, 1928).

2. Amid the chaos of France as it faced partition and enemy occupation, GM wrote Alfonso Reyes, indicating that she was immersed in rereading his edition of late Medieval Spanish literature, with particular attention to Gracián, and that she had advised Victoria Ocampo to look to the past: "I told Victoria Ocampo in Buenos Aires that it was good to continue with her books looking backward, toward the past. She was delighted with the editorial success of 'Vísperas'" (Letter, GM to Alfonso Reyes, 20 September 1939; *Tan de usted*, 122–123).

3. GM had sent Gracián's *El héroe y el discreto* to VO from Madrid or Barcelona early in their friendship, in 1935, as she indicated in G.3.

4. GM originally wrote "Gabriela" as her signature, then crossed it out, and wrote "Lucila" underneath, possibly to disguise her identity. She uses her given name again to sign G.39, and VO addresses her as "Lucila Godoy" in V.9.

ʕϿʕ

G.34 [Letterhead: none. 4 pp., typed, pen corrections, hand of GM.]

[BRAZIL.] 6 JANUARY [1942]¹

Dearest Votoya:

I'm walking around, my body like glass, and what's more, with some splitting headaches brought on by lots of reading and poor eyesight these past months. But it matters that I clarify some things for you and I'll write you, short and to the point, without expecting an answer. When I was with you, I remember that at times I'd understand you and you'd understand me more with gestures and looks than with words. *It's the only good understanding between beings;* I believe less and less in letters.

When I speak to you about "rotten France,"² I'm doing what the primitive as well as the civilized person does: one can't speak without generalizing; *only thus does one speak.* I know very well that leprosy never covers the whole body and that cancer isn't liable to move beyond one organ. Not only are there good people there, there are those who are saints to me, such as Maritain. But I don't hesitate to tell you that the France in which I lived a year, half of it in wartime, was a country in dissolution.³ Nor am I afraid to add *that the most vital viscera of the coun-*

try are rotten. I don't know if it's on account of my passion for mythology, but I'll give you some five examples, of the kind that fall to the bottom of the heap.

In Nice, I had the Chilean consulate in the building where your
consulate was, and a gentleman, a friend of your family, worked there.
The offices of the refugees, Jews, Czechoslovaks, etc., were on the same
premises.

Beautiful France of the wide-open arms had begun to hunt Jews
and emigrants in general.[4] They took the men and brought them to live
on a *poudrière* [powder magazine] located . . . in Antibes, and every half
hour they'd send the news over the radio, directed to the Germans, that
a concentration of *Germans* had formed at such and such a place. Three
Jewish families, friends of mine, knew that their men were sleeping in
this secure place. All the refugees with money were doing business with
the French officials. They were allowed to leave every fifteen days,
thanks to medical certificates that the doctors offered and gave out, for
hefty fees. The doctors would be replaced and then the bleeding would
begin again. They [the Jews] left, promising to stay in their homes, and
then the police went off to look for them. The rest of the families were
periodically summoned too, by the police, the unspeakable French police. I went to one of those summons, to accompany some unfortunate
people, and I found myself among a kind of damned flock. The Chief
of Police in Nice, or rather, the official who is one civil grade below the
Prefect, said something to them that I don't know how to describe to
you, a peroration or some such thing. He was insulting, threatening,
joking, in jailhouse language or gangster talk. Never in my life have I
seen anything like it, in terms of outrage, mockery, and cynicism, in
order to collect money. I left there with my head spinning, like someone about to collapse, and I went to see the bishop of Nice, an academic and a man of the world, as little like a bishop as he could possibly be. I told him that I couldn't stay calm and sleep at night after what
I had seen and heard. He heard me attentively and courteously; he told
me that he already knew all that, but he hadn't found anyone who'd be
responsible for the reports in order to give them to his friend, the Prefect. I answered him that he could use my name, since I was going
away, and I understood that nobody would want to provoke a police
corps of that sort. I spent the whole day with Connie, going hither and
yon, because I wanted to wear myself out, to get to sleep. At nightfall I
stepped into the small hotel, the one I showed you, and I was surprised

by a man in the dark, in the doorway, who threw himself at my feet. It was the Chief of Police and he was kissing my hands, begging me, for his children's sake, not to reveal what I had seen, not to my government or to the Chilean Legation in France. (The police wouldn't let that family leave for Chile, for no other reason than to extort from them what money they still had.) He promised that he would let them leave for free, *in exchange for my silence*. The man, now inside in the reception area, was crying like a wretch, *with his filthy face stuck to my knees*. He was a Czech of some kind, but there were the same types in every department.

Shortly after arriving in Nice, your consul had sent his secretary, a French girl, to me to say please relinquish any kind of official errand on behalf of my countrymen, since they would (or I would) provoke the police, with the worst consequences. When the war came, there were some thirty Chileans on the Côte d'Azur, and they were advised to leave the country. They were on a sight-seeing trip. I asked that girl the meaning of the consul's message, and she explained to me, her face burning, that all the official divisions extorted substantial bribes from travelers and that any consul who accompanied them would impede the operation. *The French administration* was disgusting.

Then there was the trial of an ex-consul of Chile in Nice, an ex-millionaire married to a Russian countess. It had to do with keeping his house, a mansion purchased in downtown Nice. I went to the public hearing, without the interested party knowing about it. And I saw the indecency of a trial manufactured on the grounds of robbery, by my countryman, of thirty-two doors from the house. He had asked, *in extremis*, for proof that they were taken, and by whom. It was declared that he had burned some and carried away others . . . I went to see the house: the doors were quite old, and there was no sign whatsoever of either putting them on or taking them off; the building stood whole and well preserved. The one who mortgaged the property had himself named head of the Property Owners Association of Nice — a powerful post — to carry out his brave deed. He acquired a house worth two million francs, paying only three hundred thousand for it. I saw the file afterward: it was shameful, the cynicism. *Civil and criminal justice fell into the same category*.

And that does it, for today. I'll continue later. It had already fallen to me, years before, to pay a judge, by my hand, by my hand! to get a Spanish maid out of jail in Montpellier.

You believe, Votoya, *with an absolutely literary criterion,* that a country lives or dies through its elite, that through that elite a country is lost or saved. And it's not so. A country lives through its average man.

When that average man goes bad, the country falls flat on its face. The usual Frenchman that I saw during eight years, when I first lived there, the Frenchman that I saw in the small towns, in the provincial cities, in everyday life, isn't what V.O. was seeing in her hotels or her houses in Paris. *Victoria will never know a foreign people while she doesn't LIVE WITH THEM and live with them as a poor person, which isn't possible.* I have lived among them, with them. I have the deepest disdain for their morality, and I believe that the remotest one-horse town in our hills retains, more than they, the only morality that I ask of human beings: a natural one, that is, *animal morality.*

You know that I haven't tossed all this and as much as I know to the winds or to the windstorms of the newspapers. Because I, too, have my Frances, some two Frances, from the past. And of the present one, I have a little sliver of Catholics — to whom I'm bound. The shouting in the Pacific against Europe — Europe as such, as a whole, and European culture as such, as a whole — strikes me as simply indecent on the part of some few resentful or ignorant people who take this opportunity to see people brought down. But it's something else to believe that, by the fact of having created some more or less good books, the French have the right to send all decency to the devil, to persecute the Jew and the Spaniard just a little bit less than Hitler, and to forget the A B C of decorum, *that decorum which my friendly tribes maintain, and the ones I left.* . . .

Dearest, thank you for the photo for Conni. The piece about San Isidro came and a copy of *Sur.* In another letter I'll talk to you about them. A thousand thanks, again. I'm waiting for the book of articles, which hasn't come yet. A hug from the three of us.

Gabriela.

6 January.

1. The year is deduced from the letter's internal reference to *San Isidro, un poema de Silvina Ocampo y fotografías de Gustav Thorlicher,* which was published on 27 October 1941. The text appears in GM's library at Barnard College, Columbia University. San Isidro, a suburb of Buenos Aires on the River Plate, is the location of VO's ancestral home, "Villa Ocampo." This mansion in the Argentine Belle Epoque style is where VO and her family spent weekends and vacations when she was young, and where she lived most of her life and died

on 27 January 1979. The house was deeded by VO and Angélica to UN-ESCO in the late 1970s, with the intention that it be maintained as a conference and translation center.

2. It appears that here GM is answering VO's objection to this term as too strong a condemnation of her beloved France (G.34).

3. GM's stay in wartime France apparently spanned nine months, from her arrival in March 1939 (by the evidence of these letters) to at least January 1940, when Vargas Saavedra indicates that she sailed to Rio (*Tan de usted*, 39).

4. GM's witness to the persecution of Jews and emigrants, described here, evidences collaboration predating the official Nazi occupation of southern France.

Ⴂၟၟ

G.35 [Letterhead: none. 3 pp., pencil, hand of GM.]

PETRÓPOLIS [BRAZIL.] 3 MARCH [19]42

Dear and mute Votoya,

This letter was meant to convey only some things about the *unspeakable* death of S[tefan] Zweig and the news that up to the present day, March third, your book hasn't arrived, that only the *San Isidro* arrived.[1] Can you believe it: books requested from Argentina — bought by friends there — for that rather urgent anthology, have arrived *forty days* after being sent. That's why your book still could arrive . . . It's unbelievable.

It bothers me, and makes me somewhat ashamed, to have to ask you for a material favor, aside from the moral ones that I owe you. In order to close on a house that we want to buy here, *which is very, very important to me*, I asked the N.Y. Life [Insurance Company], where I've had a life insurance policy for the past ten years, for $850 and I asked Palma Guillén for $250, so I need a thousand dollars. Palma answered me from Havana — she's on her way back from Europe — saying that she sent me a check by airmail. The one from the N.Y. Life came, but in a check against their own bank, which can't be cashed here, despite that bank being known in any large capital city. The Bank of Brazil has sent to N.Y. to cash it. The check from Palma — just like the other one that was sent and should arrive — in normal times would have taken eight days at the most. But I receive airmail letters from the United States that take fifteen [days]. *My closing date is the fourteenth of this month.* I don't want to back out because I paid a deposit, as is customary, with two thousand dollars that I must not lose. I'm asking you to back me up if possible and to replace those thousand dollars of mine that are still traveling and that could arrive too late. And I ask you not to think that I'm making up a big story about economics, in the literary bohemian style!

I have a few days to wait, as you see. It could still be that both things arrive this very week. That's why I'm telling you that you should answer me by telegram whether I can or can't count on your help and that you shouldn't send me anything until I tell you to in another telegram, in case my mess is worked out in a normal way. If you can back me up, I'll remain calm about the closing in these upcoming days; if you can't do it, then I must think of another route, one that's rarely used and seems ugly to me. The immediate mortgage on the property would be very simple if it didn't involve *a judicial closing*, but that's what the business is, the latter. The property costs 200 *contos*, that is, $10,000. The money that you could loan me remains quite safe, in case it falls through — I'm not yet on the verge of dying. . . .

I very much beg your pardon; it disturbs me a lot to get you mixed up in these bothers and concerns. I've done no business with checks or changing money since the war started, since I had a fund of a thousand *reis* to live on; this matter has caught me without knowing anything about the hopeless delay in airmail letters, because of the censorship, previously just English but now Yankee as well.

To sum up: first, tell me if you can loan me those thousand dollars, but tell me about it in a telegram; second, don't send anything unless I telegraph you — in case my money still hasn't arrived from the U.S.A. or Cuba. [Note added, hand of GM]: You would have to send the money by telegraph, because of the urgency. Address: Chilean Consulate, Petrópolis — Brazil.

And, Good God, may that book arrive. I received *Sur*, with "La loca."[2] There's something else to send you, and they're going to copy it.

A hug from me, and from this ugly person.

Gabriela

You've probably read my letter to Mallea about Zweig and my request for justice. This death has left *us* I don't know how to tell you. *Us*: the three of us loved him much more than he knew and more than we knew ourselves.

---

1. The book mentioned as not having arrived yet would be VO, *Testimonios II*, published in December 1941.
2. "La loca," one of GM's most celebrated poems, was later published in *Lagar*.

♾

G.36 [Letterhead: none. 13 pp., pencil, hand of GM.]

[PETRÓPOLIS, BRAZIL.] 7 APRIL [1942]

April seventh: This day was for writing to you, and to Palma.[1] But people came and they've only just left me at 5:00. Since I haven't slept for two nights — because of other visitors — I'm falling down with sleep, but Basque determination plants me here, on paper, and I won't go to bed until sending you my regards and something more. Thank God I now have Palma in Mex[ico]. I got her out of Switzerland against the wind and the tide. Although they've wanted to make this war as middle-class as possible and the neutral countries are said to be so good, Palma had some vestiges into which she fell and remained, for a while. It's futile to want to keep the tragedy at arm's length; it sticks more than stepping on a scorpion. There she is, but she can't come, on account of the problem with the ships. Let's see if she comes and I can have her strength close by, because I need the strength of various creatures to live through what remains of this horror that is the quarrel of the educated and the civilized and the scrupulous ones, etc.

How much I wanted to pass this day with you! Like that other one, when you didn't know that your birthday was mine too. It was my misfortune, you having been born on the other side [of the Andes], so close, but my having been born in another class and another people. Without a drop of Marxism or nationalism, I know that the two are separate. Even worse yet, I believe, having known you late, almost in my last years, because you might have helped me a great deal to live with my whole spirit when I was young, during my hard and frightfully lonely youth. What I needed was to know that I had someone within reach. With no more than that, I would've been a little happy.

The strength that you give, without knowing it, is, in the first place, your truthfulness. One believes you *without* words, on seeing you. You breathe this. Then, seeing you live courageously. Then, knowing that you love some of the things that matter to others of us. Then, that you're balanced, that you don't wear the marks of dementia that almost the whole group [of writers] wears. I tend to talk about the "filthy Saxon," but I only disdain them [Anglo-American women] in regard to supernatural life. All the rest, I respect and tolerate.

Perhaps you will have passed your day cloudlessly; here, there was an electric storm, one of the tropical ones that you perhaps know. You will have strolled with your giant steps, with your young lioness' walk, along the sand dunes — if people didn't spoil the day for you. The face changes a great deal, from one year to the next, after age fifty, and I haven't seen you for four years. Your portrait says nothing of the changes. They tend to be a pinch around the eyes and/or the mouth. And in this pinch is what's been lived, its record. You must have the war there. I have it more in my face.

Seeing you is something that I don't see happening soon. No one knows anything about tomorrow. I would like nothing but to be here, in this house hung with thick shrubs (the forest), drinking down something of the unconsciousness or the dream of the land. When I go out, walking along a street, I enter into a somnambulant state that isn't agreeable at all. But I could just as easily stay here as be made to return to Chile — and then I would go looking for you, along the way — or maybe I'd have to go to the U.S.A. if it goes badly for me! I can't tell you anything for certain.

On the fifteenth [of April 1942,] W[aldo] Frank[2] arrives. It's so very good that he's arriving and can pull us somewhat out of this black hole in which the death of the Zweigs has left us. And it will be good to hear what he and his friends think, what they make out, as far as something can be seen, what they desire and what they fear.

Criollo Nazism is based in fear, more than anything else, and then corruption. The ideology thing comes at the end. Maybe that's why Zweig believed that we writers can do nothing. Because it doesn't have to do with ideas, at least not among our poor Americans, I think. The middle class — the same one, in France, that talked its head off to make a bit of a living — throws everything to the devil, and that's the famous class of the intelligentsia. And the people, I don't believe that they'll do anything but want "the thing to thunder," without understanding what "the thing" is and how it's going "to thunder" and with what result. The same old story. The "prophesiers" can still keep on saying total foolishness.

Again, many thanks for that so very calming telegram. Palma's money came at last, more than what was requested, and there was no reason to ask for yours. But I thank you for your generosity and your quick goodwill, the same as if I had used the loan, down to the last *peso*.

Today, the seventh, they advised me that as far as they know, the papers have arrived from Rio, in Petrópolis. We'll see if the closing finally happens.

And in that regard, never send anything to me in Rio. The book took almost a month to arrive.

I'm not sure whether I told you that this anthology is, more than an anthology, a collection of pieces about creole America and that I have eliminated even the prettiest pages of what's been written among us women that doesn't deal with the land and peoples here.[3] That's why I believe that you should have sent me, preferably, a part of the story of your childhood. It's high time, Vic. If you've developed more of the one about San Isidro, this would work for me, in this regard.

I like this second series of *Testim[onios]* more than the other one, even though there's more in the first that appeals to my "very limited and unilateral" taste. You are beginning to get yourself in order and not waste what you write, to regularize your work. That would be quite enough, already, without its being everything. Reading in Spanish is still lacking, even though it might bore you. I was rereading the *Poemas solariegos* by [Leopoldo] Lugones[4] after many years, and I had you there with me, page after page. I really love *that* Lugones. He left various commonplace books. Commonplaces were what our people required of him. He was a *criollo* of your stock, a magnificent inhabitant of the earth, a smeller, toucher, and savorer of his country, squandered in for-eign imitation. Like Rubén [Darío],[5] he even imitated people worth less than him — Pascoli for ex[ample]. And so many more. I don't know what gust of wind brought him, one day, into his own, and he left, as a "testimony" of his true being, that and two other books that endear him to us. If, like me, you've forgotten it, reread the *Poemas solar-iegos*. May they cheer you up, although they may be "thick" here and there. It's the freshness of our land, of our geological animal. No one knew to carry him to his kingdom, and they let him distract and squander himself in false residences and in lying quicksand that had nothing to do with his body and his soul of idle [illegible] peevishness or playfulness. I've considered it with real sadness, with sorrow, faithful and overdue.

I won't tire you more. When I finish, good God, with this anthol-ogy, I'll tell you what that work has stirred up in me, because much of it concerns you.

Connie loves you very much, with a lovingness that puts up with all ingratitude. Yin sees you as a kind of myth and maybe doesn't even be-lieve that he saw you except for what I've *told* him about you.

A hug. God help you live the horror with your soul intact.

Gabriela.

— Best regards to Angélica and to María Rosa. G.

[Hand of Connie Saleva, added, in English]: Vic darling. My best wishes and my best love — (late but sure). Always. *Connie*

1. VO and GM regularly exchanged birthday greetings following GM's April 1938 visit to VO's house in Mar del Plata.
2. Waldo Frank was on a second lecture tour of South America. When he arrived in Buenos Aires, he was attacked by Nazi thugs because he was Jewish and pro-Communist. VO and María Rosa Oliver were the only friends of his to help him with his injuries and see him safely to the airport. The police never acted on the report of the incident (Meyer, *Against the Wind and the Tide*, 141).
3. The anthology that GM describes was to collect texts from throughout Latin America and was contracted by a U.S. publisher; see G.39. Further information about this anthology appears in *Tan de usted*; in *Recados para hoy y mañana*, ed. Vargas Saavedra; and in *Proyecto*, ed. Arce and von demme Bussche.
4. Leopoldo Lugones, *Poemas solariegos* (1928). Like other Lugones texts, this book had a profound effect on the work of Jorge Luis Borges. GM's copy of Lugones' *Antología poética* (1942) was heavily marked up by GM and may have been the volume she was reading at the time of writing this letter (*The Gabriela Mistral Collection, Barnard College Library*).
5. Even more than his friend Lugones, to whom GM compares him, the modernist poet Rubén Darío led a wandering, dissolute life shortened by alcoholism.

∞

G.37 [Letterhead: none. 2 pp., typed, pencil corrections, hand of GM.]

[PETRÓPOLIS, BRAZIL.] 30 MAY [1942]

Dear Votoya,

I've been wanting to tell you something that you should know for almost a month, but there was the move, there was Waldo [Frank], a lot of hustle and bustle in the Chilean delegation here, and all this has taken much of my time.

In the most recent issue of *Sur* — you already know that very few reach me — I read one or two notes, in the magazine section I believe, where some opinions published in *Estudios*, the Chilean magazine, are reproduced.[1] It struck me as bad that you were printing them, even if it was with a critical intention or as mere information. Review it yourself and maybe you'll tell me the reason. I must inform you about those people. Five years ago, when I went through Chile, I met up with two groups of young, reformist Catholics, *both of them very interesting*. Both came to see me and I liked hearing them. The first group has the bad name of "the Falange," and it has been getting purer, more distilled. They're democrats and follow Maritain, more or less. I believe that they are the only Chilean souls there who understand me and in whom I have confidence. The other group is as refined as the first, *they follow Maritain less and publish our best magazine, which is Estudios*. Jaime Eyzaguirre directs it — I see him as an extremely intelligent Jewish type and very studious.[2] He offers classes in the Catholic University, in philosophy, I believe. I met him after he'd married the daughter of a friend of mine, a woman for whom I have utmost respect — even now that I suspect she's Nazi — because she's very worthy in her interior life, in her total submission to the experiences of the soul and in her devotion to her family. She was married to a German, Phillippi, a very ethical man, and who on that account left her poor. My friend's name is Sara Izquierdo — the Izquierdos are Jews as well. . . . I insist on blood because only in this context can I manage to understand Sarita's type of mysticism. It's a really extraordinary family; she's a kind of matriarch, *but a saint*. (Oh, God, a Nazi saint!)

I was with her on two occasions, but each of them for a long time, and I saw that her religious culture, which is both old and very modern, is German in its modernity, and I heard her praising German Catholicism very highly. I heard some admirable comments from her about Rilke's poetry. She told me that she's indignant about our total ignorance of the German mystics, etc.

Some years ago, Sarita was in Europe and I met up with her in Paris; she was repulsed by the . . . filthiness of the city and of its people, within themselves — I, very much in agreement with the latter . . . Every time I see her, the lofty air in which she moves leaves me a little faint, along with *her total lack of mediocrity in all aspects*. But each time, I find her more Saxonized. — She also reads a good deal of English.

Let's return to Jaime, her son-in-law. I was hit very hard by the last issue of his magazine that I received, with its attack on the U.S.A., at such a point in time, and there I smelled something quite serious. In

Chile, he told me that his magazine, so daring — a defender of the
Jews, for example — was produced with funds from the office of the
archbishop, but that with each issue he feared that they'd withdraw the
subsidy. He's poor, although he comes from well-to-do people. On
reading the most recent issue, the fear that comes to me is that Jaime's
Catholic current corresponds to a substantial line of Nazis among
Catholics, including some members of the high clergy, which would be
quite serious. It's very strange, the fact that those LEFTIST Catholics
who never campaigned against Yankee imperialism before, would do so
now, right now, when it's important to be with the United States. I was
never Yankee-fied, and the Americans know it well, but it occurs to me
that only the Nazi types, and the subtlest ones among them, would
have chosen this moment to stir the embers of hatred.

The shortness of time and *my eyesight, which has declined by a half,*
haven't let me write a private letter to Jaime before sending him a public one, which doesn't strike me as excessive and might be useful.

Summarizing: I consider the sections reproduced by *Sur* as serving
not to report on, but rather to give publicity to their *bad ideas!* Since
they're very well written, they can leave their poison in many readers,
and so I think that *Sur* shouldn't cite them except to respond to them,
categorically and caustically.

Votoya, there are many things to tell you, and I'm going to take this
proclaimed but not practiced approach of *short but frequent letters* with
no obligation that you respond. But let me know that you're receiving
my letters because there's been, and still is, a Fascist hand snatching my
correspondence, maybe in Rio, and copying what interests them. . . .

[Waldo] Frank left me very content with something he said as he
was leaving. The rest was a pure waste of time. He contents the soul.
He's a lovely spirit, devoted to the supernatural — I suspected it myself, but I didn't know it. With what he told me, he left me very much
comforted and very joyous, you know? That really made me very
happy.

A big hug for you and for María Rosa — whose letter I never received. God watch over you, Votoya, for all of us.

Gabriela

I haven't seen MacLeish's message to the South American poets.[3] Can
you send it to me?

1. *Estudios* magazine is noted in *Sur* 88, no. 78 (January 1942).

2. GM's correspondence with Jaime Eyzaguirre has been published by Luis Vargas Saavedra, "Once cartas a Jaime Eyzaguirre 1940–1946," *Mapocho* 23 (1970): 19–29.

3. GM probably refers to an address the poet and Librarian of Congress Archibald MacLeish gave to dedicate the Library of Congress Hispanic Reading Room as a place devoted to studying "the greater brotherhood of the human spirit." Mistral knew MacLeish: she later signed a petition that he sponsored, asking for Ezra Pound's release from incarceration at St. Elizabeth's Hospital. Mistral also intervened with MacLeish, trying to obtain a post for Alfonso Reyes in New York at this time (*Tan de usted*, 133).

ʚɞ

G.38 [Letterhead: none. 1 p., typed, single-spaced, pen corrections, hand of GM.]

RUA 10 DE MARCO, 47. [PETRÓPOLIS, BRAZIL.] 24 NOVEMBER [1942]

Dear and distinguished Victoria Ocampo,

These lines are sent principally to introduce you to de Gaulle's representative in South America,[1] who is traveling on a partially educational mission and who strikes me as a person well worth receiving and being heard by you. The French have such a debt of gratitude to you that he must meet you. He has spoken to me about *Sur* and *Lettres Françaises* with intense gratitude.[2] I want to tell you that among the French living in Brazil since the war emigration began, this is the Frenchman who has been most to my taste and has given me hope for his people. It must be that his quality as an Alsatian gives him a patriotism that's *unquestionable, sober, and strong*.

It's been quite some time since I've written you, my dear, so dear despite our differences — with which we were born, because they aren't differences of time . . . — and it's because, aside from the ups and downs of life, my eyesight is very bad now, with an old kidney infection that has worsened, and I must use the scant clarity of these eyes to write two things: my consular duties and the letters with which I incite, like a horsefly, the lazy and the fearful in my land and elsewhere. Every week "I do the horsefly" . . . and more, because despite my consular rules, I'm speaking my truth about the war in short articles or "public letters," also short, which is what my eyesight allows me to write.

I sent you an anguished cable about Nicolau [d'Olwer]. I received three cables about his case, two from Mexico and one from Chile, from a Catalan who corresponds with him. Or he "used to," since for three months we (the friends of Nicolau, his brother, and his brother-in-law, a French Catalan) haven't heard a word from him, not *one*.[3] Which means that he could be a prisoner of Laval.[4] It's very hard for me to do these errands for him. Nicolau d'Olwer belongs to the curious genre of specialists: being known in America has never mattered to him, because all of America, he says, is dedicated to forgetting or disdaining the classics. This man who knows four Eastern languages is, nonetheless, known in Syria — where the friend I'm introducing to you has worked — in Persia, in Egypt. And this man, now called a leftist by the likes of Franco, worked year after year in the School of Latinists at Chartres, which has many ecclesiastics. And this man has published six books about the races and cultures of the Mediterranean, defending the famous Greco-Roman Latinity that Señor Franco is said to embody.

With the emotional heart of a *paysan* that I have, I thank you for all that you may have done for him. God reward you for it, giving you the health, joy, and strength to live through these appalling and unworthy years.

A long time ago, before M[aría] Rosa left, I sent you, by way of her, a fine message from the Minister Graca Aranha, who heads the Intellectual Cooperation group in Itamarati, that is, in this country's foreign ministry. He's the son of the famous novelist who wrote "Canaan." He told me that they would really like it if, on your way to the U.S.A., you were to stay here some days *as an official guest of the Intellectual Cooperation Institute.* We've talked quite a bit about you, and I was happy to hear from him that he was in Buenos Aires on business some years ago, and that he very clearly understood what your country owes you and that your staunch literary taste makes you criticize the boorish local tastes. He's a great reader and, moreover, he knows how to listen, and by way of social conversations, one understands countries. . . .

I hope that you're persuaded and that you come. M. Rosa must have told you how well they received her, how they loved her and the good job that she's done for Brazil in literary concerns, etc. She left content, and I believe that she'll return, because we all want her to return here.

Again, Votoya, thanks and thanks again for *your permanent and unbreakable nobility.* A hug from your

Gabriela

1. On 28 June 1940, the British government recognized Charles de Gaulle as leader of the free French.

2. *Lettres Françaises*, a French cultural magazine edited by VO's protégé Roger Caillois, in exile, was published in Buenos Aires (July 1941–1947). It published the first translations into French of Jorge Luis Borges' stories in 1944.

3. GM's efforts on behalf of Nicolau d'Olwer also appear in her letters to Alfonso Reyes (*Tan de usted*, 137–143); see also G.40, and GM to Eugenio d'Ors (*Castilla*, 242–244). After the Spanish Civil War, Nicolau d'Olwer married Palma Guillén and went into exile in Mexico, where he established a second career as an authority on Mayan and Aztec manuscripts. GM made several efforts through friends to find him a secure place to live and work.

4. Pierre Laval was appointed as Vichy's foreign minister on 28 October 1940. Although dismissed from that post on 13 December 1940, Laval returned to office on 18 April 1942. Here, GM refers to his role in supervising deportations from southern France (the *"relève,"* beginning 22 June 1942).

ℒℴℴ

G.39 [Letterhead: none. 2 pp., typed, pen corrections, hand of GM.]

ADDRESS: *ONLY* CONSULATE OF CHILE, PETRÓPOLIS, *BRAZIL.*

10 DECEMBER [1942]

Dear, bad-mannered Votoya:

First, I didn't write you out of rage; then, because some things have come up which had to be done, and of the tedious kind. We fulfill our duty to you, since we mention you almost every day, wanting to and not wanting to as well. . . . No, that cable didn't come, that is, it didn't arrive. There were letters, one in one year; and knowing what's happening with the mail, I sent you two with individuals, which you didn't receive. This is the story, told from the Brazilian side. . . .

Although you advised me some time ago that you were going to the United States, you still haven't made up your mind.[1] Look: I believe that it's quite important for you to go. You're free, you speak the language, you have cultured friends there. And you'll be able to see and know what's happening there, and to tell some of us what should or can be done here. Because the majority of the Yankees that come know nothing, poor things that they are, and some big fools, as Connie says. They're really indescribable. I hope they don't make war the way they travel; I hope that they don't deal with the Japanese as they deal with the world's theater: some dullards that really make you want to cry. I don't dislike them, no: I prefer them to your French, because they aren't rotten cheese, not yet, and they have their best years ahead of them, their youth, into which they haven't yet entered.

This business of having photos made of me is of no importance to me, none at all.[2] I'm interested, very much so, in the two of us talking, since the mail isn't functioning anymore, and in a short while it will be even less useful for communicating. If it's possible, stay some three days at the least; one can't say anything worthwhile in less time. If you come for the day, there's no reason for me to come down or you to come up to Petrópolis.

I've had two or three hard blows in these two months. Perhaps the worst one was today, reading that the Japanese — the renegade Mongols, the only unnatural ones — are already flying over Panama.

Your instinct, not your intelligence (since the latter is in such a state that it's useless —), has freed you from being bourgeois, despite being a rich woman. It seems that the precipitous fall of the French — perfection of physics — is due to that, from their arriving at the peak condition of the bourgeoisie. The English fall at an angle, still maintaining themselves in the air — look at how they're starting out with the Japanese — and the Yankees are in mid-apprenticeship in that method, hopeless as it is. May this war save them. I really fear that the semibourgeois countries of our America could be the worst-behaved ones in what's coming. Oh, if only there were still Indians! They'd know what the land is and they'd know *the elemental words*, the primary ones, that must be said. They know the other ones that don't save anything because they don't come out with the force of blood and *they don't burn*.[3] I mean that you've freed yourself — and at what cost — from being bourgeois. Stay that way, stay as you are, don't become bourgeois as you age, Votoya. End up without becoming stingy or a grub.

Your indigenous servant holds on to her health by sheer will: there's one bad day for three good ones, but this isn't the disaster that my life was in Europe. The Yankees have told me to go there; I should, but with my weak health I'd be no good; if I steady myself, I'll go in spite of everything, because I know very well that everyone should do something. I haven't been sitting around wringing my hands, you can believe that.

I was very interested in that debate in your group. Yes, I believe in groups, I believe in that alone for this moment, except the groups of the Kabala.[4] Because that, when published, is finished. The less one speaks, the more one does these days; the less one explains, the more one manages to really achieve something. The other part is nice, like an athenaeum of cultured people. Pardon the crudeness; you know that courtesy is something that I never learned and that I'll die without.

Rosita Chacel has now obtained a Brazilian passport. But she still hasn't arranged her return trip, that is, her right to return. And here's where this sort of procedure is really delayed. You'll congratulate her when you see that in Brazil she valued . . . [The remainder of the sentence is erased; page ends.]

. . . nothing, that she loved nothing, that she doesn't want to retain anything, and if she returns, she'll be even more unhappy. See if they can keep her there a while. I haven't managed to get her to enjoy anything here, not even the land. To the Spaniard, *Mother Earth never matters*, one way or another.

Here, I'm deep into a kind of Iberian anthology for your gringos, the United States. It's nothing but a book that could be called Ibero-America described by its writers. I've searched what I have for something of yours to include and I haven't found anything that might be American, except that trip to Patagonia, which isn't of use to me in this case because you deal with a minimal detail of your country, a little piece. And since the book shouldn't go out without something from you, I've put in an essay of yours, about Güiraldes, instead of mine.

I haven't seen *Sur* in a long time, but now it's beginning to come. I would have subscribed if I didn't have certain monetary commitments that have devoured my surplus. Thanks for sending it; it's good to find you in *Sur* when you can't be had any other way. I sent some verses and others will be coming.

Nor do I hear any news from María Rosa Oliver after a letter from Nice, more than three years ago. I wrote her about a thorny matter, but she could have written me back, keeping her hands away from it. I hold her in much esteem and moreover I love her.

Some verses from *Silvina* really impressed me.[5] They're the best, they're magnificent. Here's an Ocampo woman who has set herself to writing with her blood. You haven't wanted to, you've watered down your blood, at least with regard to writing (not for living, thank God), with the distilled water of French. Read that subtle and accurate judgment by A[natole] France about the two languages. You'll believe him, if not me. Silvina tells me that she's going to do a book. I'll write her a long commentary, because she GAVE me much in what I've read of hers, and it will give me the occasion to say things that I like saying.

I don't know Roger [Caillois],[6] and since I don't know him *on a per-sonal level*, I only know his lovely essay about the Greeks in relation to the fall of France. The parallel is an extremely bold one, but I liked it very much. It cheers me up that, in Argentina, he's been saved from making *ugly Vichy-ism*. . . . I doubt that the arrival of his girlfriend will make him happy. Man is an "unfaithful animal" and must be tired of so many lives, because he doesn't know how to love for long periods. Maybe you've done him a poor favor, bringing her. But you did her a service for sure, God keep you, beautiful Votoya!

Connie — whose name you don't remember (praised be the Mar del Plata friendship) — continues dedicated to you in spirit, since in body she can't serve you, because the two great big Chileans monopo-lize her and keep her fed up — Yin Yin and I.[7] Her face fills with joy at the mere probability that you might come this way. Send word, you hear, send word, because we live outside of Petrópolis, and the mails from Rio to here take . . . three days.

I won't bore you more. We admire you a lot, we love you even more. Watch out for your hope and joy in this moment of the world when one walks around like a sack of broken glass, because there's no *bone of the soul* that isn't broken. A hug from your three . . . Brazilians.

Your Lucila.[8]

1. VO traveled to the United States under the sponsorship of the Guggenheim Foundation in May 1943, visiting Alfonso Reyes and others in Mexico on her return to South America.

2. VO wanted to send the photographer Gisèle Freund to take photos of GM, just as VO had done with Virginia Woolf.

3. Indigenous identity in GM's work often correlates to silence (Rubio, "Sobre el indigenismo y el mestizaje en la prosa de GM"). Speech made more pow-erful by the almost successful repression of elemental emotion appears throughout GM's earliest volume, *Desolación*, and in *Lagar*.

4. "Kabala" is a code word that GM uses to refer to spying motivated by wartime factionalism, as is evident from her earlier use of the word: "It's a shame, dear Victoria, *a complete shame* that we live in times when excellence doesn't matter a bit, what only matters are some insolent badges that people wear on their chest or in their flesh, of this Kabala or that, of the tribe or subtribe, A to Z" (G.10).

5. Although best known as a short story writer, Victoria's youngest sister Silv-ina was also an accomplished poet (Klingenberg, *Silvina Ocampo*).

6. Roger Caillois traveled to Buenos Aires in 1939, at VO's invitation, to give a series of lectures. While Caillois was in Argentina, the war broke out in Eu-

rope and his stay, planned for three weeks, lasted five years. VO helped Caillois establish the French Institute of Higher Education in Buenos Aires. Also, with VO's financial and moral support, he founded and edited *Lettres Françaises* (1941–1947), a literary journal in support of free France. Caillois, twenty-two years younger than VO, became her lover in the early years of his Argentine stay and later a devoted friend for life, a close relationship documented in *Correspondencia (1939–1978)* (1999) as well as in VO, "Roger Caillois." He died in December 1978, one month before VO's death.

7. In late spring 1943, Consuelo ("Coni") Saleva prepared to move out of the house she shared in Petrópolis with GM and Yin Yin. The nature of the events that brought this about is not clear, but this letter suggests that GM understood that Connie felt the pressure of demands from GM and Yin Yin.

8. "Gabriela" is crossed out and "Lucila" is written below in GM's hand.

ΩͻϹ

V.1 [Letterhead: none. 3 pp., in French, hand of VO.]

SAN ISIDRO, 23 DECEMBER 1942

My dear Gabriela:

Thank you for your letter, which I *really* needed. I don't know if my book [*338171 T.E.(Lawrence of Arabia)*[1]] could *bore* someone, but the fact is that not many people have spoken to me about it, and I have the impression that it's fallen into a void.

What you say about its style proves your goodwill toward me. The Spanish translation is *weak*, like all translations.[2] I don't know and probably never will know how to write in Spanish, and it's *criminal folly* to persist in having translated into Spanish what I can only express in French.

Please, Gabriela, if your eyes permit, read the French text (the original) of my pages on Lawrence. I ask you this as a favor and a service. Afterward you'll tell me if you sense the difference between the ease and freedom with which I handle French compared to my clumsiness and stiffness when I write in Spanish.

I *need* you to talk to me about *T.E. 338171* once you've finished reading it (if possible, in French). These are important pages for me, because I've tried to put into them my interpretation of the unique character of a man whom I profoundly admire and respect. I'd like to know if I communicate to the reader what I've perceived and felt as a result of reading Lawrence and living in his company for months, and by my being fascinated with him to the point of believing *that he was alive for me*. I'd be grateful if you'd tell me how it strikes you and if you find that (out of laziness) I've neglected to develop certain points. The style is very direct, I think. I mean that my thoughts carry no verbal ornamentation beyond what's strictly necessary. But I think that my style doesn't seem *borrowed* in French, as it does in Spanish, and that it flows more naturally.

I've written a kind of prose poem about Lawrence (I refer to him this way because I don't know what name to give him). I'm sending you one of the only two copies that I own. Perhaps I'll try to give it better shape one day. In it, I talk about the circumstance of his death (his accident in Dorset). I went to the offices of *La Nación* to see what was said about that accident at the time. I found nothing really interesting, and I've written this poem with no intention of publishing it. I did send a copy of the book to Winston Churchill, only because he admired Lawrence, although I was convinced in advance that he wouldn't have the time or curiosity to read it.

And now a few more lines to tell you that in your last letter there was only one poem, "Manos de obreros" [Workers' hands],[3] which I like *a lot*. When we publish it, must we include "For *La Nación*," which will seem odd? Would you rather publish it in *La Nación*? I didn't receive (and maybe you forgot to slip it in the envelope) the poem, "Ultimo árbol" [Last tree].[4] Try to send it to me. I don't care if it has appeared in *El Mercurio*.

I'll write you a longer letter as soon as I can. Right now, on the eve of my departure for Mar del Plata and the New Year,[5] I have a thousand bothersome things to do. I think I'll go to New York in March.

A hug for you and another for Connie, wishing both of you what one wishes for those one truly loves.

V

TO T. E. LAWRENCE [6]

(Seven years after his death.)

That Monday, the 13th of May 1935, a Monday like any other to me,
(The morning papers reported the death of Pilsudski,[7] Laval's
     meeting in Varsovia,[8] a prize awarded to Leni Riefenstahl by
     Goebbels for her film *The Triumph of the Will*)[9]
As the leaves of the plane trees in Buenos Aires were turning yellow

and children were playing on the lawns in summerlike weather
(25 degrees Celsius in mid-autumn)
The roads of Dorset, invaded by springtime, saw you go by in a rush,
    for the last time.

Silence about you in the press: they didn't know yet. Silence in my
    heart that didn't yet know you.
You were nothing more to me than a famous, unremarkable name,
Your uniform, your colonel's rank,
The title of your book[10] — such a show of pretension and repeated
    seven times — said nothing of value to me.
Childishly absorbed by things that didn't deserve my attention at all,
Happy to possess what was never mine,
At the moment when I lost what truly belonged to me
— The smile of your friendship —
I was so poorly prepared for this misfortune that I didn't feel it.

I would have had a right to my share of your voice and your glance
    since we were both born in the same century,
Since I was a child when you still were too,
Since I was afraid of the dark, of thieves in the night,
When you were learning valor with your fellow cadets,
Since I climbed up the towers of Notre Dame without skipping a
    breath to look at the gargoyles,
When you were crossing la Beauce on your bike to be refreshed by
    the beauty of Chartres
(I see you leaving the sun as you enter the cool peaceful shadows of
    the cathedral),
Since we made the journey of life together,
In time;
Since I am your compatriot in time, a country more vast than all of
    Europe and the Americas.

But I didn't know anything that May 13th when you were taking a
    telegram to the post office
To arrange a meeting that you would never attend,
And if I had been given the choice, I would have preferred another
    era to live in.
Not now! Because I've learned that this era is yours and mine
And there is nothing to change and, what's more, nothing to prefer.
That May 13th, autumn here and springtime there, our sky was
    overcast

(I've searched in the old newspapers for the weather forecasts)
And the temperature was rising. It was gray and heavy; an autumn
    day, provoking but not upsetting,
While on the Dorset road (was it sunny?) blood was covering your
    face and the quivering shadow of the trees was tender.

Two days after the grand ball at Buckingham Palace and Vargas was
    coming to visit;[11]
In the midst of this news, a cable: Lawrence of Arabia, motorcycle
    accident, head fracture. I ignored it.
Days went by and you didn't regain consciousness.
I read about that as if it were unimportant.
The news of an exhibition of Italian art in Paris interested me more.
It would be so lovely!
Seventy-two hours unconscious, they said. Who cares!
And they spoke (as in a detective novel) about the flight of a
    mysterious automobile,
About important plans for the defense of Great Britain that would
    disappear with you.
They said that you weren't the man who lay dying in a hospital
    bed, in Wool.
Lawrence wasn't Lawrence. (Shakespeare wasn't Shakespeare.)
These lines that fell beyond my concern vanished quickly
And the only thing that stayed with me from reading the paper was
    the intention to go see Douglas Fairbanks (senior) jump through
    windows in his new film about Don Juan.
The Massilia was floating into Buenos Aires, a port crowded with
    transatlantic ships.
You, wrapped in the Union Jack, oblivious to the eulogies of
    Churchill and Shaw, in turn praised and criticized,
You, dead.
And I heard about it without understanding, without feeling
    impoverished by it, without being wounded,
Without suspecting that you were going to become me on the day I
    opened your book, and that this would not be easy,
Not at all easy to carry your death on my breast
As others carry the Cross of War or the Legion of Honor,
Those medals, those ribbons that you would hang around the neck
    of your dog to make fun of yourself.
"... He became his admirers."[12]
Auden said it of Yeats when he died and I say it of you.
Because there you are too, become me.

There you are condemned to count on my love for you in order to
    exist,
On my love and on the love of a few others
"Scattered among a hundred cities,"
We are necessary to you, I am necessary to you
(You who had learned to give up everything)
Even more than those stars subject to your will — your indelible ink
    in the sky —
That even so would disappear with the secret you told them
    — The secret that you ordered them to proclaim —
If it weren't for my eyes that prevent them from going out,
If it weren't for my attentive solitude that situates them again in the
    heavens each morning,
At that perilous hour when they disappear, like you,
At the hour when, invisible and present, like you, they lie in wait
To see if we will know how to find their silent place again in the
    tumult of the rising day.

It is I now who is charged with preventing your stars from
    disappearing
Like the markings of a child on his slate when class is over.
They wouldn't exist without my hand to retrace them
Where your hand first wrote them.
You made them become part of the words I pronounce
Which make your voice live again in my mouth,
Your voice that my mouth irremediably transforms
The way that everything not touched by death does —
"The words of a dead man
Are modified in the guts of the living,"
From now on, king of Arabia, you can no longer exist except to the
    degree that I exist,
You become what I admire in you,
You become what I am capable of admiring:
Nothing more.
You become what I am, and I wouldn't want to be too embarrassed,
    too ashamed
By what I'm going to give of myself to keep you visible, to keep you
    living;
Not too ashamed of the mouth that you will make use of hereafter to
    pronounce your words.

Since May 13th
All powerful and defenseless, there you are open to our love.
How many of us are there to love you in such a way that you may
    live?
Names matter little in this battle against death,
Names never mattered to you, writer or soldier,
Even when in the whirlwind of swords and blood
You became a little white speck in the desert
And your Arabs no longer dared wear this color
Because it had become, for them, your emblem.
Even when you wore yourself out searching for the precise word and
    the perfect rhythm of a phrase
After having lived the precise gesture and the perfect rhythm of
    courage.
But we, inhabitants of another desert, we will have to carry your
    color
And your golden dagger and your exact words,
Gathered together and secretly hung like the medals that you refused
On our breast, over the dark and steady place of the heart,
Over the exposed and vulnerable place of the heart whose beating
    you devoted yourself in vain to control
(Why did the brain seem to you more worthy of respect?)
And which struggled five days, in your absence, to avenge itself of
    your disdain before giving in;
This heart, mysterious measure of all things —

                                              V. O.
                                              December 1942

1. This book, originally written by VO in French after Lawrence's death in 1935,
   is both a short biography of T. E. Lawrence and an interpretive study of his
   character and motives as a leader of the Arab revolt against the Turks, with
   British aid, during World War I. VO described her work as aiming "to trace
   the development of a moral conflict in him that grew and grew and was interrupted only by his death" (338171 T.E., 21).
2. The Spanish translation was published in 1942 by Editorial SUR. The original French was published by Gallimard in Paris in 1947, and an English
   translation was published by E. P. Dutton in New York in 1963. VO's sensitivity to the pitfalls of translations, evident throughout her life, was the result
   of having her earlier writings translated, often poorly, from French to Spanish. Many translated works published by SUR were done or commissioned
   by VO with an eye to maintaining the highest standards of the art. In 1976
   she devoted an entire issue of Sur to "Problemas de la traducción" in which
   she applauded a UNESCO initiative to regularize and professionalize trans-
   lators' rights and responsibilities (17–18).

3. "Manos de obreros" was reprinted in *Lagar*.

4. "Ultimo árbol" was published in *Lagar* with a dedication to Chilean poet Oscar Castro, whose work Mistral did not know until after his death (*Tan de usted*, 215).

5. Mar del Plata, on the coast south of Buenos Aires, was the location of VO's summer home, "Villa Victoria." Built in 1927, it was prefabricated in Norway, in the traditional Nordic wood style, and shipped and assembled facing a large expanse of lawn and gardens. VO was very fond of the ocean climate and loved to swim and walk on the beach, often with friends or neighborhood children.

6. This poem in free verse, written in French, is typed on six standard-sized sheets of paper carrying several corrections and inserts, along with the date and signature "V.O.," all in VO's hand.

   VO did not choose to publish it under her own name; she did, however, publish it some years later in *Sur* under the pseudonym "E. Astolat" (*Sur* 188 [June 1950]: 7–12). Given her book about Lawrence, many readers of *Sur* must have realized the real author's identity. VO's choice of self-effacement may be explained by the fact that she did not consider herself a poet; she may also have felt the poem was too revealing of her emotional core, too intimate a testimony of her almost religious passion for reading. For her, reading certain preferred authors had the effect of a kind of symbolic transubstantiation in which she "became," through identification or imaginative understanding, the object of desire and shared in his/her being as it was "translated" for future generations. This was why she begged GM to read her book on Lawrence in its original French and tell her if she had conveyed the vividness with which she had experienced Lawrence's life through his literature. GM's response to this letter, if any, seems not to have survived.

   T. E.'s brother, A. W. Lawrence, wrote an introduction to VO's book in which he said: "This woman, from another end of the world, had presumably been confronted by far greater barriers to understanding the man she never met, whose problems arose in physical and spiritual environments necessarily unfamiliar to her, and from circumstances which must seem no less strange than the events of remote centuries. I found that she had passed through the barriers as though they formed no obstacle, and that her book gave the most profound and the best-balanced of all portraits of my brother; I had, and still have, no doubt of its accuracy (and I knew him, I think, quite well)" (*338171 T.E.*, 13).

   On the subject of VO and T. E. Lawrence and the relationship between her admiration for him and for Gandhi, see Meyer, "VO and Spiritual Energy."

7. Marshal Pilsudski surrendered his powers as head of Poland in 1922, then resumed power by coup in 1926, instating a military dictatorship with Fascist overtones.

8. In 1935, Pierre Laval had proposed a plan to halt Italy's invasion of Ethiopia by appeasing Mussolini. Laval went to the Polish capital, Varsovia, on a

diplomatic mission and departed just hours before Marshal Pilsudski's death
was announced on 12 May 1935.

9. Leni Riefenstahl made this film in 1935 with Hitler's support.

10. A reference to T. E. Lawrence, *The Seven Pillars of Wisdom, A Triumph.*

11. Getúlio Vargas led a revolt in Brazil, in 1930, and established a dictatorship.
    He was scheduled to arrive on 22 May 1935 for a two-week visit to Argentina.
    A detailed schedule of his visit was published on the front page of *La Nación*
    on 13 May 1935.

12. This phrase and the next ones in quotation marks are cited by VO in English
    and quoted from Auden's elegy "In Memory of W. B. Yeats" (*New Republic*, 8
    March 1939, 123). VO was evidently inspired by Auden's modern approach to
    the poetic elegy. For an analysis of Auden's poem, see Edward Callen, *Auden:
    A Carnival of Intellect.*

ღღ

G.40 [Letterhead: "Aerograma. Panair do Brasil. S.A. Panamericano (illeg-
ible) System." 2 pp., typed, pencil corrections, hand of GM.]

[PETRÓPOLIS] BRAZIL. [LATE 1942, UP TO MID-1943.]

Dear Vic,

I've just received an extremely detailed letter about the German invasion of the Mexican Legation in Vichy.[1] That's how I know that all the
Spanish refugees there were taken prisoner. My last news about Victoria Kent was this: more than a year ago, I learned that she was there
and what she needed was for *nobody to bother her in her refuge.* You may
remember that for lack of credible information, I made the mistake of
encouraging a series of Yankee women's groups to act in her favor.
Then I left her in peace, and I haven't heard a word more from her. It's
very probable that she didn't stay there this long. But now I begin to
think: with the *blessed* foolishness of innocent people, who still hope for
some morality from people who don't have it, she could've stayed in the
Mexican Legation up to now. *And I've thought that maybe you know something about her that could calm me.* You know that only your government
and mine can do something for those *unhappy* Spaniards; the remaining unfortunate American countries lack the good grace to do so.

I deeply appreciated your telegram about the action on behalf of
Nicolau d'Olwer. I sent you details about him with a French friend. I
beg you to tell me, *in a quick note,* if you receive that letter, which should
reach you in two weeks, at most. This request corresponds to the fact

that, as you know, I never know whether or not my letters arrive and at least half of my correspondence suffers the fate that you're familiar with, through the work of a Fascist trio that, up to the present, I've decided not to denounce to the Chancellery in Rio, because I feel sorry for the children of one of these villains.

My letter was intended to give you details about the career of the Spanish humanist for whom you've taken active steps, in a true act of faith in me, in your concern for him and championing of him while knowing almost nothing. For you, I'm adding the following to that information. A year ago, when I first took action so that he could leave jail with provisional liberty — (an action directed toward the Vichy government, which had imprisoned him at the request of the Spanish government), I learned about the total iniquity of Madrid with regard to its compatriots in trouble. The Peruvian minister, García Calderón, received from the Vichy government the declaration that Spain was accusing him of not accounting for the money from the Bank of Spain that had been in his charge. I sent this to Nicolau, and I learned that said funds were set aside to give to the Spanish refugees from the Pyrenees — some hundred thousand — a minimal assistance of food and clothing, until the end of the war and that by resolution of the Republican Governmental Junta, to whom the money belonged, he could not declare the location of that money. Only now do I know that it was in the Mexican Legation, because the press has said so. There were some twenty million francs, grabbed by the Germans, on account of which all those poor people are left without food and will have to do forced labor, maybe in Germany.[2]

Nicolau had been named legal consultant in the Mexican Legation in Vichy. *It seems* that he was found there the day the Germans sacked it, the same day they also invaded the Brazilian embassy.

Nicolau was, at the end of the [Spanish] Civil War, director of the Bank of Spain, a post that Azaña begged him to accept because of his profound faith in him. He defended the funds deposited there, not just Franco's funds, but the French funds too. A French minister of relations called him to his office to tell him that he would guarantee the custody of the Republic's funds if he were to hand over that astronomical sum. He refused, and on leaving the palace, he found out that *they wouldn't let him leave France ever again.* He lived in Paris, at first, then in a village near Vichy, in a refugee's and philosopher's poverty, and his sister likewise. When I came here, I left him my scanty furniture, because

I saw the bareness of the two rooms that these people were occupying, people who had been *great señores in Cataluña*. The rest of his life was in the letter that they will be bringing to you.

Again, a thousand, thousand thanks for what you've done for him. I owe to him, Votoya, much of my passion for the classics and considerable advice about philology (he did the Catalan dictionary with Pompeu Fabra, and since Catalan and Provençal are close twins, I have often sought from him the words that I doubted in Provençal poetry).[3]

I believe I told you, but I'm not certain, that my eyesight has gone down by more than a third on account of an old kidney infection that has become more acute. That's why I've neglected my correspondence. My eyes are clear some three or five days after each treatment; then, the darkness comes, until the new treatment. They say that it would be better to take out the kidney, but I don't have faith in the local doctors and I can't go to the United States yet. *Understand, in this way, the scarce letters.*

Tell me how they responded to your efforts, in order to orient me about *what remains to be done.*

Yin is very weak on account of his terrific growth, and I have let him stay with me in order to give him some months of overfeeding. Connie always thinks of you. And I give you a hug, amid the inferno that the newspapers bring and on the day that your France has been cleansed of its misery with the business of Toulon,[4] content with your contentment, which is mine as well and is, like yours, marked with mourning for so many dead.

Gabriela.

1. The letter mentioned may be from Palma Guillén, dated 29 April 1943, which describes an invasion having taken place on Monday, 26 [April 1943] (Arce and von demme Bussche, eds., *Proyecto*).
2. Spanish Republicans, among the first deportees from France, were sent to forced labor camps in Germany.
3. The influence of Provençal poetry on GM, evident in *Tala*, especially appears in the sections "Cuenta mundo" and "Materias." They describe the physical world in luminous detail, using a seemingly elementary language of ordinary things infused with sensual and metaphysical significance.
4. On 27 November 1942, French sailors had scuttled the French fleet at the Mediterranean port of Toulon rather than deliver it into the hands of the Germans.

{ΟΟ}

V.2 [Letterhead: Hotel Montejo, Paseo de la Reforma 240, México, D.F.
4 pp., in Spanish, half-size hotel stationery, hand of VO.]

[MÉXICO, D.F.] 14 OCTOBER 1943[1]

My very dear Gabriela:

I sent you a telegram from New York and don't know if you received it. You can imagine the impact that the news of poor Yin Yin's death had on me. Angélica wrote me.

What can one say at such a sad moment, dear Gabriela. I've been talking a lot about you with Waldo [Frank] (in San Francisco) and with Alfonso [Reyes][2] here. We can't accept the distance that keeps us from being with you at a time when one needs so much the affection of those who really love us. Happily, Alfonso tells me that Palma is with you now, and I know that you couldn't have a better companion.

They operated on my tonsils in New York — a lost week between the hospital and convalescence — then in Santa Monica I fell and hurt my knee. I'm still limping around. But none of this has any real importance. Just passing things (I hope). I'm taking the plane to Buenos Aires next Wednesday (20 October). I've been anxious since the first days of May, and I truly want to return home to my land and to rest a little.[3]

Dear Gabriela, how I regret that you are so far away from us! How I'd like to spend days and days with you. Through Alfonso I've had news about you, but that's not enough for me.

Much love to Palma. Tell her that I know the best thing for you is that she is with you.

A great big hug from one who remembers you often with friendship and tenderness

Victoria

P.S. As soon as I get to Buenos Aires, I'll write you at length. Please send me news of you, even if only a few lines.

[In margin on first page, sideways]: This country [Mexico] is both extraordinary and moving to me.

Forgive me for writing you on paper so poor that the words look unclear. I haven't any other.

1. GM's and VO's correspondence continues in Spanish after October 1943, with the exception of V.7 on the death of Pierre Drieu la Rochelle.

2. VO first met Reyes in the late 1920s, when he was Mexican ambassador to Buenos Aires. He returned to Mexico in 1939 and lived there the rest of his life. VO and AR had an extensive correspondence, reprinted as *Cartas echadas*; see Meyer, "VO and Alfonso Reyes: Ulysses's Malady," 307–324; VO, "Alfonso Reyes". GM's friendship with Alfonso Reyes began in 1923.

3. In this instance, VO was returning to Argentina via Mexico after five months in the United States, primarily in New York and California. This was her second visit to the United States, the first having been in 1930. This time, she had been invited by the Guggenheim Foundation to give a series of lectures. VO was also eager to observe the country during wartime and particularly the status of women in the war effort. Her essays about this visit include "U.S.A. — 1943" (*Testimonios III*, 211–288). VO was in the United States in June when a military coup in Argentina, led by Juan Perón, overthrew the government of President Ramón Castillo, beginning a dictatorship that continued until 1955.

ʕϿʖ

G.41 [Letterhead: none. 3 pp., typed, signature and postscript, hand of GM.]

RIO DE JANEIRO, BRAZIL. 26 OCTOBER [19]43

To Victoria Ocampo (To Victoria Ocampo, to Ema Cosío Villegas, to Dr. Pedro de Alba, and to Margot Arce, in many places.)

If I don't write to you like this, in four copies, I don't know when I could write you separately, and it's past the time to thank you for your letters and your company from afar and to tell you in detail the evil tidings that came into my house for the third time and worse than before. My Yin, my "little boy," now more *"little boy"* than ever because of the madness that took him from me, he didn't go because of an illness, Emita, he was killed. And writing these three words still seems like a dream to me. I'll be out of my mind and unable to touch stable ground for myself until I understand this absurdity. I'd feel relieved, I'd rest if only I understood, even though understanding has nothing to do with recovery or acceptance. The reasons that they give me, that they gather for me, that they find for me — almost all of them turn out to be invalid, or stupid, or weak. The most convincing and most immediate explanation is that a gang of hoodlums mistreated him with words, in a hateful high school, full of xenophobia. But I didn't even send him there *and he could have left at any time.* They called him "the Frenchy," with a joking tone that they now give to the word in the world of refugees; they laughed at his little hump, which wasn't more than a bend in his little spine. But one of the rascals would show up when he was in mundane places, whenever he saw him with girls or family members (to throw in his face some slip-up with flirtatious women) in front of older, "experienced" women. These fellows would visibly torture him: *his sensitivity was so excessive that he couldn't hide it.* I had begged him — toward the end — which it was when I learned about it — to live at home and go out less often. But he was sociable and wasn't even aware of the wickedness of the locals. He didn't know that a foreigner, even if he is part of a consul's family, always turns out to be an interloper or a vagabond for the ones from within the country. (The only sin of which I accuse myself is having imposed my errant life on him, for he was clearly damaged as a result of his wandering existence, rootless and irregular, on that account.) The school gang convinced him, in the end, that the girl he loved was talking badly about him and considered him unpleasant. And what's more, they convinced him that that girl was above him and was inaccessible. In all aspects — class, lifestyle, education, even physically — she was inferior to him from head to toe. He believed them because his marvelous intelligence *never helped him to understand.*

When I saw that his adolescent crisis was very strong, and when most recently I saw his obsession with that girl, I wound up telling him that, although it bothered me that she was German and although I had never seen her, he could marry her and bring her to this big, empty house, since the houseguest, Rio Branco, had left, as well as Connie, who works in her embassy in Rio.[1] He answered me that he wasn't thinking about marriage.

We were living a kind of idyll, because being alone had brought us much closer together; he knew my complaint with my heart and he took care of me with delicacy and indescribable tenderness. And no one can make me comprehend that this boy, who would get out of bed at midnight when he heard me breathe poorly, killed himself in a normal state of mind, without their having made him go crazy, using one of those drugs that abound in the tropics or that other gangs use these days. He was living the present exactly as he liked: he didn't enjoy visits and he had a house sense that seemed Arabic: just his own family and not even the outside air. . . .

Another reason, the second one that they give me, is that he was temperamental. The ones who tell me this don't know my people. But I never saw a Godoy who wasn't worse than I am, who didn't live, torturing himself, and who didn't manage to live until seventy or eighty.[2] *It's our normality*, and I didn't worry too much about the small peculiarities of Yin Yin. I'm worse myself.

The explanation of his birth, which was with forceps that damaged mother and child, and quite a bit, seems more reasonable to me. His little head had five or six bruises and a large scar on the nape. They tell me now that between the ages of fifteen and twenty an adjustment of the nervous system is made in a very delicate region, and that in some cases, the system collapses. But there haven't been major, palpable symptoms of this collapse.

An older or mature French woman was going around looking for him, from S[ão] Paulo to here, and about this last story I don't know anything other than that she asked him to abandon his family and go off with her, *which he had rejected outright*.

In the last three days, Yin had done various things that proved that he didn't think of the horror that would be consummated: moved furniture to his room, from one floor to another; *detailed projects for later on*, enrolled in associations, paying the annual inscription fee; and much more.

You will all understand me that I don't think that a drug killed him, but rather that they worked on his brain until they drove him crazy. And here my suspicions don't focus on only three members of the gang but on some two groups that were searching him out, just like the serpents that vex the world even *in its remotest corners*. One of these groups I threw out of this house rudely; the other never showed up here. Two of them came late, after my little boy was already dead, and I don't know with what purpose, but clearly signaling the types they are. I was in bed, since for nine days I couldn't walk; Connie and a friend and colleague, two bumblers who don't recognize malice, received them, but they didn't find out anything about these low-life figures who'd never appeared in the house before.

This is as much as I can tell you in a letter about the material facts. Like someone walking in her sleep, during the last week in which he kept me company, *I had conversations with him that I would only have had by divining his risk*. I let him know that, finally, I had rounded up the necessary sum that I had always sought to have for him so that he could finish his education if he wanted to continue studying, or else he could begin some small business, toward which he was inclined, in order to give himself the freedom to read and write. He would compose drafts of his novel very, very well, in a clean and sober language without a single commonplace, with a very Godoy-like depth of pessimism, with a rare elegance of syntax, lacking the vice of sentimentality, with irony, and *with a sharpness and subtlety that I never saw in people of his age*. In order to lighten his sadness brought on by his evil companions, I told him minor details of my life and this fact: that I've done all of it with only about six friends, who have helped me in everything and who have sufficed for me. He had two, both of French blood. (Here, an explanation for Victoria: Yin never fit in with this country nor with South Americans in general; our confused way of being and our habit of lying and of hypocrisy vividly repelled him. Maybe I sacrificed him, bringing him from Europe. But, how was I going to stay there myself, or leave him behind in the middle of the dreadful war that ensued?)

Don Pedro knows, Margot does too, that this child wasn't a portion of my life; he was life itself. In him began and ended my reason for working, my joys and my worries. I haven't had a personal life for some time now. More than ever, during these years in Brazil. The war has stripped naked so many sad truths about my *criollo* American people; it has made me see them so blind and so lacking in any *proximate* remedy. The passion I had for them that absorbed and consumed me was abating or extinguishing itself. The house was him; the day, him; reading, him. I know that God rudely punishes idolatry and that this doesn't just mean the cult of images.

Oh, but I have to return to my old heresy and believe in the karma of past lives in order to understand what phenomenal crime of mine has punished me so suddenly, so intensely, with my Juan Miguel's night of agony in a hospital, so frightful despite the incredible stoicism with which he put up with the burning coals of arsenic in his poor, dear little body. I have to put my Christian beliefs aside and give ear to the many Brazilians who've repeated this to me like a litany: — It doesn't come from now or from here, but from a dark shore that you don't know, this blow, this whiplash and this ash.

It's not consolation that I seek, however, *it's seeing him*, and in dreams I tend to have him, and in sensations of his being present in wakefulness as well, and I go on living from what I receive from both things, and from nothing more than this.

Palmita came late to save him with her camaraderie and *with her lucid love, which isn't mine*. He knew of her arrival, and I can't understand that he went away either, already having the certainty of her travel in two weeks. He adored her and gave her his full confidence, more complete than what he gave me, as if he were dealing with a girl of his own age.

Now no one is left to me but an ailing sister, confined to bed, seventy-two years old. Poetry never was something so strong for me, strong enough to replace this precious child with the conversation of a child, of a boy, and of an old man, that never failed to keep up with me, because in many matters he took the lead. There's no book of any sort that can dazzle me like him; there's no company that covers my right side like his, when I move along these streets of cold and hard foreign places; nor is there in me the gift of forgetting such an experience. I have it woven into me every five minutes. And I'm living on two planes, in a dangerous way. It's useless to tell you more, because I haven't said anything in three pages. *All of you, pray for him occasionally, even those of you who don't believe very much.* I see better than ever the uncertainty of eternal life, and a single thought calms me down and gets me to sleep every night: that I was going to leave him soon and live my afterworld alone and now I'll have my afterworld with him, in a short while, before long.

I embrace you all, I am grateful for your words, and I love you, as much as you all know, and more.

                                                                Your *Gabriela*

26 October [19]43. My Yin died on the fourteenth of August, two months ago. It seems like yesterday: so does my unhappy memory drip with freshness, my poor, living memory.

[Note added, hand of GM, directed to VO:] This letter went off to look for you in the U.S.A. — God reward you for the consolation that you gave me in your cablegram.[3]

  1. That Connie was not happy living with GM and Yin Yin is suggested in G.39, dated 10 December [1942?].
  2. GM's memory here is imprecise: her father, Jerónimo Godoy Villanueva, died at fifty-two (Alvarez Gómez, *Jerónimo Godoy V.*, 20), although her paternal grandparents lived to old age.
  3. This cablegram seems not to have survived.

ɔⱭ

V.3 [Letterhead: none. 1 p., hand of VO.]

SAN ISIDRO, 9 DECEMBER [19]43

My dear Gabriela:

I was deeply moved by your letter. I'll try to answer it soon. This is
only to tell you that I received it.

Roger [Caillois] and I talk a great deal about you. I'm so happy to
be able to do this and to know that you two got along[1] and even more,
since he truly likes and admires you. You were, he told me, very good
and generous to him.

I spent ten days in Mexico on my way back from the United States.
What a strange, extraordinary, and magnificent land.

I'll write you as soon as I have the tranquillity I need to find a way
of telling you (in French) what I think and feel. Love to Palma. For
you, an embrace and my affection as always.

Victoria

1. Roger Caillois traveled to Brazil to spend time with GM after Yin Yin's
death. They met again in Paris in December 1945 after GM's acceptance of
the Nobel Prize in Stockholm. During her stay in Paris, GM gave Caillois
some of her poems to translate into French. In a letter of 29 January 1946,
Caillois wrote to VO: "Gabriela says that you intimidate her a great deal: she
says you're both animal and celestial, like the animals of the zodiac. (I think
she even said "divine"). It makes me feel very happy to be able to talk this way
about you with someone who loves you. She says she loves you much more
than you know (and that she's told you so)" (*Correspondencia (1939–1978)*, 181).

ɔⱭ

V.4 [A telegram sent by VO from Buenos Aires to GM in Petrópolis on
the occasion of their mutual birthday, 7 April.]

[DELIVERED] 8 APRIL 1944

Remembering you with love, and a hug,

Victoria Ocampo

ʻOʻ

G.42 [Letterhead: none. 2 pp., typed, faded typewriter ribbon, multiple pen corrections, hand of GM.]

PETRÓPOLIS, BRAZIL. 27 APRIL [1944]

My dear and admired Votoya:

I'm in the countryside and I don't send telegrams except for when I go down into Petrópolis. My address now is *Post Office Box 43, Petrópolis, Brazil.* — I thank you very, very much for your affectionate telegram. Your words, even a few of them, always bring me a *special* strength. I've dropped loads of people in recent years. For being useless, because they just took up space, and they served no interest for my soul. And that's why I'm staying *in voluntary solitude,* and some delayed messages of the kind that matter to me are entirely necessary for me to continue living my own travails and this terrible penance of the world.

The *Sur* issue dedicated to the United States hasn't come. I went to Rio some days ago and was with the man you recommended, Professor Zobel, whom I liked quite a bit.[1] He gave me your letter, *voluntarily exaggerated* (according to Saint Paul's charity), for which I thanked you then and I thank you now. We spoke about various things involved in Pan-American exchange and we'll continue talking. I believe that the most important thing is that those Yankee people *know how to choose who they bring to the U.S.A.* They toss money around like children, and the general rule is that *although they might want to,* they don't know how to choose from among our candidates. Some time ago, the Guggenheim Foundation sent me some grant proposals to review, by professors from various countries. I always send them criticism that rigorously conforms to the truth, thinking that those who go will always prove to be the *test* [English in original] of us, the worst, the bad or the good. But since they, the Americans, continue believing in *quantity,* they think that they're doing well when they triple the number of people receiving grants. They will learn, little by little, as long as they listen to those who don't ask anything for themselves and thus have free souls.

Votoya, since the time, six years ago, when I saw you in your country, until the day and hour in which I am writing to you, I have the impression that fifty years have passed, such is the upheaval, blood-drenched and all, that has happened to the world that was ours. And it seems somewhat ineffectual to write you because there would be so much to say about it. It disheartens me, then: the poor paper and the poor hand that can't even indicate with a finger the total of things to say.

Yes, it was extremely pleasant for me to know and deal with Caillois. You know that I have opinions and prejudices about the French. The first thing that I enjoyed in him was his *real* youth, because the first calamity of his people is having allowed decay to win out. Then, his magnificent educational background, steeped in classicism, but with generous glances toward the popular. Then, his lack of vanity in which one has a respite from the Hispano-American plague of infantile self-love. Then, his enormous talent — you already know that I never put intelligence before anything. Then, the artistry of words, a fine hand because the other four senses are fine. And I very much liked knowing that he holds the people close, which ensures that he won't be finished by middle age, that he has humus, meters of it, *deep down*. This Pampa thing, despite the fact that it couldn't be written joyously by a French person, is among the best examples *of its genre* that I have read about the lands of this world, and this is a kind of reading to which I often turn. It's a pity we talked so little. We'll continue some day, with you, I hope.

On various occasions I've thought that you and I should see one another. I hope to have more strength. When I go down to Rio and speak with a few people, my strength is entirely used up. Ever since I've been living *for myself*, with no obligations of any sort, as the lesser animals live, with no more reason than myself, my strength — the internal kind — is half of what I always had. That's why I now read some books that are foolish to me, and *I write and copy out prayers*, because I've fallen into a terrible state ever since my poor little boy, my sweet, fourteen-year-old love,[2] turned his back on his house and on the poor woman who had him as a reason for living. He was driven crazy by three half-wits, by three pieces of walking garbage. You'll pardon me, but I cannot understand that his whole mind failed him, to the point of his being unable to see the nothingness of them, and of the others who sought it, the physical and spiritual nothingness, the denuded and palpable nothingness: a hole full of nothing.

On account of this weakness, which is more, much more, than my heart, and is ultimately of the soul, *of the very ends of my being*, I haven't told you of my desire to see you in Uruguay. Connie isn't going off to Puerto Rico yet. If I can pull myself together, I could go with Palmita to meet you and Connie would look after the office in Petrópolis.

I read in *Tiempo* magazine, the Mexican edition which is very well done, about the reception that they gave you in that country. And I enjoyed and was moved by your words about the land and the people there. There are various Mexicos within Mexico, and the country isn't wasting itself, like other ones: it gives food to the soul for a long time and it remains, *and it lasts.* I continue feeding from it. The passion of the Indians, they gave it to me, and someday you'll understand it from me, perhaps now that the white man is seen clearly as rotten and *falling into pieces.*

I read somewhere, I don't know where, that A[ldous] Huxley is in a religious crisis or he's joined up with some unnamed sect. This interests me, in him and ... in you.[3] Because I've been told something about you, too, *but more vague.*

In a notebook, I copy out selections about J[esus] C[hrist] taken from the most diverse and most opposite sources — eliminating only the ones written by the poor devils who call themselves rationalists. Many lights come into my sight, new lights, that help me. I believe that this can take me *somewhere.* In dreams I also receive some true crumbs of life.[4] In this way I keep on living.

On my table in the bedroom in which I work there still are the two notebooks full of your "Message." The one that was begun and didn't get finished, and which I kept and subsequently put aside because one can't deal with your Gallicism, at this time, without its seeming malevolent. I put great value on the confluence of foreign cultures in you, but that's all beside the point now. Those foreign cultures are one of your keys, *but they aren't everything, that I know.* I persist in believing that Racine and Company had to have distanced you, *fabulously,* from the expression that your body and your temperament both dictated to you, that you gave them the strongest juices of your being, that you performed for them a kind of blood holocaust, similar to the Jews, that you swore a kind of oath to them, to leave behind you the act of writing in your language, your personal one, which is better than mine in *freshness and warmth,* and in plasticity and *movement.*

On the other hand, your literary demands, which resemble a hemp-grinding machine, make me watch *too much* what I say about you, what I write. Crudely put: you make me afraid, *you rob me of the looseness and the lightheartedness with which I write about others.* You continue to subdue me, *you make me correct too much.* And with all this, *you dry me up and* you give me a curious uneasiness, caused by discontent with what I've said. But here are the two notebooks, until God be willing. I haven't seen you in vain; *I must have seen you in order to tell about at least a side and a half of you. Be patient with me.*

I've worn myself out now with this machine's old ribbon. I hug you tenderly.

Gabriela

27 April. I've just read some serious things regarding a book by María [Rosa], which I'm not familiar with. I've ordered it. She went off in that direction, but I still hope that she doesn't continue where she's going, *which is to her detriment, and to the detriment of many.* G. Best regards from Palma.

1. Professor Zobel served as a consultant to the Guggenheim Foundation, which had underwritten VO's 1943 trip to the United States.
2. In noting "fourteen years," GM apparently refers to the length of time she and Yin had been together, even though he seems to have been with her from infancy and was apparently eighteen years old when he died.
3. VO's interest in Huxley's work dated back several decades. One of her most interesting and revealing essays was "Huxley en Centroamérica" (written in 1934 and published in *Testimonios I*; see also V.23). GM was interested in Huxley as a kind of guru. On GM's meeting Huxley in California in 1947, see appendix, "About Gabriela."
4. On dreams and their importance for GM, see her various *ars poetica*, ranging from the "Decálogo del artista" (1922), in *Desolación*; "La flor del aire" (1938), in *Tala*; or "La desasida" (date not known, from 1938–1954), in *Lagar*, which begins: "In dreams, I had no mother or father, no joy or pain." Further discussion of dreams and their importance for GM appears in *Otro suicida*, ed. Vargas Saavedra, and in Rojo, *Dirán*.

ΩΩ

V.5 [Letterhead: "*Sur* directed by Victoria Ocampo, monthly magazine, Calle San Martín 689, Buenos Aires. Cable address: vicvic.baires." 1 p., typed.]

MAR DEL PLATA, 6 MAY 1944

Dear Gabriela:

I sent you a telegram on the seventh of April, remembering that seventh of April that we spent here together. I don't know if you received it.

By now you must have in hand the issue of *Lettres Françaises* in which the translations of your poems appear. The translations are very good, but what can't be translated is the flavor of what you write in that language so much your own that it seems invented by you.

Wouldn't you like to come spend a few weeks (or whatever) in San Isidro? I'd so like to have you at home with me again and to be able to talk to you about so many things. What can we say in letters?

If Palma is with you, give her a hug for me and tell her to come along too.

With my love, as always, and a hug

Victoria

∞

V.6 [Letterhead: none. 1 p., typed, signature and postscript, hand of VO.]

BUENOS AIRES, 31 MAY 1944

My very dear Gabriela:

I received your letter, which I'll answer this week. I read it to Roger, who was very happy and moved (I told him that your praise was, as usual, too excessive — and he thinks that when you exaggerate, it's me you're talking about, which is true).

We want to know if you liked the translations. As soon as you re-ceive *Lettres Françaises*, send us a few lines.

Love to Palma and to Connie.

A hug and my love, as always

Victoria

[by hand] P.S. Why don't you come here for a few days or longer?

∞

G.43 [Letterhead: none. 4 pp., pencil, hand of GM.]

[PETRÓPOLIS, BRAZIL.] 7 APRIL 1945

Votoya:

Today's the seventh. I want to write you at some length, but guests will be coming. And moreover, I'm limp. I remember that I've lived too much, that I haven't been happy except in dealing with trees and pastures, that "I came in vain" for Yin, in vain, too, for others. And I don't want to be a weeper with you.[1]

I tell you, then, this only, and I'll continue later. Take care of yourself and live. You've done brave and happy things, and of high quality. In *Sur*, you've defended almost everything that had to be defended. You've written at least two things of the sort that your Yankees call "inspiring": the pieces on Emily [Brontë] and [T. E.] Lawrence. (Is H.D. Jewish?) You've changed the direction of reading in some three countries, and with that, you've seasoned our still colonial culture with ineffable ingredients. And, the only thing that you may have been lacking, perhaps, you've turned your face and ear toward the invisible, in good time, leaving yourself space and time to know enough before leaving this odd thing that's the planet Earth.

Be happy, then, and thank the Lord for all that, today, while I ask Him why I came.

Palma and I have been reading *Sur* in these months. The part related to criticism — the part in small type — I never read because of my eyesight. That's what I've come to. I have greatly celebrated in you the blade — or the colander — that you have for choosing your people: the rigor and the delicacy. (In the book reviews, I miss only J. L. Borges, who stayed — at his ease — with Cinema.[)] — I'm missing issues of [*Sur*,] the magazine. Many.

The war is coming out of its bottleneck. You also served us, you did, in washing what was washable from our decorum as sub-Spaniards and sub-Indians who didn't want to go off to fight. — Now, Votoya, steady your arm for the feces of war, that is, so that the sewers — or pipes — don't overflow and toss the stopped-up and fermented filth into the streets and plazas. Retain for this — in sequence — your arm, your strong voice, your instinct for deep cleanliness, your brain, your soul, and even more, your spirit. I hug you. God keep you.

7 April.[2] Gabriela

1. Evidence of GM's depression appears in the upcoming months and is confirmed in letters that Roger Caillois sent to VO (January and February 1946), describing his impression of GM during her visit to Paris, where she spoke of her depression, wanting to die, and desire to see VO [in appendix].
2. This letter, G.43, was sent with G.44.

ಬಿ

V.7 [Letterhead: Villa Victoria. 1 p., in French, hand of VO.]

[MAR DEL PLATA.] 11 APRIL [1945]

Dear Gabriela:

I thought a lot about you on April seventh . . .

Perhaps you know that Drieu la Rochelle,[1] whom I'm incurably fond of and have known for fourteen years, committed suicide in Paris. The news brought me a sorrow that I feel time and again in the bottom of my heart and that no reasoning allays. One always blames oneself so much for things after someone departs. Even when it's absurd to do so.

Did you receive my little book?[2]

I send a hug and my love, with all my heart.

Victoria

1. VO met Pierre Drieu la Rochelle in Paris in April 1929, during her first trip back to Europe after her very intense affair with Julián Martínez. Drieu was a handsome young man with a seductive, refined manner, but his tendency toward cynicism put Victoria off at first. As they came to know each other over extended talks and visits, they became lovers and traveled in France and Europe together, despite Drieu's being married to a much younger woman. The amorous relationship did not last, but their friendship did. In 1932, Drieu came to Argentina to give a series of lectures, which were warmly received. Several of the books he wrote after this visit were influenced by his experiences with VO and Argentina. Drieu was becoming more and more attracted to Fascism and Hitler's Germany, however, and he actively collaborated with the Nazi occupation. He committed suicide on 16 March 1945, shortly before the Allied invasion of Europe. His will named VO and André Malraux as his literary executors. VO wrote about Drieu in several of her essays and in her memoirs (*Autobiografía* V, 67–175; "Pierre Drieu La Rochelle: Enero de 1893–marzo 1945"). Also see Dominique Desanti, *Drieu la Rochelle ou le séducteur mystifié*.

2. Probably a reference to VO's very short book in French (11 pp.), *Le vert paradis* (1944), which contained four essays she wrote about her affection for France and England as a result of childhood readings and travels.

ʕΟϽ

G.44 [Letterhead: none. 4 pp., pencil, hand of GM.]

PETRÓPOLIS, BRAZIL. 25 APRIL [19]45

It happened, Votoya, that I came to Rio and I left behind, up there [in Petrópolis], what was written for you on the seventh.[1] I'm sending it in a separate letter. I've received here your lines about D[rieu] la Rochelle and about a book of yours. (It hasn't come yet; it could be up there [in Petrópolis]; they only send me the letters. I'll let you know.) It makes me very happy that you're working. I didn't know that about Drieu. Yes, it must have grieved you a great deal. But, who can guess, good God, what anyone carries inside of them? One doesn't even know it oneself. We women don't know what sudden move we could make to-morrow. He and Gueheno[2] [*sic*] (is that how it's written?) — I liked them, and not just a little. Giono really amazed me. He zipped over to Pétain's side, as you saw. I understand this more — maybe because I've reread his book. Look: the passion of the earth has some mud, heavy with traditionalism, that speaks above and beyond ideas, which aren't ideology but something worse, on account of being strong, hot, and compelling. I don't know what unsuspected routes or reefs there were in Drieu that brought him to those depths. (The depths aren't always gloomy or . . . low, or wicked.) You'd taught him the *plumb line*, Maritain's and yours, which permits both of you to yield without giving up, and to comprehend without accepting. Oh, it's becoming very hard to live and even to think. But maybe you'll stay on the impervious side, like María [de Maeztu]. One believes that one can save and at least warn someone. And — as I now see with Yin — I neither saved nor warned. Because they are beings that need pure divination at their side, Votoya, and for this, only the Angel.

Don't torture yourself. Pray for him. Briefly, but often. I'm certain that it gets there, because I receive word back from them.

It seems that the war is coming to an end: it's moribund. But the other thing could follow it, right away.[3] I'm beginning to become exasperated. We still can't sell those houses, so we can leave. And for myself, I fear being uprooted on whatever day that I wake up in an executive mood and put my foot forward. When I do it, I don't stop, and they can't stop me.

A thousand thanks for your telegram. It came to me [illegible] in the countryside, and it gave me great happiness that you remembered. I prayed for you on praying for me.

Gabriela

1. Refers to G.43, 7 April 1945.
2. Guéhenno is also mentioned by Caillois, in a letter to VO (*Correspondencia [1939-1978]*, 176), as having participated in a debate about "committed literature."
3. GM here recognizes Latin America as a major front in a Cold War arms race between the Soviets and the United States.

:OO:

G.45 [Letterhead: none. 3 pp., pencil, hand of GM.]

[MONROVIA, CALIFORNIA.] 22 SEPTEMBER [1946]

To Vict. and to María Rosa:

For ten days I've been going around feeling ill. I've had a tragicomedy at home. They sent me an Italian-Mexican (married to a Mex[ican]), along with her Spanish lover and two impossible children.[1] They're drunk, and moreover, it seems that they're on drugs. It's too much to tell the rest. Getting rid of them has cost me plenty. They've initiated proceedings for "damages," they've terrorized the maid, and they've turned the house into a hell. And during those days Votoya's lovely letter about Roger [Caillois] came.[2] I wrote to the French consul — I can't get out of it, on account of official courtesy. —Whether he answers yes or no, I'll be free to do something after next Monday, with the Univ[ersity] of Calif[ornia]. I would be very happy to see you here, to have you here under the tree . . . where I spend the day. And to engage in conversation is the only thing that counts: not writing.

I hope to answer Vic. from time to time. I begin with this: I believe that in the chaos of our poor and rotten world, the universal use of alcohol counts for a lot. My trip through Europe was a passage from table to table, official and unofficial, where there was drinking with a kind of rabid euphoria, at first, and then, of ecstasy, and in the end, stupefaction. Please, keep these and the rest of the words to yourself! One can't speak these terrible things except from mouth to ear! There can't be healthy thinking in those people, María Rosa. Ideas don't count for anything. Today, as always, what counts is a body without poisons serving a soul likewise.

It seems, Votoya, that the war was made — by everyone — carrying a line of trucks with drinks behind each battalion. The mothers sometimes say that their sons came back to them, turned into alcoholics. I know that your country is sober. But you know that the rest— except Uruguay and Brazil — without going to war, also live in an alcohol bath. That's why it's indispensable that women who are *still* whole and clean-blooded vote. In part, you'll say. Yes, but in large part.

This opinion isn't dictated to me by my experience of the thing. But what I've lived has made me see, like the back of my hand, that alcohol not only stupefies but leaves no decency whatsoever, which is more important than anything. It's a kind of demonic possession of the powers and a hurricane of madness.

I'm writing to both of you from bed. My [blood] pressure has risen to twenty-six, and my heart is bad as well. I hope to recover in a month. I have my dark-skinned angel: my cook from Mex[ico], who tells me stories at night and helps me in the garden in the daytime. Let's see if she lasts. No one lasts, in service, in this country. I didn't know the extent to which the feudal custom that we call *servitude*, without a good understanding of the word, is being suppressed here.

Now we have in front of us, Votoya, the nightmare of G[onzález] V[idela] in Chile.[3] He's to become presid[ent] today. He was my ambassador in Rio, and I know him all too well. God sends me the worst calamities. They say that they want to take me out of the U[nited] N[ations]. I'll see if they let me retire while this man is in power. (I don't believe that he'll last.)

I hug you both. (I don't believe that Votoya is coming.) God keep you.

Gabr

1. GM mentioned her legal and other difficulties with these employees in California to many of her correspondents (*Vuestra Gabriela*, 89; *Antología mayor: Cartas*, ed. Vargas Saavedra, 406, 425; Arce and von demme Bussche, eds., *Proyecto*; also see Arturo Torres Rioseco [*Profunda amistad*] and Fernando Alegría [*GM íntima*], who spent much time with GM during her residence in California).
2. VO evidently wrote to GM about Roger Caillois' impending visit to California, asking her to receive him. This letter has been lost.
3. Gabriel González Videla became president of Chile in late 1946, following the death in office of the elected president Juan Antonio Ríos.

ᛊᗡᗡᘔ

G.46 [Letterhead: none. 7 pp., hand of Connie Saleva, pencil corrections, hand of GM.]

[MONROVIA, CALIFORNIA.] 2 JANUARY [1947]

Dear Votoya,

The hand that's writing this will be familiar to you. It seems that she [Connie] came back to bring me to the hospital. I've had a diabetic at-tack. By the symptoms, I realize that the illness is an old one. It's good to get better, but it would be better to be with Yin Yin.

It's curious that in the days [you've: *sic*] been in bed, in the hospital, I've had a curious entrance experience in your Mar del Plata house. I remember little of the rooms, but I do remember the lavender sitting in each one of them. I wrote some verses; they are too long, and you should toss out all that's superfluous.

I'm grieved by the disappointment that you're not coming. I wanted not only to see you, but to converse with you a long time about what's happening in your land, in mine, and in the other ones. Letters don't leave me with *any sensation of communicating with anyone.*[1] At the end of the prewar period, I remember that I wrote Mallea a letter telling him that it was necessary to reach an agreement, even among four or five people, *about what had to be written,* and that the lack of communication would end up damaging all of us. He didn't answer me with even a word. Here, I had two long conversations with María Rosa, and for me, they've been very helpful. I was going to write the article that I owe you about your magnificent lecture for women, asking you for verbal clarifi-cations *about various points.*[2] You're lazy, and it's not a matter of you an-swering me with a letter, plus the moment is so thorny that one can't write, without rhyme or reason, about certain points of ideology.

All this isn't to say that I'm trying to demand anything of you. But you, *someone who wants to be Argentine only,* you must know that what-ever is to be done, if it's to be useful, has to be planned with a view to South America, *almost* entirely.

I'm very much letting go of the world. I don't know if it's because of my illness or because of Yin. But I'm conscious that I'm acting badly, and suddenly a kind of anguish for everyone grabs me. Such bitter thoughts and expressions come into my head when I write poetry, that gathering only images of plants and animals is a kind of mental cure for me.[3] And I would like to write only about them for that reason, to cure myself. But I know very well, I repeat, that one shouldn't think about oneself *and that this is almost a crime, yes, a crime.*

What is happening to your land, as it takes on a Com[munist] color (and those who believe in totalitarianism have to take it), has already happened to my country and, some say, to Bolivia and to Paraguay. When everything is threatened, *asphyxia will drown all of us who've remained silent.*

I thought that you would go to the Nordic countries, which are the only healthy ones, and which should be talked about. You didn't go. I asked top-notch women from there to show you the Swedish way of life, at least. With regard to Italy, I preferred that you not go, because that makes one want to weep. That trip of mine did me great injury, and the famous strength that you saw in me in Washington was *sheer willpower.*[4] Since Paris, the illness had already begun wearing down my body (ten kilos less).

Perhaps María Rosa would like to lend you a hand [for writing], my lazy, spoiled girl. (Don't be bothered by the possessive, because at the hour of truth, those who don't know one another use *"tú"* and unexpected pronouns among themselves. . . .)

During some days of desperation, without a secretary and without a maid, I began to think about going to your country. Daniel Cosío sent word to me, by way of Palma, about the extent to which that wine had turned to acid.[5] My greatest need is to understand, *to see,* even partially. You must know that my head is very slow, that solitary thought does me no good in cases like this one, and that I only have some *flashes of understanding* from one afternoon to the next. The Inquisition called the mystics "the Illuminated Ones," and in me there's a lot of paganism, but a bit of natural transcendence. To have been close to you would have been an enormous rest and assistance, perhaps a cure as well.

Without coming up with a solution about what has to be done — what has to be said — I mean, to be written — and in the state of weight loss and tiredness that I've come to, I've only concerned myself with saving some drafts of verses and with writing verses, because prose, in me, always leans toward something that resembles social pedagogy. Palma is tied to her husband's work (ambassador of the poor Spanish Republic in a country with 60,000 Republican refugees) and can't help me either. From the discretion of her letters, I see that she doesn't trust her thoughts to paper.

You see, then, what it means for me that you haven't come.

Maybe you don't know what a calamity it represents for me to have the Boss that I have down there. At this point, I would be in the street if it weren't for that N[obel] P[rize]. The strange thing is, Votoya, that yours and mine [Perón and González Videla], apparently so opposite, go hand in hand!

I haven't even the slightest desire to read, and to lose that appetite is something very bad for me, since in my *unrelieved* solitude, this is like "the last straw."

Pardon this sad letter from a hospital, you who always keep your spirit intact and dislike whining. If you liked reading long things, I'd ask you to review the Apocalypse of Saint John and, above all, the last three books by Merezhkovsky, the ones about his conversion. I understand that he died in exile, and completely abandoned, like all prophets.[6]

I ask you to send me, in return for the verses, some seeds of your lavender.

Tell Caillois that I was finally able to speak with someone in his consulate, in a Santa Barbara school, and that he promised me two more lectures. We'll see if he follows through; they are apparently entirely superficial people and as lightweight as thistledown. As I lacked the language, his errands were done for me by strangers. If I can move around when he arrives, we'll go together to talk in each place. Although it isn't said here, Latin languages are in full decay and really they don't matter to anyone, since the ordinary American doesn't manage to learn languages.

A hug from Connie and from me and an *"hasta la vista"* that I say to you with real sadness.

2 January. Gabriela

1. Age and distance contributed to GM's increasing frustration with the inadequacy of correspondence.
2. GM may have been referring here to VO's stance in opposition to Perón's granting women the vote in Argentina purely for his own political motives (Meyer, *Against the Wind and the Tide*, 147–148).
3. GM describes the act of writing what became *Poema de Chile*, which her later correspondence terms a "purely objective poem." Writing *Poema de Chile* became a vital necessity for her, keeping her alive despite her growing anguish and solitude.
4. GM and VO saw one another briefly in Washington, D.C., a few months

after GM was awarded the Nobel Prize. GM traveled almost constantly from November 1945 to September 1946, going from Brazil to Sweden, London, Paris, Rome, New York, Washington, and finally to California.

5. GM refers here obliquely to the Peronist takeover in Argentina.

6. The last three texts that GM notes by Merezhkovsky (Russian writer [1865–1941] Dmitri S. Merezhkovsky) probably refer to the trilogy *Christ and Anti-Christ*, consisting of *Peter and Alexis* (1931), *Jesus the Unknown* (1934), and *Jesus Manifest* (1936). Merezhkovsky was known as the author of texts such as the *Romance of Leonardo da Vinci*, *Freud's Christian Unconscious*, and *Death of the Gods*.

ဘင်္

G.47 [Letterhead: none. Envelope to VO postmarked Monrovia, California, 21 April 1947. 2 pp., pen, hand of GM.]

[MONROVIA, CALIFORNIA.] 19 APRIL 1947

Dear Votoya, always remembered.

I forgot, for the first time in years, that your seventh was my seventh, that your day was mine.

I just lost my sister, Votoya. She was *the only one I had left* — and there's no hyperbole here. I'm left somewhat stupefied. Praying for the last one that left me often separates me from the rest of reality: I'm with them, literally with them. Pardon me; you didn't know this. . . .

I received a letter from your new editor at *Sur*. I had written, earlier, a very long one to María Rosa in which I told her about a very long poem, that possibly wouldn't work for *Sur*. There are some hundred verses and it's a "*Recado*" [Message] about an imaginary journey through Chile.[1] They're resentful, there, that I'm not going to visit. The doctor just canceled another of my trips to Washing[ton] for official duties.

To placate my compatriots, I've written that to them. I told María Rosa that if the "*Recado*" doesn't work for you, I'll send you something else. It won't go out as a submission to *Sur* for at least a month. I need *to verify* information — minute details about plants and little places.

Coni remembers you, always affectionately.

Thank you very much for that cable "full of memories."

God watch over you amid each storm.

If you pray, pray for me too.

Gabriela

19 April P.S. *It seems* that in another month I will be in S[an]ta Barbara. L[os] Ang[eles] is hell for me. I want to go there [to Santa Barbara], first, because of a clinic, then, because the city is sweet and delicate, then, to avoid contact with certain honchos of the Neolithic type who come here and disrupt my tranquillity.

G.

1. GM here describes an early version of *Poema de Chile*.

ஓஓ

V.8 [Letterhead: Villa Ocampo. 1 p., hand of VO.]

[SAN ISIDRO.] 1 AUGUST 1950

My very dear Gabriela:

This isn't a letter, as you'll see. It's just a few lines to ask you a favor.

Sur will be twenty years old in January 1951. And to celebrate this anniversary, we want to publish a double issue (December–January). This issue *cannot* appear without something of yours in it. Send us *whatever you want*. But please, send it as soon as possible.

I think of you, and *we think of you*, continually. I love you and we love you.

With a hug from
V

ஓஓ

G.48 [Letterhead: none. Envelope postmarked 24 January 1951. 5 pp., pencil, hand of GM.]

HOTEL ITALIA, RAPALLO [ITALY.] 21 JANUARY 1951

Cara V. O.:

I ask you to pardon my silence after the favor you asked me. The decision to leave America and to come to the "little hell" of Europe has been a long "mystery" — in the sense of ancient ceremonies, celebrated *underground*. . . . It was very difficult for me to see clearly, to see that our lands are, for the Lord's little animals, very blessed places to live (to be lived), and for the descendants of Adamites, very bitter to chew. In the end, here I am. They recite, almost in my ear, "the barbarity that's coming," but it neither moves nor excites me.[1] Crazy, senseless, blind and all, Europe is still a great human entity, a creature to whom one can listen to its speaking of what it did, before, and for years on end.

Various times, seven or ten, my brain has focused on that *prologue* for you. It's been a long time since we talked and maybe you no longer remember that I'm a very irrational Being who, through effort, can sometimes be very rational. Try to see *my rationality, dressed up as absurdity,* this time. Why, I say to you, and how did it occur to you that I might be able to write a prologue for a book of *yours?*[2] I've written, with some brazenness, various prologues for books of poems, saying a bunch of silly or made-up things. But the essay *is a very serious thing.* And ... *I don't know how to think,* V.O. I know nothing about "intellectual speculation." *I don't conjecture.* Be good and understand me, even though I may not be explaining the situation to you.

Ask me something else and I'll obey you, despite your bad behavior — your oversights, unforgivable for those who love you. *This thing that you're asking me is too much for me.*

I haven't sent you anything for *Sur.* When my packages arrive, I'll send some poetry.

Your social essayists — you have several in *Sur* — should send you, at this point in time, something about what's happening ... about *feeding* (what human beings eat, what they live on). There are places where the Mag[azine] moves on cat's feet — the one with the big boots.[3] And they don't see it. They live with sleep in their eyes, the ones who own primary things.

I suppose that some stupid women or intelligent men will have heard something like the above from me, since they spin stories about me being a *bolshie* [Bolshevik]. . . . The earlier ones turned me into an insufferably pious, *damaging* woman.[4] Add to that, the fact of my hanging out with gringas, American women professors. I'm still hanging out with one, to give them pleasure, and she's quite a person.[5] They've been insulting women, *in groups.* And since I was going around with them, both the men and women, the street slang also fell on me: Yankee W[hores]. . . . go back home!

You, who didn't want to hear the *whole* story about my poor little Yin, you can't understand *how much* I'm horrified by xenophobia. And I didn't know, I didn't, that that country [Brazil] had become xenophobic, above all in the rural areas. I left. Some day they'll drag me back to

Chile. But I trust in the poor bit of memory that I have to remember that our tropical countries are pure xenophobia and . . . an angry rash formed by envy. Some day I'll tell you the whole story. It's not too much to tell you in advance that even the best ones are mixed up in *that*, such as D.C.V. and his wife [Daniel Cosío Villegas and Ema]. They loved me, but *they felt* the same as the others: *the itchy feeling, that one more foreign woman was living among them.*

Maybe I offend your country if I don't tell you that only once, many years ago, did I experience a roguish attack from Argentina. I owe many things to your country that you don't know about.

It's easier for me to see you coming to Rapallo than to run into you on our continent. I wish it were so! But if the thing that almost everyone awaits comes [war? death?], I may not see you again. My diabetes has improved (due to an Indian herb from Mexico), *but not my heart.* And it would be good to see you here, here, in this world. Because it seems that in other worlds, reencounters are rare. . . .

I haven't had a letter from my María Rosa. She was going to go to Mexico. And I was always putting off until tomorrow the letter in which I was going to tell her this: in Mexico they don't love our countries, and especially not Argentina.

Tell her this. I'll write her when I find a house. I'm still looking, and the hotel makes me feel very lazy about writing.

A hug from
GM.

1. Writing from Italy, GM apparently thought another war was imminent, given her own experience of war in her lifetime: World War I in her youth, her presence in Mexico following the Revolution, in Spain prior to the outbreak of the civil war, and in southern France on the eve of the German occupation. She could also have been referring to possible repercussions from the Korean War, which began in June 1950.
2. This refers to VO's *Lawrence de Arabia y otros ensayos* (1951), with a prologue by Guillermo de Torre. Torre later published an expanded version of this prologue along with essays on GM, Güiraldes, Reyes, and Mallea (Torre, *Tres conceptos de la literatura hispanoamericana*, 1963).
3. GM here compares *Sur* magazine to the folkloric character "Puss in Boots."
4. GM describes and mocks the extreme and inaccurate aspects of her public image.
5. This refers to Doris Dana, who traveled and lived with GM from about 1950 (in Mexico) until GM's death in 1957 (in New York).

ɷ

V.9 [Letterhead: Villa Victoria. 1 p., typed.]

[MAR DEL PLATA.] 17 FEBRUARY 1951

Mi cara Lucila Godoy:

I would never have wanted or dared to bother you by asking for a preface to essays that only have a passing interest as testimonies. Since
Aguilar publishing wanted a preface right away, and since I didn't want
to ask anyone for it (because I detest bothering people with requests of
this kind), it was [Ricardo] Baeza's idea to ask you. I told him to leave
you in peace (despite how much I would have been pleased and proud
to have my little book carry a few lines from you at the beginning). I'm
so sorry that, in spite of my protest in an effort to save you the bother
of saying NO to a request, these people didn't pay me the slightest attention. This very day I received a letter from Aguilar asking me if I'd
heard from you, and I learned that they made the request IN MY
NAME. Well, they've used my name without asking permission. I
don't want to ask anyone for a preface, because I know it puts people in
an unpleasant bind. Please forgive this (since it wasn't my fault), and
don't think about the matter anymore.

I'm working hard right now. That's why I'm not writing you at
length. I always have plans to go to Europe, but I don't know when I'll
be able to carry them out, as things aren't going so well here. And we're
poor as church mice.

Until soon, I hope. With a big hug from

Victoria

ɷ

G.49 [Letterhead: none. Envelope postmarked, typed address to VO,
"SUR," etc. 2 pp. pencil, hand of GM.]

RAPALLO [ITALY.] 7 MARCH 1951

Cara Votoya:

I don't know where you are because your letter came saying that you
were coming to Europe. I very much want to see you, and hear you
"outside of time" and without an immediate departure. . . . Be it as it

may be — crazy, hysterical, or amnesiac — Europe continues to be a magical spot . . . You know this well.

I've lived an awful winter here. Because of the minimal heating in the house, because of a great "lethargy" in my body, and because of the bad food. (This is a city with few "townspeople," and the hotels carry off the cooks.) I'm not a *delicate* person except when I'm ill. My weight dropped from eighty-three kilos to sixty-nine. . . .

The topic of the war, Votoya, is too broad. Don't even broach it. It seems that the European semifederation that they're working on has improved even the air. Which doesn't keep us from having the Mediterranean so full of ships that it doesn't seem what it is, a little pond.[1]

I've decided to stay here, even with war. I'll go off to the places that *border Rapallo.* The Mexican experience is something that I don't want to repeat with another group of South American nationals: I the Communist; I the religious fanatic; I the Yankee sympathizer, I everything, anything but myself.

The fat issue of *Sur,*[2] magnificent, really magnificent. How well you do everything that you do, V.O.! God watch over you. (I don't hear anything from María Rosa.)

Gabr.

1. With the formation of NATO (the North Atlantic Treaty Organization), U.S. fleets were regularly stationed in the Mediterranean.
2. The "fat issue" that GM regards as "magnificent" would be the twentieth-anniversary issue, *Sur* 19 (October–December 1950).

ΣΘ੮

G.50 [Letterhead: none. Envelope postmarked, typed address to VO at *Sur,* Argentina. 1 p., pencil, hand of GM.]

RAPALLO, [ITALY.] 8 JUNE 1951

V.O.:

I've written you in regard to your coming to Europe, and there's been no reply. I beg you to tell M. Rosita that [I haven't] written her on account of my miserable eyesight, which I must use sparingly.

I asked you to tell me if you're going to come to Italy and when. Because I really want to see you and hear you.

I'm going to Naples: I've lived my worst winter on the famous Riviera, almost entirely in bed with sciatica. Everyone is puzzled by the lack of sun for four long months. They say that the world is now *Other*. . . .

I was very moved to receive *Sur*. Thanks! I'm going to take out a subscrip[tion] when I get to Naples. Because I still don't have a house there. God keep you, great and beloved Votoya.

Your Gabriela

ΩΩ

V.10 [Letterhead: Villa Ocampo, with the address of *Sur*, San Martin 689, added, hand of VO. 2 pp., typed.]

BUENOS AIRES, 22 JUNE 1951

My very dear Gabriela:

Two lines — because today I haven't time to write you as I'd like — to thank you for your affectionate letter. I don't know yet when I'll go to Europe. I hope in September, if I manage to get organized from an economic viewpoint. This isn't easy to do in times like these that we're living. You live outside our America, and so you don't know the thousands of small and large obstacles that accost us every day and that are difficult to conquer.

I've lived here for years struggling to keep alive a magazine that probably doesn't serve any purpose (or so I think in moments of depression). I can't make up my mind to shut it down. I can't make up my mind to have done once and for all with those preoccupations that rob so much of my time — time that I'd like to use right now to write, for better or worse, my memoirs.[1]

I don't know if you've heard that [Count Hermann] Keyserling,[2] in his [memoirs], devotes a chapter to me (which, according to his wife, is the most important one of the whole work). Although this chapter is full of praise, I find it unjust (even in the praise), and I've felt compelled to write a *mise au point* [a rejoinder]. It's a little book entitled *The Traveler and One of His Shadows*. I'm sending it to you along with the large book by Keyserling (which is very badly translated). You don't have to read the whole chapter to find out what he says about me. It's enough to begin reading on the page where my name first appears and

continue to the end. It's true that in my own country no one has accorded me the importance that K. does (on a whim of his own). But
there are several things in the chapter that, for reasons too long to explain, have bothered me a great deal. It's a long story.

Roger Caillois and Daniel Cosío Villegas liked my little book a lot,
and Roger thinks that someday it will find a place in the history of literature. Here, up to now, it's not had much impact, despite the penchant for scandal that this little village has. We live *sous la cloche pneu-
matique* [in a vacuum-sealed jar]. And emptiness kills all sound.

You may know that SADE [Argentine Writers Association] has
awarded me the prize of honor that, in past years, [Ezequiel] Martínez
Estrada, [Jorge Luis] Borges, [Eduardo] Mallea, [Arturo] Capdevila,
[Ricardo] Rojas, and [César] Fernández Moreno have received. I'll also
send you some pages that I read in answer to Borges' short talk on the
occasion. I think that this time I managed to say what I wanted to.[3] I
don't know if I've said it *well,* but I said it.

This is all my latest news for now. With regard to news of another
sort [Perón's government] . . . it's not appropriate for a letter. Letters get
lost and often end up in unscrupulous hands. I'll see that this one, as
innocent as it may be, is mailed to you from Montevideo. That way, I'm
more assured it will get to its destination. As you can imagine, *je ne suis
pas en odeur de sainteté au près de notre gouvernement* [I'm not in a state of
grace with our government] . . . even though I don't get involved in political matters of any kind.[4] But I do say what I think. And that's a mortal sin. Each time I have to obtain a good conduct certificate (every six
months),[5] it's the same old story. That's what I'm going through right
now. I'll tell you more when I see you.

What I want more than anything is to have time and enough peace
to write. I don't know if that's possible.

A big hug from

Victoria

1. Victoria began to write her memoirs formally in 1952, although selections
   had been published before that in her *Testimonios.* Excerpts would also be
   published as "Las memorias de VO" (*Life en español,* 17 September and 1 October 1962). Although the "complete" Spanish version was published posthumously in six volumes (*Autobiografía I–VI, 1979-1984*), these texts do not go
   beyond the early years of the founding of *Sur* in the 1930s.
2. Victoria was enthralled by Keyserling's works (*The Travel Diary of a Philosopher* [1925] and *The World in the Making* [1926]), and arranged to meet him in

1929 in Germany. Their fateful encounter is described in various of her later works and in Meyer, *Against the Wind and the Tide*, 73–91. After reading Keyserling's fanciful notions about her in his posthumous memoirs, VO wrote a response to his version of their relationship (*El viajero y una de sus sombras: Keyserling en mis memorias*, 1951). She also wrote about him in her *Autobiografía V*: 9–63.

3. VO's speech, later entitled "Malandanzas de una autodidacta" (Misadventures of an autodidact) was given on 13 June 1951 and published in *Testimonios V*. This is one of VO's best autobiographical essays, focused on her upbringing in a patriarchal society and her early efforts as a self-taught writer.

4. Although VO had no interest in politics per se, she did take a public position against the dictatorship in that she and other *Sur* writers regularly spoke in favor of liberal democratic values, which was enough to make her persona non grata in the Perón years.

5. Certificates of good conduct, necessary for Argentine citizens who wished to leave the country, were used to control the activities of political opponents. Although other authors of prominence, such as Jorge Luis Borges, received a certificate of good conduct, VO had to wait until 1955 when Perón was overthrown to travel outside the country.

ဟုိ

V.11 [Letterhead: none. 5 pp., hand of VO.]

PARIS, 18 SEPTEMBER 1951

Very dear Gabriela:

Your letter — which was sent to me from Buenos Aires — reached me in Lisbon. Angélica and I disembarked the day before yesterday in Cherbourg, after enduring a day and night of high seas that sent everything that was on the tables to the floor and made the chairs, baggage, and passengers roll from one side to the other. We still haven't rested well after those rough blows (some travelers were hurt, and they say the *stewarts* [*sic*] were frightened). But *tout est bien que finit bien* [all's well that ends well].

These are a few lines to send you a big hug and to tell you that I always remember you and love you.

To say that life has become unpleasant in Argentina is to say very little. In order to get my certificate of good conduct, I was given two appointments (six months apart) at seven in the morning with the special section of the police, eighth district (where they torture people and use the electric prod on them, etc.). They interrogated me for hours. They searched *Sur* and my private residence (*pour la forme* . . . since they hardly looked at anything). You should know that about two or three months ago crosses appeared on all the doors of people in the opposition (whose only crime was not giving in to Peronism). In my case, they put *two* crosses. This distinction honors me. But of course it's not at all pleasant, and since I live alone in the outskirts and drive my own car, coming home by myself late at night, I sometimes felt enervated by these untraceable threats.

You should also know that those of us who are not addicted to the royal couple are (with the decline of the peso, the freezing of rents, and everything else) poor as church mice. In order to keep the magazine going, I have to make *real* sacrifices (sometimes I wonder if it's worth it . . .). We've had to sell properties just to come and breathe a bit in Europe. Criticism of anything the sweet couple does is considered a crime of treason against the fatherland, and they put you in jail. That's what they'd do if this letter fell into their hands, for example. I warn you that they open correspondence, and mine (my telephone, too) is no doubt thoroughly scrutinized. In a Peronist newspaper, under the nice title "National Traitors," they once published part of a letter of mine to a friend.

Imagine them accusing me of Communism . . . me! I say *me* because I <u>hate</u> that brand of totalitarianism as much as I hate the Nazi one. This has cost me some very bitter arguments with María Rosa,[1] who each day is more sold on Communism and, to my way of thinking, more blind, confused, and on her high horse in this mistake. One can't talk to her about these things. At least I can't, because *de mon coté* [for my part], I also get riled up and irritated without being able to help it.

All this is very painful and sad. I would have liked to live a while outside Argentina, but the fact is that I can't afford to do it. I didn't take the precaution of withdrawing funds when so many others were doing it. I haven't concerned myself or been preoccupied with money matters. Now I regret it and think I was very stupid.

I don't know if you received my little book about Keyserling (in answer to a chapter about me that came out in his memoirs). In your letter, I think you're referring to *Soledad sonora*.[2] Nothing much, Gabriela, nothing much.

With regard to the magazine, if you only knew how difficult it is to do the little we do. If you knew the struggles and headaches that any effort of *that* kind means today in Buenos Aires!

The world is out of joint [English in original][3] . . .

Paris fills me with nostalgia. I've lost almost all the friends that used to make my stay here pleasant. I have some projects that I'll try to accomplish, without any illusion *de les mener à bien* [of it doing any good].

You can't imagine how sorry I am that you couldn't write a few lines for the book that Aguilar is going to publish in Madrid, since fools want prefaces no matter what.[4] And you're the only person who can talk about what little I've been able to achieve with *human feeling* (the only thing that interests me).

I'll send you news again soon. Please write me on the typewriter if at all possible. I have trouble understanding your letters in pencil, which blur so easily.

With love and hugs,
Victoria

I'm staying at the *Hotel de la Trémoille, 14 rue de la Trémoille, Paris.*[5]

1. María Rosa Oliver's ideological commitment to Communism led her and VO to many differences of opinion on political matters over the years, and put stress on their friendship. Although Oliver was confined to a wheelchair after childhood polio, she traveled frequently and often visited VO in San Isidro and Mar del Plata. María Rosa Oliver's writings about VO appear in her memoirs (*Mundo mi casa*, 1965; *La vida cotidiana*, 1969).
2. *Soledad sonora*, VO's fourth volume of essays, was an exception to the series of volumes that generally came out under the title *Testimonios*. This volume appeared in 1950.
3. Quoted from T. S. Eliot's "The Love Song of J. Alfred Prufrock."
4. Here, VO seems to forget that she had disclaimed an earlier effort to convince GM to write this preface. It seems obvious here that she indeed supported the request that she attributes to Baeza and Aguilar.
5. This was VO's preferred hotel in Paris for many years.

ιον

G.51 [Letterhead: none. Postmarked envelope, typed address to VO, at *Sur.* Reverse, hand of GM: "I opened it — in case it wasn't convenient to mail it." 3 pp., pencil, hand of GM.]

SALITA SCUDILLO, 17, CAPODIMONTE, NAPLES, [ITALY.] 18 SEPTEMBER 1951

Vic. as ever:

I write you at my second pause in your book *"El viajero"* etc.[1] I'm saddened by what's said there and by what you don't say, out of generosity

— and charity — values that accompany you and never leave you. You know that I read *in portions*. I'm going to leave for Rome and I want to *forward* these words to you. Take care, increasingly, of "your weakness," which is giving lodging to vagabonds "from the four points of the compass." Distances done, I've lived similar experiences, and for years. Right now I'm living one of them. . . . And yesterday, reading you, I made *a vow* never again to offer lodging to strangers . . . or acquaintances. They're insatiable, with monumental greed and vanity. Your case is much worse, Vic, because the wives of the guests particularly claw at you. How awful! Give them, the men or the women, the price of their days in a hotel in Buenos Aires and nothing more. It's dangerous even to become their "intellectual guarantor," because newspapers and magazines become poisoned toward you, thinking that you're only capable "of loving foreigners."

I've been grieved, reading your little book, page by page, Vic. But at the same time, I've delighted in the good prose and the command of the text and of the tone. I send you a very tender and emotional embrace.

Note my address.

Gabriela

— When will you come this way? Italy is, despite everything, Europe's most wholesome, sweetest part.

P.S. — I forgot the main thing, Vic. I recall being in B[uenos] A[ires]. At the table, in your house, you received a letter or cable from K[eyserling] asking you for money to transport him and . . . his family to B[uenos] A[ires]. I vaguely remember that your comment was that you would send him monetary help, but not for that general transport. The little pamphlet or book or article, or whatever it is about him, must also contain that scrape. (They're never wounds, Vic.: they are scrapes, those kind that in the tropics become a sore and smell badly, in one day.)

Forget the poor man. In regard to our people, if they comment, you already know: our America has no solution, aside from ten centuries or twenty of *living*, of existing. It's full of children who play with mud instead of playing with comets. Another hug.

G.

1. GM refers to *El viajero y una de sus sombras*, which describes VO's literary relationship with Keyserling.

இஇ

V.12 [Letterhead: none. 1 p., hand of VO. No place or date indicated.]

[PARIS. 19 OR 20 SEPTEMBER 1951]

Dearest Gabriela:

Yesterday I sent you a letter, and this morning yours arrived. I don't know exactly what address I sent it to, so I'm sending these lines just in case.

I'm going to Rome, but I still don't know on what date (though I think soon). I can't deny that I feel deeply heartsick for many motives and reasons. What's going on in Argentina is hateful and depressing. It wasn't worth it to stay there as I did, depriving myself of everything that appealed to me so much in other *culturally* civilized countries, in order to end up like *this*. *This* [life under Perón] means ignorance of all the values that matter to me in life.

A hug,
Victoria

இஇ

G.52 [Letterhead: none. Envelope postmarked, typed address to VO in Hotel Trémoille, Paris. Reverse: Conde 1664 Belgrano. 2 pp., typed, pen corrections, hand of GM.]

VIA TASSO 220, NAPLES, [ITALY.] 26 SEPTEMBER 1951

So very dear Vic,

Doris Dana remarks to me that you've asked me not to write you by hand. And I grab the typewriter after three years or more, to keep from tormenting you with my handwriting — although I try to make it come out fine. . . .

Your letter has moved me very much;[1] I've been needing it for months now, and not writing you has been, in large part, a fear of hurting you since I'm an outspoken woman and the Argentine matter can't be dealt with, except with ugly words. . . . That thing about the doors being marked — copied from the age-old persecution of the Jews — *sent chills down my spine.* That was publicized in Europe, despite the Argentine money that circulates among the journalists. There have been jokes and even *mockery* in the press about the royal couple.

I mean that it's a tremendous relief for me to know that you're in

Europe. Try to stay here unless the earthquake also arrives, shattering our tranquillity.[2] For now, your friends breathe easily, knowing you're distant from life under the police, or rather, under scrutiny, which apparently exists in B[uenos] A[ires]. I breathed easily on seeing your handwriting and the postmark. I won't keep silent about the fact that maybe you've chosen the *most feverish* atmosphere for resting. Because Paris is more developed than Rome, *much more*, for those who don't go for peace or relaxation.

Today, the twenty-sixth, I note in the newspaper a sudden rise in temperature in the international news. You're less nervous than I am and you'll know how to do a better reading of the press. I ask that when you can, you send me just a few lines if this heat wave is going to continue. . . . I'll do the same.

You're useless for rural life, my dear Vic, and I believe that many of us have to become villagers or leave Europe. And I don't want to leave Europe, because it would mean returning and falling onto the tip of Ibáñez' sword. . . . The world has come to that: a hunt is beginning.[3] People advise me to take refuge in that boring country called Switzerland. I believe that its mountains would console me: you don't know how much I miss the mountains of the Valley of Elqui. . . . But I don't believe I'll go there. To an Italian village, maybe yes.

Going back: there have been various invitations to go to Nice, for meetings. I haven't gone because of that French climate, which strikes me as malarial.

The most serious thing that I've read about our peoples — in the very little that they send to me — is, first, that an alliance of the three kings of the south was being arranged. Then, great silence and some little note about how the Chilean population saw this as a bad thing.

Our people don't improve, Vic. Carlos Ib[áñez] is heading straight for the presidency and a self-exile of quality, of quality. They tell me that he'll pull it off, *and with a large majority*. Years ago, "the Horse" [Ibáñez] left me pensionless in Europe and, what's more, . . . without a passport. His flunkies turned down my request. And now, six years of his second presidency are walking toward me. Chew on this fact: his candidacy has been pushed by a women's political group. My future bread, already confiscated, matters much less to me than this filth of Chilean Fascist skirts. There's more: the majority of those women, the leaders, are Catholics. . . . And they are, naturally, from Santiago: our peoples rot from the head, first. We'll see many more disgraces, Vic:

our countries are living a grotesque but nonetheless serious hysteria. We'll see many more disgraces, and our old age will become plenty hard. But there exist some Very Delicate Forces, which are scarcely visible, and they, even so, act *when things come to a head*. They arrive, yes, they show up; but even more so, they always console the persecuted, with His presence, I repeat, and here I'm not telling you anything that resembles hallucinations.

Flag waving and nationalism, Vic., are the forces whose grease fattens these so-called "national" or "patriotic" movements. They live on those VIRTUES, like on pig's lard. It's a real industry, and journalism makes itself a fortune by it.

Read your Bible at random: it always offers counsel, it always answers, and that great voice that it has strengthens, sets aright, almost raises the body's heat. . . .

Yesterday, there arrived an invitation to a lively get-together of the handsome Brazil of the mulattoes. They're extending an invitation, expenses paid, to a congress or conference *on Latinity*. Naturally I'm not going. I'm waiting, tenser by the day, expecting M[arta] Salotti or someone else to take Yin's little body from Petrópolis and bring it with them to me. But I'm afraid that my government, which plays up to people the comedy of how *they take great care of me*, might call me, drastically, if the situation in Europe gets worse. If that happens, I'd ask to stay in Uruguay.

In Chile, we have a deluxe candidate for president, a Mr. Matte, a "white" man, liberal and with an irreproachable life. But nobody thinks he has a chance, no one, and everyone is sure that "the Horse" will come out ahead, *and with a strong majority*. I was forgetting: the education minister called me, some days ago, for . . . a national homage.[4] I answered that I've been sick, and I am, but I'm not in a state that keeps me from sailing.

I'm hungry to see you and to hear you. Where? Tell me. If you don't want or can't take the boat down to Naples, *tell me what I should do*. My house is Via Tasso 220, Naples. The consulate is still separate.

I ask you to read one or two newspapers for yourself and for me. I'll write you about our situation, which is normal up to now, except for this morning's news.

I live with an American writer and professor, Doris Dana. Only now has she decided to stay in Naples — out of concern for me. She's very serene, and one sees no alarm of any kind in her. But the occupation of the port by American troops is annoying the people — read here, the local Com[munists].

May God hold you in his hands, V.O., beloved soul. You are strong; I was, I no longer am. Your

                                                                        Gabriela

1. The letter mentioned is V.II (18 September 1951).
2. Another reference to the renewed war that GM anticipated, perhaps as a result of Cold War enmities.
3. GM marks her awareness of Cold War politics as a witch-hunt.
4. GM was awarded Chile's National Prize for Literature in 1951.

ΩΟΩ

G.53 [Letterhead: none. Envelope postmarked, typed address to VO, Hotel de la Trémoille, Paris. 3 pp., pencil, hand of GM.]

VIA TASSO 220, NAPLES, [ITALY.] 6 OCTOBER 1951

Cara Vic:

We're moving — I don't have furniture, but stationery, yes. And in this seething mass I can't find the two clippings that I was going to send you about "the present-day Eva — Domingo."[1] I repeat that the Italian press is very decent about this point and that it flogs the couple with ridicule.

I also repeat that I want very much to see you and to hear you, and that I can go to see you at the border — to Nice — but *only if you can't come here.* My health is very delicate. Today, for no reason, a kind of cardiac faint *came over* me. The loss of Yin, Vic., not only left me extremely impoverished; it was also a bite *from an Amazonian beast* out of my old flesh.

I still don't have an answer from you to my earlier letter. But I'm writing you again because maybe I didn't give you my new address. It's Via Tasso (the name of the poet, born in Sorrento) 220, Italy.

Don't suffer, Vict. Your country was the most sensible of our twenty-one countries. The time to go crazy had to come. The whole world is catching the fever. (Keep up your strength, Vic: we all need it.)

It seems that you're going to keep on doing *Sur.* I haven't sent you anything, I believe, because I'm only continuing that long poem about Chile — purely descriptive. It requires me to read and to preserve the little strength that I have.

I believe that an invitation to that meeting in Vienna has probably come to you. Maybe I'll go to it. But I need to know that it isn't full of Communists. Or perhaps you have the other invitation for India. Both things would distract you, Vic. I want to know you're somewhat happy. I'm not one of those women who believe that suffering helps: a theory of this sort is absolutely Spanish, that is, morbid, an inquisitorial type of thing. Protect your joy.

Pardon what I'm going to tell you if the matter is disagreeable to you. If you're thinking that *clean Argentina* would be helped by writing about its crisis, or if some Europeans are already doing so, I would help that movement of conscience. Tell me something about it so I can get to work.

Don't feel obliged to write me at length. What I need is to hear from you every two or three weeks. Right now I know nothing, and *this disturbs me. Drop me a note.*

All the old and ongoing affection of
Gabriela

1. Eva (Duarte) de Perón.

ιοσι

G.54 [Letterhead: none. Postmarked envelope. 3 pp., pen, hand of GM.]

NAPLES, [ITALY.] 5 NOVEMBER 1951

Cara Votoya:

I know nothing about you, following that announcement about your arriving in Rome. And I'm writing to you in Paris . . . although maybe you're in Rome.

You might not be thinking about coming to Naples, and that's why I'm getting ready to leave for Rome at the first word from you. But up to now, that word hasn't come.

My eagerness to know this comes from my fear that they're going to call me to Chile. The rags-or-rubbish dictator certainly *doesn't want that* — it's the street people! They organized a rally over there, apparently 70,000 people — middle-class and workers — and they spoke about everything, even that I should return. And it really gives me the jitters! I'm relieved to know that the king isn't pleased with that. But now his wife — herself, in person — is going around collecting money to reconstruct the house in which I was born[1] ... — and where I lived for the forty-day quarantine, after my mother gave birth.

The point of my wearing you out with all this is that I run the risk of not seeing you, which really "gets" me. If you don't want to come yourself, I'll go to Rome. The good gringa who accompanies me should be arriving today.

I don't know your address, so I have to entrust these lines to your consul in Rome, giving him the chore of getting them to you, one way or another. (My sec[retary] just tracked you down in Paris.)

I don't have any serious ailment, but I do have a tremendous listlessness, worse than in the tropics ... and I don't like this one bit.

I'm asking you a difficult favor, Vic: obtain from someone in Buenos Aires — a man or a woman — who knows *something*, Good Lord, something that might be true and clear about what's going on in Chile. On account of the small print, I don't read the newspapers from there; what's more, the right-wing press is a total lie, and the left-wing is fanatical and extremist. As a result, I'm in a starless night. . . . (How beautiful they are, Votoya, our starry nights! I never know if I'll see them again!)

I live amid a flood of letters that eats up my day, and that *Poema de Chile* that already has eighty or ninety quatrains; but a lot of things are missing.[2] Some helpful books have finally arrived, which will let me continue adding things, correcting and inserting others.

I don't know, dear Vict, *very dearly beloved*, if you're in a situation where you can escape from events and empty your mind of them. [Rudolph] Steiner can help you with that: there's nothing better, these days, than *to buddhisize* yourself, a bit. Don't laugh at me. (I don't know how that infinitive is written ... Italian keeps damaging my Spanish).

Send me a few lines. I'll go down to Rome. Not to Paris — because it's very far away.

I haven't heard from María Rosa either.

P.S. — I wrote you about your last writings. Some days ago.

G.

1. Here GM indicates her awareness of being monumentalized in ways that contradict her own lived, historical experience and that reveal the fissures of gender within national politics.
2. This marks the first time GM uses the title *Poema de Chile* to refer to the long narrative poem she was composing during the last decade of her life.

ɔɔ

G.55 [Letterhead: none. Envelope postmarked, typed address to VO, "Embajada Francesa ante Vaticano, Via Piave, Roma." "Express mail." 5 pp., pen, hand of GM.]

VIA TASSO 220, NAPLES, [ITALY]. 10 NOVEMBER 1951

Victoria, so very dear:

I sent a letter to Rome. Maybe you're somewhere else, and I won't manage to locate you.

It's been some days now that I've been writing a substantial letter for Chile, aimed at seeing clearly amid the situation that's heading straight toward *us*. The right wing has had the cynicism to launch the candidacy of Ibáñez. In addition, groups from the so-called center are joining in the chorus. According to letters that sensible people write and . . . in code, the Horse (that's what they call him) could be a sure thing . . . They continue to speak of the secret pact of the "Pacific Cloverleaf," Brazil, A[rgentina], and Chile.

For me, Vic, all this means leaving this consulate in March or September, and my head's been full writing letters to find out where I'm going. We *criollos* from the Pacific have bad karma; we live in this tragicomic farce that repeats itself without respite.

Even so, every day I remember you and commend you to the Lord, the only Person we have in our reach . . . although this is something that many don't believe. I only ask Him for inspiration, a direction for you and for myself.

The first effort that I'm making is to someone who, by turns, has loved and detested me: [Jaime] Torres Bodet. I'll tell you what he answers me.

A letter from María Rosa [Oliver] has come, asking for a signature on behalf of a destitute prof. I sent it to her, by cable. And so it continues. And it will not stop, Vict., except *when it "comes to a head,"* and among the people of our countries, the point or degree of "coming to a head" is delayed, not in being produced, but *in being seen.*

For some time, there's been talk of a secret accord among the ones who belong to the Pacific pact: G[onzález] V[idela] is a great big buddy of the Brazilian corporal. There's been a lot of talk about an Andean interview between your bogeyman and mine. But it still hasn't happened. Or it has, and we don't know it, Vic. . . .

The middle class behaves very badly. Its affectations are costly, and its unrest is called a fur coat, a house on Huérfanos and Moneda Street, and jewelry. What a fright! Even Chilean Communism has begun to go bourgeois. Everything goes bourgeois. The only Chileans with whom I "exchange letters" are [Jacques] Maritain's group.[1] In them, too, the alcoholic ferment for luxury and balloting for high posts is also under way. (I no longer know how balloting is written . . .)

The elimination of this fever is so distant in time, Vic, that neither you nor I will see it.

Every time that "the earthquake" has fallen on top of me, I rested my spirit — I raised it up — remembering that Uruguay is a country of refuge. And some days ago I paid a courtesy visit to their consul in Naples. What happened to me then, I still don't understand . . . I arrived, I greeted the consul, who didn't stand up. I ask him about some of *my* people in Montevideo. He didn't give me any news. Suddenly, peering out from a doorway, was this woman, his wife, who yelled: "Is that the famous one, is that really her? Is it Mistral?" The man didn't answer a word. And she kept on shouting. Until I — a visitor without a seat — left. . . .

Some kind of intrigue must be going on in this, because Juana [de Ibarbourou], to whom I wrote a letter some time ago, making no request whatsoever, didn't answer either. (It had to do with a general, literary matter.)

Gossip, Votoya, the small-minded, stupid, and dirty little *criollo* gossip comes and goes like the tides, on our unhappy continent. And writers, Votoya, don't clean their furry tongues — I'm not sure of this word either: between Portuguese and Italian, my poor Spanish is liquidated.

Be patient, great and beloved Votoya, be patient; it's a brownish gray virtue, vulgar and pedestrian, but it's more helpful for living than the capitalized Virtues.

Some vulgar little devils, as dirty as dogs without a master, run from north to south through our towns, to the big ones, the medium-sized ones, and the little ones. We won't see the cure for them, my little one. Sometimes a happy convalescence appears in them, some healthy color. Then they relapse.

Forgive me, Vic. *I don't believe in white lies for consolation;* I prefer to look, face to face, at the sores. I'm hurt, sometimes I cry, but the end is an acceptance of reality, thinking . . . of karma.

Your old Gabriela loves you and thinks of you often.

1. "Maritain's group" refers to the cadre of young Chilean lawyers, influenced by the reformist Catholicism of French philosopher Jacques Maritain. They broke from the Conservative Party in the 1940s to form the then National Falange Party, subsequently renamed the Christian Democratic Party. Members included the future Chilean president Eduardo Frei, along with Radomiro Tomic and his wife, Olaya Errázuriz de Echenique (Frei, *Memorias*, and *Vuestra Gabriela*).

ဆင်္သီ

G.56 [Letterhead: none. 5 pp., pen, hand of GM.]

[NAPLES, ITALY. SEPTEMBER - NOVEMBER 1951]

Dearest Vict:

You're thinking I'm dead, but I'm not dead yet. And I remember you as if remembering you were a sacred tradition, plus a sweet habit.

I was in Rome, where I usually go to a kind of Intellectual Coop[eration Institute] that the Italians are trying out for me. Little is accomplished. Although, Vict., it's time for the writers to do something for the "Peace Round." But things have discredited the word, and it's truly something . . . shameful. That's what I have to call it, looking at the face opposite my own. And that face, Vict., almost always gets frozen stiff, or becomes livid when one names the other thing, war. But they continue to do nothing, sick with fear, with pure decadence. Because love and fear are vitality, but this, this is agony without death.

It's probable that I'll go to this Venice get-together, with Th[omas] Mann; [Paul] Claudel, who detests me as a "hateful person" . . . in poetry — and [Roger] Caillois above all.[1] *I want to know if you're going. Please tell me.*—I can't *keep up* with the business of the Argentine peso and I have a bit of money there. Because in Naples, *they don't declare the exchange rate in the banks,* saying that they don't know if there's been a new drop. Tell me about it *without going to any trouble;* do it by way of M[aría Rosa Oliver]. What is she doing? Pardon her, Vict.: we pacifists are living a minor tragedy. It's unnecessary for me to explain her to you, *unnecessary.* We cannot stop being with her. In my case, because of the children.

Perhaps I've told you that my health is very delicate. The current heat afflicts my heart; but Naples is my only possible place, because in wintertime my circulation is very bad in cold places.

I'm anxiously awaiting the end of the term of the half-man who rules over us. But, ay, maybe the Horse will follow. That's what Ibáñez is called by the very ones who are going to vote for him . . . Look at the political conscience of the *criollo*. I'm expecting that the "layoff" I had some years ago will be repeated for me. (My *pension itself* was canceled). Matte is a first-rate person, but since they don't believe that he'll "make it," many will vote for him — "the favorite son," or for the Horse.

I hope that you continue writing. Although you don't need to hear it, I already told you and I am telling you again to take advantage of this, *your best point in time*. Do it, *be true to yourself*. Get away from people, go off to the countryside, and write. This is *your hour*.

I don't know anything about *Sur*. I'm able to send you a little check. Don't laugh. I'll send others as frugal as this one. They are to ask you, *later*, for the issues of *Sur* that I don't have.

Oh, Votoya! My magazines — yours — I need them, in order to read them for the third time. That's how I read, insisting on what I've missed. But I can't open the big box of books and *Surs* because . . . I live, thinking of the probable "uprooting" if "the big one" comes. This is how I live day by day, sacrificing things that it pains me to keep closed up in big boxes. I live in a provisional house, *with nothing of my own* except medicines. Without Spanish, except for *the little books* that arrive. Happy are those who don't believe in the witch — the war. I believe. And you? Tell me; maybe you'll relieve me.

Doris [Dana] went off to her country [the United States]. Now she's coming back to keep me company. Now and again there's Palma, who *works* in Rome. Fortunately, the house has a palm tree and a little garden, plus a terrace that looks out on the sea.

I believe that I had told you that there's material of mine for a book.[2] But I still haven't finished a *Poema de Chile*, which is completely *descriptive*, and I'm missing plenty of information. Everyone promises me help, but no one sends me things that are *concrete*. I don't know how I can get out of the jam I'm in.

Tell me if you're going to go on this trip to Venice. In that case, I'll ask permission from Cuco-Coco[3] — he's a total wooden monkey, but "he gives the orders," and he didn't let me go to Vienna. And so one's left without a *truthful* report. Every time that he [Chilean President Ibáñez] does something to me, his wife goes out into the streets of Vicuña — my city — to beg for money to buy the house in which I was born and lived . . . forty days, the forty-day period following my

mother's giving birth. . . . Our people are at once explosive and hypocritical, crude, and sly.

God keep you in health and joy. He has loved you more than you
know. . . . He's hidden, but very attentive. . . . A hug from your old

Gabr.

1. The congress in Vienna, honoring Thomas Mann (to which Pablo Neruda
   helped provide an invitation for GM), was planned for 6 October.
2. The book mentioned as finished would be *Lagar*. G.59 also describes *Lagar*
   as a finished book.
3. GM seems to be playing on the name of the Chilean ambassador to Italy,
   probably Eduardo Cruz-Coke, doctor, writer, and political figure.

ಬಃ

G.57 [Letterhead: none. 3 pp., pencil, hand of GM.]

220 VIA TASSO, NAPLES, [ITALY.] 7 DECEMBER [1951][1]

Dearest Vic., more loved than you know:

Tomorrow I'm going to clip press notices that I've set aside for you.
They come from Buenos Aires; they seem to be from a correspondent
who hasn't sold out. I should send you that straightaway, in a timely
way, but my eyesight is very poor, as you already know.

I know, Vic., that you're a great one for eating, likewise for your bed
(that is, for getting your sleep). For both reasons, I haven't told you to
come to us in Naples. Today, I'm reading something in the press that, if
it's true, would make you prefer Naples to Paris, despite everything.

Although it might be ingenuous, I'll tell you this: this house is *as
much yours as it is mine*; it's a little apartment: a living room, two bed-
rooms, an office. There's a garden and pretty views of the sea. Since its
exposure makes it seem "ripe for a bombing," Doris Dana and I are now
looking around regularly for a house *further in*. Almost all of what's offered is for sale and not for rent. *But we'll find something*, yes, God willing. I would leave the office in the center of town; there's a sec[retary]
who attends people there.

Now they've added the province of Naples to the city of Naples for
me. I'm thinking of taking a trip through my radius. (I've told you that
Doris has a car.) You'd be able to see this countryside, which is well
kept and *beautiful*, and Doris would bring you to Rome when you

wanted: she has great esteem and liking for you, including a certain special gratitude because you love her Yankeeland. . . . She's "very personable," and I know that you will like her, Votoya.

Big cities bring no peace, Votoya, not for writing or for *existing*. . . . And keep it in mind, if the "Nameless One," the war arrives, they are *the worst place* to be.

I promise — if it's ingenuous, pardon it — to give you peace and some sweetness in any one of the little towns, green and sweet, in the outlying regions. The most difficult thing is . . . the cooks. But that, too, can be found, with enough patience to continue looking for one. . . .

I know that there are difficulties in getting money out of Argentina. Tell me if you need some now. Or tomorrow. No one knows what's coming, Votoya. (Every time that I write this name, I see the little boy who called you this. . . .)

Don't do what our *criollos* do here: read the press *to feel the pulse* of what's coming. You must read every day, and change newspapers from time to time. . . .

I'm asking for two little words from you. I'll continue to look for a house . . . *for three*. A faithful hug from your

Gabr.

1. On this same day, VO wrote her sister Angélica from Paris (*Cartas a Angélica*, 93) confiding that she (like GM) was losing patience with gossip: "Every day I feel less capable of conversing at lunches and dinners and every day I am more disgusted by mundane literary flutter." Also see V.13.

∞

V.13 [Letterhead: *Sur* (crossed out on first page). 4 pp., hand of VO.]

PARIS, 26 DECEMBER 1951

My very dear Gabriela:

Thank you for your very affectionate letter and for your offer. But I can't for the moment (will I ever? I doubt it) stay much longer in Europe. I have things that demand my attention in Buenos Aires. You forget that — whether it's worth the effort or not — I have a magazine there and a small publishing house. Do you remember when you used to tell me over and over that I couldn't leave America? Well, I've stayed in America. But I don't know if for better or for worse.

Paris fills me with uneasiness. The rivalries, intrigues, and "*arriv-isme*" of its little literary world upset me. Besides, it's hard for me to live enclosed by four walls. And Paris, however pretty, is *that*. The trees, the ocean, or the river (the big one, mine) are almost indispensable to me. And however much loneliness I may experience . . . I prefer *that* loneliness to this one.

I'm now planning to go to New York if only for fifteen days. But guess what, when I looked at my passport I realized that my visa had expired in November and I have to renew it. I don't know how much time that will take me. If it's too much, I won't be able to go to the U.S.A.

Nor do I know the condition of political affairs in Argentina. Peronism doesn't let me live and work there in peace. And so what I *want*: trees, air, space, is being affected by the underground rumbling of "the new Argentina," as they refer to it. In a certain sense, I'm calmer here. But *not* in a city like this.

In regard to what the newspapers say . . . I give them little credence. And what's more, I don't understand a whit of what's going on in the world, which I think is populated by madmen.

I've spent five days in Berlin at the invitation of the French minister of that section of the capital. I've visited the four sectors (American, English, French, Russian). I've spoken with people, smelled the city, gone into stores, theaters, "cultural houses," and restaurants. My impression is that there's as much chance of resolving this as there is in a bag full of squabbling cats. They all cordially detest each other. General Mathewson (American), with whom I ate, a nice gentleman who speaks Spanish perfectly, told me: "The more money we give Europe, the more they hate us." And I think that's true. The envy that the United States awakens in Europe is frightful.

Berlin's Soviet sector is very poor, and it's still very destroyed and full of rubble. Not much light at night. People very miserably dressed. The Allied sector, thanks to the dollar, has a very different look, and there you can find practically whatever you need.

I had a conversation with [Bertolt] Brecht, who's director of a theater in the Russian sector. Unfortunately, we weren't able to talk for a long enough time. He struck me as very pleasant, but of course, ideologically misguided.

In general, Berlin leaves an impression of great sadness, especially if one knew how it was before the bombing of the last war. The neighborhood I lived in is gone. In 1930, I spent fifteen days across the street from the zoo. Drieu la Rochelle was in the hotel, and we would go out to see Berlin together. What we saw is today just a mound of rubble, and the new trees in the zoo are one meter tall.

I'll keep you posted about my *doings* as soon as I know if they'll give me my visa quickly or not.

Lots of love to your delightful companion and a big hug for you from

Victoria

[Written sideways in the upper right-hand margin of the first page]: Torres Bodet, whom I only saw for a moment a while ago, pays no attention to me . . . nor does he have reason to. What do I represent nowadays other than my small personal value? Nothing.

[Same page, in left-hand margin]: María Rosa is in Brazil, working for Peace with the Communists.

∽∾

G.58 [Letterhead: none. 2 pp., hand of GM.]

[NAPLES, ITALY.] 6 [JANUARY?] 1952

Cara Vict.:

I was happy to see you, despite the ash that fell on the end of our conversation — the whole thing with Yin. Thanks for the time that you gave me.[1]

Vic, I'm writing you in a hurry, because I'm going out to eat. And I'm writing, all "bristling," after reading the newspaper for *today, the sixth.* I don't know whether my newspaper has joined in the fever, but the debate that it reproduces, which must be textual, of [Soviet Foreign Minister and Ambassador to the U.N.] Wishinski's [*sic*: Vyshinsky's] discussion — I don't know how to write this name — with [U.S. Secretary of State Dean] Acheson, seems to me the *hottest* thing that I have read since I arrived in Europe.

I strongly suggest that you read your newspaper; at this point in time, it's necessary. (What makes me uneasy, personally speaking, is that at the first thundering signal of war, they will call me to Chile, and I'll fall between G[onzález] V[idela] and Ibáñez. It's pretty horrifying to me.)

I read *Il Mattino*. If you read *Roma* — it has fewer news services — our information will be good. But I will also try to read a French newspaper.

I'm sorry to alarm you, but I need a few lines from you in order to know your reaction after reading that nameless *debate*.

A hug. Oh, I didn't speak at all with Angélica. The thing with Yin made me clam up. Please send her my excuses: I really do love her. Because you love her, and because she [Angélica] *is her name.*

Gabriela
Via Tasso 220.

1. GM refers here to the brief meeting she and VO had in Rome in late 1951.

ιοο;

G.59 [Letterhead: none. 6 pp., pencil, hand of GM.]

[NAPLES, ITALY. APRIL OR MAY 1952?]

To V.O.

I don't know whether it's a sin of my imagination — although I don't have much — or what, but these last months have been pure silence, injurious to me, and with no motives on your part, Vic.

Life has become for me a storm of correspondence that I can't deal with anymore. To this I add the frequent exchange of visits, on arriving at each country. This lasts — this looking into one's poor face — some three months. Now it will be Naples. Before leaving, I want to have this time with you.

Vic., the Ligurian winter — which has scandalized the people of Rapallo themselves, has been very humid and very strange, because in addition there have been some curious *phenomena* in this sea, and it seems that I absolutely depend on the heat. In summer I was much better, but in the end the infection of tropical insects came. The cold leaves me without a drop of energy and the heat did me in, [as] in the Yucatán, *three hours* of cardiac collapse. (You should have seen how sweet it was to go to sleep like that!) Three brutal injections from my American doctor pulled me out of that great sweetness that was, ah! simultaneously, a brief death and the *néant* [nothingness] or *the Vacuum* — like *that of the Buddhists.*

Enough of my calamities. I thought I'd go to Naples, and since I'm getting better, they already authorized it. (They call me a prisoner of vagrancy.) I believe I'll go in the middle of June. Maybe before.

Thank God — and your parents, you're healthy, Votoya. May he take care of you.

I believe that the worst that's happening to us is *a stoppage* of criticism — not the literary kind, *the other kind.* Because whoever does it [criticism], they either hurt the newspaper or they create a kind of void that not even the Inquisition would produce. This hasn't happened to me yet, although there's some of it already. Listen: at an urgent request from L[uis] A[lberto] Sánchez, and *knowing,* besides, those superlatives about the intention of P[eru's] government with regard to Haya de la Torre, I wrote to a compatriot, Alej[andro] Alvarez, who was writing about the thing with the Hague.[1] (Get M. Rosa to tell you about it.) I wanted to tell him what H[aya de la Torre] is like, based on the fact that he lived in my house in Mex[ico] years ago. The letter was delicate and exact in its details, precise, decent. He answered, in two and a half lines, that he "always served justice!" (And they served it so murkily that the sentence is a yes-he-is and a no-he-isn't, at the same time.[)] [Alejandro] Alvarez (in the Hague) is the president of the tribunal.

They are creating an atmosphere so different from the pretty one of the *Earthly planet,* that I tell you with an almost universal sensation, that is to say, an almost bodily sensation that day to day, I feel that living is too much for me, that living is a business punished by I-don't-know-who, us, certainly, but perhaps a type of demon that we overlook.... A demonic one.

I would tell you much more about this sensation, but it would tire you (come, Votoya, come).

In Santiago, they took an article of mine about Peace — "The Accursed Word" — and the Communists reproduced it in ten thousand copies — and they added to this a kind of propagandistic *enterprise* or odyssey.[2] And listen well, a minimal amount of mail always comes to me from Chile, and now, all of yesterday's mail was full of *that thing* and the like.

I haven't seen *Sur* for a long time. I would like to find an article of mine that followed the other one and is called "Yellows." It refers to the Chinese. I was a journalist for twenty years and I know something, something very small *but ineffable,* about the soul of those poor people.

But I don't believe that you can give me lodging in *Sur* with that objective.

El Mercurio canceled me after sixteen or twenty years, *without a word.* They paid me for articles and didn't publish them. I wanted to get into *La Prensa*. (Mallea eliminated me from his *Supplement* [to *La Nación*]), and when they had already accepted me, the cavalry of *La Prensa* began. I could tell you so much more. But now I'm worn out by so little! (Mallea asked me for poetry and not prose. And I find poetry in a newspaper to be very *strange.*[)] I continue producing — verses, but five years after Yin's death (passing). Because I have, now, a certain illusion that I reach him and that he comes each *time that I need him* … and my poetry, lately—there's a book, *"Lagar"* [Winepress], which is scarcely, hardly, "for the newspaper people."[3]

I hope, Votoya, to correct what I wrote about you and to publish it *when your book comes out.*

A single little spark tends to console me. Perhaps women can make this world somewhat sane — with or without the vote. But at this moment I say, ay, ay!

Tell María Rosa that I am *always* waiting for her. Shortly, Alone [Hernán Díaz Arrieta] will arrive in Naples, at my house. Then, a Chilean, a good poetess, Olga Acevedo, an ex-Communist. María Rosa should come to Naples. I will have what she needs *in some two more months.* I love her very much, although I'm also remiss with her.

Italy is calm in comparison to other countries. It isn't crazy: it takes care of itself — and I love it all over again, with the love of old age, which is better than that of youth.

I've been waiting for you all this time, V., but I still believe that you'll come, that you'll come in my door, in that house that I still haven't found. … (Ask in Rome), ask the people in our embassy.

Indications of the time: My cook comes into the room with breakfast, and she gets furious because I haven't gone to Mass. And I ask her, why does she get irritated if she's a Communist. And she tells me that she's as much a Cath[olic] as a Com[munist] … that the two things go very well together and *they've worked it out.*

I'm writing tomorrow to M[aría] R[osa]. May you join me in living, far or near.

A hug of … reconciliation.
Gabr.

1. After Raúl Haya de la Torre sought asylum in the Colombian embassy in Lima, Peru, the case went to the International Court of Justice in the Hague. The Court denied Colombia's right to grant asylum. Alvarez, along with three of the four Latin Americans on the court, wrote the dissenting opinion. The court's decision was then amended exactly as GM goes on to describe ("yes-he-is, no-he-isn't"): Peru was not obliged to offer Haya de la Torre safe conduct, and Colombia was not obliged to hand him over. By 1954 the case was resolved when Haya de la Torre was symbolically handed over to the Peruvian minister, who put him on a plane for Mexico.

2. GM wrote "La palabra maldita," about peace and the Cold War, in November 1950, while she was living in Veracruz, Mexico.

3. GM's volume *Lagar* is the least "popular" of her poetry volumes.

PART THREE

LETTERS 1953–1956

MAR DEL PLATA, SAN ISIDRO, BUENOS AIRES, PARIS, NEW YORK, AND
SANTIAGO DE CHILE

*Letter from Victoria Ocampo
in Argentina, July 1954.*

Gabriela Mistral circa 1952.
Photo courtesy Museo-Biblioteca
Gabriela Mistral, Vicuña,Chile.
Collection of Elizabeth Horan.

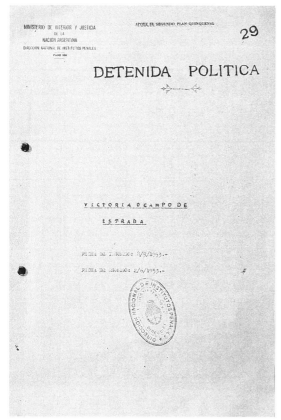

Copy of Victoria Ocampo's prison detention file.
Collection of Doris Meyer.

Victoria Ocampo circa 1961.
Collection of Doris Meyer.

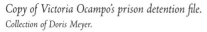

V.14 [Letterhead: Villa Victoria. 1 p., hand of VO.]

[MAR DEL PLATA.] 9 MARCH 1953

My very dear Gabriela:

Don't be surprised that I haven't written you. When I see you, I'll explain why. I always feel close to you.

Roger Caillois wrote me that he was planning to meet with you at
some congress or other (in celebration of the Martí centennial, or
something like that).[1] Did you go? Are you staying in Naples? I'm enclosing an article that I find interesting.[2] You'll notice that my Argen-

tine compatriots don't even mention the publication of *Tala* in Buenos Aires, nor where you were staying when you were visiting this country. That will give you an idea of how, out of pure patriotism, they wipe certain things from the map. Those things *don't exist* for them. *Ainsi va le monde.* [So goes the world.] So now you see how little good it did me to stay and work in this land, as you told me to . . . and as I was willing to do without anyone telling me.

I can't write letters, which should only be for those to whom they are addressed. If you suspect that other eyes will read them, you lose the urge to write.

A big hug,
Victoria

1. GM's three essays on the Cuban poet José Martí, each presented during a visit to the island, demonstrate the importance of his work on her intellectual and poetic formation. "La lengua de Martí" and "Los 'Versos sencillos' de José Martí" were originally given as speeches on 28 July 1934 and 30 October 1938, respectively, at the Institución Hispanocubana de Cultura. This letter refers to the keynote address that GM delivered on 28 January 1953 for the Martí centennial in Havana, Cuba (reprinted in *Gabriela anda La Habana*, 65–82, 83–96, 111–116).

2. No record of this article remains.

∽∾

G.60 [Letterhead: none. 5 pp., pencil, hand of GM.]

[NEW YORK. MARCH 1953 OR LATER]

Victoria, dear:

I'm doing this, writing you, with no hope of any kind. Doris and I have already written, and we've had no response from you. You know how such a thing in these times creates despair and a loss of hope.

When I read these and other things to Doris, I lose all hope and am more and more taken with the idea that we're rolling, like stones in the cordillera, toward an end, a place that exists and that we don't know, where we're all going to end up, just like that, not knowing where and when.

I've always been a pessimist, Vict., so you can imagine the point I've come to. I'm writing you from that condition but at the same time with a seemingly brave desire to see someone who's confronting the calamity, so that I can join in and help her if it happens that we still have individuals who *do that*.

In an old letter,[1] I remember having described to you the face that I saw on almost arriving where you *were or are*. I have that face alive and in front of me, which is why my letter can't *taste* either sweet or serene to me.

I don't manage to have any clear hope on my own. I believe that I was telling you this same thing in another letter. You, who are a strong person and capable of doing great things because you have a lot of people in your country — even though they may be lazy, and even including you with them — you should indicate to me a few people who can and want to do something. The worst thing is that I'm not in my country or in another Hispano-American one; wherever I turn my eyes, I find only strangers and foreigners.

I'm going to tell you about something that seems comic but it's more: it's tragicomic. In my earlier letter, I already told you the fact of the matter, although not entirely. One never knows who the person really *is*, the one who's sitting at your side. Try to remember my previous letter. I don't go to "posh gatherings," but the illustrious place [Columbia University] where that one was held *obliged* me to do so, because I taught there, many years ago. It suddenly struck me that that *illustrious* Institution was worth the sacrifice. And right there at the table, surrounded by extremely honorable people and without anyone being drunk, my neighbor began to elbow me and tell me off-color things, in the manner of a picaresque novel. I had your business [troubles with the Perón regime] all thought out and ready, to ask him to help. The fancy gentleman had been my boss in better, decent times. But I couldn't do it, because of what I already told you in my earlier letter. It seems unbelievable. What can he be doing, in his Illustrious University, that dirty, roguish old fellow! It wasn't as if this man had been drinking: he had all his wits about him.

Vict.: I've often thought about the numbers of high-ranking, powerful people you've always had, and in important places. If you have friends in one of those cities who aren't like that dirty old man, tell me their names. I forget, with fabulous speed, both people and their names. I tend to believe that monks and nuns are the only beings to whom one can speak clearly and directly.

I just finished reading something about powerful Colombia — the country. Someone who was persecuted there has told me things that make the Inquisition look insignificant. Pablo N[eruda] had told me about it and I hadn't believed it, or even taken it into account. Ecuador — a pleasant country, and one that's begun to "pretty itself up" — is very divided as well. Consider the geographic picture and you'll be chilled, with shivers.

Oft-remembered Vic: Nothing from you. We know that you're busy, but we ask you for a letter in return because we need to know if you're coming. Send a postcard, that's all. I've always liked that way of knowing "yes" or "no." I'm content with that and my head won't be spinning around, night and day.

If you sometime pass by the stands where newspapers, yours or mine, are sold, buy them for me and send them along. We'll be very thankful. They're [the Chileans] angry because I don't return — I went a short time ago. My people don't write me, in any manner of writing! In any case, tell us if you'll be coming or not.

At present, I read the *Christian Science Monitor* in order to learn about . . . my people. Doesn't this seem very sad to you? Ever since I was a girl, I sought knowledge; I'm sixty-three, and it seems that I achieve nothing. The only ones who don't let me down are the cat, the mother cat, and the little ones that she's carrying in her little belly . . . When I go out, I buy three newspapers, in case they deal with South America. Nothing in the three of them. It would be better to continue reading . . . advertisements.

A hug,
Gabr.

Now, the most important thing: at her own expense, Doris has acquired the house from which I'm writing you, which is very pleasant. You can consider it yours, since it belongs to her, and she loves you as much as I do.

I want to know this very soon. Doris isn't with me yet and I'm in this house, the one from which I'm writing to you. Neither of us knows whether you're really someone who *can* leave where you are and come to the United States. If you can send a cable, send it. Then we'll be able to know the rest and be relieved of our present anxiety about your health and about the upcoming days. Take care with the text, so that it can get to us. Send it *to Doris*. And soon. Think about it well and answer with care. (Doris and I think about you, day in and day out.)

No more for today.

Lucila

1. Refers to G.46, in which GM imagines/recalls entering rooms in Villa Victoria, VO's Mar del Plata house.

ɷɷ

G.61 [Letterhead: none. 5 pp., pencil, hand of GM.]

[NEW YORK. MARCH OR APRIL 1953]

Dearest Vic:

I hope that this letter has more luck than my last one. I want to continue hearing something from you every fifteen days at least.

It tends to happen to me, dear, that I get the feeling that all *my people* have died and . . . myself, as well. . . . To explain this to you I'd have to write a great deal, and I believe that you're bored by tiresome letters.

In truth, I've been left without a single specimen of what we call relatives, with no one. When I realize *this, that* other thing comes, a kind of shame in still being alive, in my having them without their having me, like a *fraud* or being stood up for a *date*. It's a curious thing, and it happens to me more and more. How horrible it is, Votoya, this living with no obligation whatsoever.[1]

This morning I left my room and I went to my books to pick up something that would push me to write. For all this — I'm sorry — I blame New York. I believe that if I were to begin my day hearing a rooster crow or hearing a shout in Spanish — from someone who'd tell me "Get up!" — I wouldn't be in this ugly, depressing mood.

A merely mediocre poet lived some of this, and two of his verses come into my memory: "For whom do I plant a rosebush? For whom do I want to be good? Why do I continue living, now that I don't have you?" These lines are poor, but *the primal* is liable to strike one more strongly than the polished. The quote is from a second- or third-rate Spanish poet, vaguely folkloric, but without popular origins.

Thank God that you have a family, Votoya, and a country, not *perpetual* foreignness.

Doris is very good for me, very good; but it gives me a certain remorse to monopolize her. I know that she's losing her life with me, her life.

That word, "care," Votoya, we pronounce it without clearly realizing what it means. It's the same or worse than "slavery."

You'll say again, why don't I return to the Valley of Elqui and stay there with an orchard. I would have done it if that indecent Coni hadn't robbed me of all my savings (some fifteen thousand dollars).[2] I can't go back there to live. They retire us with a miserable pension and I have two fat expenses: doctors and medicine, and . . . travel.

I've wound up realizing this: the sea strengthens me; I'm close to it, and after a week, I'm another person. I tend to believe that good health — and *strength, above all* — comes from the sea. The earth is a raw element, almost without a soul, inert, boring, and overwhelmingly bourgeois.

I'm going to return to it, the sea, in my "trial and error," and to see for myself. But oh, the best sea is the tropical one and in this climate, dear, on the land there's something *of death and of dirt* — even at a short distance from it. With great vanity, I call the sea "my husband" . . .

It's hard to grow old and hard to die, Vict. And despite all the religious literature, we know nothing of the other world. I've read a great deal of religion; perhaps I've read too much; even so, my faith doesn't help me much. (There's a strange appetite — almost an obsession in me — *to be* with my dead ones.)

Doris is the perfect companion, the best that can be found. But at times the thought runs through my mind that an old woman, without realizing it, might not make a person of her age happy; yes, that, and what's more, it could age her.

Enough of troubles. I beg you to help me with this: my eyesight is poor and I tend to waste it on books that aren't worth sacrificing my eyes. Could you, Votoya, send me a list — your own, I repeat — of French books? Do you know that I have around a thousand in my house in Santa Barbara, but that I don't have someone to pack up at least a hundred of them and send them to me? (This isn't a request, Vict.; it's only to tell you something about what occurs with vagabond drifting.) I requested and received a quantity of things that don't help me: all the works of a Spanish collection. But the minimal poetry that it includes are only verses that, I repeat, I already knew from when I was twenty or thirty years old. . . .)

What I'd appreciate having from you is something that isn't old and common knowledge, the names of *what's new and good*. Forgive me, and pass this request along to someone else.

Doris and I think about you constantly.

If they were to follow our consular regulations with me, they'd call me back. But, but, but they don't do it. How great it would be to eat the peaches and apricots of the Valley of Elqui!

I take comfort in reading books about the sea, I repeat. But *I'm running out of them.*

> A hug, a great desire to see you. Love from Doris.
>
> Gabriela.

1. GM's survivor guilt after the loss of Yin Yin is expressed here and in much of the poetry that she wrote during her last decade of life. Her expression of mourning relates personal loss to the Holocaust (see "Luto" in *Lagar*) and to the genocide of Native Americans (see, e.g., *Poema de Chile*). Echoes of the phrase, "like a fraud or being stood up" appear in "La abandonada" (The abandoned woman) from *Lagar*: "Everything is too much and I'm too much for myself, like a party dress for a party never held" (*Poesías completas*, 596).

2. No evidence supports GM's accusations of theft regarding Coni. The two women may have disagreed during GM's stay in Mexico in 1950, but it's not clear what the origin of their dispute might have been.

∽∽

G.62 [Letterhead: none. 5 pp., typed, double-spaced; final page with corrections, hand of GM.]

[NEW YORK. MAY 1953]

About the Victoria Ocampo Case[1]

All we Hispano-Americans living in the United States have been much moved by the brief reports from the American press regarding the imprisonment of Victoria Ocampo, a feminine figure without peer and the director of *Sur* magazine, a quality publication to which the best writers and the most civil consciences of Europe and Spanish America are connected.

On the South American continent, it can happen that people sometimes ignore the small but qualitative group to whom they owe almost all of their cultural life, and it's because mere politics is too absorbing of general attention. If it weren't for this, the figure of Victoria Ocampo would be untouched and untouchable, since she's lived a life absolutely dedicated to the task of creating and maintaining a magazine of the quality of *Sur*, a publication worthy of esteem and also veneration among the twenty-one countries that speak Spanish.

Argentina is the Hispano-American nation most saturated by Europe, and Victoria has been, for us, a kind of missionary who has allowed us to receive the rich, boundless European message. Because of this fact, which we all know, it is hoped that Europe will also take part in the debate opening up with regard to the illustrious woman who just entered prison, mixed up with common criminals. "The cases of an error of this degree are very rare in that great republic," say many. But some years ago a traveler called Latin America "the great ruiner of Liberty." It was a French academic as I remember. I didn't find out whether anyone answered him or not, because in those days a great silence fell on us, partly from shame and partly from laziness.

I live far away, and from here I'm useless, alas, for this prisoner number such and such — and here the hand that's writing this story, albeit thirdhand, freezes up. I'll just spell it out for those who don't know her. For three days now I've been following her, going and turning around at the door of the prison, going up to her cell and saying to myself, "All this must be a dream." I'm too used to dreaming, and I lie on the pillow of my sickbed hoping that someone will suddenly say to me, "The news about Victoria Ocampo being in prison was all made up, just a story."

I hope that by this time my dear, close friend has been returned to her home, to her books, and to her noble occupation of serving the diffusion of culture in our continent. The first words that her friends exchange, on meeting one another, are these: Is Victoria free yet? But none of us knows anything for certain, and a well of silence forms around us, one that's full of anxiety for the beloved creature.

The story is turning out to be true. What is she doing in her cell in these very moments: Victoria Ocampo, the Argentine wont to defend culture, truth, justice in her homeland and in the rest of the others who share her blood? What sentence have her judges pronounced on her, in these moments? And what will women on the whole do for her, Argentine women and the women of the twenty-one homelands of her language and her people?

Alas for our women on this occasion of direct responsibility for us all! All women, without really knowing it, owe a lot or a little to this imprisoned woman who perhaps continues to contemplate her docket number. Until now, we women have had few occasions to live such a categorical, vertical solidarity. Victoria Ocampo has worked expressly and tacitly for us women. She belongs to us despite national borders;

she has bettered us with the creation of a publishing house and a magazine with few equals, dedicated to reading and to the chore of weeding out the mediocre, teary-eyed, and poor character we've had in every circumstance in the Spanish American language. Anyone knows that publishing isn't a matter of "profits" in our America, and that this lucid and noble Argentine woman accepted losing money and more money in order to purge, slowly and surely, the poor quality of our readings. In that hard business, half-literary, half-didactic, she finally met with success.

Many times I've heard slanted judgments such as this: "We don't like Victoria because we don't like her social class, but we read all the books that come from her press." It's a case of receiving without gratitude, and in this matter, alas, we're legion.

The press in America and in Europe owes us the details of this lamentable occurrence due to the very fact that in "the Victoria Ocampo case" an illustrious person and an artful crafter of our civilization will be judged.

Europe has the duty to open a debate about so serious a matter, and the United Nations and UNESCO have the chance to shed light in the blind alley of a criminal proceeding whose details are unknown to us.

Our presentation of a timely commentary on so painful a matter has to do with the fact that Victoria Ocampo represents what's truly first-rate among South American women.

For more than ten years, there, at the mouth of the great river, this creature who's loyal to her people and to her sex has fought for women's suffrage with splendid insistence. The whole mass of Hispanic women is indebted to Victoria Ocampo for her lucid and noble attitude in the chapter of "human" rights.

It's not too much to add Victoria's charity to the debts already noted. Some years ago I put the original manuscript of my book *Tala* into her hands, telling her that the proceeds from it would go to the poor children of my homeland, Chile.[2] She immediately declared to me, "The printing of *Tala* will be free, so that the small legacy might wind up helping my children more." What more could one ask of a woman than to launch a project at a total loss?

She has been lavish with deeds like this, and the chapter about her being a "Mecenas" is a very long one. Because of her great modesty and notable courtesy, Victoria Ocampo has never spoken about this or other numerous and profound courtesies of hers, of which many people are unaware.

Now and only now do we have the opportunity to bear full witness, standing by this civilizing woman; at this very moment she should see us come to her side — alas, to her jail cell! — with a word of unquestionable solidarity. This is the moment to accompany her, to make known what's been ignored: that the silence of many men and women is only the child of ignorance with regard to her trial and imprisonment, which moves from being incredible to seemingly fantastic.

Even now, as I write, I'm unaware of what lies at the bottom of the case against her. But for twenty years now, I've known her broad, sturdy decency as an Argentine follower of Sarmiento and an ultrapatriot. Moreover, Victoria Ocampo has no idea of lying and its associates, which are fear and hypocrisy. For all these reasons, we who are her friends will give full credit to Victoria Ocampo when she enters her plea.

Regarding her lively and even excessive patriotism, this I also know by way of her long, involved conversations, which I recall in full. It's because of this ample knowledge of her conscience that I can write these pages without knowing the circumstance of her actions in these painful years. I've seen palpable evidence that a nobility as level and constant as the blood's pulse governs this great woman in her life and her civility.

Because of my fifteen years' wandering in foreign lands and my faithful reading of the most truthful local newspaper that I can find, I've encountered many cases of that misfortune that's called "judicial error." This exists under all suns and under all regimes, but particularly in young nations. We belong "to yesterday," and by way of being the children of new peoples, we err because of our temperamental quality, by now famous in the world. We live from passion as much as the Oriental peoples whom we disdain.

It could be that this is but one more judicial error made by our people, and for that reason, perhaps, it will be annulled soon, very soon. It's always been a noble thing to recognize an error, and the revisions of an important court case have been absolutely necessary and have produced the best outcome.

This is the hope of many absent Hispano-Americans, particularly we old ones who, rolling through foreign lands, more or less know that Justice, even amid the deepest commitment to getting it right, tends to fall victim to haste, to twisted reports, or to feverish patriotism. Even the famous trial of Marie Antoinette is read today with sorrowful astonishment at its crass errors.

All of our America follows, with avid eyes, the cause of its great woman, hoping that yet another judicial error won't produce one of those sentences that ruin a life and that stand out in History as documents that old and young read, sobbing. Among the friends of Argentina, myself included, we're awaiting the text that the press hasn't yet submitted. With true anxiety we wait for the newspaper, the latest mail, or the calming telegram.

[no signature]

1. "About the Victoria Ocampo Case" is a previously unpublished essay written during a period when GM hoarded her dwindling energies for writing poetry. It follows the last two major essays that she wrote, "La palabra maldita" (1950) and "Mis ideas sociales" (1951). "About the VO Case" stands out for its eloquent defense of VO and for GM's calculated effort to avoid angering the Perón regime in the hope that they would use the "judicial error" excuse and release VO. No charges were ever filed against VO (V.15).

2. GM seems to have forgotten that she had designated the proceeds from the sale of *Tala* to go to the Basque children, refugees of the Spanish Civil War, in the Residencia de Pedralbes (G.9). Given the difficulties that Argentine publishers encountered in Chile (described in G.19–22), SUR probably published *Tala* at a substantial loss. Whatever profits SUR might have realized would have been in permissions fees from subsequent reprintings, such as by publishers Espasa-Calpe and Aguilar.

ᖆᖆ

V.15 [Letterhead: *Sur.* 2 pp., hand of VO, with 7 pp. typed attached statement with corrections, hand of VO.]

[BUENOS AIRES] 17 JUNE 1953

Dear, dear Gabriela:

Thank you for everything. I didn't learn about your cable until after they let me go.[1] In the Peronist newspapers, they said that, *despite* my offenses, they let me go on account of your cable. I haven't committed any sin . . . at least not of *that* political kind. I've written a *"rapport"* so that you know what happened to me. *I beg you to be <u>prudent</u>[2] and not say it came from my hand.* They'd probably put me in jail again.

I'd like to leave here in August. But I don't know if they'll give me my certificate of good conduct. I'll keep you posted.

From the bottom of my heart, I thank you for everything.

My love to you,

Victoria

[Written sideways in margin of first page]: I'm sending the *rapport* to Victoria Kent as well.

Statement:

I didn't leave Mar del Plata after the month of December. No "political" person came to my house. My guests were the same as always: Pepe Bianco, Enrique Pezzoni, Antonio López Llausás, Lola E., and Rosita C. None of these individuals had a connection to people involved in politics. Naturally, we spoke about the dictatorship and P[erón] and about all the arbitrary measures and abuses that we learned about through the press or indirectly from others. All of this was discussed clearly and boisterously. But this was the full extent of the subversive activities of the residents of Villa Victoria, and mine in particular. Half of the Argentine Republic was doing the same thing. I've heard people talk this way in the street. So I spent the summer working on translations, on my memoirs, and swimming in the ocean. I didn't even go to the casino. My diversions were the movies and canasta (with people who were visiting me). *Un point c'est tout* [And that's all].

On April fifteenth, the day when P. spoke from the balcony of the Casa Rosada, Angélica and I were alone in Villa Victoria. We turned the radio on. But since the speech resembled (at least at first) others that we had heard so often, I left the radio on and went out for a walk in the garden. After a few minutes I came back, and it was the wife of the gardener (who was listening to the speech on her radio in her room) who came running out to let me know that two bombs had exploded. I shrugged her off, saying that she spent too much time imagining things. At first, I didn't believe the news of the bombs. She and the other servants are my witnesses. This is what my participation in the terrorist conspiracy of the fifteenth of April amounted to.

On the morning of May eighth, I was getting ready to work (I was alone in the house with the servants) when I was told that the police commissioner wanted to see me (I found out later that they had come to San Isidro looking for me at 3:00 in the morning). The morning visit of this individual surprised but didn't alarm me in the least. I was a million miles from imagining that he was coming to arrest me. To keep him from waiting, I had him shown into my room and received him there (I was still in bed). He entered, followed by an inspector, and said he had orders to search the house. Would I please get dressed and accompany him. The two men (there were four more, downstairs) went into my private office (the next room), and I got dressed. They looked all through the house, read my papers (this is what irritated me the most and made my stomach turn, not because my papers and old letters might incriminate me, but because they dealt with *private* matters, my private life, *sans rapport* with politics). I witnessed the operation with horror. When they concluded their task, without finding anything, they wrote out a statement that they made me and two witnesses sign. Then the police commissioner told me he had orders to take me to headquarters. I asked why. He replied that those were the orders and that was that. At headquarters, an officer took my fingerprints, and I waited. I waited. And I waited. Finally, the commissioner sent for me in his office and told me that he had telephoned the negative outcome of the search to Buenos Aires, but that they needed me URGENTLY in the capital, and so they were sending me there accompanied by an officer. I went back home with the commissioner to get a change of clothes, my toothbrush, etc. (a little valise), and left for Buenos Aires on the bus, in the custody of an officer in civilian dress. We got to Buenos Aires at noon (delayed by fog). In the Political Affairs headquarters, they led me into an office where I found another detainee (it was the former administrator of *Sur*, Nelly Saglio, a member of the Socialist Party, but as innocent in matters of a terrorist conspiracy as I was). We were told that we were "incomunicadas" and not to speak to each other. They kept me until 3:00 in the afternoon, sitting there on a very hard chair. Then they took me to another office to be interrogated. They asked me if I knew so and so, the ones suspected of planting the bombs. I told the truth: NO. They asked me if I knew anything about the conspiracy. I answered: NO. They asked me what I lived on, what my income was, what investments I had, and what contacts I had with the Communists, etc. I told the exact truth about everything.

I also asked what the reason was for the interrogation and the arrest. They replied that it had to do with investigations relating to the terrorist conspiracy. I said that it didn't justify my arrest, since I knew absolutely nothing about it. And I added that after keeping me sitting in a hard chair for fifteen hours (not to mention the trip from Mar del Plata and the wait in the headquarters there the day before), the least they could do was to leave me in peace and respect the RIGHTS OF THE AGED. The inspector laughed in my face and told me that I didn't look aged.

I went back to the office and waited there again with Nelly another hour or so. Happily, my family had learned my whereabouts and had sent me some food. We had just devoured some sandwiches when they came looking for Nelly and me. We left the Political Affairs headquarters accompanied by two guards. They put us in a police van and deposited us, *sans autre forme de procès* [without any kind of judicial proceedings], at the Buen Pastor prison for women. There I spent twenty-six days. I was able to see, from behind three sets of bars, the closest members of my family (my sisters and their children) once a week. The schedule (prison style) was as follows: mate tea at 6:30 A.M., brought by a poor young woman who had killed her evil lover. The nun accompanied her. We stayed locked up (bars and padlocks and much rattling of keys) until 11:00, when we would go out to walk in the courtyard where the prison wash was hung. At about 12:00, we went back to the cell. They brought us lunch, and then we would stay locked up with the lunch leftovers until 5:00. At 5:00, mate tea again and a walk in the courtyard. At 6:00 or so (it varied), back to the cell with much rattling of keys. Dinner was at 8:30 P.M., and we stayed there with the leftovers of the meal until the following day at 6:30 A.M. We could go to mass at 6:00 if we wanted to, Sundays at 8:00. But nobody went to mass (I went on Sundays) except for two Peronist women who were locked up with us: one because she really wanted to go (an unhappy girl, accused by a fellow office worker of being anti-Borlengui [the minister of the interior]; the other, because she was a "bootlicker" (that's what we called her) who wanted to get on the good side of the nuns and get a little air. The chaplain, with whom I spoke, was a Spaniard and a follower of Franco (good comfort for suffering souls). In other ways, despite being very coarse, ignorant, and insensitive, he really didn't seem a bad type. Definitely not cut out to be in that profession.

We were eleven women: five Socialists, one Radical, two progressive Democrats (*whatever that may mean*) [English in original], two Peronists, and myself. But we knew that there were more political prisoners in other sections of Buen Pastor, some in isolation cells.

We were able to supplement the unappetizing meals by purchasing oranges, cheese, dulce de leche, chocolate bars, and bananas — in limited quantities, naturally. We wore the checkered smocks of *droit commun* prisoners. They took our wristwatches. We only had one change of clothing. *Le tout* fit into our night table. Because the heater wasn't working right, we couldn't have hot water most of the time. I voluntarily *never* used hot water, even when they gave it to us. I would wash myself at 6:30 with cold water and made do quite well. But some of the other women, poor things, had rheumatism and couldn't do it.

I asked for paper and a pen. They told me that wasn't in the regulations unless I was writing a letter, which would be read by prison authorities before being mailed. I asked for a Bible. There wasn't one. After fifteen days, I managed to obtain one (which a priest smuggled in to me when he heard my request and took pity). We were able to get some books, as there was a library for the prisoners (but not for political prisoners; in some ways our jail system was *stricter*). But the books were simply impossible to read. They were books for the mentally retarded, of course. I asked for St. John of the Cross, the *Confessions* of St. Augustine, St. Theresa. In the library, they found a *dépareillé* [dog-eared] volume of the *Confessions*. The priest with the gentle soul (he didn't belong to the prison staff) brought me St. John and St. Theresa. I also obtained some selected passages from the *Quixote* (for schoolchildren). The political [*sic*: criminal] prisoners, on the other hand, *had their own books*. Among us, the eleven women who lived together, there was great solidarity. All of us were ONE, except the Peronist M. She made our lives miserable, but I felt more pity than hatred for her. In fact, I didn't really feel hatred for anyone. The miseries, the weaknesses of humanity, and also its moments of generosity never appeared so evident to me as during those twenty-six days, and I'm glad to have had the opportunity to live them. These are not frivolous words. I've never felt as I did during those days the meaning of togetherness in misfortune and the warmth of human tenderness among strangers. Sometimes I felt profoundly happy when I would see that one of the girls (they were quite young) who were locked up with me would worry about me, think of me. And whatever I could do to distract them I did with childlike joy. I ended up being the clown of the group.

The worst thing was not being able to sleep at night and being awake for so many hours in the darkness, surrounded by snoring.

Three of the Socialist girls (a seamstress, a nurse, and a student) spent forty-eight days locked up for having cried when they saw the fire at the Casa del Pueblo (the Socialist Party headquarters). Two of my companions there told me they had been tortured with the electric prod after their eyes had been blindfolded. One was just a girl of twenty.

The last day of my imprisonment a prostitute joined our group for having hurled insults at the president. She had already spent thirty days locked up in San Miguel prison. I'll tell her story some day. She was a colorful person.

The sisters were by and large good (this is *my* opinion; others found them cold and inhuman). Toward the end, they ordered two women jail guards to watch us. They weren't bad types either.

While I was in jail, an inspector came one day to interrogate me. The interrogation consisted of asking me if I knew X, Y, Z, etc. Some of them I knew, others I didn't (they had taken my address book from Mar del Plata that listed the telephone numbers of my friends and relations). They especially interrogated me about my youngest sister [Silvina Ocampo], or rather about her husband [Adolfo Bioy Casares] and his relationships. As I didn't know what this was about (although I was sure that *they weren't involved in political affairs*), it made me very uncomfortable. I went back to the cell trembling for the first time. All my companions noticed it, and when I saw that this upset them, I gathered the courage to overcome my discomfort. Happily, this interrogation came to nothing, and they didn't bother any member of my family. There was no justification for doing so. But in this unfortunate country, there's no justice worthy of the name these days.

Twenty-six days after I entered prison, a nun came to our sleeping quarters and said (we were already in bed): "O. is free by order of the minister." The nun was pleased to bring me the news. She was not an intelligent woman, but she had a big heart.

I was almost ashamed to be getting out of prison and leaving five women behind (only six of us were left). I was sure that none of them was guilty of any crime, except the Peronist M. And I didn't know anything for sure about M. beyond what they said about her: that "she knew too much" (some reference to a government branch).

None of the telegrams or petitions sent by foreign writers was published in any newspaper of the Republic. The request of the Mexicans was mentioned in *La Prensa* without giving names or saying what it was about, just adding that the request had no importance and that another Mexican newspaper had declared that, for many years, I had been *a spy for the FBI.*

Three days ago, *La Prensa* said that I was given my freedom based on a request by Gabriela Mistral, but that they would continue investigating my infractions of the law and a trial would ensue.

What infractions and what trial are they referring to? I have no idea. They must have been inventing it. I haven't done anything beyond being anti-Peronist and decrying *à haute et intelligible voix* [loudly and clearly] the monstrous dictatorship that is crushing us.

Victoria Ocampo
Buenos Aires, 17 June 1953.

1. GM telegrammed Perón on 27 May 1953: "Am profoundly shocked by news of Victoria Ocampo's imprisonment. I beg Your Excellency to liberate her in consideration of her great contributions to Latin America and Europe. Will be grateful for your intervention." When VO subsequently learned about this telegram, she was unhappy with GM's choice of words, particularly the part about asking Perón for help. VO later said she believed that the intercession of Prime Minister Nehru of India was responsible for her release. GM also telegrammed many influential people in Latin America and Europe (including Herbert Matthews of the *New York Times*, Alfonso Reyes, Ernest Hemingway, Rex Stout of the Authors' League, and others), asking them to pressure Perón on VO's behalf (Meyer, *Against the Wind and the Tide*, 159–166).

2. Underlined three times in VO's letter.

ʇᏅᎥ

G.63 [Letterhead: none. 3 pp., pencil, hand of GM. Envelope (postmark removed) addressed to VO at *Sur*.]

[ROSLYN, NEW YORK. SEPTEMBER 1953]

Sister Victoria, so very loved:

I'm missing you a lot and not just me — Doris too. You've always gone to Europe or you've come here, but you don't come now, when I'm in the United States.

Your great head, plus your lucid eyes, plus your knowledge of our vegetal world, that and much more would help me with the "revision" of that descriptive *Poem of Chile* that I threw myself into writing.[1] The verdure, the vegetal world, still isn't in it. I barely have a few books with just a few species of flowers . . . ay, from the garden. I need trees, and it's so aggravating not to find something about indigenous flora. (Someday I'll go to live for some two months in your Pampa; I'd really like to live there about two months and write what a foreign woman could write about it.) And I had taken *that* as finished, and it turns out that trees are missing. Beyond the Chilean palm and the *araucaria* as well as the *maitén*, I don't have any more, *dear* [English in original].

For some two months now I've been living with very low spirits, despite the fact that I'm with Doris now. But it matters little: I have to return to the place of my life, but before then I must go to Cuba and maybe Canada. I'm no longer consul; the mere recitation of "Cordillera" and "Valle Central" has doubled my delirium for vagabond drifting.[2] Come help me, dear. I'm not telling you this with stupid pride; I believe that no one can give me back our vegetation like you can. The Argentine flora and ours are very similar.

I suffer from the following fact: almost all of our gardens live from pure European botany. In my lap I have two lovely illustrated books of flowers that we call ours: *all are European, Vict.*, all of them. We must have indigenous ones, but we inevitably scorn them.

I must be very whiney, to call on you a third time.

Every time the mail arrives, Doris asks if there are letters from you.

I understand, given that glory of gardens, orchards, etc., that you have, that you're staying close to it. Maybe my vagabond drifting comes from the fact that, for now, I don't have any home base in my country, not a house, not a single family member. It makes me a bit ashamed to be living, Votoya.

Today I'll try to do something more so that you'll come. To help me with this future book, I hope. As a collaborator. Come, Vict., come, please. Your old

Gabriela

1. Throughout the last years of her life, GM was engaged in composing *Poema de Chile*, which recounts an imaginary journey the length of Chile, with herself as a phantom in the company of an Atacama Indian boy and a *huemul*, a variety of miniature deer, native to the Andes, nearly extinct. The earliest sections of *Poema de Chile* were published in *Sur*: these texts, written immediately following GM's visit with VO in Argentina, describe the waterfalls, lakes, and volcano that GM visited in the south of Chile during her June 1938 trip (G.19). Writing an extended objective description of Chile's plants and animals apparently came to GM during her 1946 residence in California. Although GM considered *Poema de Chile* unfinished and did not publish it during her lifetime, it was published posthumously as an incomplete work.

2. "La cordillera" (Mountain range) and "Valle de Chile" (Chile's Central Valley) appear within *Poema de Chile*.

ⓘⓞⓘ

G.64 [Letterhead: none. 4 pp., pencil, hand of GM. Apparently written shortly after VO's release from prison (2 June 1953).]

[ROSLYN, NEW YORK. AFTER 2 JUNE OR LATER 1953]

To the dearly remembered and loved one:

You know that we matter very little to this country in its newspaper services. I have understood your silence as a matter requesting calmness and no more. This is why, relieved by the news of your liberty, I haven't written you. But I don't like it, not knowing if two or three of my letters reached you . . . I believe that there's peace in your house by now. Praise God! I think about you and I almost see you in your house, going back to reading, listening to music, conversing with your friends. Praise God! — When something like that happens, I silently repeat to myself the expression: "We're a bunch of raving lunatics."

I'm in this house of Doris' again, and since she knows you and loves you very much, you crop up in conversation, day after day.

I believe that it isn't too much to tell you that, here, your friends weren't indifferent to what happened. As I live in two houses [in New York and California], in Doris' house I don't have the original of our

cablegram that you might not have seen. "We breathe freely at last."
Now I'll say: we're breathing and with great relief.

We think — Doris and I — that we shouldn't recall that outra-
geousness, that unspeakable absurdity.

From time to time, more or less every two or three years, they call
me to Chile: the government. On these trips, dear Vict., I haven't traveled through your Argentina, nor have I gone to see you, because I'm
careful not to ask favors that they might not grant me. If I'm called a
fourth time, I'll try to buy the tickets myself. But I still think of my
third trip as reminiscent of that horrible moment of near shipwreck in
which we said good-bye to life, Vic. (I believe that I told you). Doris
and I live on hope (Bless her!). We plan to go see you wherever you
may be. But I think that because you have fewer friends here than in
France, you'll soon go over there. Tell us something about this.

It seems, dear, that they've destined me to this city: New York. It's
made me happy, because of Doris and her house, but I'll never understand New York, and I will live, leaving it and returning to it, which is
not at all pleasant. They've only given me the job of offering talks about
Chile and its Boss. Maybe you know that story about my clash between my Pres[ident] and this country. It's just as well, because our
staff has given excuses and explanations.

Now your visit might not be pleasant for you because of the raw
winter that's also long. Regarding the tickets, I can manage the one for
coming but not the return. But if you were to have any trouble again
there, we'd put the two together, the one for coming, and the one to return.

What you've lived through, Vict., deserves your paying close attention to the situation and moving forward according to *how you see it*.
Your judgment is very lucid, and your experience is vast.

With regard to your travel tickets, I no longer remember their total.
I think it's not too much to tell you that soon I can send you the ticket
to come here. If you stayed here, I'd get that return ticket. (I believe you
know the indecent Coni's brave deed: she stole *all* my savings, which
were some ten thousand dollars or more.[)]¹

Should you make up your mind, dear, tell me, and give me the exact
figure.

I don't know the current value of your money in U.S. dollars.
They've given different rates here. You should give it to me; the agen-
cies aren't much to be trusted here because *they inflate* the prices. I need

to have the cost of a trip from Buenos Aires here, but tell me in your money and in dollars. Until later, dear, very dear. Doris says the same as I do.

G.

1. As noted on page 198, there is no evidence for GM's accusations against Coni.

ɩ⊃ʚ

V.16 [Letterhead: Villa Ocampo. 2 pp., typed, signature and hand corrections of VO.]

[SAN ISIDRO] 29 SEPTEMBER 1953

My very dear Gabriela:

Thanks for your letter.

My trip to the United States or Europe no longer depends on my will. I don't know if you know that they've denied me a passport.

I'm trying to ascertain through a friend what kind of steps I would have to take for them to give it to me. Of course, there's one type of step that I can't and won't take.

Can you imagine that simply by my going to talk to the minister about my passport (this bit of paper depends on him, and not on the police) they would portray me in the press as tendering a public *mea culpa*. How could I then prove that it was untrue? What Argentine paper would dare to publish my denial? My name would be linked to the Democrats (read Conservatives), who in my opinion have been completely wrong. Perón won't give them what they want; in fact, he will use them, divide them and thereby weaken the party (as he has just done — in spite of his promises — with the Socialists).

I'm prepared to demand my passport, since they owe it to me. My only crime is thinking freely. I'll tell them that. If they give it to me, *tant mieux*. But if they put a price on that little bit of paper, I won't pay it. I won't sell myself for a passport.

I'll keep you posted on what transpires, in veiled terms, of course. Naturally we still have postal censorship. I've got someone to mail this letter for me (Gustavo Pittaluga, who's about to leave for Havana).

I'd really like to give you names of plants for your poem. But don't look down on European plants. Don't become a nationalist (*côté* indio), my dear Lucila. What's more, lots of purely American flowers are today much beloved in European gardens, like petunias and zinnias, dahlias and coxcombs. And many have come from Persia and India . . . beginning with the very *répandu* [widespread] jasmine and the *paraíso* (*Melia azedarach*, with its purple flowers that smell of lavender and that grow around the door of every proper farmhouse in the province of B.A.), which, although it is a shade tree, in springtime (right now as I'm writing you) it also produces those marvelous perfumed clusters that fill the air of all the northern suburbs (Vicente López, Rivadavia, Olivos, Martínez, San Isidro, San Fernando, Tigre). That aroma comes in through the windows of the commuter trains when they stop in the stations. It's a smell that has accompanied every one of my springtimes as long as I can remember, and I remember smells (a sense that's as sharp in me as in some animals). Oh! How I have loved and continue to love the pleasures of this land and many others! Did you know, Gabriela, that we have here many plants from the Cape of Good Hope and from Australia? We're so used to seeing them that we can't imagine they're not ours. Do you believe that the eucalyptus from Australia is less *ours* than the Peruvian *aguaribay* or the Argentine *timbo* and *tipa*? I don't.

Yes, we'd have a lot to talk about regarding plants. A lot. It would even make us forget everything else.

A hug for Doris. Tell her that I always think of her.

And what's this about your not being consul any longer? Explain this to me. And what will you do? Don't come to live in this part of the world for the time being. Stay out of *this*. Do you remember how you used to tell me that I wasn't American enough? . . . and that I should stay in my own country and work on its behalf. You wouldn't complain about me now. I've hardly lived outside my land these last few years. And sadly, it hasn't done much good, has it? A sacrifice in vain.

A big hug,
Victoria

[Sideways in the margin]: Furthermore, now I know I have to set a good example.

ℭ

G.65 [Letterhead: lined paper. 4 pp., pencil, hand of GM.]

[ROSLYN, NEW YORK. EARLY WINTER, PERHAPS NOVEMBER 1953]

For my *Victoria*.

Very dearest and very much in mind:

I'm writing to you from Doris' house. I don't clearly remember if you've met her. I'm here because without any request from me — none whatsoever — they've posted me here, to New York, the most difficult of cities for me. And I think, from whom did this nomination come? From people who saw me in ill health, it seems. You know that these doctors are admirable.

My ailment is nothing new: it just expresses itself in various ways. Once it completely blinded me. The doctors didn't recognize a diabetic crisis in this, and they made me lose years. In the end, I finally understood and I taught it to my doctors. And I started on a diabetic diet, which is indispensable.

I think that you might be pleased with this assignment of mine [to New York], but I see no indications that you're coming. Doris constantly explains it to me, saying that you're getting all your affairs in good order. Even so, I need to hear from you in order to rest easy. Send me a few clear lines to keep me from being so anxious. The same thing is happening with Doris: she expects you from week to week. I need to know if the response that I received, totally polite and accepting of my request (from your government), was true or not. Doris and I are worried by your delay. Send me a cablegram or a post[card] if you're going to be further delayed. Every day, D. and I anticipate news of you, of your coming. If your health takes a bad turn, also advise me by cable or with a quick letter.

Be a good girl and write me. It's necessary to know what you've decided. And soon. Write the envelope to Doris, who isn't a gadabout and rarely goes out. The newspapers don't concern themselves now with either your country or mine. Postcards are best because that's what arrives soonest. We're concerned by your silence and because winter has arrived and didn't bring you . . .

Send postcards if you don't have time for more.[1] And soon.

A hug from the two little persons who so much desire to see you arrive. If there are difficulties in traveling, tell me so right away.

Another hug from Doris.
Your old *Gabriela* (continued)

The publicity about Argentina here has come to an end. The newspapers say nothing, which tends to make me become optimistic, something I almost never am.

Doris' house could be enjoyable for you, on account of the woman of the house and the trees, because it's outside of terrible New York. If you don't like the area, you can go with me to a place where there's no winter, to New Orleans, where the beautiful river makes me as happy as having the sea close by. I need to know what you enjoy.

I hear very little about my country. My people only know how to send me pampering letters that don't say anything, and the press here does-n't bother with small countries (and my family no longer exists, Vict.).

1. VO's concern about censorship would have dissuaded her not only from writing postcards but also, perhaps, from writing more letters unless she could send them with a friend leaving the country. See V.17.

ಚಿ

V.17 [Letterhead: Villa Ocampo. 5 pp., hand of VO.]

[SAN ISIDRO] 26 DECEMBER 1953

My very dear Gabriela:

I don't often have the occasion to send letters with friends who are leaving B.A. When they agree to mail what I write, then I write. Oth-erwise it's hardly worth writing, since we suspect there is censorship, and thus one can't unburden oneself even in letters.

Now I'll give you the latest news regarding my passport. [Ber-nardo] Canal Feijóo, who, ever since I got out of jail, assured me that he could obtain it for me, finally told me that I wouldn't be able to get anything without first visiting (and asking to be heard by) the minister of the interior. The objective of this requirement is to make the one who asks for a hearing appear repentant (for what? For being anti-Per-onist). The newspapers publish notice of the visit without saying what its purpose is. And the minister spends an hour giving a sermon to the visitor explaining the marvels of the regime and the lack of patriotism of all the Argentines who don't recognize the prodigious material, moral, and spiritual advances of the new Argentina.

If it were a question of going to the minister and saying: "Mr. Min-ister, what's happening with my passport? What reasons do the police have for not giving it to me?" I wouldn't mind doing it. But I fear that they will make me appear like someone going to offer *excuses*. Like someone working out a deal. And I can't permit that, do you understand? It's not a question of vanity but of basic dignity. A passport *isn't bought*. I won't buy it. They either give it to me properly, or they can keep it.

Recently, Congressman Nudelman, who has made a big campaign against inflicting torture on political prisoners (I was in prison with two women who were tortured with the electric prod), has been working on getting me my passport. And look what's happened.

On the twenty-fourth, I left for Mar del Plata. The doctor had told me that I needed solitude, rest, and quiet. I really feel I need this. I am, as they say in France, *à bout de nerfs*. I took an express train and got to Villa Victoria at 2:00 in the afternoon, happy to be at the sea again. At 3:00, Nudelman phoned to tell me that he had spoken with the chief of investigations and the chief of police. It looked as if they were ready to settle my case, and they wanted me to go see them on the twenty-sixth at 7:00 in the evening. I had no recourse but to take the train again on the twenty-fifth, Christmas Day. I left Mar del Plata at 4:00. Angélica wanted to wait in the car for me at the station, but I said no because I don't like her to get tired. I got to B.A. at 10:30 at night, and took the subway to Retiro station, in order to catch the train to San Isidro. At Retiro I had an unpleasant discovery. Due to a derailment, the schedule of all the trains had been changed. There would be no train to San Isidro until the morning. And so I got in line (a long one) to get a taxi. I waited and waited. End result, I got to San Isidro at a little past 1:00 in the morning.

Today, Nudelman made a date to meet me at the central police station at five minutes to 7:00 in order to go with me to see the chief of investigations. We waited in the chief's office for *one hour*. He didn't come. His secretary said that she didn't know where he was. Nudelman explained that we had an appointment for 7:00. The secretary advised us, after an hour's wait, to leave and return another day.

I had returned from Mar del Plata in response to their call. Nudelman, a national congressman from the Radical Party, went with me. But we were stood up.

What do you want me to do, Gabriela? You complain about your country. What couldn't I say about mine, with even more reason?

I could leave via Chile. But if I go beyond Chile without a passport, I couldn't return. Monday, Nudelman will have an interview again with the chief of police, and we'll see what he finds out.

In addition to the passport matters, I've had other displeasures. An associate of mine at *Sur* turned out to be a bad person. It's a very long story. The fact is that I'm going to have to dissolve the corporation and lose a lot of money. My lawyers didn't dare bring a suit because, given my situation as *persona non grata* and the fact that justice doesn't exist nowadays in Argentina, the case was lost in advance.

This is the news, dear Gabriela, but there's no reason to get upset. So many people have worse things happen to them! Why shouldn't they happen to me too? I'm going to wait until Monday to finish this letter and send it with a friend who is going to Montevideo.

I do hope you will let Victoria Kent know everything I've written you here. A hug for you. Until Monday.

[no signature]

ဃ

V.18 [Letterhead: Villa Ocampo. 3 pp., hand of VO. This letter continues the previous letter written three days earlier.]

29 DECEMBER [1953]

[Conclusion of preceding letter]

Yesterday at 7:00 I returned with Congressman Nudelman to police headquarters. After we waited for an hour, the chief of investigations received us. The mere image of police officials (tall or short) has such a disagreeable effect on the pit of my stomach these days that the only thing I want is to "make my getaway" as quickly as possible. This chief asked, "Why do you want to go to Europe?" I thought the question was offensive and would have liked to answer "Because I want to," but I acted like a gentle sheep and answered that I had been invited to perform "Perséphone" in Turin and give lectures at the University of Puerto Rico. We spoke briefly about nothing in particular (what else can I talk about with the police?), and then they drew up a request that went as follows: Mrs. So-and-So has been invited by Stravinsky for etc. and by the University of Puerto Rico for etc. She would go first to Turin and then to Puerto Rico, etc. She requests her passport, which has not been given to her. "This is the sole reason ..." and then I signed. This will be sent today to the minister of the interior, the chief of investigations assured us. *We suppose* that they will answer, or rather that the minister will answer (if it occurs to him) ... Congressman Nudelman told the officer who was expected to deliver the petition to tell the minister that he was also supporting the request. I don't know how much clout an opposition congressman can carry, but Nudelman has waged an effective campaign against torture (the system used by the police to make the guilty or the innocent, either one, confess).

I can't tell you, dear Gabriela and Victoria (Gabriela, please do send this letter to Victoria, who has been so concerned with *my case*), how churned up I feel inside after a visit like this. The mere fact of not being able to shout at them: "You're acting like despicable cowards! There's no justice! No truth! Nothing matters to you!" . . . makes me feel like choking. And if these words were to come into their hands, they'd put me in Buen Pastor again for lack of respect.

If I have any more news before Mrs. X leaves with this letter, I'll write you again.

Please, let me know as soon as you get this letter. Say that the letter in which I sent the list of books I needed has arrived.

I'll be in Mar del Plata. The address is: Villa Victoria, Matheu and Arenales, Mar del Plata, Argentina.

A big hug for you both, with love and appreciation

Victoria

∽∽∽

G.66 [Letterhead: none. Postmarked envelope addressed to VO. 3 pp., pencil, hand of GM.]

[ROSLYN, NEW YORK. 29 DECEMBER 1953]

My very dearest:

Please excuse the pencil and the occasional jumpiness of my fingers: we've been expecting you all this time, Doris and I, and she'll continue to expect you . . . whether you come or not. I, my Vict., must leave for Cuba on account of two things: first, the winter, which is always hard for me in this country; second, because I must go to give two lectures about my country.[1] Perhaps you remember the unemployment that Pres. Ibáñez decreed for me, years ago. The man has returned and I don't want him to throw me out, using the slightest excuse. I realize that he hasn't forgiven me — and even less forgotten my *disobedience*.

And hear me out: the disobedience was not believing myself capable of serving four embassies at once. That unemployment was *the worst in my life*.[2] All my friends fled from me like the plague, dear. Then I threw myself into the swim, I set out to write prose: two hundred articles and more. Now I'm old and, furthermore, I realize that *prose* isn't my thing. You know that I've given myself the trouble of writing some sixty stanzas that are absolutely objective — horrors! Now I'm going to begin correcting them and . . . making them decent. It's a descriptive poem.[3]

Well: I'm headed off to Cuba, in order to keep from having to do hack work again, another two hundred and more. According to Alone, what's saving me now is that Swedish prize thing [the Nobel Prize]. I don't exist as a Chilean to my boss.

Once winter's over, I hope to go to Canada.

But between these two things, my trip to Cuba and the other to Canada, I'll have twenty days or more *to see and hear you*, a celebration that I'm looking forward to and that makes me smile with sweetness and joy when I think about it.

But, but, why are you so late? Drop me a line, *a little telegram*. Then I'll be able to get my plans to jell . . .

Doris loves you very much, and you won't need me very much. There are some books here that you probably haven't read, just a few because my library stayed, alas! in my house in California. I had to leave it on account of an ex-peon who was *my boss* in Calif. and who treated me as if I were an animal. They've finally sent him somewhere else. But when I think about the three whole days that it takes to travel from Santa Barbara to here, I resolve to stay here. Up to now, my consul general in New York behaves well toward me. He's married to a *first-rate* woman, an American. I don't know how much longer I'll have the relief of being supervised by someone decent.

We'll talk for a long time here about our affliction. But don't keep me waiting much longer, Vic., my dearest girl. I need, in fact, *your advice and your vision*. Mine is short, very short. Because of *the pessimism* into which I'm slowly slipping.

A hug. Gabr.

1. *Gabriela anda La Habana* documents GM's various trips to Cuba. Despite GM's plan in this letter, written at the end of 1953, to visit Cuba amid a chilly winter in New York, her January–February 1953 visit was her last.

2. Facing ill health and old age, GM's fear that the Ibáñez regime would again leave her unemployed while abroad apparently led her to agree to a visit to Chile under that regime's sponsorship.

3. How much of the "descriptive poem" to which GM refers, *Poema de Chile*, was completed by this point is unclear, given her habit of continuous revision.

ℒ❀ℐ

V.19 [Letterhead: Villa Ocampo. 1 p., hand of VO. This was a continuation
of the previous two letters, possibly mailed all together.]

[SAN ISIDRO.] 30 DECEMBER 1953

Dear Gabriela and Victoria [Kent]:

I've seen, in the company of the radical Congressman Nudelman, the chief detective, who is a very important person on the police force. I explained my situation to him. I told him that I had to answer *yes* or *no* to the people who had invited me: Stravinsky and the University of Puerto Rico. He took account of everything and drew up a note (which I signed) that said exactly and simply what I've just written to you. This note was sent yesterday to Minister B. For the moment, there's nothing to do but *wait*. We'll know within a week if the minister accepts the note or if he will require me to ask for my passport in person. I have no intention of giving in. How is it possible that an innocent person, who was a prisoner for twenty-seven days, be made to beg for a passport as if she were *guilty?*

With love and hugs from this grateful friend who misses you and wants to see you.

Victoria

ℒ❀ℐ

G.67 [Letterhead: none. Postmarked envelope addressed to VO at *Sur*,
forwarded to Mar del Plata. 2 pp., pencil, hand of GM.]

[ROSLYN, NEW YORK. 12 FEBRUARY 1954]

Cara Victoria:

Here, we've been awaiting you for some time.[1] In case you have postponed your trip for something like a month, please drop us a line.

If these words come to your house on time, I beg you to do me a big favor:

I'm missing many books published in Argentina. I need Spanish, French, or Latin American ones, all good-quality books published in the last two years.

Today I asked Marta Salotti to buy them for me and bring them; but since I don't trust *her choice in my reading,* I'm asking you as follows: send Marta a mere list of books. (*The ones corresponding to the last two years, dear.*) Because ... although Marta reads a lot, she doesn't have my taste *in literature;* I believe that we only agree in ... pedagogy ...

It's a big favor that I'm asking of you, dear, but I can't use anyone but you for this. Dictate that list to someone and send it to Marta Salotti, *straightaway,* please. She'll pay for them with those few monies of mine and then she'll bring them to me in her baggage. Marta Salotti's address is Franklin 1832, *Buenos Aires.* Oh, how happy I'd be if you could do me this favor. The number of books in Spanish, in Italian, and in Portuguese that I can find in this city is minimal, Votoya. You know that not reading in one's own language is very, but very impoverishing. Please forgive me for this bother by considering the situation.

Doris and I await you every day, just so, incessantly. If there's any difficulty, I'll even dare go to the ... ones higher up to ask a favor. But give me a sign. Come, come ...

A hug from Doris and
Gabriela

And a rapid response about your plane.

1. Evident here is GM's inattention or misunderstanding of VO's difficulties in obtaining a passport. This miscommunication caused frustration for VO, as is evident in subsequent letters.

ᖇᖇᖇ

V.20 [Letterhead: Villa Victoria. 6 pp., hand of VO.]

[MAR DEL PLATA.] 21 FEBRUARY 1954

My very dear Gabriela:

I'll draw up the list of books for you right away. But I warn you that the majority of the books that are published in B.A. are translations.

Please tell me if they interest you as well. For the time being I'll send you *my* translation of *The Living Room* by Graham Greene.[1]

I still don't have any news about my passport. The worst part is that my petition has gotten *no response*. I've heard that they gave Borges his passport and certificate of good conduct. He hadn't received them until now. I don't know by what means he obtained them (he didn't want to visit the minister of the interior either). But Borges wasn't in prison for twenty-seven days, as I was. And the twenty-seven days of *unjust punishment* appear to be a powerful reason for not excusing the evil that one has suffered.

I don't know if I told you in my last letter that I gave up my trip to Turin, where Stravinsky had invited me to do the recitation of "Persé-phone," as I had done before under his direction in B.A., Rio, and Florence. This sacrifice wasn't easy. But now it doesn't matter to me. I won't say I'm happy, but I do have a clear conscience and the assurance of having done the only thing that my sense of dignity allowed. Many people think that I'm an idiot and no more. Well it seems that few people think twice about going to the minister to ask for a passport if they can't get it through the police department (which is the usual place). But since I don't consider myself a criminal or a political conspirator, but rather a person who has kept her freedom of thought, I don't choose to act (under pressure from the dictatorship) as if I really were a criminal political conspirator.

If you want to, or if you can *make inquiries as to why* they aren't giving me my passport and certificate of good conduct to travel, it would be good, even if only out of curiosity: just to see what they're going to invent to justify an attitude that is totally arbitrary, unjust, and infuriating.

I see in the newspapers that my old friend, now the French ambassador to Washington and influential ex-minister from the *Coopération Intellectuelle* (do you remember those days?), is lunching with our ambassador to Washington, the representative of a government that physically and morally tortures innocent people . . . *Ainsi va le monde.* I no longer believe in the good faith of any politician, any diplomat, or any person tied to monetary interests. Amen!

I'm living quite alone. I don't see María Rosa as I did before (although I've invited her to come here, to bathe in the sea, because I know that otherwise she'd have no summer vacation). This is because her blind Communism (disguised as pacifism) gets on my nerves.

Since I don't want to broach political subjects in her presence, and since politics is truly her passion these days, we are inhibited in our conversation. I understand that her *mission* (pacifism) will be taking her to Europe again soon. The government doesn't seem to have an eye on her as it does on me. I think that her Communist faith fills her life, which is fortunate in her case. It's a pity, for those of us who don't think like her, that *that* is her faith. I regret that I don't have a sufficient amount of meekness and Christian charity to not get angry when she brings up, with a religious tone, her preferred topic: the marvels of the Communist system and how maligned that party's leaders are, since they're really incapable of cruelty.

Well, dear Gabriela, I'll continue another day. Tell Doris that I send her a hug and thank her for her note. Another hug for you and the true affection of

Victoria

P.S. I'm sorry to tell you that the María Rosa business is painful for me.

[On a separate page]:
It's best to write always to *Sur.*
My address is: *Sur,* San Martin 689, Buenos Aires.
And until April: Villa Victoria, Matheu 1851, Mar del Plata, Argentina. The rest of the time I'm at: Av. del Libertador General San Martín 1799, San Isidro, Prov. de Buenos Aires, Argentina.

1. Between 1949 and 1959, SUR published four Spanish translations of Graham Greene's works, all done by VO. VO also translated and published Camus, Faulkner, T. E. Lawrence, and Dylan Thomas (among others).

∽∾

V.21 [Letterhead: Villa Ocampo. 1 p., typed, with 2 pp. of addendum containing the Neruda poem critical of VO.]

[SAN ISIDRO.] 18 MAY 1954

My very dear Gabriela:

I'm sending you these lines, which are not meant to be a letter (I'll write you at length soon), to accompany the copy of a poem by your compatriot, the poet Pablo Neruda. It appeared in his last book, *Las uvas y el viento* [The grapes and the wind]. No need to tell you what I think of a poem like this . . . You can more than imagine.

A big hug for you and for Doris from
Victoria

"NOW THE DANUBE SINGS"[1]

Old Rumania golden Bucharest
how you resembled
our infernal and heavenly
republics
of America.
You used to be pastoral and shady.
Thorns and rugged terrain hid
your terrible misery,
while Madame Charmante
rambled on in French in the salons.
The whip would fall
on the scars of your people
while the elegant literati
in their review "SUR" (no doubt)
studied Lawrence, the spy,
or Heidegger or *"Notre petit Drieu."*
"Tout allait bien à Bucarest."
The oil
would leave burns on our fingers
and blacken our nameless
Rumanian faces,
but there was a chorus
of sterling pounds
in New York and London.
And thus
Bucharest was so elegant,
and the ladies so delicate.
"Ah, quel charme, monsieur."
While hunger
hovered about carrying
its empty fork
through the black suburbs

and the wretched countryside.
Ah yes, gentlemen, it was
exactly like Buenos Aires,
like Santiago or Lima
Bogotá and São Paulo.
A few people were dancing in the hall
exchanging sighs,
the Club and the literary reviews
were very European,
the cold was Rumanian,
the hunger was Rumanian,
the lament of the poor people
in the mass graves was Rumanian,
and so life went on
from one generation to another, as on my continent
with the prisons full
and the waltzes in the gardens.
Oui, Madame, what a world
it was, what an irreparable
loss for all
the distinguished people!
Bucharest no longer exists!
That taste, that style,
that exquisite mixture
of putrefaction and *"patisserie!"*
It seems terrible to me.
They tell me
that even the local color,
the picturesque ragged clothes,
the beggars twisted like poor roots,
the girls who, trembling,
would wait at night
at the entrance to the dance hall
all that, horrors, has disappeared.
What shall we do, *chère Madame?*
Somewhere else we shall start
a review "SUR" for cattle ranchers
profoundly concerned
about *"métaphisique."*

1. Written in 1953, the poem was published in Neruda, *Las uvas y el viento*, 359–362. In an interview published in *Pro Arte* (28 November 1952), Neruda had accused *Sur* of publishing the work of "international spies" and "colonialists, spreading the pernicious influence" of writers like Faulkner, Eliot, and Heidegger. When *Sur* rebutted these remarks in an anonymous article in March–April 1953, Neruda wrote this very sarcastic and political poem. As is evident from these letters (see G.19–22), he had been working as early as 1938 to undercut VO's efforts to publish and distribute books throughout Latin America (King, *Sur*, 141). By the 1960s, however, Neruda had changed his opinion of VO. At a PEN meeting in New York, Neruda praised both VO and her work. Translation here by DM, previously published, it appears with slight differences in Meyer, *Against the Wind and the Tide*, 116–118.

ΩΩ

G.68 [Letterhead: none. 5 pp., pencil, hand of GM.]

[ROSLYN, NEW YORK. APRIL 1954]

Dearest:

I'm still expecting the long letter that you've been promising to send me. That's why I kept quiet. Doris and I have been expecting you all this time, and it's because of this waiting that we haven't written you. I'm a curious animal who becomes discouraged when there's a lot to say. I send out nothing but short things, straightaway. It's an absurdity that resembles "all or nothing." But I feed on absurdities, my dear.

These days I haven't had bad things, just not knowing "nothing about nothing" in Chile. (You know that the American press scarcely notices our peoples unless we have an earthquake there.)

I believe that I told you about something that strikes me as a kind of fable: I know nothing of my people except for the letters from my good friend Congressman Tomic, *a Yugoslav*. My godson [Tomic's son] is named Gabriel. I don't know how to thank his father for taking care of me. Do you understand the loss of all my people? Sometimes a letter arrives from a saintly woman, Blanca Subercaseaux de Valdés. Now she gives me nothing but news of her household because she's gone off to the countryside with all her people. It's a good thing: if I were living in Chile, I'd go off to the last mountain in the Valley of Elqui. My Montegrande mountains number more than a hundred.

I'll only go if they make me retire, because people must retire at half pay and one can't live here on that.

It makes me very sad to think you're so far away, Vic.

I don't know if I've told you that when I believed that I could or should leave this job, my good friend Ester de Cáceres, Uruguayan, found me a supervisory post for rural schools, something ideal for my situation. Since they let me be, I didn't take it. I had doubts about not taking a job from such good, personable people as those.

Here, I depend on a boss who's married to a wonderful American woman. He asks nothing from me, work-wise. I don't like it, but I don't argue with him about it: it seems that his care for me is sincere.

It's been nearly two months, at least one and a half, since I've written. That poem — geographical and . . . vegetal — about Chile has worn me out. It occurred to me to put it together using a single rhyme. Craziness. I've never made poetry that's straight description; I have to correct it a great deal, and in order to do this, I'm taking a rest.

Dearest: I learned this a long time ago: it's very restful and even healthy to write things that are absolutely objective. (Try doing it yourself: to rest the soul is almost a form of hygiene; in any event, it works (or uses) only *the memory* that is called objective, merely *objective.*[)][1]

It rests me from my cares to water Doris' plants, a few of them that face the street. In addition, there's a little forest inside the house. This does me even more good, but it doesn't need me . . . Some six or ten minutes from the house is a semi-sea, a sea that's small but pleasant to look at, *almost without hearing it.* Because of having almost everything that I really *need* here, I'm feeling more and more peace.

I owe to Buddhism, dear, a certain ability to concentrate, that is, to plant a single thing, a single pleasant thing, in the center — if there is one — of my being. I can stay like this for hours and hours: it brings me *to life* again, like something that eliminates all the rest: everything disappears and only that thing remains. Try this. What's more, dear, Buddhism gave me the power to cut out, as if slicing away, what was injuring me. I can be thinking about something and suddenly I *let go* and pass everything by, the tree-lined street or the pretty female cat or the record that's playing.

Forgive me for telling you these things. They're commonplace and important at the same time; they are a true power of the mind. If they're forgotten for a day, they should be recovered quickly. It's a great truth that our mental life "is in diapers." One can make of it a living far from all obsession and much sadness.

Now, the poet [Pablo Neruda]. I will never understand how that woman [Delia del Carril] got to the point of not defending her women friends in front of her husband, of not making him see clearly those with whom he spent time, and above all, not defending them. She's gone gaga with pure love. It's a love resembling those ailments that take over the entire body, leaving nothing for life's normal things.

I remember, dear, an "ugly face" that you once made at me, just because I alluded to this: to the fact that it's one's duty not to surrender oneself, as with all of one's being and especially all one's conscience and one's past.[2]

I don't know that book. I don't recall Pablo [Neruda] ever giving me a book of his. I know that he dislikes me, but listen, much less than his wife does. She's given me advice about *intelligent life* — that is, about blowing one's own horn or something similar. The love of old women is like that. She *seems* more Com[munist] than he. That's how she wants it to appear, but I still don't believe that about her: the part about her ideas. She's come to the point of a kind of ultra "theater" of *her* political convictions. I've stopped liking her because I'm not convinced by her pseudo-insanity and even less by her Com[munist] theater. Sorry, Vict.

Doris and I think about you a lot. If she weren't enslaved by her work — she does "treatments," plots for film projects. She has a *very sane* soul, and not just pretty, but a healthy soul that does good to her women friends, which is very rare in our people, Vict.

I don't want to tire you more; tell us what books from here interest you . . . A hug from Doris and one from me. We think about you very much. Your not coming has hurt us a great deal.

G.

1. GM is again insistent on objective reality as a value for her writing. Interest in lyric as reflecting an objective reality is manifested in a significant movement in poetry in the United States at this time: poets Charles Reznikov, Louis Zukovsky, and GM's correspondent Archibald MacLeish were all interested in this movement.
2. This recalls GM's advice to VO about her relationship with Mallea in G.18 in which she urges VO to "devote your life to him, sparing no effort."

ʚ⁄ɞ

V.22 [Letterhead: Villa Ocampo. 2 pp., typed with corrections,
hand of VO.]

[SAN ISIDRO.] 27 MAY 1954

My very dear Gabriela:

We're still here trying to be patient. They haven't given me my passport, and I don't see that they have the slightest intention of changing
their attitude. They treat me like a dangerous person who threatens
the peace and well-being of the Republic. Why? I don't know and
never will, since I haven't been involved in political *"activities"* (as they
call it). It's an exasperating and depressing situation.

On another topic, I'd like to ask you a favor, or rather, I want to ask
you (and answer me in complete candor) if you would be able to help
SUR with a certain matter. This is what it's about: we have already
translated a book (I'm enclosing a page so you have an exact idea of
what it's like)[1] that I find very useful as a reference tool. Unfortunately,
the printer is asking a lot of money to do it, and SUR is always short of
money; as you know, we are only concerned with putting out books of
the highest quality (and my fight with my partner [Juan] Goyanarte
was because I refused to give in on this point). SUR is a cultural, not a
commercial, enterprise. And that, in these days and in totalitarian
countries, is the height of madness . . . from the point of view of the
peddlers and bootlickers. Well, getting back to the book, whose title is
Clío, it occurs to me that if some Spanish-speaking universities bought
a given quantity of this book, which is so useful and unique in its
genre, that would enable the publication of the work, which we
presently can't do for lack of funds. It would be another matter, of
course, if we were members of the P[eronist] Party. But we aren't, and
we never will be (unless the gentleman undergoes a "conversion"). I
wrote [Francisco] Ayala[2] about this, and he answered that the level of
the Puerto Rican students was not sufficiently high for *Clío* to interest
them (it's as if he told me that a dictionary wasn't at the student's
level . . .). He also told me they could buy about twenty copies. We
haven't written back to say no, but of course, twenty amounts to nothing. We'd have to place at least a thousand copies (which doesn't seem
like a lot for Latin America. Or doesn't Latin America exist?). What
other university do you think we could approach? It fills me with despair that such an important book isn't printed immediately.

I beg you to think about this and give me some advice, or recommend some people whose opinion could be influential.

Write me. I want to hear news from you.

I'm about to publish a little book about the diary of Virginia Woolf, which I'll send you as soon as it's out.

A big hug for you and another for Doris.

Victoria

[by hand] P.S. I'm sending this letter with someone who is leaving for N.Y.

1. The information to which VO refers was not included in the archived letters, and the details of this project remain sketchy.
2. Ayala became a good friend of VO, a frequent visitor at her *tertulias* in San Isidro, and a regular contributor to *Sur*. Ayala had met GM in Spain before the war and spent considerable time with her in 1945 in Rio de Janeiro, where he had accepted a temporary professorship.

ʕᴑʔ

G.69 [Letterhead: none. Postmarked envelope addressed to VO in Buenos Aires. 5 pp., pencil, hand of GM.]

[ROSLYN, NEW YORK. 1 JULY 1954]

Dearest:

For the first time I'm a little annoyed with you, and this comes from your asking me something *very agreeable to me*, but you don't give me any information about it.

In the first place, you need to say the probable number of pages in that World History as well as the price at which the book will be sold *to the public*. Students, who would give you a *voluminous* clientele, will ask the price first of all. Those same young men and young women will come more or less from the middle class, and that class really reads a great deal, although they're presently experiencing a crisis caused by the rise in the cost of living in our various countries. My country has become quite inclined to reading, for example, but its people constantly deplore the high cost of books that began a year or two ago.

Droves of students presently show up at the libraries in Santiago and Valparaíso. This is called scarcity of books, at least of *supplementary* texts. I don't know if your History would be of this type. I believe that it would have to be of this character. (Your Frenchmen make that type of book marvelously well. The Germans make it even better, which we *now* buy rarely or never. They nonetheless continue making them, directed to the Nordic countries and even to the English, it seems.[)] I have the impression — it could be an error — that history matters very little to the Americans. They think that it matters very little to people who are making it — like everything — "with no expense spared," with a speed *that seems unbelievable.* Once I heard, right here, a judgment similar to what I'm telling you. (When my present big shot threw me out of the service, I gave classes here, in Columbia Univ., History of Latin America — applied only to the principal countries *and to their past.* I understand them without admitting that they're right about this. My only pleasant memory was teaching the marvelous "Empire of the Incas." There's a French book, put out by a big company, about that marvelous matter.) Despite this and other things, the book that you're projecting will be popular in a few more years. The current age, Vict., is *skating over history.*

Of my travels through our countries I remember that in the circles surrounding me in each *criollo* country, there were a few erudite, little old men who tended to write texts for the university or secondary schools. I was moved by their holy perseverance and the holy patience they had for interesting, alas, a very few of their students, not to mention the rest of their readers. History is clearly at a low point with regard to young people in the universities.

You know, Votoya, that up to the present the French are the most famous authors of school texts; even the Germans can't be compared to them.

(Today, the fashionable text *must* have many colored plates.)

I suppose that your text will be in Spanish; I need, what's more, to know first of all, before everything else, the probable price of this History. I must have this information immediately.

In case your History doesn't aspire to be a *school* text — they're the only ones that make money — but one for professors and educated people generally, you can be somewhat optimistic about the sales. Success won't be immediate. I repeat to you, that history doesn't much interest the middle-range reader either. History, a noble woman, only matters to mature, conscious people.

If you're going to continue with other editions of books of this kind, launch one that spreads science written "in the French manner," that is, with some amenity.

(Yesterday I brought back, from a French bookstore, a great big book, with marvelous color plates. I'm half-crazy about it. But the size, and the paper, and the cover and *all* must be extremely costly. I go wild, seeing well-done, plentiful engravings. I bought it because the sea is the passion of my old age, Vict. This is an ideal book, almost great for adolescents. The engravings are worth as much as the texts themselves, and what's more, they would make boys and girls brim over with enthusiasm. But take a look at that price. The collection has three works in it. I have it complete now, and I'm going to give it, woe is me! *the little eyesight that I have left*. Review it yourself, if you have it.[)]

Are you going to make a mere history, or something similar? Please pardon my ignorance: I want to tell you that some are already doing it with the same precious richness of this sea book. The publishing house of this work is yours? I ask you because of the technical question of the numerous engravings. This book has at least two thousand, and they are perfect, Votoya, *perfect*. (Naturally, geography is more graphic than history, but I've wanted to tell you about *the fiesta I had with it yesterday*.) My love for the sea borders on vice. Some days ago, it surprised me and literally bathed me. I was drenched. My companions, two American women, professors, were very startled.

I will try to go to Columbia [University] tomorrow. Despite what I owe them, I haven't shown my face over there. I'll do as much as I can with the people that I don't know, sending them a kind of circular.

The Univ. of Pittsburgh, where I had to give a lecture, surprised me a few days ago: the city and its college surprised me. Although the only job that I have to do here is give lectures, I'll do it quite rarely: <u>my body no longer wants to obey me</u>.

For now, although you may already have them, I'll send you history school texts used in the university and in secondary schools.

Regards from Doris, who loves you very much and will do as much as she can for your request. She was a prof. She doesn't like pedagogy. She'll take me to Columbia tomorrow, or first to the big bookstores here. A big hug.

Gabr.

I'm missing details in your letter.

∽

G.70 [Letterhead: none. Postmarked envelope addressed to VO in Buenos
Aires. 3 pp., pencil, hand of GM.]

[ROSLYN, NEW YORK. 1 JULY 1954]

My dear and remembered one:

We've come, and for a few days, to a tourist place, not to stay, but . . . to
continue toward . . . Chile.

For the first time they're calling me back. There's a new minister
and he's quite a fellow. That's why I'm obeying him immediately. But
even so, deep in my bones I have *a crazy fear.* Of crowds. In the middle
of them there are always spying intruders and among these there are
women, there are the "good sisters" and the colleagues always waiting
for my job to become vacant. There are the men or women who send
me anonymous letters, and there's a poverty among the women that
splits my soul in two. When they arrive, they say that they aren't coming to beg but rather . . . to get a look at my face and to know that I'm in
good health.

Because I know that I'll be delayed in writing to you from there, I'm
taking advantage of this day.

I just finished reading that book by Alone. He isn't a bad person,
Vict.; he's only a Frenchified man who always disagrees with me. He
doesn't know, *he can't be faithful.* For example: I haven't spoken with him
out of some kind of repentance regarding my "democracy." I've done as
much as can be done to have him see clearly and to know that I'm not a
Socialist but a kind of ingenuous democrat.

I know that he'll understand *nothing* about me in this sense, nothing
about anything along this line. He'd even laugh out loud, or he'd cover
my mouth.

More and more, Vict., I'm horrified by the tropical and nontropical
misery of our countries. At least nineteen of them. And by now this is
a kind of obsession in me. And I feel that almost all we *creoles* are condemned now and for all time because of that: because of what we see
day by day and let run and run like the water of our rivers, but a water
that was filthy.

Alone holds you in great esteem, Vict., but maybe without understanding you. Here and there he conjectures about you, and his face
becomes tender and happy when he's right.

But at the same time, it always turns out that I'm resigned to his understanding nothing or almost nothing about me.

When he likes people, it seems that he turns off like a faucet and tries, at all cost, not to understand but to argue.

Even so, I believe that he is walking toward you like all those who may not know you, but who *conjecture about you*.

Returning to my trip: I intend to escape from Santiago to my Valley of Elqui and stay there as much as I can. *I can't put up* with Santiago: I leave that city as if driven away. The important thing is for them to leave me in my mountains to finish off that *Poem of Chile*. I'm going to go over what I've done in rough draft, and when I finish the twenty or more stanzas that are missing, I'll make a beeline for the countryside where I was raised.

I have some kind of sore with which I must be careful, because that's really bad in a diabetic.

If you please, dear, send me your news as soon as I give you my *stable* address.

Doris remembers you as much as I do, and she continues needing to know about you, even though you might be at peace. Write to her.

A faithful hug
Gabr.

ɷ

V.23 [Letterhead: Villa Ocampo. 3 pp., hand of VO.]

[SAN ISIDRO.] 11 JULY 1954

My very dear Gabriela:

I'd like to tell you about a lot of things, too. But what to say and where to begin? To begin with, my desire to travel is now a kind of obsession. I feel like a prisoner here; and this feeling increases rather than diminishes. It was a year ago June second that I got out of jail, and they still haven't given me my passport.

I write. I work at *Sur*. Generally, my days don't change much. In the mornings (I sleep four hours at most) I either write or do translations for *Sur*. When I have time, during the week, I go out with my fox terrier, whose name is Dingo II (I had the first one back in 1920). We walk. I eat lunch alone (since I live alone in this big empty house out of love for the place. I would prefer a house with two rooms). I get in my

car and drive myself to Buenos Aires. I leave the car in a garage and go
to San Martín 689, at Viamonte Street. At *Sur*, I do a variety of things
for the magazine and publishing house, from correcting proofs to fighting with printers when they don't do what they're supposed to. . . .

At around 7:00, those who work at *Sur* or those who go there (Pepe
Bianco, Murena, etc.) leave to go to some café for a drink. I don't drink,
so I don't go with them. I stay by myself. Sometimes I go to a movie
from 8:00 to 10:00. And I return alone, by car, to San Isidro. If I don't
go to the movies, I eat alone in my room. Saturdays and Sundays, I stay
here and Angélica comes for the weekend. A friend or two visit me on
those days.

That's what my life consists of.

I don't see María Rosa. She's completely absorbed in her politics
(you know which kind). I can't approve of her activities. She travels a
lot and (oh mystery!) with ease . . . I feel affection for her, but I can't
converse with her. Her absence has left a void in my life, as you can
imagine.

I'll send you a list of the French books you ask for.

Have you read *Camus*? I recommend him to you. He's among the
very best now in France. Great talent as a writer and he's a man of free
spirit besides.[1]

[André] Maurois has just published a life of Victor Hugo, very interesting, as it's well documented. He had published one of George
Sand that I liked. Of course, Maurois is not one of the premier writers.

I'm sending you my little essay that I wrote about the diary of Virginia Woolf.[2] And I send you a big hug.

Victoria

A hug to Doris.

I'll send you information about *Clío* —

[In the upper margin of the first page, sideways]: Can you find out for
me the Onís' address at their country place?

You'd like Aldous Huxley's latest book: *The Doors of Perception*.

1. In 1949, Camus accepted VO's invitation to visit her in Argentina, where he
   stayed at her home in San Isidro. When his play "Le malentendu" was
   banned by the Perón government, Camus showed his opposition to the
   regime by refusing to give any public lectures in Buenos Aires (VO, "Albert
   Camus").
2. *Virginia Woolf en su diario* (1954).

ՇՃ

V.24 [Letterhead: *Sur.* 1 p., hand of VO.]

[BUENOS AIRES.] 2 AUGUST 1954

Dear Gabriela:

I'm sending you herewith some information about *Clío*, in case you can make use of it.

Thinking of you every day and yearning to travel —

Victoria

ՇՃ

G.71 [Letterhead: none. Postmarked envelope addressed to VO in Buenos Aires. 3 pp., pencil, hand of GM.]

[NEW YORK, NEW YORK. 9 AUGUST 1954]

Very dear and very silent Vict.:

Your silence grieves me, Vic., and I don't believe I deserve it, no!

I've had no news from you for more than half a month. Now I'm writing you to complain about your forgetfulness and to tell you that it seems that next month, that is in September, I'll be traveling to Chile.

A very lengthy cablegram has come to me. It has a politeness that I have never encountered in official cables. It's an invitation from the ministry of foreign relations to go to Chile — without my remaining there, it's understood. This gentleman is a grandson of our hero Arturo Prat, and he's not a politician. I can't manage to comprehend that my country's situation (economically) could be so grave that they're now resorting to nonpolitical persons who have moral value sufficient to save the regime and *the country itself.* The author of our economic debacle isn't the current president, but the previous one, Vict., the crazy and stupid González V[idela], who gave me such hard times. (He's . . . a zero, and *the Freemasons* are trying to reelect him.)

You should know that the Freemasons have been governing us for more than seventy years. Perhaps I hadn't told you that I live a life of wandering because of them.[1]

I decided to resign from official teaching because of this "Precious Creature" [Freemasonry]. One day, a gentleman, a stranger, came on foot to my high school to tell me this, at the door of my office, with a scowl and an officious voice: "I've come to advise you that, being a person displeasing to Freemasonry, you will have to leave the directorship of this high school."

Following that came the break with the sub-secretary of education, another Freemason, a friend of mine, who showed up, not at the high school but at my very house, to declare that he was bringing his friendship to an end. After this, I was no longer heard by the minister regarding the needs of the school that I governed: a public high school, a Liceo.[2]

In the same week as these swindles, Vict., the invitation from the Mexican government arrived. I accepted it. I returned from Mexico to Chile and there came that offer from the League of Nations: a directorship in the Institute of Intellectual Cooperation. There, I worked under the precious and, *to me, saintly* — [Henri] Bergson: I worked there under him, such a marvelous soul, *words can't say*. Then, Madame Curie came to us. (I don't believe I've told you these things.)

I don't know the reason for this call for me to return — I'm sending you a copy. I can't understand it. (I don't know the minister of foreign relations).

I hope to go to my Valley of Elqui if they don't keep me in that capital city *that I never loved*, and I hope not to remain in it for more than a month and a half. I'll go by boat, not by air. That is, I'll go down to Chile from the Panama Canal, toward Valparaíso. (Oh, at this very moment an Italian-Chilean visitor reminds me that there's no way to avoid our cordillera, either coming or going. What a pity, Vict., what a pity!) *All heights, even medium-sized ones*, are prohibited to me, because my heart is *damaged*.

I'm going to ask you a favor: Give a little thought, for me and on my behalf, to the matter of us *seeing each other*.

I don't yet know what ship I'll take.

A faithful hug

Gabriela

1. GM believed that her not being strongly anti-clerical led the Freemasons to reject her.

2. GM's use of the term "governed" to indicate her work as director of a Liceo suggests the disciplinary, administrative, and political aspects associated with the job, one of the most prestigious then available (1918–1922) to any woman in Chile.

ʿƆƆʿ

V.25 [Letterhead: Villa Ocampo. 2 pp., hand of VO. No date on letter, except the year 1954 appears to have been written by VO, after the fact, in the
top right-hand margin.]

[SAN ISIDRO.] MONDAY [AUGUST–SEPTEMBER 1954]

Very dear Gabriela:

If you never receive letters from me, I assure you it's not my fault. I've
written you several times and I've also explained with an excess of detail (if I remember correctly) the reasons why I'm not leaving Buenos
Aires, or rather San Isidro (I spend most of the time here). Things
haven't changed. And as long as they don't change, I won't be moving.
Not even to go to Chile. Either I leave with my passport and my certificate of good conduct (which I believe I deserve), or I don't leave.

You can imagine how much I'd like to see you and Doris. You don't
tell me if she stayed in the U.S.A. or if she's gone with you.

I'm working a lot (it's the only way for me not to get depressed). I
think I'm going to do a record album. Recitations of French poets:
Baudelaire, Verlaine, Mallarmé, Rimbaud.[1]

Don't forget to tell me how it went or how it's going in Santiago
and the famous (thanks to you) Valley of Elqui.

You complain! But . . . what would you say if you'd experienced with
your compatriots what I've experienced with mine?

A big hug and all my affection,

Victoria

A hug for Doris and another for the Valley of Elqui?

1. This multi-record album was recorded and made commercially available
   by SUR in 1954. VO was highly regarded for her public recitations, primarily in French, a talent she acquired as a young woman studying theater under Marguerite Moreno, the noted French actress.

ʂɔɕ

G.72 [Letterhead: none. Postmarked envelope with return address: G.M. c/o Radomiro Tomic, Calle Enrique Foster 0350. SANTIAGO de Chile. 5 pp., pencil, hand of GM.]

[EN ROUTE TO CHILE. LATE AUGUST OR EARLY SEPTEMBER 1954]

Dearest:

Although I wrote you just a short time ago, here I am again. It's to tell you about my upcoming — and unforeseen — trip to Chile.

My Chileans have invented the calling of consuls with greater frequency. I'm one of the consuls who turns up there the least. That's how it is, Vict., despite the fact that I really tend to miss my countryside, in a few spots.

When I wrote you — a very short while ago — I believe that I forgot this information. Because I hadn't "realized" it either: the part about the *obligation* to go there.

I'm bored to death by those curious meetings in which only the "little jealousies" and twisted gestures of colleagues are seen and felt.

My real treat — and my relief — I repeat, would be to see and hear you. In three telegraphic words, tell me if you're coming [to Chile]. I well remember that you don't like crowds of people. But maybe you'd like the countryside. I'd try to save you from those types of young and older men who only want to be heard "by right or by force."[1] If you were to come, my blood would be less acidic walking those Santiago streets. I already told you that seeing you and hearing you is the only thing that matters to me. Doris says the same thing.

Although I'm not a good observer, I can see that our people of the south are deserting the area, and in a bit of a rush.

These days I feel very much a woman from another time, that is, an old woman, and on that account, nothing of a futurist. But there is, Vic., something else, more serious, that can *get to me*: the *locaíno* boys [the sons of landowners] and the ones who live and breathe Communism. They shouldn't be on their own "remaking the world," as they say. What's more: there's bad politics in that.

Listening to them, I sometimes believe that among them there are a few little souls, purged of vanity. They're few, but they do exist.

Having said this, I'm *still* going to spend a few days alone with them. Their conversation often gets to me, but I hear them in order *to make out, distantly,* just a bit, *what's coming,* what *they're bringing.* When I manage to get them to talk at length, I manage to learn something, they clarify things somewhat for me.

I detest the *tricky ones* and the ones who wait in ambush and the ultravain ones.

(It's been a long time since *they appeared* here.[)] That's why they remind me of my last experience with Neruda, I believe, something like a year ago or more. I told him — sorry — but broaching the fatal topic of politics, the most unpleasant little person turns out to be your friend [Delia]: the biggest "Red" and the biggest authoritarian. P[ablo] is diminished by fanaticism and constant electioneering. Maybe you know it. Patience: I'm working on that, be patient . . .

Needless to say, the others — at the other extreme — also *bore* me when they're fools and fourth-rate preachers.

At times when they're really ugly, they become merely entertaining. Has that "Neptune" thing come to you yet? It just came to me. Those ones, it seems, are only playing. They've devoted themselves to . . . Neptune, and since I'm traveling, coming by sea, they include me in their games.

As in so many other things, it turns out that these people, *being Yankee sympathizers*, have more humor and more of a comic spirit as well. They maintain something of the "English grandpa" about them.

I really miss your letters, that is, your news. Send a line. Doris is grieved by it, too, and you'll give her joy.

Now something else. Do you employ someone you can ask to do the following?

The fact is that if I go back to subscribing to *La Nación*, *I sit down to read it almost all the way through*, which is terrible on my eyes. After reading *La Nación*, could you make a little mark, and pass it to one of your employees to put my name on it and toss it into the mail?

You'd help me a lot, with this. Our newspapers offer little, and what little there is, is poorly selected. I need to know, at the least, something about *the South*. Don't be upset that I'm sending you off to help me so that I don't totally lose what my people are doing over there, so far away, so far!

I'm not asking you to put together some kind of big package, or anything frequent. I only need to glance at more or less important notices. I repeat, that I don't want to lose *all of my southern life*, that is, everything that matters to me to understand and follow from afar.

My address has been sent to you various times. Your silence worries me. I become concerned whenever my people are silent.

I also beg you to give me a small list of important books, of the sort that can't be overlooked.

A faithful hug from Doris and me.

Gabr.

[Postscript added, hand of Gilda Péndola[2]]: Gabriela had forgotten that she constantly receives *La Nación,* and she asks me to tell you to pay no attention to her request. We will arrive in Valparaíso on September 8 and we will probably return with the *S. Isabel,* which leaves Chile on October 6. Gabriela would really like to see you again. Greetings from the girl from Rapallo.

Gilda Péndola

1. "Por la razón o por la fuerza" is the motto that appears on Chile's national seal.
2. Gilda Péndola (a young Chilean-Italian woman who had met GM and Doris Dana in Rapallo, Italy, in 1950 or 1951) accompanied GM and Doris Dana on the journey to Chile and back (Spinola, *GM: Huéspeda,* 28).

꒰ꆤꀯ꒱

V.26 [Letterhead: Villa Ocampo. 1 p., hand of VO.]

[SAN ISIDRO.] 9 NOVEMBER 1954

My very dear Gabriela:

How is your health? Tell Doris to send me a few lines telling me about it.[1] I'm taking advantage of a friend's trip to send you these lines. Here nothing has changed concerning my passport. Someone has promised me that he'll check into what's happening . . . but I no longer even believe what they say. People are afraid of asking for something with regard to those of us who aren't considered *en odeur de sainteté.* There are two hundred students locked up and a very long list of people who can't leave the country. I'm on that list.

A big hug and another for Doris

V.

1. VO clearly suspects that GM is deteriorating, based on her recent letters and forgetfulness.

∽

G.73 [Letterhead: none. Postmarked envelope addressed to VO. 2 pp., pencil, hand of GM.]

[ROSLYN, NEW YORK. 10 JANUARY 1955]

Dear:

I leave for New Orleans tomorrow. The winter in N.Y. doubles my rheumatism. Doris is staying here. You can come with complete confidence, if you're coming. I sent a short letter to Papa [Perón] saying that I really need someone to help me with that poem and that I lack geographical information about your country, that I know little about the northern part, etc. No answer has arrived yet, but this was only four days ago, and I believe it takes eight days both ways. Doris and I are very anxious. She'll send me a cable, to wherever I'm staying, should you arrive.

I beg you not to look badly on my going where I'm going. You can rest here in the house with Doris and go down to New Orleans *whenever you want.*

With my rheumatism returning, I'm useless for working, and with nothing to do, I turn toward the saddest things in my life.

If you aren't interested in seeing the South, I will come from there to see you in this house of Doris'. I've already told you that she loves you very much.

Please bring me some *catalogues* from your bookstores. I'm forgetting Spanish. But don't buy me books, because I have *mountains* of them, it's only that I don't know the latest ones. I'm interested in the catalogues to see if I find new things in poetry. I just need catalogues.[1] I repeat this because you might bring duplicates of books that I already have with me.

Doris and I are looking forward to you like a *fiesta.* I say no more because I'm going to pack my bundles: more books than clothing. . . .

Until later, dear, God willing. A hug from your old lady.

Gabriela

---

1. GM demonstrates continuing interest in writing poetry that would be up-to-date.

ᔕᘓᔓ

G.74 [Letterhead: none. 3 pp., pencil, hand of GM.]

[ROSLYN, NEW YORK. EARLY FEBRUARY 1955?]

Dear, very dear:

We received your letter and we're staying very calm. We hope that in a little more time you'll appear in the door of this house. We all know that you like to travel and that won't surprise anyone.

In this city's newspapers, which I always read, it's been almost a half-month since there's been any bad news from your native land, dear little one.

I'm in Doris' house, which gives me much peace, and I'm reading a small book that brings me great, great peace. Although I've read many works of this sort in my life, this book, which is only a hundred pages, showers me with faith and hope. May you find it in your country and read it slowly. It's English, but I'm reading it in Spanish. It's called *The Interior Life: Series of Addresses.* Don't dismiss it for being very small. By giving me much peace, it helps me.

And you, dear, help me out by sending me a list of what you read with pleasure. I can't — you know — read much, and I choose with great care.

We don't have a letter from you with the latest information, I repeat. Try to get someone of confidence to write for you. Remember that life abroad is somewhat sad on account of this personal absence — of those we love. It increasingly happens that people forget the ones who are far away. You can ask me to get books that matter to you (that interest you).

Regarding things in the news, Vict, I don't know anything about my people. And here I say "women friends," not "relatives," because I've no one left. In my previous letter, I believe that I've told you what happens in the spirit when this occurs and women friends also forget.

(I've been entertaining myself writing this long poem about Chile. Today I've thought of making it longer, like this: adding plants and flowers. I don't have anyone, either, to tell me about the ones from Chile.[)] (They must be the same as yours, but no one explains them to me.[)] I've told you about the dearth of letters when one is absent for more than *a year.* The last one to send me "news" got tired. I was paying for them. One day I forgot to pay for them, *and he has been silent to this day* . . . That's too much for me. I don't believe that he's dead; it was Alone, the critic, not someone poor, to be sure. I'll see about getting started again. Right now, Doris tells me that . . . she just finished reading an article by him about Pablo [Neruda] and myself. This doesn't matter at all to me, since he's already written a great deal; it matters that he tell me if he's gotten out of his situation, which was a bad one. I wrote to people who are in touch with the regime. My Old Man — the president — doesn't read anything. There's no response up to now. Poor Alone has many who resent him, and they must be the ones responsible for "the silence" that is "death," there. — Doris just told me that he's alive and still writing. — That relieves me. — I was reading *all* of his things before. This semiblindness came, and naturally I canceled articles and letters. — I'll go back to writing him . . .

When I went to Chile, the people rained down to the point of not letting me sleep. One day the doctor was alarmed and he ordered me "to cut it out," the excessive number of letters that they were sending me, *even from Patagonia*, where I also lived for about five or six years.[1] People cared for me very much. I don't understand this. They're very sensitive, *overly so.* I traveled in the provinces, something that really wore me out. I'm waiting for the summer, to continue traveling, doing the same thing. In this country, Vict, no one bothers with what our continent writes, and this is something that my people don't want to understand. I'm left astonished by my trip to New Orleans. The group of women prepared everything, and the people rained down, the women especially. I'm waiting for summer to go someplace else to do more of the same . . .

Write, Vict., I'm really much surprised by your silence toward someone absent who needs your communication. A hug

— Gabr.

P.S. I hope that this letter gets to you.

1. GM's memory fails her, here: she lived only two years in Patagonia.

≈

G.75 [Letterhead: none. Postmarked envelope addressed to VO in Buenos Aires, forwarded to Mar del Plata. 5 pp., pencil, hand of GM.]

[ROSLYN, NEW YORK. 18 FEBRUARY 1955]

Our dear:

We remember you every day, and not seeing you here with us really grieves us.

I sent you a message with your countrywoman. I've had no response to that. We suppose you're busy. It's enough for us, for Doris and me, to know about your health, and that's why we're writing you again.

I never saw you idle or unemployed. I suffer only in winter, Votoya, because I can't live with the elements and this is, for me, very troublesome. I've wanted to go down to the sun, to the coast, but they tell me that I'll just find it somewhat tepid. But how long the winter is here, and sunless, dear. I only read, I don't write.

I'm somewhat calm with respect to Chile.

The president has the people on his side. I saw him, a little while ago, healthy and rejuvenated. He treated me very well [two half lines erased], but the ladies in high positions don't like me. They pay me only minimal courtesy.

If you ever get sick, call me; I'll go or Doris will.

My trip to Chile was without anxieties, that is, without problems. I was surprised by the mass of women (all of them unknown, I believe) who received me at the station. I asked them what politician were they expecting . . .

But but [sic] no one took me to the countryside, and I went . . . to see the plants whose names I don't know. So few, so many years! The family that gave me a place to stay, on account of who they are, kept me away, day in and day out, from these poor little things [the plants]. This hurt me very, very much. Next time I'll go straight to the Valley of Elqui. Naturally, I went there, but I could only stay two days.

Victoria: I've come to a stop here in that work with which I need your help. I've had no answer from you, and this troubles me a lot. I'm a person who greatly needs the help of her friends. I'm thinking, how will I be able to obtain your precious help, if it's personal. I can't ask you a hundred things about agriculture, about those things that can't be made up because they come from nature: names of grasses or herbs, that is; things from the cordillera, more than a few animals. You'll understand very well that because I went out at age fourteen to work in a little school, I only know the botany of the Valley of Elqui.

In the letter that I sent, I mentioned my desire for your knowledge to help me, but I've had no answer this time. That work requires daily consultation.

Unlike you, I don't know our native animals. I myself don't understand why I didn't return by way of where you are, in order to consult you about these two things, plus the cordillera about which you also know so much!

Dear, there's no more than this: either you help me or I'll write of plants, animals, and cordillera, all of them invented . . . How awful!

A hug from Doris and another from me. I'm going to pray to San Antonio. He does everything for me. Another hug.

Gabriela Mistral[1]

[Added page]: Your two letters arrived, with your answer about the books that interest me from your country. A thousand thanks. I'm sending a hug from Doris and from me.

Gabriela

---

1. In this letter concerned mainly with *Poema de Chile*, the poet signs her most "public" name.

ℭℭ

V.27 [Letterhead: *Sur.* 2 pp., hand of VO.]

[BUENOS AIRES.] 9 MAY 1955

Dear Gabriela:

Yesterday was the conclusion of the second year since I entered Buen Pastor prison. I've asked again for my passport from the Central Police Department, as does every citizen who is entitled to receive a certificate of good conduct. I made the request seven months ago (normally they give a passport in five days). Up to now they haven't given me anything, and each time I go to ask for my papers, they answer: "Being processed." This process can last a lifetime, I suspect.

My friend suggested to me that you should write to the minister of foreign relations, Remorino. You might say that I haven't gotten my passport and that *it surprises you a great deal.* That you would like something to be done to settle the matter, *which mystifies you;* and what's more, you're very interested in seeing me (as soon as *I can* travel) . . . or something like that. But please, don't make it look like I'm asking to be pardoned for crimes I didn't commit. In that case, I'd prefer *never* to have a passport. Do you understand?

I'm sending this letter only to explain *that* to you. Evidently, the letter you sent didn't produce any effect. Which doesn't surprise me. It would be better to send your letter to Remorino (if you write him) through the Chilean embassy.

How are you and where are you? I'm working on things for *Sur* more than on my own things. I've translated several books for my publishing house.[1]

A big hug for you and another for Doris.

Victoria

1. VO was probably referring to her translations of T. E. Lawrence's *The Mint*, Colette/Anita Loos' *Gigi*, Graham Greene's *Loser Takes All*, and Lanza del Vasto's *Vinoba*, all published by SUR in 1954 and 1955.

ΩΩ

G.76 [Letterhead: none. Postmarked envelope addressed to VO at *Sur*. 3 pp., pencil, hand of GM.]

[NEW YORK. 19 MAY 1955]

So very dear Vict:

My silence is not forgetfulness, no. In this house, two little souls remember you, day by day. I believe that by now you know that I sent a second cable to your president, asking him the favor of your coming here, so that you could help me in a job for which I'm no good because I don't have your knowledge of French, etc. I declared myself wholly lacking the capacity for that work. *And that was no lie, or anything like it.*

Doris and I have been in tension, week by week, and no kind of answer has arrived, dear.

What I don't remember, Vict, is whether I sent you that letter by way of that schoolteacher, [Marta Salotti] the woman that I used other times, or if it went to your address. In any event, your silence, which is already long, makes me think that it's failed. There's still someone to whom I can turn: it's my president, who was here with me various times and very cordial. But I don't know, Votoya, if that would displease you.

Just tell me; don't be hesitant with me. Because you're so far away, I can do nothing but write you and not as completely as I'd like. If you authorize me to do this, if you agree to come with us, you'll wait for my second letter, the following one, that is, and in the meantime I'll wait for the result of my request to Señor Ibáñez, who has been here in N.Y., but has had to leave on account of Chilean matters. I believe that this time I'll ask Alone to speak with my president about your matter, on my behalf, *in my name*. He, Alone, tends to spend time with my president, who sees him on a familiar basis.

Because I hadn't gotten your last letter, *your answer* that is, it didn't occur to me to bring up the matter with him, himself, given the fact that I now know of the friendship that ties him with your president.

Don't laugh at me, now. I have — in me — *an almost childlike devotion*, a most ingenuous faith in San Antonio, the Italian, that is, *of Padua*. I stay away from bothering the saints, but every time that something *presses on me*, I ask him, my Italian. — It seems that the Spanish saints have never protected me . . .

If you had answered me straightaway, and by cable, all this would've been done already. This beginning of summer is very lovely here and pleasant, and Doris' house has woods, and the woods have a little river in front of it. And if you want to laugh, you can play with the cats, a Siamese and one of her kittens, ultrablack, who is my favorite.

I believe that if you're really coming you'll stay a little while in France or you'll come directly here. I like both things. We have the sea close by, dear. I call it: "my husband," and I go out to see it, like a person . . .

Answer me in two words: I'm coming soon, or rather, I'm coming later.

A big joyous hug.
Gabriela

ҁѺҁ

V.28 [Letterhead: Villa Ocampo. 5 pp., hand of VO.]

[SAN ISIDRO.] 31 MAY [1955]

Dear and remembered Gabriela,

No. I don't think it's worth the trouble to write to Ibáñez, and moreover I think it could even be counterproductive. I don't think our president would pay any attention to you in regard to this matter. The reasons, I have no idea. And as you well know, I've never had a role in or
interest in politics of any sort. My only sin is speaking out freely and
saying: this is black, when I see it's black, and this is white, when I see
it's white. And for *this*, I will not ask forgiveness, nor will I ever, as long
as I have my wits about me, God willing.

I've gone five times to the police department to see if my passport
was ready: NOTHING. They always reply: "It's being processed." Last
night I went back in order to speak with a commissioner who deals
with what they call here "social cases." I knew that this gentleman had
received men and women who had been prisoners, like me, and that he
had given them their passports. *He didn't even receive me.* He had his
deputy tell me (I was waiting *outside*) that my case has been in the Security Council since May thirteenth . . .(security of the Argentine nation, which evidently would be threatened if I left the country . . . do
you believe it?). It's madness. And so there's not even any point in trying to obtain a passport *that* way. If there's another way, I don't know it.
It would seem not.

Dear Gabriela, you don't understand the mechanics of what is happening here, nor does Victoria Kent. Here, justice and truth have no
weight. At least, that's *my* personal experience. I can't tell you more.

Do you remember? . . . how many times you told me that I had to
stay here. That this was my place. Well, I've stayed, Gabriela, and this is
the result. If it had done some good, I wouldn't complain. But I'm
afraid it didn't.

In addition, here I can't *do anything in public*. Not the most innocent
and least political thing.

One example: Stravinsky invited me to do "Perséphone" with him in
Turin. They didn't give me a passport (this was last year). Now they're
going to do "Perséphone" (with another director, naturally) in Buenos
Aires. But of course they're not going to do it with me but with a French

woman who will do it very badly. I am the person Stravinsky chose personally to do the recitation. I've already done "Perséphone," not only at
the Colón in Buenos Aires, but in Rio and in Florence in May (of 1939).
I am Argentine (here they say nationalist). But none of that counts, dear
Gabriela. No institution would dare to ask me to do "Perséphone," because they know I am not in favor with the government.

That's my situation.

I don't know if you got a letter in which I asked you to write to the
minister of foreign relations, who seems more or less well disposed toward me. You could simply tell him that *you don't understand* what's happening with my passport and, as you would like to see me, could he
clear up the matter, since you gather that it could only be due to *error*
that they're not giving it to me.

A hug for you and for Doris
Victoria

P.S. I'm sending you this letter through a friend.

ƆƆ

V.29 [Letterhead: none. 1 p., typed by VO.]

BUENOS AIRES. 10 JUNE 1955

Dear Gabriela:

A few lines to tell you that it appears that my case will be resolved
soon. I haven't and don't want to comment on this to anyone, because
in this country people go around gossiping and inventing things *à
longueur de journée* [all day long], as the French say.

The matter was taken care of through an old friend of mine.

I'll write you soon giving you more detailed news. Until I have the
papers in hand, I don't want to have any illusions. They've promised
them to me by Monday (today is Friday).

A big hug for you and for Doris.
V

{ɔ͡ɔ}

G.77 [Letterhead: none. Postmarked envelope addressed to VO at *Sur*. 2
pp., pencil, hand of GM.]

[ROSLYN, NEW YORK. 20 JUNE 1955]

Very dear Vict.:

Here we continue waiting for you. I believe that in the end, when you
decide, you'll wind up, as other times, opting to remain there. But I
tend to remember committing errors in my life for which I have not
forgiven myself.

I'm not comparing myself to you, Vic., I am — to be sure — remembering stupidities that I've regretted later.

Every time that I return, the flow of my life is liable to deceive me,
and how! My vagabond drifting, Vict., has real causes. You're a person
so surrounded by friends, our cases are incomparable. Worse yet for
me would be to compare your situation to mine. That foolishness has
never occurred to me. Now that I'm growing older from week to week,
it very much weighs on me that I've been too compliant and obedient
to my advisers. No one should live according to the pleasure of our
egoists who complain or smile at our decisions.

Now I'm going to resolve something: it might be foolish, but I must
resolve it for myself sometime, because I've always obeyed my "elders,"
as our old men or bossy ladies say.

My physical necessities are clear. I have to rest my heart and my
nerves today and not tomorrow. Oh, may God give me strength to live,
sometime, a life of my own, the one that old age dictates to me, plus the
dirty little advising world. In the end, I don't have anyone anymore, and
my sixty-four years are speaking to me now and they're almost shouting. Do what you want and no one else. God help me. Pray for me. I
pray for you, often.

Vic: ask the Holy Spirit for illumination.

And that I'll see you again in this world.

Write to me by way of Doris

A hug. Pray to S. Antonio and to S. Pablo.

Your old Gabr.

ගියට

G.78 [Letterhead: none. Postmarked envelope addressed to VO at *Sur* in
Buenos Aires. 3 pp., pencil, hand of GM.]

[ROSLYN, NEW YORK. 1 AUGUST 1955]

So very dear Votoya:

Here we're anxiously awaiting "the Second Coming." That's what we say
in Chile, the ones from the Valley of Elqui. You know Doris' address,
which is also mine. — It seems that I *must* go off to Cuba. An awful
thing just happened there, but I have to go. (But, *just now*, an order's arrived, to stay here *in addition* to my work as a general consul. When I
receive orders along this almost military line, Votoya, it makes me want
to retire. But I'm stopped by the fact that retired people have to return
right away, since they're paid in Chilean currency and Chile's finances
are in very bad shape.[)]

   Furthermore, there's this: some months ago, I asked to return to
Chile for two months, knowing that my people constantly criticize me
for my absence. There was no answer to my note, and I can't move unless I'm *called*. Today, today, I'll show up to receive my orders. Just so,
like the military. I should retire again; but the situation before isn't like
today's. For fifteen or more years I've been living away from my country, and this creates a very great solitude in me, and according to what a
"witch" who came to this house said, *everyone hates me* back there because of my being away.

   The 200 percent optimism of Doris sometimes relieves me, although I know very well that Doris hasn't the slightest idea of *criollo* reactions, no idea whatsoever, and she understands nothing of our In-
dian-American world. If you write her sometime, try to get her to
realize [English in original] this fact. She's very intelligent, but I don't
manage to accomplish this in her. Votoya, I always seek her advice
about my more important matters; but when she answers me, I see that
she accepts neither my version nor the solutions that I find for this
blind world *that worries me night and day*, dear. In any event, I believe I've
fulfilled my obligations by sending the ministry [of foreign relations]
that official letter with my declaration that I want to return for a while,
for whatever time they want to give me. You may guess that I'm doing
it to see if I should retire, plain and simple. (Please tell me the exchange
rate for the Chilean peso in Buenos Aires.) (They've only authorized

me to go out and give lectures.) I was going to go to Cuba and then the awful matter came, as you know. I would go to Canada, but, I repeat, the cold there is a serious consideration for my rheumatism. When I pass by some cemetery, I think that I could *stay* here. But I'm a *criolla* and nothing but a *criolla*. Nor do I want Palma to carry my bones to Mexico.[1] I'd rather that someone carry them to Guatemala. . . .

Some people would pray for me. — You understand this, which is such a forceful thing: people today — Chileans — because of my absence are as foreign to me as the Yankees with whom I live. I'm not talking about Doris; she invents something pleasant and sweet for me every day in her house. Today, visiting us, is a Bolivian woman who just lost her husband, the writer Antonio Iglesias.[2] The house is becoming Hispano-American for her!

Our Vict[oria] Kent has found herself a jewel of a *girl* [Louise Crane] nearby, who very nobly houses and feeds her. May God watch over her, because she has surely spent her savings. Vict[oria Kent] looks happy; only her face *falls*, yes, *it falls*, when speaking about Spain — she's very patriotic.

Vict., I still don't have an answer to my last letter. Send us a few words, but send them with some frequency. I want to know about your health.

If Marta [Salotti] goes to see you sometime about my concerns, meet with her, dear. She has always been a good soul to me.

A great faithful hug.
Gabriela

Also a big hug from Doris[3]

1. A failed land deal in Mexico may have changed GM's feelings toward that country (see Palma Guillén, Letter to Luis Vargas Saavedra, *Tan de usted*, 153–155).
2. This woman was the Bolivian sculptor Marina Núñez del Prado, about whom GM wrote an essay in October 1952.
3. This line added, hand of Doris Dana.

ɷ

V.30 [Telegram from VO.]

[BUENOS AIRES.] 9 AUGUST 1955
GABRIELA MISTRAL
15 SPRUCE ST. ROSLYN HARBOR, NY

I hope to see you soon. Hugs.

Victoria

ɷ

G.79 [Letterhead: none. 2 pp., pencil, hand of GM.]

[ROSLYN, NEW YORK. AUGUST 1955]

Dearest and much remembered:

We received your cable, which has made us very content. Now comes the waiting. I would like to know if there is someone, or some friends of yours in that department,[1] in case of difficulties, that is, so that we can turn to them. I mentioned something of this in my earlier letter. It wouldn't be too much to give me the name of the Chilean ambassador in B[uenos] A[ires].

Doris tells me that there's no need to take any kind of steps right now because you already have your passport. (I'm the one who's anxious, because of that phenomenon that I told you about before, Vict.) I've seen so many twisted things in the world *today* that I've fallen into a kind of massive pessimism and I don't believe that anything good will happen to me, that is to say, anything *happy*, and your visit is a precious joy for us. If on receiving this letter your trip plans are going well, send us a line to reassure us so that I don't *rave nonsense*, something habitual with me, I repeat. (Remember that we live in New York now.[)]

God watch over you
Gabriela.

In this house, Vict., you're remembered every day. Our sorrow is not being able to be near you. The information from the newspapers strikes us as very brief, not enough to understand the facts or what might happen. "But that things will pass on to a normal level is certain."

Doris and I understand your reasons, although we're both very saddened not to see you soon.[2]

I believe in the Good Fairy of your native land. Don't you believe, Vict, in a spirit or Power that nations have?[3]

Even so, we say that if something were to happen, you can and *must* send us a cablegram about your tickets. It's not too much to ask you not to wait for something to happen for you to send a letter: send a brief cable. For example: It's time now. Or better, another phrase.

The winter, like every year, makes my bones ache; but D[oris] doesn't have rheumatism.

A hug
Gabr.

1. Probably the ministry of foreign relations. VO was trying to get her passport validated, a process that took over two years.
2. There was probably another letter from VO, now missing, given the fact that here GM expresses regret that VO will not be coming soon.
3. Belief in the power of prayer and, specifically, the intercessory power of saints characterized GM's popular religiosity and folk Catholicism. This belief was probably not shared by VO.

ःOःः

V.31 [Telegram from VO.]

[BUENOS AIRES.] 7 NOVEMBER 1955
GABRIELA MISTRAL
15 SPRUCE ST. ROSLYN HARBOR, NY

Thanks. Not interested in ambassadorship.[1] Letter to follow. Hugs.

Victoria

1. VO was offered the ambassadorship to India by the government of Major General Eduardo Lonardi, who overthrew Perón in an armed rebellion in September 1955, promising to restore democratic leadership. VO was an obvious choice for this post, given her long-standing association with Indian culture; this was principally through her friendships with the poet and Nobel laureate Rabindranath Tagore and with Prime Minister Jawaharlal Nehru, but also through her writings on these authors and on Mahatma Gandhi, whose philosophy of nonviolence deeply influenced her life. See VO, "Tagore en las barrancas," "Gandhiji," the special issue of *Sur* (259 [July–August 1959]) dedicated to India, the special issue of *Sur* (336–337 [January–December 1975]) devoted to Gandhi, and *Testimonios VIII*, 25. GM and Doris Dana sent VO a telegram congratulating her on the ambassadorship, which VO declined for reasons expressed in the next letter (V.32).

ːᙣː

V.32 [Letterhead: Villa Ocampo. 6 pp., hand of VO.]

[SAN ISIDRO.] 8 NOVEMBER [1955]

My dear and always remembered Gabriela and Doris:

Thanks for the cable. At the start of the revolution, or rather the beginning of the government of Lonardi, a friend called me to tell me that my name had been proposed as ambassador to New Delhi. He asked if I would accept. I answered that I thought it was unlikely. I can't physically deal with tropical countries in the first place. And in the second, I can't stand diplomatic life, that is, the meals, the lunches, receptions, etc. In the third place, I don't know anything about that *métier*. In spite of all this, my friend (*porte voix* of some member of the government) insisted, etc. Word got out, and it ran in the newspapers and on the radio. They interviewed me on television. And, despite my pointing out that the appointment was only a rumor and *that I wouldn't discuss the topic*, they introduced me (without my knowing it — the people who saw me on television told me) as the future ambassador, etc.

Mario Amadeo, *entre temps*, had declared that he had great esteem for me, but that he was *allergic* to anything relating to "women in public positions." That says it all. The one who was opposed to my appointment, given my sex, was the minister of foreign relations himself. Needless to say, in view of what I know now, I wouldn't accept the appointment coming from him (Amadeo), even if he begged me on bended knee. On the other hand, I don't think the offer would be officially made. The ideas of the minister and his manifest antifeminism would prevent it.

All this to inform you about my personal situation. Beyond this and the inevitable difficulties confronted by those who govern after a twelve-year dictatorship, the revolution has been a miracle, and there are very good people in the government, like the president, the vice-president, Busso (minister of the interior), and the minister of public education, who is behaving with great good sense and effectiveness. The negative points are the nationalism and clericalism of some of the gentlemen who are in positions of power. But even so, we are breathing freely. One can speak and write. And breathe . . . for now. And we owe a lot to the ones who risked their lives to reconquer the country [VO's note at top of page: especially the navy]; it was a country occupied by thieves and torturers, without scruples or any sense of duty.

Returning to me: of course, I'd like to take a trip. But our financial situation is disastrous, and the new government will only be able to remedy this over time. Traveling is almost beyond our means now. But as soon as things stabilize a bit, I'll try to arrange things so that I can hop over to Europe — and to the United States. I need it. I've had a pretty bad time of it, as you can imagine, in recent years.

We're now preparing an issue of *Sur* about the revolution. I've been busy with this and other similar things . . . (talks, radio).

We are recuperating from the horror of a government run by an egomaniacal gangster.

Excuse this letter that says little of what I'd like to explain to you.

Yesterday I went to the travel agency to find out what the new fares were. It shocked me. We'll have to swim there.

A big hug and all the affection of

Victoria

ගිරි

G.80 [Letterhead: none. 3 pp., pencil, hand of GM.]

[NEW YORK. LATE 1955?]

For the very dear and much remembered one:

For some time now we've gone without a single bit of news from you, Vict. We don't know if that thing ended, or if you're in good health, or if you are coming, either. It seems that you've forgotten these two little persons. We're yours and to dispose with as you wish. Not a thing, nothing.

I've told you about the crisis with my eyesight. That happened some time ago, and I remember that I wrote you immediately. A short time ago, I told you about what winter does to me: it's called "a little death." It has to do, I believe, with my heart being unwell.

Your silence, so extensive and, I believe, damaging to me, *I can't understand it.* When I don't understand something, it hurts me more and more.

You've left me not knowing whether you've gone to Europe or elsewhere in your country. Tell me what's happening, Vict. If my letters have tired you (I write at too much length, but it's necessary to tell me so, with the trust that we have[)]. Doris is also worried about this strange thing. Is it, as happens with various people, that you're bored by answering because so many people write you? If you were to write me that in your own hand, I'd understand. Don't *discard* your people, Vict., and above all, don't give them this long and incomprehensible silence. Answer Doris if it suits you; she can't understand this situation either.

The two of us are reading two newspapers in order to see if the difficult part has already passed.

Yesterday I read a long article. I believe that they spoke of the peace that your country had obtained. That reading gave me joy and great relief.

If I were in Chile, I would have gone to see you more than once by now; but I'm very far away. (Chile now moves its consuls after they've stayed long in one place.[)]

Doris and I don't know anything here about [illegible] because she's involved in her things and because I realize that our countries [illegible] don't give much calmness.

Write, Vict., we love you very much and we can't understand such a long silence from you. That's enough. We don't understand any of this, dear. *Has some letter of mine displeased you?* Why doesn't anything of yours arrive? I don't remember anything that could be *"a motive."* If it's about your health, you should come to this country and live with us. This is a consulate, and there's no trouble from anyone. Our countries don't provide peace, it seems.

If I still don't have news of you, I'll have to ask strangers, and I don't like this at all. If you're sick, give me more details. If you're silent, I'll have to appeal to people I don't know, something that does *not* agree with me. I'm almost regretting what I wanted in my earlier letter. The cause of this insistence lies with you, my dear.

I believe the local press is good, Vict., even though I'm living this absolute silence with regard to news. By this, understand, it's necessary for you to reassure me with respect to your health and your calmness.

A hug from Doris and from me.

Gabriela

ᏯᎧᏋ

V.33 [Letterhead: Villa Ocampo. 3 pp., hand of VO.]

[SAN ISIDRO.] 20 DECEMBER 1955

My very dear Gabriela and Doris:

Gabriela, how dare you say *"forgotten"*? How little notion of reality you have! If you could see how I've lived in these recent times (before and after the revolution, first aborted, then triumphant)! I have no time for anything, and I *dream* about going to N.Y. and Paris to see my friends.

I'll give you specific information.

As you know, I have a publishing house and a review (which now function separately, since there are people who want to hold stock in the publishing house, but no one wants to be burdened with the *magazine*, a money loser).

The publishing house, in these difficult times, produced 14 percent in earnings. The review left me with a loss of 84,000 pesos (and, of course, I don't have that much in annual income and I have to pay for it out of capital). As you see, my financial situation is not spectacular. We anti-Peronists are more or less ruined. *Sur* was on the list found in the Central Bank of institutions and individuals condemned to "economic death." My house in Mar del Plata was the first on the list of houses that should be burned down.

The government of Lonardi, like that of Aramburu, is largely <u>antifeminist</u> . . . if not to say *completely*. Aside from one woman *judge* (appointed by the minister of the interior), there is *no one* of the feminine sex involved *in any way*. My appointment to New Delhi never went beyond being "conversation," do you understand?

We are, and I am, *very* grateful to the government and happy (you can imagine), or even more, *delighted* to have come out of that horrible dictatorship of Perón and his gangsters. But *for me*, the difficulties *go on*. And I think they'll continue. This country isn't mature enough for some things, and its men deserve, in a certain sense, the Eva Peróns. The women who don't kick them around don't matter to them. They give in to force, to violence, not to merit. That's the truth.

Dear Gabriela, don't scold me. I don't deserve it, I assure you. My life has not been easy or pleasant.

Dictate some lines to Doris and tell her to write me acknowledging receipt of this letter and letting me know *that you understand it*. A big hug,

V.

[In the margin of the first page, sideways]: Merry Christmas and Happy New Year to you both.

ᘛᘚ

G.81 [Letterhead: none. 2 pp., pencil, hand of GM.]

[NEW YORK. NO DATE OR POSTMARK; AFTER 1955]

Cara Victoria:

I'm extremely worried about your silence. I've had no response from you, to my letters (three at least, more likely four).

It makes me want to send this letter by way of the Chilean consulate, but I know that you've nothing to do with my Chileans. Marta Salotti doesn't please you — or me either, Victoria.

I've read, with joy, the news from Argentina. All of it is good. Why are you being so silent? I don't understand any of this.

The only news I have is my move to New York, the city that I call "Frightful," that's what I call it. Doris and I think about you constantly, as I've said before. Answer this letter, or better yet, call.

How's your health? I hope to know about this: *I know nothing of you.* I hope that your books, always excellent, give you joy. What I no longer can hope for is that you are coming.

I was in Chile at my president's call. I left there exhausted by the official visits, very tired. I couldn't pass through your Argentina because of the mountains, yours and mine. Mine are worse than yours, and I avoided them, by doctor's orders. I have heart disease, you know that. The older I get, my heart is more delicate and traitorous.

I'm going to ask you a favor, dear: I believe in the field herbs more than in my D[octo]r. I believe that I'm "healthy medical material." But I've forgotten various of "my medicinal herbs" here. I can't get them here, and that's why I can't ask my Chileans for them. And they don't believe it and only smile at my request. Maybe you know something about this. I'd be very thankful to you if you could check this forgotten information for me. Take care of your heart, Vic. It's very *jealous,* and when it's damaged, it gives very serious surprises.

Ask me for the books that you can't find there.

Why don't you come? Doris and I still don't understand it.

A lovely hug. May I see you again in this world.

your Gabriela

ༀ

V.34 [Letterhead: Villa Ocampo. 3 pp., typed with corrections,
hand of VO.]

[SAN ISIDRO.] 4 JANUARY 1956

My very dear Gabriela and Doris:

Happy New Year.

I received your two letters, Gabriela, in which, as usual, you complain about my silence. But one of them begins like this: "We received
your letter . . ." so my silence is relative. No?[1]

I wish nothing more than to come to New York, and for several reasons. To see my friends, you both, and that city I ADORE. To eat griddlecakes and doughnuts (I don't remember if it's written this way) and
cinnamon toast.[2] To go to three movies a day when I feel like it. To go
to the theater (which now must be *"beyond my means"*), and to walk
through the streets and hear repeated a hundred times a day "watch
your step" or "you're welcome."[3] And many other things like that which
would seem insignificant. The peso isn't worth anything. It's pointless
to write you that at this moment one dollar buys three pesos, because I
don't know if it will be the same tomorrow. But the peso matters little
(it matters, of course, for those of us who are anxious to travel) in comparison with the supreme happiness of living again, spiritually, like free
citizens. Although it's true that those who had spiritual freedom never
lost it . . . it was very costly to sustain it.

I have continued to struggle with a thousand difficulties. This year,
for example, *Sur* has given me 85,000 pesos in deficit — a deficit that
for my pocket is catastrophic. Since the month of June, no one has
been buying books or literary magazines. Nothing mattered to anyone
except the politics of the moment, the here and now (and rightfully).
And so the publishing houses and literary magazines (and *Sur* is the
primary and most purely literary one in the country) went down the
drain (as we say here). The twenty-five years that *Sur* has just completed were thus celebrated with a net loss of 85,000 pesos. But of
course, no one learns of this type of sacrifice and, basically, no one
cares. Everyone imagines that I have money to give and to lend, which
today is absolutely, totally false. Peronism has practically bankrupted
me . . . as with the majority of those who opposed it. Probably (if the
situation doesn't improve) I'll stop publishing *Sur* next year.[4] I've made

up my mind to publish it this year as a last effort . . . I've published it in difficult times, during the dictatorship. Now I don't have the same moral reasons to keep on doing it.

As you know (or perhaps you don't), a list was found in the Central Bank naming people and institutions who had been condemned to "economic death." Naturally, *Sur* was on the list. The government continues with its difficult task. I feel sorry for them. The French ambassador told me that he has rarely known a group of men so fundamentally disinterested and desirous of carrying things out well. And he added: *"Ils sont touchants."* But, politically, he finds them naïve.

This evening my dinner guests will be Alicia Moreau de Justo (the only woman on the Advisory Council, put there by the Socialist Party, not by the government, which doesn't appoint women, as I wrote to you), Tito [Alberto] Gainza, and the minister of works and planning, Raúl Mignone (the only minister who isn't antifeminist).

Friday I'm going to talk on television about my experience in jail and about the changes that I think should be made in the women's jail.

All these things keep me busy and concerned, as you can imagine. I really need a rest. This year has been quite active for the Argentines, and especially for those who weren't on the preferred persons list of the deposed government.

Well, dear, this is the news. Don't complain about my silence. I work as much as I can so I don't become useless.

A big hug for you both. And I hope to see you in my beloved New York.

V.

[by hand]: P.S. If I could only write in some North American magazine!

I'm sending you by diplomatic mail the issue of *Sur* dedicated to the [Argentine] revolution.[5]

1. It's not clear what letter VO refers to here. It could be G.79.
2. All the food terms appear in English in VO's original letter.
3. All the quoted terms appear in English in VO's original letter.
4. *Sur* ceased regular publication in the early 1970s. Special issues appeared sporadically after that, including one after VO's death in 1980 (No. 346) containing tributes to her, and another in 1985 (No. 356–357) with selected works by VO.
5. *Sur* 243 (November–December 1956).

ʊʊ

G.82 [Letterhead: none. Postmarked envelope addressed to VO at *Sur* and forwarded to Mar del Plata. 3 pp., pencil, hand of GM.]

[ROSLYN, NEW YORK. 9 FEBRUARY 1956]

Cara Votoya:

I wrote you days ago to learn how you are, and I've had no response. Before that there was another letter from Doris and me. We had a letter from you that made us hope we'd see you soon. But the awaited one hasn't come. That's why I'm bothering you with these lines.

I've been appointed, as I've told you, to give lectures about my little country and the topic of immigrants. This seemed to interest Chile, but I've been learning that my compatriots — the ones that come here—aren't interested in the matter. This is very stupid: they fear competition from *the high-quality immigrant*. I'm not yet writing to the minister and I continue to watch. The president understands — it's no joke that Chile visibly lacks specialists, above all in scientific branches, and they don't think about what it means for a country to lack scientists. They think about nothing but competition. I'm troubled and angered by this silliness and this small-mindedness that has no eyes for looking out toward the world.

I'll keep on with it until I can, in some way I don't yet know, make the president understand this matter.

I would like to know, Votoya, if the European specialists that you've brought to *your* country have worked with real success and in what branches. Sorry to bother you with this.

I'm going to transmit whatever I can see on this matter to my president. He isn't a foolish old man; he's sharp.

It's been quite some time now, I repeat, that the press here prints nothing on this topic: people setting out for our America and on account of this substantial, serious matter that fills me with shame: the complete lack of young men in Chile — and let's not talk about the women — who dare study anything but little books of second- or third-rate literature.

I'm sorry to be bothering you with this. I'm pretty bored with reading what's *consumed* in our high schools and in Latin American *universities*. Included in this letter is a clipping from *La Prensa*, a newspaper here. It's *the only one worth anything*. It does nothing but what you'll see in this issue.

I don't know, Votoya, if you're still publishing your magazine so that I can subscribe to it, or if, understandably, you're tired. Tell me if in Buenos Aires there's another one that isn't full of affected little poems by girls who only want to get married . . .

[The remaining half page is blank, no signature.]

ᘰᘯ

V.35 [Letterhead: Villa Victoria. 3 pp., pen, hand of VO.]

[MAR DEL PLATA.] 26 FEBRUARY [1956]

Dear Gabriela:

I don't understand how you can ask me about *Sur*. I thought they were sending you the magazine, which continues to be published, and which just celebrated its silver anniversary at the beginning of the year. UNESCO published a very nice note of praise on the occasion of the anniversary. In addition, the November–December issue was an extraordinary one, dedicated to the outcomes we hope will be achieved by the change of government.

Evidently, I haven't written you that this past year was fatal for the sale of quality magazines and books. The review had an 84,000-peso deficit. And given the state of economic misfortune in which we find ourselves in Argentina on account of the devaluation of the peso (we anti-Peronists, who put up with the consequences of so much thievery), this amount is really terrible for my deflated pocketbook (the pocketbooks of the anti-Peronists were the only ones that didn't inflate under *justicialismo*).[1]

To sum up: I'm making a supreme effort to carry on. Twenty-five years of existence for a review (and of those twenty-five, ten of a dictatorship determined to demolish culture and freedom of thought) is no small thing. Generally, the magazines that are lucky survive in conditions that are normal for a dog — in France there are exceptions to this.

Now, as you see from the paper, I am in Mar del Plata resting. I'll try to obtain the information that you're interested in, but I don't know anyone here at the beach who can give it to me.

Argentine magazines? Although it may seem boastful, I don't see any of real literary importance being published at the moment. But I'll send you a list of the ones that are serious, or try to be. One is *Criterio*, the Catholic review (which has been published for years also). It has the defects of Hispanic American Catholicism, although it's the best we have in that vein. I think another review, the primarily philosophical (José Luis Romero's) *Imago Mundi*, is no longer appearing.

Please, if you can't answer me right away, tell Doris to write me a few lines answering me about *Sur*. Because in the issue about the revolution there were two articles of mine in which I told things about my stay in jail that will perhaps interest you. I would have liked those articles to be published in the United States, but I have the impression that it's useless to try *to get into* the magazines of that country. Only *Vogue* has published my things on two occasions.[2] And if I hope to travel, it would be very helpful for me to earn a few dollars . . .

If you don't have the November–December issue, I'll send you a copy of my articles, as the issue has sold out.

A very loving hug for you and another for Doris

Victoria

I'm going to dedicate the July–August issue of *Sur* to women.[3] The antifeminism of the Argentines is a lamentable sickness, aggravated by the false feminism of the Peronists and the disastrous models of womanhood that Peronism used for its political ends. In this issue, we'll talk about the problems of women in all kinds of situations, according to what the contributors choose. I'd very much like you to send us something — whatever you like.

1. *Justicialismo* is the term used by Peronists to identify their political ideology.
2. As of this date, VO had published two of her essays, in English translation, in *Vogue* magazine: "Memories of Virginia Woolf" (1946) and "Fani" (1953).
3. This issue did not get published when VO intended. The reasons for this are unclear; however, it may have been because the editorial board did not concur with her feminist point of view. Clearly, VO had to negotiate her publication wishes with a more conservative majority of men on the board, and this time, one might speculate, she lost. The issue dedicated to women appeared some fifteen years later, in 1970–1971 (combined issues 326–328), and is noteworthy for the international and multicultural nature of its contents.

ℭ

G.83 [Letterhead: none. Postmarked envelope addressed to VO at *Sur* and forwarded to Mar del Plata. 2 pp., pencil, hand of GM.]

[ROSLYN, NEW YORK. 29 FEBRUARY 1956]

Dear Votoya:

I'm writing you on the day after arriving. It was a pity not to return by way of Argentina and not to see you on that account.[1] But you're free, thank God, and you can come whenever you want. I always miss you. — What I'm telling you isn't anything like adulation, it's a fact, repeated over and over and wherever I may be or live.

Ever since I came back, I've been awaiting some news of you, here where I live and Doris — who, as our grandmothers used to say, was "smitten by you" — lives.

We live in a totally forested place. It's beautiful in the summer. Come here if you can. There's a great silence that some find sad, though very sweet to me, sadness and all. Although people sometimes come, there are no strangers on a day-to-day basis.

I still don't know if you're living now in the sweet peace that they always had in your native land. They tell me so. The people I've been with didn't know how to answer this for me, in detail.

When you see this house, you'll be pleased by its vegetal peace: complete silence.

I say all this, even though I know the distance between us, because I have this habit: not accepting the fact that all of my people are far away and that I'm living in foreign lands *per vita*. It would be very bad for me to declare this *to myself* and every day.

Be with me, for a few moments. In this way: writing me twice a month, for example. And I ask you more: send me *the list* of French books that have been published.

A long hug
Gabriela

1. This is an example of GM's state of mental confusion about time. Her last visit to South America was in September 1954.

☾∞☽

G.84 [Letterhead: none. Postmarked envelope addressed to VO at *Sur*, forwarded to Cordoba, Argentina. 5 pp., pencil, hand of GM.]

[ROSLYN, NEW YORK. 15 MARCH 1956]

Cara Victoria (Votoya, sorry[)].

I've been here [in Roslyn] ever since I arrived, frozen stiff. The cold is something that seems like nothing, but it literally knocks me down. There are two or three small heaters in the room where I write. Even so, they're practically worthless.

I still fear, dear, that your precious spirits may wane a little or a lot. This has been worrying me for a while. The slightest bodily discomfort is liable to bring our work to a halt. People don't know about my great sensitivity — exaggeratedly so — to insults or simple dislike. That Nobel P[rize] not only distanced various people from me, but they stopped writing me, and this lasts up to now. For two — maybe three of them — my memory, I repeat, is bad — that Nobel P[rize] killed them for me, up to today. And though I've told them and *shown them* the negative answer that I gave to four people trying to seek and find capable people for me, people to increase the news of support, they've remained in immense silence, even so.

The others, the majority of them not friends but mere "acquaintances," are also staying silent. I don't know how to tell you how much it's hurt me to see their faces changed toward me, up to the present day.

Various times, Votoya, I've wanted to tell you these things. I've restrained myself because I know that in that type of person, in that sort, what's called the temperament is never cured.

Our president, a military man and all, sees and feels this, and although I've never touched on this —"telling" this indecent fever of anonymous people and that loss of old friends — one night he spoke to me about it at length, about what happens to him and a hundred things more.

"Don't give them pleasure by suffering," he told me. "They'll learn about it and they'll get worse."

Everything said above is so that you add on envy as being a racial illness *with no cure*, Vict. I've always believed this. Now I know it.

You know full well, probably since you were a little girl, that in our race, this is incurable, fatal. I've looked for ways to understand and . . .

to cure even half of this furor in my people. It doesn't work. They're going to die of their *cancer*. Call it that: it's cancer and it stinks because that's what it is.

Now, understand that my little life only now (today) stopped short. I've gone around doing "things" that are asked of me and that are impossible or useless to do. (Difficult political matters, too long to recount to you.[)]

I don't know what to do to make them leave me in this lovely peace facing the forest and the other peace of the trees, which I don't manage to obtain. It would be so lovely!

The winter, dear Vict. is my worst enemy. I'll dance when it leaves.

Now listen: I don't know if you know that despite the decline — relative, but decline — of certain economic powers, this [erased word] country doesn't decay . . . nor does *it decline*. This must be the result of its common sense: what we look at and hear, laughing, or rather, this word and its meaning. Surely, I repeat, the United States will save them. — When I recover, when this roguish, perverse season passes, and my bones don't feel cut through, as if with a knife, I'll tell you more. We'll try advertising *Sur*. For this, dear, it's necessary to have "our" people helping us. — Right here, V., they lack superior people to value their best magazines.[1] I'll have some of them sent to you. The unfortunate thing — don't forget it — is that here something like *Sur* can't prosper for us. Impossible. But there are certain circles of discontent, people who can achieve something with their criticism. There's a standstill: the ones who can understand *Sur won't say* so; they'll keep quiet about the fact that they like *Sur*. Even now, I haven't heard them say anything favorable to us, Votoya. And watching faces as they speak, for they don't know how to hide their truths, they "give something away," and this "something," Vict, has no cure because it's in almost everyone and it's a hard and perhaps definitive thing.

I owe them some things of importance, such as support in the matter of the Nobel P[rize], worth a great deal, to be sure, except that . . . the Swedes aren't at all admiring of this country. They criticize the lack of things that they have. And in this the Swedes are right. Someday I'll tell the Swedes about you.

I'm astonished at the United States nominating a Swede [Dag Hammarskjöld] for a high-level post of an intellectual nature. I'll tell you about it another time. And another time, I'll write you about something that you may not know: the Canadians, a mixture of French in the blood, and opposed to the Yankees.

Dear: Doris has made her own house here now; in three days or less she's finished her housewife's chore. A hug. Another letter will go out tomorrow!

G.

1. It's not clear whether GM means "Chile" or "the U.S.A." when she writes "here."

ΙΟΟΙ

V.36 [Letterhead: none. 2 pp., hand of VO.]

PARIS, 23 JULY 1956

My very dear Gabriela:

I've been in Paris for exactly one week. They sent your letter to me here. Thank you for the lovely photos.

As soon as I finish what I have to do here, I'll go to London, where I also have some things to take care of. I have to read some letters of T. E. Lawrence which are in the British Museum, and I have to talk with someone. I've come alone, by boat. I'm in the Hotel de la Trémoille, 14 rue de la Trémoille. I hate to live in cities, especially in the summer. Here I have a room whose only window opens onto the walls of a small patio. This room (a holy horror; for me, anything that involves enclosure is a horror, even if it were in a palace) costs 2,200 francs. It seems this is cheap for Paris . . . The prices of everything one sees are fantastic. And the meals give you indigestion by their sheer expense. The surprising thing is to see how many people there are roaming the world.

I spoke for a minute to Nehru, on the seventeenth. Unfortunately, the only day he spent in Paris was a day full of interviews, talks, and official visits, which didn't give him time for private conversations, ones very far from politics as ours would have been. I'm going to publish an issue of *Sur* devoted to India, and I'd like to have for that issue a few lines written by him.[1]

I'm still not sure what I'll be doing or when I'll do it.

The humid and heavy summer weather, a rainy summer, depresses me and tires me out a lot. Also, I have to be my own secretary and servant, which bores me, since I'm a demanding boss and I don't like disorder or lack of punctuality.

All my friends are on vacation, so in that sense my trip has been poorly timed. But I wanted to see Nehru, even if only for a minute.

That's all, dear Gabriela.

I don't have much desire to see people. Up to now, you could say that I've seen almost no one.

I'll write you again as soon as I have something definite to tell you with regard to a possible trip to N.Y. (if my very reduced means permit).[2]

A big hug and another for Doris

Victoria

[In the top margin of the first page, sideways]: The Pan-American Union [now Organization of American States] has published an index of *Sur*. Ask the Department of Cultural Affairs in Washington to send you a copy. Bibliographic Series 46. Columbus Memorial Library. Don't forget.

1. The special issue on India was *Sur* 259 (July–August 1959).

2. VO evidently went to New York and visited GM at home and later in the hospital. On 2 December 1956, she wrote a letter to her sister Angélica describing the visit:

"Yesterday morning I went with Victoria K[ent] and Louise [Crane] to Roslyn (Long Island) to see Gabriela. The place where she lives (where she is dying) is lovely, full of trees and small houses (sufficiently far apart so as not to bother each other). Hers — which belongs to Doris, who is with her, leading a life of filial abnegation that one rarely sees in such absolute form — is on *a hill* [English in original]. From every room (with modern windows that take almost a whole "side" of a wall; others are about 1 meter 70 from the floor, narrow and long, and go all around the room) you can see the nearby woods; really they're more like a plantation of trees with space between them, so they aren't overwhelming. In the distance, one can make out some hills . . .

The modern house, with a good garage and an enviable car parked in front (Angélica, find out for me if one can bring back a car), is surrounded by an unfenced American-style garden. Inside are good-sized rooms, an excellent kitchen, and that damnable heating that every American house has whose temperature I've experienced (I feel strangled by that incubator-type heating. In the Crane house I live with my window open, which naturally lets in a glacial draft, and they keep closing it whenever I leave my room).

Gabriela's thinness and weakness are like those of a concentration camp. She was in bed in a kind of pink flannel nightgown. An Indian. Everything Indian about her has been accentuated by the illness: her color, the slowness of her movements, the immobility of her face, where only her mouth opens slightly and with difficulty in order, it would seem, to let out a wisp of a voice and hesitant words.

She was pleased to see me. But time no longer exists in her head. I mean that she mixes up different times. She asked me: "How will things end up in Italy?" I suppose she was thinking about Mussolini's Italy. And to the other Victoria [Kent] she said that they would end up winning in Spain (I don't remember the exact terms).

She has retained her picturesque way of speaking. She can talk about everyday things without delirium: food, which she has no desire to eat; the cigarette she wants . . . and then doesn't smoke; the cat she loves so much, etc. She had a pack of cigarettes in her hand. She took out one after another, *elle les roulait* between her fingers, and then they would drop onto the coverlet. Then she'd take out another cigarette, as if she didn't realize that she'd already taken out several. After she lit one, she would then grasp it on the lit side without noticing (that is, she almost touched the burning end). Suddenly, she gets out of bed, and in her pink flannel nightgown, with red socks instead of slippers, she begins to walk like a priestess through the rooms.

The nightgown hangs on her body as if her body didn't exist and were only a rack with a head instead of a hook. The cat climbs onto the bed, and she looks at it as if in a daze. She didn't ask me about all that had happened in the Perón era. She, who wanted so much to know those things and asked me so often for details . . . , made no allusion to the prison. She told me she never went out, never budged from the house (four days earlier she had come back from the hospital). All in all, it's a painful spectacle. Gabriela has that anxiousness of people who are near death. But she doesn't realize anything. Of course she recognizes people (at least yesterday she did): she asked me to take off my glasses so she could see my eyes. I didn't know what to say to her, nor how to act. *I am no good with ill people* [English in original]. I get inhibited.

We ate lunch there. By that I mean that Louise and Doris went to buy some of the *hamburgers* that I detest, a cake that seemed made in a perfume shop (that kind of inedible American cake), and cheese (which was good). We sat down and ate in Gabriela's room, but since she got tired, we had coffee in the *living room*. It's really awfully sad to see her end up like this . . . a little along the line of her lifelong somnambulism, but now a sinister caricature of herself. She doesn't want to eat. She doesn't sleep.

[. . . .]

At 3:30 I went back to New York, and Victoria K and Louise went on to Connecticut to spend Sunday in Louise's country house. I didn't want to go because I don't want to pack again right now. . . ." [Translated by DM from VO, *Cartas a Angélica y otros*, 101–103]

Appendix
Added Writings

[This poem by Mistral, whose origin Ocampo describes in the selection "And Lucila Who Spoke Like a River," was written in Mar del Plata in 1938. Mistral placed it as the final poem in her collection *Tala*. In this poem, Mistral, the perennial wanderer, identifies Ocampo with her homeland and bids Ocampo to protect the freedom of speech and cultural expression of America.]

"MESSAGE TO VICTORIA OCAMPO IN ARGENTINA"

Victoria, the shore you brought me to
has sweet grasses and a brackish wind,
the Atlantic Ocean like a colt's mane
and cattle like the Atlantic Ocean.
And your house, Victoria, has lavender
and — all veridical — iron and wood,
conversation, loyalty, and walls.

Bricklayer, plumber, glazier
measured without instruments, measured by looking at you,
measured, measured . . .
And the house, which is your scabbard,
is half mother and half daughter to you . . .
Diligently they made it for you of peacefulness and dreams;
doors they gave for your fancy;
a threshold they spread at your feet . . .

I don't know if fruit is better than bread
or the wine better than the milk at your table.
You decided to be "the terrestrial one,"
and the Earth serves you willingly,
with corn ears and oven, vine stocks and press.

The children run through the house and garden;
they cleave your eyes coming and going;
their seven names fill your mouth,

the seven graces make you laugh,
and you become entangled with them in the abundant grasses
or you fall down with them going over sandbanks.

Thank you for the sleep your house gave me,
in the fleece of merino wool;
for every blossom of your ceiba tree,
for the morning when I heard the wild doves;
for your idea of a bird bath,
for so much green in my wounded eyes,
and the mouthful of salt on my breath:
for your patience with poets
of the forty cardinal points . . .

I love you because you're Basque
and because you're stubborn and ambitious,
aiming at what's coming and hasn't yet arrived;
and because you're like nature's bounty:
like the corn of plentiful America
— plentiful hand, plentiful mouth —
like the winds of the Pampa
and like the soul of almighty God.

I bid you farewell, and here I leave you
as I found you, sitting on the dunes.
To you I entrust the lands of America,
to you so like the ceiba, so knife-erect,
so Andean, so fluvial,
so like a blinding waterfall
and Pampa lightning!

Keep your Argentina free:
the wind, the sky, the granaries;
free education, free prayer,
free song, and free weeping,
the *pericón* and the *milonga*,
free lariat and gallop,
the pain and happiness, free!

For the ancient Law of the Earth;
for what is, for what has been,
for your blood and for mine,
for Martín Fierro and San Martín
and for Our Lord Jesus Christ!

[From *Tala* (1938); reprinted in Gabriela Mistral, *Poesías completas* (1958), 587–590. Trans. Doris Meyer, reprinted in Meyer, *Against the Wind and the Tide*, 163–164.]

ℒℴℷ

[The following piece by GM was written in 1942, after various earlier and apparently discarded drafts mentioned in G.5, G.8, and G.19. Mistral both celebrates and condemns her friend's talents. What bothers her most is Ocampo's preference, even in her forties, for writing in French rather than in Spanish. It seems that her difficulty in putting her portrait of Ocampo into words stemmed precisely from the disjunction she could not reconcile between her friend's very creole nature, on the one hand, and her Europeanization, on the other.]

"VICTORIA OCAMPO"

There must be many Victorias in Victoria, since I myself know at least four . . . One is the godchild of France who knows all the phrases, verses, and fairy tales learned from her French governess, around whom creole Spanish was never heard.

And next to the devotee of the Seine and Racine, there is another Victoria, who escapes across the Channel, knowing that the Seine can't give her everything — for example, the strong wind of adventure and a certain freshness of institutions found in a newer metropolis, Paris-like but poorer. This Victoria reaches the other side and sets herself up on the shore, so unlike the first, eager to receive the gusts from the Channel or the Mediterranean, not to mention other gifts she can find only there: a poetry less ingrained in the flesh and a prose more permeated with music and grace.

And behind these two Victorias of foreign-leaning mind, behind these two big whims of hers — which some interpret as a vice and others as childishness — there is a magnificent Argentine woman (*argentinaza*) who, as soon as she tosses away the mirror in which she contemplates and distorts herself at will, becomes completely and unexpectedly Argentine and laughs at those of us who fell for her tricks, as if saying to us: What were you thinking? Did you believe, my foolish friend, that one can have a pampa as wide and vigorous as this, and a river like our Plate, and that one can live with Martín Fierro snoozing by the hillside and not carry it in one's soul just as in one's body? Do you think it's possible to walk with this long greyhound stride and breathe with this llama neck and enjoy these endless sand dunes if one is from the Loire Valley and dreams of Piccadilly?

From the moment when one realizes the hoax or the little white lie, when you see her face or her gait up close or hear the echo of her Spanish anger, all the rest of her black legend collapses, falling on top of us like an avalanche of sand.

And this Victoria will be the one left after the English ivy or the European bougainvillea is ripped away. Before us is the naked stone, the stubborn, massive block of total Argentineity that seems never to have been taken from the quarry; the great woman (*mujeraza*) of the River Plate who, forever after, whatever anyone might say about her, will, for you, be only this loyal image and likeness of her own geography. No one will ever make you believe again in the Victorias of the smoky, fraudulent mirrors.

This *criolla* Victoria is mistress of all the openness and boldness that name and wealth can give to living, and yet, she is consummately timid when it comes to life itself, to speech (she would say "expressing herself"), to spilling her rich human marrow on paper. She seems to protect herself with words, and her word must suffice as mental opinion!

The great literatures she frequents, the best of the classics and the moderns, have given her, with regard to writers and texts, a kind of superstitious reverence and fear similar to what we women and children feel toward complex machinery, or when we imagine the gold cargo of a Spanish galleon . . .

This is the only way that I — also feeling dazed and daring in taking on this great task — can explain the very long road and the scandalous amount of time Victoria Ocampo has taken to convince herself that she has her own treasure, as wide as the avenue of the Paraná River, to offer and pour out.

She has only recently begun to suspect what richness she has but not to understand it with zeal and knowledge, from sea to mountain range. This treasure is from a life of happy submersion, completely soaked in living. The large, Mexican doe–like, woman's eyes of our Victoria have seen the morning countryside and have unfolded the tapestry of a hundred or more cities; her delicate doe ears know by heart this world's tree of music, which has moved its outermost branches for her. Her enormous desire to capture the nature of places and people of means and experience has made her accumulate the wealth of an essential wisdom and an art of living, which she neither measures nor counts, since she's still not convinced that she possesses them. Because she doubts this, and because of her incredible timidity and a superstitious fear that has an Indian-like quality, she has had a foolish habit of seeking ratification, help, loans. In a similar way, in the Elqui Valley where I lived as a child, my girlfriends and I used to play blindman's bluff, but with a twist to it that I don't know which one of us invented. The blindfolded girl whom we turned loose in the orchard, feeling her way past plum trees and vine roots, would suddenly hear us shout: "The river! The river!" And if she was a scaredy-cat — nowadays I'd call her "imaginative" — she'd stop in her tracks, raise her arms, and become very pale or red-faced. She would sense the river there, one step away . . .

The legend of Victoria will make some people laugh at the comparison. I don't care. In matters of writing, Victoria Ocampo is the frightened little girl of my Elqui Valley.

Smart as she was, she paid obeisance to the Masters and showed that very South American fetishism of book worship. Thus her tendency to walk a zigzag path, consulting her fake gods, insecure in her intentions, and fearful of using her native language because it wasn't taught to her in her infancy.

Pedagogically speaking, I know very well that such a pyramid of superstitious scruples produces a kind of apathy that passes for professional ethics. I know that it's a noble sentiment and even considered a sign of good breeding. But I also know that, for some South Americans, their European idolatry and their doubts about their own spiritual and verbal capacity have wounded them like a paralysis.

I am more than familiar with the symptoms of this *criollo* infirmity: the river of images is dammed up; one mistrusts the ambient language, even though it bubbles with life, like the ceiba tree; homegrown wheat must pass through triple foreign sieves; and one goes around every day wasting precious tactile and visual experiences simply because they happened in a mountain village or along a path that smelled of farm tools and cattle.

But this drab and humble treasure was precisely the one that the good Sarmiento gathered up, accepted, and worked with. And the reason for his success was, among other things, his willingness to give credit to his surroundings, to their domesticity, and to write about them, giving them value, beauty, and honor. This was his first concern or, as they say, right at hand.

On his left side, secondarily, he carried his library, which never became a suffocating blanket because on his right side he carried his Argentine pampa or his Chilean mine or his schoolhouse, bumping him at every step, like one holds on to a lover or a child so as not to lose him.

Victoria Ocampo began her work with three books of essays. All three are good, not lacking fine chapters or sections. One of the bad things that can befall a writer is to be successful at going out on the limbs of her being, playing about and distracting herself, and thus delaying her descent to the trunk of her being. It's strange when you can't see a human being whole, like looking at an animal in the water just lying there on its side, or maybe its back, just showing its hide.

Victoria lay back for quite some time on her ingenuous hide, play-ing cleverly with the genre she deemed most hers — the essay — which, for others, is merely a form of commentary. She did this out of modesty, not presumptuousness, as some suggest. The really pre-sumptuous people are those like me, who throw themselves into the churning swell of the sea. Victoria tried to glimpse, gloss, skim over the theme of woman in her debut publication, *De Francesca a Beatrice.* The subject seemed so right for her to express there, in torrents, her own self, or rather, her magnificent femininity. But it didn't happen; she did other things, but not as much as she could and should have. It's impossible to touch Dante without having a gigantic bibliographic mountain fall on you, suffocating and choking you. In this book, Vic-toria, who is daring when it comes to living but not when it comes to writing, behaved not just reverentially — with tact, hesitation, and modesty — but fearfully. The mountain of predecessors frightened her. Who could attempt to handle, much less lift, that continent of il-lustrious paper, she must have said to herself.

After that would come pamphlets, also the result of timidity, then two volumes of *Testimonios,* which included what was in the pam-phlets. But in the second volume of these testimonies — finally! — like opening the shell of a nut, there appeared the almond of her voca-tion, her ability, her talent. In the essay on Emily Brontë, one sees through to the nucleus of the Victoria who had spent years of inti-mate communion with Emily Brontë and Virginia Woolf. Years of not just reading about them in European criticism but of having the soul of Emily (the poet and novelist) in front of her like a secret box or capsule that's hard to open and peer into.

The man-genius always intoxicated Victoria, but the woman-ge-nius intrigued her. She wasn't content only to read the biographies and assessments of Emily, which were legion; Victoria insisted on going to see the moors where she grew up and left her trace, however insignificant or supernatural.

Perhaps because she's dealing with a woman, Victoria seems to have finally gained some confidence. It's about time! She is, in fact, very sensitive to the glories and miseries of our sex, to its humiliations and its accomplishments. Her splendid biography of Emily Brontë brought us, her friends, a very special pleasure: that of seeing Victoria free herself from those two thousand ties that were almost like a big soft ball of wool yarn that her Masters — great and small — had wrapped around her.

Victoria Ocampo began to see ahead of her the vast and fertile fields of labor. She awakened to a sense of her own resources: she knew how to write another's life . . . It was only natural, since she has a memory for people that is fuller and more abundant than a grapefruit tree in summer. Her hands are full and ready to share the knowledge of many types of human beings — the fibers, skin, pulp, juice of many grapes. São Paulo's Museum of Wood doesn't contain more varieties of rare and commonplace specimens than Victoria knows of women of all kinds through her vast experience. She knows the keyboard of the female gender by heart.

Why, then, did Victoria spend so many years (as did the girl from the Elqui Valley) groping in the dark? For lack of self-confidence, which we might call wisdom, but which, in some moral enterprises, could be called a waste of wealth and a left-handed estimate of the tools one has for the job.

We her friends, who rejoice at her "entry into the subject," have read this beautiful biography in which she fuses herself with her work for the first time. Reading it, I remembered the famous Victoria-of-books who casually drops a phrase, just one, about something — a book, a person, a fruit, or place — drops of pure essence, like those that come from the pine or like myrrh, drops that fall thirty feet from a vegetal heart before landing at our feet or falling into our hand.

Victoria is a temperate conversationalist, never spiteful, sometimes benevolent, and frequently admiring. The cut that she takes on books or other things when she talks strikes me as magisterial, because she makes visible the most intimate fibers, even though to do it she must part the outer layers and slice past the comments of others.

It was, then, something from her conversation which, after so much hesitation, she managed to pour onto paper in writing her testimonies. Not entirely, of course, because her writing still shows some "scholarly fears" that aren't there when she speaks.

It would be interesting to find out how her French governess, whom she remembers with gratitude, taught Victoria the classics, and whether her submission to the Masters and her need to quote them comes from that manner of teaching. There's another thing: the fatal attraction South Americans feel for the formal perfection of the French language. Victoria — a passionate person — tends to be a little stiff and cold in her structure, which is not a result of her expression but of an instrument that punishes a bit the faithless daughter of the Spanish language.

In love with the language that rubs elbows with the paternal Latin when it comes to formal perfection, Victoria still is not aware of the bad marriage that results when a passionate woman of Spanish speech expresses herself in French. It's a phenomenon akin to heresy; the unfaithful one lives the tragedy of what people refer to as "a divided love" and what the confessors call the triumvirate of the spirit.

Because, really, the other woman, the renegade, continues living next to us, like the mistress beside the lover, but the wife — or if you prefer, the mother — is situated in the middle. When the shout of joy comes, it's she who jumps up, owner and mistress of our being, which, as flesh, according to age-old custom, controls and governs.

I still remember the part of a conversation in which Anatole France clearly pointed out the risks of a Spanish writer who gives himself to French. This is more or less what he said: that the two languages have opposite and even warring mentalities. What a twenty-four-carat truth! Maybe one of the few classics that isn't damaged by Spanish is Shakespeare, whose language approaches the magnificent disorder of our own, its loose abundance, euphoria, and frenzy. Racine may be a counter-Shakespeare. Dante is with us shoulder to shoulder in his universality and passion; but again, his almost geometric, iron-rigid form has nothing to do with the frenetic bonfire of San Juan de la Cruz in Spanish, people-language, multitude-language.

For me, the linguistic tragedy of Victoria Ocampo consists in the fact that a heated and passionately tumultuous temperament like hers, when kneaded and molded by a French education from nannies and governesses, ends up acceding to their teaching and example. And to their language; like a first cousin but different, it both fascinates and opposes us. Thus is accomplished an almost inhuman damage, so fatal are its consequences.

But she's happy nevertheless, stubborn as she is. Like a wife who accepts the passing liaison because it suits her or because it occasionally makes her happy, I don't ask myself if it really makes Victoria happy to be with that foreigner, that is, the borrowed language. The subject comes up regularly in her conversation, which would seem to indicate a conflict that concerns her.

That Victoria Ocampo fertile of body and so rich in potential, full of nutrients like the ceiba or the araucaria, the Victoria of violent impulse and character as clear-cut as the cordillera peaks, the Victoria of free judgment and familiar expressions — how can she reconcile, how can she go on, *how can she live* with that anti-Rabelaisian, crystalline language that French has become, according to Leon Daudet, who knew the anatomy of his language well? How can she accept the ambidexterity of speaking Spanish and burning to write in a French as smooth as the burnished wood of a caoba tree? In what region of her brain or her soul does she suffer her linguistic bigamy?

February 1942

[From *Gabriela piensa en . . .* , 49–56. Trans. Doris Meyer and Marjorie Agosín, reprinted in Meyer, *Rereading the Spanish American Essay*, 185–191.]

ΩΩ

[In November of 1945, Gabriela Mistral was announced as the winner of the Nobel Prize in Literature. She left Brazil and traveled to Stockholm, visiting Europe and the United States over the next months. The following are excerpts from letters between Victoria Ocampo and Roger Caillois, from late 1945 until early 1947, in which they discuss Gabriela Mistral. Given the fact that no letters survive from VO to GM in this period, these pages offer some additional insight into their relationship at the time.]

"ABOUT GABRIELA"
27 DECEMBER [1945]

Dear Victoria,

. . . Your essay on Gabriela will appear in *Confluences*. Gabriela has been invited by the French government: she'll pass through Paris upon her return from Stockholm. I'll be glad to see her and talk with her about you. . . .

Roger

MONDAY, 14 JANUARY [1946]

Dear Victoria,

Gabriela is still in Paris, but it seems that she doesn't leave her residence very much except for official occasions, which, by the same token, she has reduced to a minimum. She's well and wants to see you again. (I need a copy of *Tala* for a translation.) What's more, she's had problems in Stockholm, where the Chilean embassy recently wanted to publish selections from her work with a preface by Valéry, which cost them a fortune. But she didn't want this preface that Valéry wrote because she says that the French author doesn't know Spanish or her work and that under these circumstances the commissioned and paid-for preface was neither a pleasure nor an honor for her. I think she's right. They replied to her that in rejecting a preface by Valéry she would be committing an "offense to France" — which is idiotic. She also pointed out that Valéry has written two prefaces for [Antonio de Oliveira] Salazar (whose Fascism is no mystery) and one for Swedenborg (paid for by the Swedish embassy) for a book that shows his notorious incompetence and evident antipathy, and that she doesn't want to be presented by him, despite the great admiration she has for him.

I can see you here in the same situation saying: "I don't like promiscuity."

. . . R.

Gabriela is carrying on like St. John the Baptist. She tells everyone of your impending arrival, saying that they will have to make the most of your visit.

Dear Victoria,

. . . Gabriela was supposed to have tea at Elsa Triolet's house. She didn't seem
too enthusiastic about it. Yvette and I saw her very often during her stay in
Paris (she left Sunday for Rome). Once, when we were alone, she told me
some incredible things about "the valley of Elqui." Her mother saying to her
when she went back there, "Tell me about your God; he seems better than
mine." She's given me the poems she wrote after or apropos of the death of G.
[Yin Yin]. I'm in the process of translating them. There are about seven or
eight of them, all very beautiful. She sent you one for *Sur*, "Mourning." She
was concerned to know if you had received it. She's also given me a wonderful
photo for you. I'm going to send it to you by diplomatic pouch at the next opportunity. Gabriela says that you intimidate her greatly: she says that you are
both animal and celestial, like the animals of the zodiac. (I think she even said
"divine.") I've felt very happy to be able to talk this way about you with someone who loves you. She says she loves you much more than you know (and
that she has told you so).

Her simplicity and her majesty must have impressed a lot of people. But I
have the impression that she has seen almost no one interesting (except
[André] Malraux, who happens to be a minister and thus obliged to offer her
a luncheon).

. . . Roger

[to Victoria]

I spent a long time with Gabriela bidding her farewell. She seemed somewhat
preoccupied by death. She told me that she discovered in Rome that she did-
n't want to live anymore, that she was only suffering; if I dare say, she considers herself a survivor, like one condemned and in suspension on this Earth.
She wants to see you again; she even told me a little bitterly, or so it seemed to
me, that she had proposed to you a meeting in Uruguay. She would also like
to see the Yucatán ("to see what my Indians have done"). She'd be delighted to
go with you and with us. I promised her I'd talk to you about it. And the
truth is that the idea is enormously seductive to me. It seems there is a clean
and comfortable hotel ("for the Yankees"). With regard to that, she said that
you were accumulating such a karma of "spit and polish" that in another life
you will surely be condemned to live in filth and discomfort for having attributed too much importance to pulchritude and comfort in this one. I must say
that this reasoning fascinated me. For my part, I told her that I hoped to escape that punishment (at least in regard to filth).

She's very malicious in conversation and even very [?]. I didn't know this side of her. Doubtless when I met her she was too absorbed by the recent death of G. [Yin Yin].

When we were leaving, she said to Yvette, "May God bless you, child, I think that someday you too will pray." She didn't say anything like that to me. I was a little put out, but I think she didn't dare say it to me.

...R.

28 JANUARY [1947, FROM CALIFORNIA]

Dear Victoria,

...

I took a bath and got on the bus to go meet [Aldous] Huxley in Beverly Hills.... I liked him very much and, as you said, he's extremely pleasant.

You're right, Huxley really does practice mysticism, and he does the exercises every day. "I couldn't live without this."...

I was supposed to go to Gabriela's [in Santa Barbara]. Besides, she wanted to know Huxley (being a Buddhist), but he had never been able to meet with her and vice versa. So he and I went together to see her (Gabriela had sent a friend in a car to get me). I can assure you that the contrast between the two of them was worth it all: Huxley didn't want Gabriela treating him like a more advanced mystic than she was, when it was evident that, of the two of them, she was the mystic. He couldn't stop observing her like a psychologist observes an odd case, and he knew that I was aware of it, which just increased his indignation and caused him to be even more evasive of Gabriela's questions and to reject her deference.

You can't imagine to what extent his intellectual side reappeared in her presence, showing that it had never disappeared! And I was acting as translator for both of them.

...I miss you a great deal, and I'm convinced that if you had been there the conversation with Huxley would have taken on another aspect, since you know the points of view of both of them. We could only grope our way.

...R.

MAR DEL PLATA, JANUARY 1947

Dear Roger,

Finally, I've received news from you. Your letter wasn't very long, and I would have liked to have known more about your meeting with Gabriela and Aldous. I can imagine the displeasure of ("cerebrodonic") Aldous confronted with ("viscerotonic") Gabriela. His temperament would have been more affected than hers. Aldous always feels rather uncomfortable with (or in the presence of) individuals who "wear their hearts on their sleeves," as they say. And even though Gabriela is essentially a complex being full of secret folds and double folds (secret, even, from herself) and in no way as simple and direct as one would think by listening to her, she gives the impression of revealing her life, her heart, to the first person she meets. She's like Carmen, who on first impulse "sings for herself" and generally ignores the personality of her interlocutor or is indifferent to it — although she may feel benevolently when she hasn't fixed on an idea or taken sides against someone. She loves passionately, madly. This is her way of loving — like yours is to be moderate in your feelings — but she's blind, and when she *sees* something, it's never a consequence of her critical sense (which is weak) or her intelligence. Never through her eyes (which are the organs destined for such use in average mortals), do you understand? Metaphorically, it's through another sense that has developed in her because of her blindness.[1] What's more, when she talks about things, the same thing happens. I've never seen her observe or smell a garden the way I do. I never saw her devour with her eyes the sky, the sea, the first quarter of a bright new moon shining in the blue, pink, and green skies of our evenings, evenings I've spent with her. She wouldn't look at anything, wouldn't breathe in things, and didn't need, as I did, to put her hand or her nose into plants and trees, or to pick flowers in order to see them up close. These divine familiar ornaments don't fill her with happiness. The shape of the figs she ate by the dozen, and which I had picked for her with love and placed on a blue-bordered plate with my own hands, didn't give her any pleasure.

And nevertheless . . . she speaks about those things she doesn't see, or at least doesn't seem to see, the things that I so much enjoy looking at, touching, and smelling.

The senses, which in me are always alert to those small and immeasurable pleasures, are, in her, latent and reserved for inspiring her pen, never her real life. She's a writer! (I suppose.) Things happen *in her imagination of those things.* I want direct contact, communication; I communicate with fragrant and green things, with the sand and sea, the trunks of trees and the clouds. It's not through my imagination but through reality that I delight in them.

During my ten months [in the United States] of cities, walls, sidewalks, and asphalt, I felt alienated from myself. "My batteries like in radios were low and the messages didn't get through." . . . I'll tell you more about this in person.

Everyone has asked me for news of you with true affection (without forgetting the minute details of your likes and dislikes). "Do you remember the *carbonada* [Argentine stew] and the pasta with chicken?" We're a country of *viscerotonics.*

I miss you — despite your well-known bad behavior — more than I can tell you. I hope we can see each other again soon. But I'd like to establish a more stable arrangement that will permit me to believe that we live together, as before.*

I missed a great deal of California and Mexico, but I wanted to go back to see Angélica and to know for myself how she was and if her depression had more physical than imaginary causes.

That perturbation — if one can call it that — that affects her to the point that she has to cover one ear in the movies in order to tolerate noises that are a little loud, seems to be somewhat better. Or else she has gotten used to it, or the suffering from it has diminished. It's nothing serious, but it is very unpleasant. I think my being here has done her good. She was getting too bored without the activity that I contribute, and without the hustle and bustle that I stir up around me. It's curious, but to people like her and Fani, my defects seem to have a calming effect. It's my defects they miss. When I get carried away by anger, they feel stunned and pleased at the same time. They've gotten used to listening to me live more or less noisily. That noise calms them. Fani would say: "The house was so quiet that it seemed empty without the señora."

Right now Tota and Baeza (whom I invited) are here, and also the ex-marquise (who invited herself).

The d'Ormessons [French ambassador to Argentina] are at X's, but they'll come later. That's the only embassy that still invites the members of the so-called oligarchy. Neither the United States nor the British embassies will do it. "How do you like that?" as the Yankees say. In those two embassies, they don't want to run the risk of offending the monarch [Perón]. That's what the world is like.

Write to me. Tell me if you've received this letter. . . . Don't eat raw vegetables in those countries lacking hygiene. Be careful also with V.D. And with your heart in those areas where the altitude has bad effects.

I embrace you and think you ("te pienso," as Gabriela would say),

V.

*Although you've aborted many of my hopes. As soon as I go away, I feel you're seduced by what adversely affects me. Our harmony is off-kilter.

[From *Correspondencia* (1939–1978), 176–191. Trans. Doris Meyer.]

1. GM was losing her sight because of diabetes, a condition not diagnosed until her residence in California (1946–1947). Her letters to VO frequently mention her deteriorating eyesight.

{ƆƆ}

[This essay was written by Ocampo just two months after Mistral's death in January 1957. It is a classic example of Ocampo's elegiac testimonial prose, drawing from Mistral's poetry to portray the qualities she loved and most vividly remembered in her friend, both when they first met, and when she was dying.]

"AND LUCILA WHO SPOKE LIKE A RIVER"

And Lucila who spoke like a river
Like the mountain and the cane field,
Under the moons of madness
Was granted the kingdom of truth.

(Gabriela Mistral, *Tala*, "We were all going to be queens . . . ," 101)

I met her twenty-seven [*sic*, twenty-three] years ago in Spain. María
de Maeztu, that very Spanish woman, took me to the house of this
very vagabond, but very Chilean, Indian, and Basque woman. We had
missed the chance to meet each other in Paris and had exchanged
messages. Our first encounter, in Madrid, was a memorable one to say
the least (I've written about it before). Gabriela, unmoving and ag-
gressive, didn't lose her nobility by being unjust, because her injustice
never sprang from the pettiness of avarice or envy but rather from a
generous and blind impetuosity, an inner torrent that was difficult to
hold back. Right off the bat she reproached me for being born in the
least American of the South American capitals; for being Frenchified;
and for not having become friendly with a woman writer she knew
[Alfonsina Storni].

Taken aback by her judgments and somewhat subdued in her
presence, I stammered that I hadn't been consulted about where I was
born nor later about the choice of who my teachers were. With regard
to her friend X, I had only seen her once and we never met again.

My side of the conversation that afternoon was an awkward attempt to explain. Gabriela's side (and naturally her way with words
had enchanted us all, in her succulent Spanish that we would never
hear again from such an American mouth) amounted to variations on
the theme of reproaches. What part of America was so sacred that it
demanded our unconditional loyalty? She assured us that, in large
measure, it was Indian America, to which she was bound by blood
(half-blood). Her insistence admitted no argument from us on this
point.

Normally, I would have lost my patience, but not this time. Out of
sheer enchantment, one might say, I listened to her with uncharacter-
istic meekness. Although sometimes one might perceive disdain or
condescension in this type of praise, I felt the workings of a beneficent
human warmth behind her aggressiveness.

Gabriela always spoke about something. She was a stranger to
what Anglo-Saxons so accurately and untranslatably describe as
"small talk." She demonstrated this to me from the very first day.

There was no preamble. She plunged fully and quickly into what she wanted to clarify. Without wasting time on pleasantries, she went to the heart of the subject that concerned her, as I saw her do many times thereafter. Once she began, she invariably indulged in diverse and lengthy parentheses, which in turn led her to new parentheses within the main one. "What was I just saying? . . . Oh yes! . . ." And she would then return to the previous juncture. Her parentheses would lead her to unrelated topics remote from the one that had motivated those fascinating extended monologues. But in Gabriela's case, the monologue was something special. It revealed to us, shining or somber, the world she lived in, a world that her imagination and lyric fancy kept alive.

> A river always sounds nearby . . .
> It's the music of my blood
> or rather a rhythm I was given . . .

It was useless to try to interrupt that music by saying: "Actually, Gabriela, the truth of the matter . . ." Gabriela would keep on talking from within her kingdom, and her kingdom was one in which pumpkins changed into carriages and vice versa, carriages into pumpkins.

Perhaps that was the hidden reality, "the kingdom of truth" Lucila was granted, that Valley of Elqui, which Gabriela saw

> With the braids of a seven-year-old,
> and white pinafores of cotton percale,
> chasing after thrushes on the wing
> in the shade of the fig tree . . .

In my house in Mar del Plata, where she spent some time in 1937 [sic, 1938], the woman who served the meals, and still does, recalled: "Señorita Gabriela would sometimes stay in the dining room talking. When teatime came, she hadn't moved. Not even when it was dinnertime. She loved Spanish figs and would eat them at teatime. We were always trying to find the best figs." How could we forget those afternoons in the dining room, blue with smoke, when Gabriela would go from coffee to figs to mate without any break in her conversation. Darkness would fall. The lights would be lit. Friends would come and go. They would sit down to hear and see Gabriela more than to have lunch, tea, or dinner. From time to time I would slip out to take a walk through the garden and see what the children were up to. There were a flock of seven of them in the house, which was transformed by

their presence. They added to Gabriela's contentment. When I would
return to the dining room, the air seemed unbreathable to me, and I
protested: "Lucila Godoy, what kind of a smoker are you? Do you
want to get sick? Tell me in two words what's been said in this den of
yours while I've been gone." Gabriela would smile. The smile would
change the almost bitter line of her sad lips and would rise to her eyes
and her half-moon brows that gave her quiet face a certain expression
of surprise, of incredulity. She smiled. Never did I experience any
other reaction from her. I was one of the many pumpkins she transformed into carriages.

She spent the seventh of April in Mar del Plata. It was her birthday. We shared the same birthday, but it was only then that we discovered the coincidence. I got up early to wish her the customary felicita-
tions. She was sitting in bed, pencil in hand, correcting something.
"What have you written?" I asked. "A message for you, for your saint's
day, as you call it." "Can I read it?"

> Victoria, the shore you brought me to
> has sweet grasses and a brackish wind,
> the Atlantic Ocean like a colt's mane . . .

It was early and you could only hear the noises of a house that was beginning to wake up: shutters being raised, careful steps, the name of
an early-rising child who was impatient to go out to the garden but
first had to have breakfast. The air had that pungent morning freshness of autumns by the sea, and it smelled of toasted bread.

Gabriela, pencil in hand, handed the pages to me one after another. "You must write it for me in ink," I protested.

> I bid you farewell, and here I leave you
> as I found you, sitting on the dunes

I understand now that she was saying good-bye that day. Good-byes
are said in advance . . . you never know when, until later. Two and a
half months ago, even one month ago, I saw Gabriela on the verge of
death, but we didn't talk of good-byes. On January second, a few days
before I left, Gabriela didn't recognize me. But even when she could
still see me and talk to me, I was already separated from her. I knew
she was dying and I didn't want her to read it in my eyes. She asked
me to take off my dark glasses. I felt that my face was laid bare. What
could I talk to her about so that could I keep the secret from her? A
secret she surely had guessed. I tried to act naturally as we spoke of

things that weren't what we were both thinking. She didn't even ask
me about my two weeks [*sic*: three plus] in jail, after having begged me
in her letters to tell her all about it; it pained her as it did my own
flesh and blood. Gabriela had been greatly concerned for my fate from
1953 on. She didn't cease asking me to tell her about my misfortunes,
my worries, or encouraging me to leave my country and come live
with her on Long Island. But when I arrived in December of 1956, the
Gabriela who wrote me those letters and had gone all the way to Cape
Cod to discuss my plight with Waldo Frank [August? 1953] was no
longer there. Absent, the ghost of Gabriela looked at me with her
green eyes. A ghost who barely understood what was happening
around her and who lived in certain parts of the remote past more
than in the present. A ghost whom I didn't dare to awaken, if such an
awakening was possible. We spoke . . . but nothing we said carried any
weight or substance, since it wasn't linked to the essence of the moment. Word sounds, word ghosts.

Just like on the seventh of April 1937 [*sic*, 1938], she was in bed, surrounded by trees whose branches and crowns peered through the
windows and surrounded the bedroom. Like that seventh of April, I
was sitting next to her, listening, looking. It was a frigid, radiant afternoon of a Long Island winter. An afternoon with birch trees, blue sky,
and an insistent wind. She knew me, I think, but without connection
to the present. "Next time you come," she said, "let me know so I can
have fruit for you." She remembered my love of fruit, but not what she
had wanted me to tell her. In the terrain of small material things (how
the cat who wandered through the house was behaving, for example),
she was on firm ground. But in that of world events . . . What was
going to happen in Italy? How would things in Spain turn out? . . .she
merely asked questions. They were Italys and Spains of the past, not
today. No mention of Argentina. And to her eyes at that moment, I
was probably closer to the Victoria that María [de Maeztu] took to
her house in Madrid than to the Victoria who had inspired her
telegrams and letters to a dictator. But I had the impression that, like
deaf people who instinctively try to cover up their deafness by pre-
tending to hear and manage to play this game with great skill,
Gabriela remained in that vague terrain almost voluntarily. She knew
she was forgetting things and she didn't know which ones. She was
feeling her way.

> I bid you farewell, and here I leave you
> as I found you, sitting on the dunes . . .
> Keep your Argentina free . . .

free education, free prayer,
free song, and free weeping . . .

Did she remember having written, in pencil, that "Message"? In 1937
[1938], in the morning that smelled of toasted bread, the request to
keep my Argentina, its education, and prayer free seemed extravagant,
but it didn't surprise me coming from Gabriela. She, the real traveler,
was afraid that I might leave my country for good, and she was determined to prevent me from doing that. With that objective, she attempted to persuade me that my presence in Argentina was necessary.
That's why, in her poem, she entrusted the lands of America to me.
Later, the moment came when she wanted to drag me away from
those lands. Perhaps she felt partially responsible (which was entirely
wrong) for my not wanting to leave when education and prayer were
not free. But even though the request of her "Message" didn't surprise
me, it did seem then to be a product of the most unfettered fantasy.
How could I have known that the end of that poem written on our
birthday would be prophetic, that our Argentina would really be
threatened, that to keep it free we were going to have to sacrifice our
own freedom, at least on a personal and material level (who can take
away the other kind?). The tone of her request was grave and urgent,
as when people say: for the sake of what you cherish most.

> For the ancient Law of the Earth;
> for what is, for what has been,
> for your blood and for mine,
> for Martín Fierro and San Martín
> and for Our Lord Jesus Christ!

But on the seventh of April 1937 [1938], I didn't know that the poem
written by Gabriela, our birthday poem, the one with the seven children, the sand dunes, the wild doves, and our Lord Jesus Christ, was a
prophesy. Nor did Gabriela know that she knew it.

> This is how I saw her:
> Spelling out the unseen,
> giving name to the foretold . . .
> In Madrid (when I was introduced to her).
> In Mar del Plata (where she spent a happy time).
> In Buenos Aires (with her friends, at my home).
> In Nice (with her nephew).
> In Rome (with her anguish).

In Washington (that night, on her way back from Stockholm, after receiving the Nobel Prize, when she told me about the suicide of her nephew—the person she loved most. She talked and talked, until dawn. When she left my hotel, I set about checking the room, looking under the bed, feeling possessed by an irrational nervousness. I was alone, but I felt that I wasn't alone, and it scared me. "Who was that woman who was shouting last night?" Gabriela asked the nurse the day after Yin Yin's death. "That was you," she replied).

In Roslyn (among the leafless trees of Doris Dana's house).

In the anonymous Hempstead hospital (seeing her live through the moments she had foreseen and described):

> When my broken neck can no longer sustain me
> (but there was the unforeseen filial arm of Doris)
> And my hand reaches for the diaphanous sheet . . .

("Take her hand," said Doris. Her weak hand lay inert between mine. Then it pulled away and resumed its agitation. "I don't like it," my mother would say, "when a sick person moves his hands like that, twisting the sheets.")

On the Atlantic Ocean (when my ship was crossing into our hemisphere) when a cable arrived. I thought then, perhaps with other words, but it hardly matters:

> I've been chewing the shadows for so long
> that I can no longer relearn happiness;
> stepping on lava stones for so long
> that my feet forgot what fleece was like;
> so many years biting the desert
> that my homeland is called Thirst.
> And after that, also with other words:

"Grant that my fervor may endure and my deception be brief. Wrest from me this impure desire for justice that still troubles me, the protest that erupts when I am wounded. May incomprehension not cause me pain, nor forgetfulness sadden me."

I remembered that one day, talking of the wounds of injustice that are so difficult to heal, Gabriela said to María de Maeztu: "What does a saint care about injustice?" Which is to say, what does he care about the injustice the world does to him? He exists on another level.

I thought that perhaps many of us had loved and admired our Gabriela and would conserve her presence intact because she under-

stood these things; and she knew that, when we manage to understand them, it is unfortunately rare that they are realized. She understood this as few people do because she passed through the world and
our lives

> Spelling out the unseen,
> giving name to the foretold,
> marvelously, mysteriously blind and deaf.
> William Blake once said:

"I don't know any other Christianity, any other Gospel than that of
the freedom of body and spirit to exercise the divine arts of the imagination. Imagination: the real and eternal world of which this Earthly
Universe is only a fleeting shadow; the world in which we will live
with our eternal or imaginative bodies when these mortal, earthly
bodies cease to exist."

I don't know if Gabriela read Blake. I don't recall her mentioning
him to me. But nothing evokes her for me at this moment like those
paragraphs of the *Prophetic Book:* "I will give you the end of a golden
thread . . . ," Blake said to us. And the same golden thread that this son
of a London shopkeeper and reader of Swedenborg spoke of is the
one taken up by Lucila of the Valley of Elqui, born of Indian blood at
the foot of the Andes.

Both of them said, don't drop the end of this thread because it
leads to the doors of Heaven:

> It will lead you to the doors of Heaven
> raised up on the walls of Jerusalem.

And Jerusalem is called Freedom among the children of Albion as
among those of America. The freedom to "chase out the devils" in the
name of Christ; the freedom to cure those who suffer "a spiritual sickness." The freedom not to behave like the Pharisees

> crucifying and circumscribing the sea and land
> for proselytizers of tyranny and rage.

That was how William Blake and Gabriela Mistral thought and felt.
That was how they lived in the real and eternal world of which this
Earthly Universe is only a shadow: the world that Blake calls Imagination. And that is how they will continue to live and meet where the
dead are found, as another kindred poet wrote: on the lips of the
living.

[*La Nación*, 3 March 1957; trans. Doris Meyer]

ೲ

[This essay, written five months after Mistral died, is Ocampo's way of sharing the extensive correspondence she had saved from her friend. Through the letters, she draws a portrait of Mistral and, through Mistral, of herself, as she meditates on the nature of letter writing. We include this essay, even though it repeats sections of GM's letters, because it offers insights not found in VO's surviving letters to her.]

"GABRIELA MISTRAL IN HER LETTERS"

Gabriela Mistral is the most representative, the most important woman of Hispanic America in our era. I don't believe anyone would argue against that. She is representative as a personality and important as a poet. I know no one who has her combination of talents and is at her level.

America (Indo-Spanish America), children, and poetry were her three constant loves. Accompanied by them, she traveled through life and the world with the strange blindness of a clairvoyant and the surefootedness of a sleepwalker. As she said:

> I believe in my heart, which asks for
> nothing, because it is capable of great fantasy
> and embraces all creation in its fantasy.

The very nature of her loves obligated her to ask for nothing.

Gabriela had no choice. In order to love what she loved, from "the high reaches," as she would say, she had to believe in her heart. Children demand it that way, and poetry too, even the most unreligious kind. And like children as well as poetry, *our America*[1] needs to be loved in the same way. And if we don't love her, her existence, just like a child's, is threatened and almost extinguished. Because the love to which I refer is disinterested love that creates what it loves and helps it to thrive.

I've heard Gabriela converse with the children in my household. I've heard her explain how her poems were born. I've heard her speak about her America with the kind of trembling one being feels in the presence of another of one's own blood who is threatened (after all, Gabriela's passion for America was perhaps the most carnal of her passions). All of this was one and the same thing: a product of the heart.

The following biographical information may be useful to those who are not aware of it. . . .

But now, let's get to the subject at hand: Gabriela's letters, the ones she wrote to me.

To communicate in writing one with another. To care for and love one another. This is the definition that the Royal Spanish Academy gives to the word "correspond." And that's the double meaning the word has always had for me. To write letters is this or it's nothing.

In the volume of letters from Proust to Madame de Noailles, there is one that is significant. Both of them were young then. Anna de Noailles, in addition to being beautiful and talented, was embarking with rousing success, at the age of twenty-six, on a literary career. Proust, at thirty-two, was still an unknown. The important magazines would continue to reject his manuscripts for some time still; high society, which so attracted this man destined for glory, admitted him almost as a favor . . . It's the old story.

We're in 1903, and Proust writes to Anna de Noailles, whom Barres would compare to the Greek goddesses: "What emotion I felt today upon seeing the helter-skelter tumult of your handwriting . . . When my father, who is as active as I am lazy and goes out every morning, came up with the mail and said to me, 'A letter from Mme. de Noailles,' Mother scolded him and said, 'Don't take away his pleasure of discovering it by telling him in advance.'" That's how Proust awaited her letters, and we know what it's like. A simple letter can bring so much joy or so much discouragement.

Insofar as this particular correspondence is concerned, I was aware of something that made me even more sympathetic to Proust's trembling upon reading the undisciplined handwriting of the young and ungrateful Anna. I say ungrateful for the following reason. Years after Proust's death, she told me:

He would write to me a lot. But in those days I was young, and my head was full of other things. Often letters would arrive from him that I didn't even read. Now I'm having them copied for me on the typewriter, and as soon as they're copied, they're brought to me. So each morning I receive a letter from Proust.

She told me this with her characteristic heartless charm. I smiled, but it seemed monstrous to me that such a thing could have happened with the letters of the very sensitive and exceptional man who wrote *A la recherche du temps perdu*. Monstrous but natural. That's how thoughtless youth can be. And Anna, giddy with success, with her beauty and her own work, Anna who only had eyes and ears for the talent of Barres, didn't notice the genius of that unconditional admirer who would write her without any illusions: "I already know that I don't matter a bit to you." It was true. She herself said in her pages of posthumous tribute to Proust:

Dear Marcel, I possess a treasure that I really didn't value when you were alive: your letters. Those letters, carefully preserved, will be read; but won't they make me suffer too much? I fear suddenly and forever knowing what my mind and my heart have lost.

Even when we value the treasure during the lifetime of the one who put it into our hands, it often happens that after death we discover that we have lost much more than we feared. That is what happened to me when I reread and copied part of the letters from Gabriela.

Keyserling used to complain that the telephone, telegraph, airplane, and typewriter had ruined the art of correspondence. "Can you imagine," he said to me, "Mme. de Sévigné writing to her beloved daughter every day if she had had more rapid means of communication at hand?" I don't doubt that Mme. de Grignan would have received one telegram after another and that her mother would have gone broke making long-distance calls. But in spite of this, I don't think posterity would have lost the joy of reading some of the extraordinary letters that rained down on Mme. de Grignan. There are people who, despite the telephone, telegraph, and whatever else there may be, are writers of letters. The telephone is another kind of medium. . . .

Ortega was of the opinion that the epistolary genre went together with femininity because the letter is addressed to only one person, not to everyone, and because, unlike men, women are made for intimacy. According to Ortega — and he and I argued and even fought about this detail — men and women can only reach their maximum expansion in two different atmospheres. For men, the public life; for women, private life. But let's take, for example, the theater arts where there have been as many good actresses as actors ever since women were first allowed to be on the stage. The life of actresses, and I refer to their work, is as public as can be. Nevertheless, they have risen to perfection in an occupation in which, according to Ortega's theory, they should have failed. Let's take another example. When a woman decided to take command of an army, she didn't fail. And yet one can't say of Joan of Arc that her maximum expansion took place in her private life. That's an exception, they'll tell me. Of course. But all the great figures of history are exceptions.

Returning to my great and admired friend Ortega, and to the epistolary genre, if the maximum expansion of men and women is only achieved in different atmospheres, as he opined, how calamitous that would be. Those expansions would never manage to coincide, since they require different climates. To carry his reasoning further, it would be as difficult for a manly man and a womanly woman to understand and agree with one another as it would be for a soaring eagle to notice a fish in the depths of the ocean. I believe, and it seems to

me difficult to deny, that one can only understand what one potentially possesses. In spiritual, intellectual, and even sentimental matters, an ill-acquired good is impossible. One can only possess what
can be paid for with ready money or its equivalent.

Ortega affirmed that women have a talent for letter writing which
men lack, and that the fruit of that talent, properly destined for one
recipient, can subsequently be enjoyed by great numbers of unknown
readers. The epistolary genre, I countered, is then only nominally private. Men, Ortega would say, are incapable of writing successful letters because they turn their correspondent into a larger public before
whom they stage a performance. But, I objected, didn't Mme. de Sévigné, a consummate letter writer, commit the same sin at times? Didn't
she turn Mme. de Grignan into her public? And did Ortega think
that Mme. de Sévigné's letters about Turena's death or Mademoiselle's
marriage were less addressed to various readers than the poems of
Anna de Noailles or the novels of Virginia Woolf?

This whole discussion had to do with lyric talent and epistolary
talent. Ortega attributed the latter to women and the former to men.
He had fallen in love with that theory and was determined to show
that reality confirmed it. I would say that being in love with a theory
and then wanting to make reality agree with it is, in itself, a markedly
masculine attitude.

In the case of Gabriela Mistral, as devoted to writing letters as to
writing poems, we find both kinds of talent — one of them somewhat pruned into shape, the other growing like a tropical jungle.

It is evident that among men as well as women, there are those
who write letters with an eye to posterity and others who don't. This,
in my opinion, constitutes the true difference. Perhaps men worry
more about epistolary posterity, but of course I'm referring to men
who write for a living, professional writers.

A short time ago I mentioned Mme. de Noailles. I've had the opportunity to read the unpublished letters written to her by Barres.
They're very beautiful. But when I read them, I had the impression
that those beautiful and admirably composed letters were destined
not just for the woman born as the princess of Brancovan, but also for
all those who would one day think of her and of him as two extraordinary individuals. One could also argue that there is nothing surprising about a great writer wanting to show off his gifts like a peacock in
order to dazzle a Greek goddess. But something tells me it wasn't just
that. It's also true that the French have or had a strict code of courtesy
that, to us, in the Spanish language, is inhibiting and blood-congeal-
ing. The first letter from Proust to Mme. de Noailles begins with
"Madame." After a friendship of eighteen years, the last letter begins

the same way. And if I remember correctly, the same is true of Barres' letters. This may not have anything to do with that glance toward posterity of which we have spoken . . . but my impression is that the "Madame," or shall we say formal attire, can be found in other parts of the correspondence, not only at the beginning of each letter.

Gabriela's letters were not composed, literarily speaking, nor even careful. They were like her handwriting. I don't know what a hand-writing expert would say about it, but it's a very slanted kind of writ-ing, like alfalfa in a wind storm. Very even, all the letters very much the same size. Sometimes difficult to decipher, especially because it was her habit to write in pencil. This writing in pencil is more proof that when Gabriela wrote letters she didn't worry about posterity, nor hardly even about her correspondent. No one who thinks about pos-terity uses a pencil. Lawrence of Arabia, a great letter writer, used in-delible ink.

I used to complain about the pencil, which, together with her handwriting, was a truly hopeless combination. Gabriela would promise to reform. I would say to her: "At least use ink, woman. . . ."

When I complained to Keyserling for similar reasons, although he didn't use a pencil, he got angry and assured me that when the Gestapo searched his home and went through his papers, they read his manuscripts in no time. "Are you trying to tell me," he said, "that the Gestapo is more intelligent than you are?"

Like Keyserling, Gabriela wrote letters in abundance. And she wrote without composing them. They were spoken letters. That's the way Virginia Woolf wrote them, too. Let's keep in mind that both women spoke in their own distinctive way, with complete spontaneity and naturalness. Being two writers and two totally different, almost opposite personalities, their command of the language enabled them to use it however they pleased. I mean to say that they used words like they used a comb. Sometimes the comb was made of bone, other times of tortoiseshell, but above all it was what it had to be: a comb.

For those who like to write letters, material distance isn't a prereq-uisite. It's common to write a friend or a relative in the same city, even in the same house. This happened between Gabriela and myself. And a letter that goes from one floor of a house to another has of necessity to be different from a literary composition of the epistolary kind — just as a live bird is unlike a stuffed one. Moreover, even if you weren't in the same house or the same city, Gabriela's letters were "snapshots." They never were like the photographs of a professional who says to the client: "Now smile and don't move."

Our correspondence began, without really beginning, with two unsuccessful encounters: one in Buenos Aires in 1925; another in Paris in 1929. Gabriela had the bad habit of not dating her letters, but these two were exceptions. The ones whose envelopes I didn't keep are today impossible for me to date with any certainty, unless she mentioned in them something about an external event or about where she was at the time.

Her first letter, written in January 1925, is brief. She was writing to me the night before her departure for Europe, thanking me for some flowers I sent to her when I found out she was passing through Buenos Aires. We didn't manage to see each other.

The second letter came to my apartment in Paris four years after that, regretting another missed encounter. Gabriela was working at the time at the Institute for Intellectual Cooperation. She says:

Only yesterday I learned that you're here. And it's very difficult for me to leave without seeing you. I'm leaving Monday. Could you favor us with a visit to the Institute . . .

I'm buried in paperwork and don't have a bit of free time. I've loved and admired you for years now. Receive these words without smiling. Affection is always a beautiful thing, whomever it comes from.

Here, a mea culpa. I was young and, like Anna, my head was full of other matters. I didn't want to sacrifice who knows what silly date to run to the Institute for Intellectual Cooperation. We parted again without even knowing what each other looked like.

A short time later, one afternoon in Madrid, María de Maeztu took me to Gabriela's house. I've related that encounter several times because it had a very Gabrielesque flavor. Right off the bat, she reproached me for three things: (1) that I was born in the least American place in South America; (2) that I was Frenchified; and (3) that I hadn't gotten to know Alfonsina Storni, a friend of hers.

After our second meeting, and almost after the first one, she began to change her mind about the first two points. Regarding the third, she realized that she could hardly blame me for that.

After those few conversations in Madrid, I didn't see Gabriela again until she came to Argentina in 1938. I've come across an unfinished letter to a friend which I never sent and in which I described Gabriela's arrival in Mar del Plata. At that time, Gabriela and I weren't writing at length to each other because we were living in the same house . . . (sometimes we would write each other from bedroom to bedroom). This letter, then, is the only document that I consider to be from that period, with the exception of the poem Gabriela wrote in my house on the seventh of April, our mutual birthday. My letter to my friend said:

I'm in bed with a cold, unable to read, not so much because of the cold but out of a monumental lassitude. I spend the time listening to the trees in the wind. And listening to the birds and to the five children in the house, who are even more strident. I really do like those earthy noises! In the midst of this lassitude and this cold of mine, and without any prior notice, that strange and wonderful woman, Gabriela, appeared obliging me to shake off my drowsiness, my trees, the birds and children, and the shouting that burrows tunnels into the night that lead to one's childhood. I'm no longer floating aimlessly.

The day before yesterday, in the midst of a torrential downpour, the telephone rang. Gabriela's secretary was calling from the old train station to let me know that they were there, without a car, and that someone should come to get them. Gabriela had suddenly gotten tired of Buenos Aires and had taken the noon express train without thinking to let me know. I had invited her to come spend as long as she wished at my house in Mar del Plata [it was March, early fall], but I wasn't expecting her so soon. At about eight in the evening, she came into my room looking like a statue. Her head has a beauty and mystery that I hadn't remembered. There's something especially harmonious in her forehead; was it the shape or proportion of it? The way her hair framed it? Her eyes are a greenish color, and even when she walks, she seems immobile. She sits down next to my bed, like a statue, that is, if statues can go from one posture to another without ceasing to be statues. For two plus hours she talks about the Spanish revolution (which she has watched, she says, from Lisbon) and the Catholicism of Jacques Maritain, whom she thinks about every day since they met, she assures me. Gabriela also believes that this man comes as close as is possible to being a saint. He is attacked from the right and the left, and the Vatican looks upon him with a certain wariness. I tell Gabriela that Maritain's Catholicism is of the highest order, as he is a Catholic convert. Certain Catholics who practice their faith mechanically can make us detest that extraordinary religion — theirs and mine — when one looks at it with unprepared eyes and heart. In Gabriela's case, it turns out that she has gone to look for Christ in Buddha. She returns from the house of Buddha carrying Christ, who naturally was there also. Christ is everywhere from the moment when a certain kind of glass-enclosed Catholicism ceases to stand between him and us. An opaque Catholicism. Life is difficult, wherever one lives it, and it is worse without Christ. Blessed are they of pure heart . . . who see him always, glass or no glass. (My heart is pure about one instant in every seven years.) I say this to Gabriela. And she tells me that understanding the nature of Grace has changed the complexion of her life. Until one understands it, one tends to grasp terribly and desperately for justice . . . and the heart bleeds. I confess to her that I am still grasping for justice. Perhaps one day I will understand Grace, since the peace promised to those who have a hunger and thirst for justice can't be found within justice itself but rather higher up, where it becomes superfluous. I refer to *justice as it applies to oneself, not to others. The ability to be happy when one is suffering an injustice is a form of Grace.*

Gabriela asks me how I feel about religion. I answer: "When I see a man like Maritain, or rather when I am around him, in the atmosphere of his royal presence (not when I read him; his books appeal to my intellect in a way that doesn't change my spiritual temperature and thus doesn't lend itself to eclosion, to germination), I say to myself the words of Pascal: 'Joie, pleurs de joie' [Joy, tears of joy]. How could his way of living his life, of judging his neighbor (or not judging), his habit of demanding everything of himself and nothing of his neighbor be the fruit of a misguided idea? Of a false conception of what man should be and what the Eternal One (this is how I most like to refer to God) is? Is it possible that an exemplary human being as admirable as Maritain can build his beliefs on foundations that are totally or partially false, feeble? Is it possible that that feeling, comparable (though less intense) to the one I felt in the presence of Gandhi (the greatest of all, in my opinion), doesn't emanate from a form of conduct in life, and especially (since that conduct is an effect not a cause) from the meaning that it gives to life, to man? From the interpretation of that mystery? And if that interpretation is mistaken, could it produce such results?

Rather than say all this to Gabriela, I was thinking it as I listened to her. Gabriela speaks without raising her voice, without gestures, without any part of her face moving, except for her melancholy mouth. I listen to her like a child who has everything to learn. That's how I feel in her presence and in the presence of those who, in telling me their own lives, reveal to me the secrets of the universe.

I came to life again to listen to her once more this morning. It's a curious sensation this feeling oneself renewed in the presence of a new person who suddenly enters our life. Ortega would make some fun of this. He'd say: "Like an orangutan, right?" He has written: "The lowly beasts find each morning that they have forgotten almost everything they lived the day before and their intellect has only a minimal quantity of experience to work from." Well, yes, like an orangutan. Why not? My experience with other people does me no good when I encounter a new person. I have to begin again, starting at Adam's rib.

Gabriela talks and talks about the civil war in Spain. She has an abhorrence of Fascism and an invincible revulsion for Communism. She tells me terrible things. Both Fascists and Communists will say that such are the inevitable atrocities of revolutions. But those disjointed lives, those men without passports, exiled, rejected from every country, and fleeing from their own, terrify us. And that's not to speak of the systematic extermination of Communists by Franco's side, and of the Fascists by the other side.

Gabriela believes that the Spanish race[2] is possessed, that a demon leads them on. The insuperable cruelty of that race when it comes to conquest (as in

America) or revolution. She repeats this to me. Her Indian blood speaking, I think.

  Gabriela doesn't know how to laugh. Or she has forgotten. She laughs all of a sudden, without motive, after the moment to laugh has gone by. She laughs with an accumulated, delayed laughter that does not appear at the opportune time. A laughter that seems to make fun of laughter itself. I never saw her cry either.

Gabriela spent almost her whole time in Argentina in my house. When she left, our correspondence began.

  In her first important and long letter (after having gotten to know one another), she says to me:

It's been a tremendous surprise for me to find you so criolla, *as* criolla *as I am, although more refined. What's more, it's been a real joy. And needless to tell you, a hope of mine. From age twenty to forty we wear cosmetics, at forty everything that isn't our bone and marrow falls away. I await in you, then, the years to come, and I do so with patience and certainty. When you live with the full volume of your blood and not with a portion of it, you will return or you will go toward Spanish, all by yourself. Until then, you should let some eager people like us send you books, old and new, written in a language that you can't help but love and that will give you absolute pleasure. Let's see what you make of Gracián . . . My letter is taking on a tinge of imperiousness that I find disagreeable. Try to overlook it.* [G.3]

Here, a clarification. I was educated by French and English governesses. In my generation and in certain social classes both here and in Europe, it was common to be concerned above all that girls learn to speak foreign languages. I say girls, because boys necessarily had at that time a different and wider field of studies. Nevertheless, Güiraldes' case was identical to mine insofar as learning French was concerned. We used to read and prefer French literature (and in my case also English) to Spanish. France was our second homeland. In reality, I've never understood why the study of French and English, and a wide familiarity with their two literatures, should be damaging, since Greek and Latin are recommended and even obligatory for any serious humanist . . . Ricardo Güiraldes was proof of the massive dose of foreign literature that can be digested by a native Argentine without losing his Argentineity. Güiraldes was fervent about everything French, but he remained on the margins of English, unlike Borges.

  Nonetheless, Gabriela had the obsessive idea that this frequenting of things French and these preferences could definitely alienate me from my true destiny, or what she imagined was my destiny. She continues to write in her first real letter to me:

Your case *wouldn't matter much to me if I had the dishonesty of the literary types, male and female, who deny you the category of "writer." But ever since I read your first book ("De F[rancesca] a B[eatrice]"), I knew that you threw yourself into literary writing, body and all. If along with those same invidious people I believed that your sphere of influence did not extend beyond a group of snobbish gentlemen, I wouldn't waste my time writing to you. The caste of snobs matters less to me than the guild of stamp collectors. But I know, principally by way of* Sur, *that you reach and influence our South American youth. The magazine would not turn without you turning, from the very depths of your being.*

I vaguely understand that you fear falling and causing Sur *slip into that creole nationalism of saddle pads and spurs and mate or tango, into which others fell and became mired. You who have the possibilities in your mind and your soul should create a superior* criollismo, *an Americanness both smooth and fine, like that of your beautiful personal manner, and identify and weed out all that our manner might lack; take care, with the most zealous carefulness, of your Spanish and that of the people who follow or surround you. Perhaps this is your duty in this world: to transpose Argentineness along more qualitative lines. Americanness isn't resolved by a repertoire of dances and colorful fabric, or by a few foolish and insolent postures of defiance toward Europe. That portion of Americanness is dealt from the left hands of jokers and fools. There are a thousand possible directions and paths to follow, and with your subtle aim, you can choose the least expected ones.*

We ask nothing of you, only a presence, as complete as possible, within the American movement . . .

Pardon my impertinent demand. Some of those of your race, whom you must love, Sarmiento, for example, would tell you more or less what this schoolteacher is telling you.

I will continue in another letter, Victoria. The topic is huge and everything that you know matters to me. [G.3]

As modesty dictates, I beg forgiveness for being on center stage in these letters. But what is interesting about them is to see how Gabriela took everything American (that is, South) to heart and how she was opposed to any flight of capital when she thought that one person or another, for one reason or another, could enrich or serve, intellectually, this America of ours.

More or less around the same time, or so I surmise because she doesn't yet use the familiar "tú" and because the letter addresses me by my first and last names, she writes:

You and Don Miguel [de Unamuno] offer counsel and support. It would be somewhat tasteless to explain that support to you, what part you have in it.

You affirm and maintain the Americanness that I so often denied you, an Americanness more physical than literary. But since the body exists terribly, Victoria, the other varieties of Americanness will come carted along, hissed at or swollen up by it sooner or later . . . Oh, Victoria, how our America resembles, in its double face, its precious guanaco of the mountain ranges: smooth to the touch, the color of toast, with a skittish air that tends to become wild and spits on the familiar and the foreign alike. . . .

You have a mission (the word is trite, put whatever word you want), . . . Be careful of the transparency (the clarity) of the message that you bring to spread and to spread with fitting insistence. Be careful of the instrument (a seismograph they call it?) so that they don't cut or alter its operation without you. And be careful of those who are being careful.

This letter will cost you effort because of its unconventional handwriting . . . May God watch over you, Victoria, the American. . . . [G.4]

To conclude this topic of my enslaving Americanism, which was a fundamental one in the letters Gabriela wrote me (as will be seen if they are published one day) and which she first denied in me and later discovered upon getting to know me, I'll cite what she wrote to me immediately after the time spent in my house in Mar del Plata:

I always live you, and have been for some time now, Votoya. Whether I write you or not, I continue living you like that (it's not fiction) — with the clays, grasslands, and the little animals of our America. You could be neither noble nor superior; I would live you just the same, because I, too, feel tenderness for our weeds. Do you remember that tremendous shrub — Goebbels-like — at that ranch you took me to, from which you had some branches cut? [G.26]

Gabriela was referring to the hills of Balcarce where quantities of *curros* grow. The *curro*, which I like so much and which has been declared a national plague, is a bush of pure thorns, the thorns forming a cross. In the fall, it has white flowers that smell of vanilla. She continues:

I see that geometry of thorns, that "look at me and don't touch," that machine gun of silence and thorns. That's how you could be, and I would still think the same way about you. Because that "repelling" plant is also truthful, and what most sums you up is your truthfulness. . . Perhaps other women in Europe could give me your culture and your talent; no one gives me your truth and your vital violence. It's the most open-air American style there is. . . .

Votoya, we almost didn't meet one another in this world. You wouldn't have lost anything by it, except for one more bite, just another, from the American corn. But you have done many good things for me: I needed to know, to know, to know, that a totally white person could be a genuine American. You can't fully understand what that means to me! Then, I also needed to under-

stand that literature doesn't destroy or cause a woman to decay inside (that is, to create cavities); that it doesn't damage her in her essence; that it doesn't rob her of a certain sacred marrow, exchanging it for some more or less beautiful phrases. The two good things that I mention to you were already a lot. But more remains, which I'll tell you about, bit by bit.. . .

In me there's hardness, fanaticism, ugliness, *that you can't be aware of, being unaware as you are of what it's like to chew bare stones for thirty years with a woman's gums, amid a hard people.* [G.26]

Her search for things American had found in me an odd field of ex-perimentation. And during our twenty-three years of friendship (I don't count the first years), which was peppered with discussions but not with fights of any kind, I don't believe she ever stopped looking at me as she did the stones, grasses, and little creatures of our conti-nent . . . even the weeds and national blights . . . with infinite tender-ness and unquenchable curiosity. Shall we say that I was, in the ani-mal realm, her favorite thorn bush. And that everything said about me should carry this botanical classification [*curro*]. For Gabriela, I represented "the most open-air American style imaginable."

With regard to what she says about herself in the last paragraph of the letter I just cited, only one of the three things she accuses herself of is correct: her fanaticism. Let's be clear about this. Gabriela didn't believe, as her letter proves, that fanaticism was a desirable trait. But the exalted nature of her love for America, or that part of it with In-dian blood, was very akin to fanaticism, as was the Americanism of my friend Germán Arciniegas. I used to say to Gabriela: "You're more racist than Hitler when it comes to Indians. Isn't that right?" Gabriela would laugh, almost flattered by the criticism. In this, she was — as am I — absolutely intransigent. There is no good fanaticism, in my opinion. I believe fanaticism is dangerous even when dealing with God, because it circumscribes, impoverishes, and falsifies him. Gabriela wasn't fanatical at all when it came to her religious beliefs. Her religion didn't diminish God, and that sarcastic statement by Voltaire, as applied to certain religious perspectives, would not apply to her: *"Dieu a fait l'homme à son image, mais l'homme le lui a bien rendu"* [God made man in his own image, but man has done the same with God]. But when it came to America, the Indian surfaced in Gabriela and she got carried away. This trait of hers, which would probably have irritated me in other people, made me feel tenderly toward her, as it was the result of her unshakable faith in this continent from which, nevertheless, she was physically distant for almost her entire life.

And yet, as we shall see from some portions of her letters, her pas-sion wasn't as blind as it seemed. Gabriela would often encounter a less flattering American reality, and she was too honest and sincere to conceal from me her disappointment and displeasure. All the countries of the world, as well as its peoples, have their good and their hateful sides. Some more or less hateful than others. How could it not be that way, given that countries are made up of people? Gabriela would submit to these truisms when, in her travels, she encountered something egregious showing that America, the innocent, was more than a little corrupt.

Once I asked her to give me some information about the period when she was a schoolteacher living in the Valley of Elqui, which she often remembered (and where I assured her she would not be able to get used to living again). She answered me with a postscript: "Don't worry about me until I die and you see the worms at work on my poor bones. Before that, what's the point?"

How I regret now not having insisted! I extract such a small amount of juice from the dry facts and dates, the cold names of places! What do I care about the exact hour of her birth, the day she taught her first class, the moment when she decided to go to Europe or when she decided to stay on the old continent, or the northern part of our hemisphere, forever (she wouldn't accept that I might leave Buenos Aires at one point, because she had it in her mind that I had a mission to accomplish here). What mattered to me was how she herself would have told me about it, how she would have described it, with what details and how much flavor, with what earnest contradictions, and what amount of nostalgia for a place where, in spite of everything, she would not return. And with how much of her unique lyricism. A lyricism that, instead of galloping, as is common with romantic lyricism, proceeded at its own pace. You can't gallop in the Andes.

In the same letter in which she talks about the thorn bushes, those machine guns of silence and spines — an admirable description — she mentions a topic that obsessed her: reincarnation.

These days I've been in a good mood, but yesterday and today I've felt almost happy, I don't dare say how happy. *The word always makes me afraid. I recently found the edition of* Les Vers Dorés des Pythagoriciens *with commentary by d'Hierocles. I read it some years ago, but it didn't have this pile of helpful notes by Mario Meunier, the Greek scholar. This version is admirable.*

With regard to reincarnation, I'm always somewhat inarticulate, or embarrassed, or considered harmlessly crazy. Coming across it again, there, in the mouth of two big, lucid, marvelous, and what's more, somewhat saintly writers, has made me lift my hunched shoulders and take up again, with pleasure, my incurable heresy. How clean and clear-cut they make reincarnation. Palmita

says that reading my Hindus she feels lost in vapors and as if galloping with
monsters. Here it's clear, unquestionable, honorable, and straight up and down.
This reading has made me happy — the word slipped out. Last night I slept as
if I were far from the cares of the world. — Let's see if I sleep like that again,
today.

No, I don't deny or become distanced from Christ, nor do I cut myself off
from Him, as they say of this great big heresy. Like Yin Yin, I believe in God
and in the gods. [G.26]

Gabriela was constantly worried about religion, about how her
friends felt about such beliefs.

I read somewhere, I don't know where, that A[ldous] Huxley is in a religious
crisis or he's joined up with some unnamed sect. This interest me, in him
and . . . in you. Because I've been told something about you, too, but more
vague.

In a notebook, I copy out selections about J[esus] C[hrist] taken from the
most diverse and most opposite sources — eliminating only the ones written by
the poor devils who call themselves rationalists. Many lights come into my
sight, new lights, that help me. I believe that this can take me somewhere. In
dreams I also receive some true crumbs of life. In this way I keep on living.
[G.42]

She wrote me this after Yin Yin's suicide. As I said before, this was the
terrible tragedy of her later years. She wrote:

. . . this child wasn't a portion of my life; he was life itself. In him began and
ended my reason for working, my joys and my worries. I haven't had a per-
sonal life for some time now. More than ever, during these years in Brazil. The
war has stripped naked so many sad truths about my criollo *American people;*
it has made me see them so blind and so lacking in any proximate *remedy.*
The passion I had for them that absorbed and consumed me was abating or ex-
tinguishing itself. The house was him; the day, him; reading, him. I know that
God rudely punishes idolatry and that this doesn't just mean the cult of images.

Oh, but I have to return to my old heresy and believe in the karma of past
lives in order to understand what phenomenal crime of mine has punished me
so suddenly, so intensely, with my Juan Miguel's night of agony . . .

It's not consolation that I seek, however, it's seeing him, and in dreams I
tend to have him, and in sensations of his being present in wakefulness as well,
and I go on living from what I receive from both things, and from nothing more
than this. . . .

. . . Poetry never was something so strong for me, strong enough to replace
this precious child . . . There's no book of any sort that can dazzle me like
him; . . . nor is there in me the gift of forgetting such an experience. I have it

woven into me every five minutes. And I'm living on two planes, in a danger-
ous way. It's useless to tell you more, because I haven't said anything in three
pages. [G.41]

Yin Yin died on the fourteenth of August, 1943. This letter was written on the twenty-sixth of October.

In the last years of her life (she would never forget Yin Yin, whose
death left her only half alive), Gabriela stayed in the United States, on
Long Island at the home of her North American friend Doris Dana.
From that refuge she wrote me:

It's been nearly two months, at least one and a half, since I've written. That
poem — geographical and . . . vegetal — about Chile has worn me out. It oc-
curred to me to put it together using a single rhyme. Craziness. I've never made
poetry that's straight description; I have to correct it a great deal, and in order
to do this, I'm taking a rest.

Dearest: I learned this a long time ago: it's very restful and even healthy to
write things that are absolutely objective. (Try doing it yourself: to rest the soul
is almost a form of hygiene; in any event, it works (or uses) only the memory
that is called objective, merely objective.*[)]*

It rests me from my cares to water Doris' plants, a few of them that face the
street. In addition, there's a little forest inside the house. This does me even
more good, but it doesn't need me . . . Some six or ten minutes from the house is
a semi-sea, a sea that's small but pleasant to look at, almost without hearing
it. *Because of having almost everything that I really* need here, *I'm feeling*
more and more peace.

I owe to Buddhism, dear, a certain ability to concentrate, that is, to plant a
single thing, a single pleasant thing, in the center — if there is one — of my
being. I can stay like this for hours and hours: it brings me to life *again, like*
something that eliminates all the rest: everything disappears and only that thing
remains. Try this. What's more, dear, Buddhism gave me the power to cut out,
as if slicing away, what was injuring me. I can be thinking about something
and suddenly I let go and pass everything by, the tree-lined street or the pretty
female cat or the record that's playing.

Forgive me for telling you these things. They're commonplace and important
at the same time; they are a true power of the mind. If they're forgotten for a
day, they should be recovered quickly. It's a great truth that our mental life "is in
diapers." One can make of it a living far from all obsession and much sadness.
[G.68]

Gabriela had learned to penetrate a realm that many of us only know
secondhand: that of meditation and contemplation.

The proximity of the sea to Doris' house filled her with well-being and contentment. We shared that passion for the sea. One day she wrote me a joyful, childlike letter. She had bought a very expensive ($22) book about the sea, a book with pictures that delighted her: "The sea is the passion of my old age," she said. And in another letter: "I have an almost sinful love of the sea." And again: "I've finally realized this: the sea gives me strength. When I'm near it, after a week I feel like another person. The earth is a brutish element, almost without soul, *boring and excessively bourgeois.*" No one shares more than I this passion for the sea. Those of us who love it and, furthermore, feel loved by it (since its presence revives us) know what vigor it imparts. But — and here I'll give a clear example of what I call Gabriela's fanaticism — the earth is not boring or bourgeois. Good God! What variety it offers us! What unexpected delights! What fantasy! It's as sublime in its diversity as the sea is in its apparent monotony . . . A monotony that's anything but monotonous. A beginning again that's always a new beginning. A visible reserve, as Valéry said: *"Masse de calme et visible reserve"* [A body of calm and visible reserve]. But my Gabriela, who with a smile would call the sea her husband, loved it so much that she had to call the earth bourgeois, a brutish element without a soul. Her fanaticism was thus always a blindness produced by an excess of love.

I said before that Gabriela suffered from a certain Americanist fanaticism, but she could also quite suddenly and clearly see our defects and denounce them. On the subject of Nazism, she wrote to me:

Criollo *Nazism is based in fear, more than anything else, and then corruption. The ideology thing comes at the end. Maybe that's why Zweig believed that we writers can do nothing. Because it doesn't have to do with ideas, at least not among our poor Americans, I think. The middle class — the same one, in France, that talked its head off to make a bit of a living — throws everything to the devil, and that's the famous class of the intelligentsia. And the people, I don't believe that they'll do anything but want "the thing to thunder," without understanding what "the thing" is and how it's going "to thunder" and with what result. The same old story. The "prophesiers" can still keep on saying total foolishness.* [G.36]

The situation of our Latin American countries worried her greatly. I intended to visit her when she was the [Chilean] consul in Brazil, but something prevented it just when she needed my presence most. Later, she wrote me from California:

I'm grieved by the disappointment that you're not coming. I wanted not only to see you, but to converse with you a long time about what's happening in your land, in mine, and in the other ones. *Letters don't leave me with any sensation of communicating with anyone. At the end of the prewar period, I remember that I wrote Mallea a letter telling him that it was necessary to reach an agreement, even among four or five people, about what had to be written, and that the lack of communication would end up damaging all of us. He didn't answer me with even a word. . . .*

What is happening to your land, as it takes on a Com[munist] color (and those who believe in totalitarianisms have to take it), has already happened to my country and, some say, to Bolivia and to Paraguay. When everything is threatened, asphyxia will drown all of us who've remained silent. . . .

Without coming up with a solution about what has to be done — what has to be said — I mean, to be written — and in the state of weight loss and tiredness that I've come to, I've only concerned myself with saving some drafts of verses and with writing verses, because prose, in me, always leans toward something that resembles social pedagogy. [G.46]

When I complained about an offense, she answered:

Unamuno, who knew the inner workings of his people, used to say that the force of envy was stronger than the instinct for preservation in the Spanish animal. In these things you shouldn't see anything but that putrid root of the race, with which one has to live, as one lives with a damaged organ, Votoya. Don't look at the personal aspect, it's collective. You are paying for having many gifts — it's the ransom that's required by the gods. But pay, aside from that, with your disdain, at least with your why should I care *about lesser types. And horseflies pester even the oxen.*

I'm a sermon giver *today. You don't like sermonizing or emphasis, because both things are prophetic. But I believe in prophetic speech . . . still. I believe in Cassandra, I believe in Electra and in the charming Antigone. Reread them and accept them, even though they aren't Christian. For me, they're more alive than the Intellectual Cooperation and its choice group of old men . . .* [G.27]

Out of the disorder of her letters without dates, written in pencil, I'm still not able to establish a chronological order. When I would read them, I'd come upon the same prophetic note — the gift she so admired in Cassandra — although undoubtedly in letters that were distant from one another. Gabriela saw what was far off better than what was nearby. She interpreted it more accurately. From the Chilean consulate in Niteroi, she wrote with terrible heartache following the defeats of Holland, Belgium, and France during the war with Germany:

. . . I've made four significant efforts to see what women and Latin American writers can do TOGETHER *with what's about to happen to us, three of them*

in your country. They haven't answered with a single word. Listen, it's the
same as always: everyone believes that they'll escape on their own . . .

I send you a big hug and my desire to talk with you ten days and ten nights,
when it occurs to you to come visit. . . . [G.31]

Concerning the rumors that reached her about me, some commenting
on my supposed Fascist tendencies (invented by the Communists),
others talking about my supposed Communist inclinations (invented
by the Fascists — this is truly an era of confusion), Gabriela wrote to
me:

I didn't believe it . . . Per cause. Fascism will befall America, vertically, if it
wins in Spain. . . . The danger for us, my Victoria, is truly mortal. [G.8]

And talking about a Spanish woman friend of ours:

I hope that she doesn't take me for a Communist. There are, as yet, some two
or three things that separate me from that party. They seem like trifles, but
each one goes to the center of the Earth . . . One is its 100 percent atheism, stu-
pid and closed off. But I don't see where Fascism could be the lesser of two evils,
I don't see it.

. . . I didn't accept going to Argentina, and it turns out that I'm going to a
Fascist country again. I always feel a vague animosity toward that country of
yours, for its neglect of the most wretched America, the abandonment of our
global problems, the "what does it matter to me" of a happy country. [G.8]

With regard to the approximately 200,000 Spanish children who left
Spain during the civil war and almost all went to England and Russia,
which was very painful to Gabriela, she insisted that it would have
been better to leave them with their own kind:

Our America, blinded by political fanaticism, has crossed its arms. . . . And
those children go to England and to Russia, as if a continent half theirs and
with their flesh and blood didn't exist! [G.9]

I repeat: Gabriela donated the sales of her second book of poems,
Tala, to benefit Spanish children. The book was printed gratis by
SUR, which doubtless contributed to my reputation as a Communist
sympathizer. In those days, Gabriela was furious with her beloved
America and with the lack of understanding and the close-minded-
ness of one of her compatriots. "I know," she wrote to me, "that so-and-
so won't understand anything about me; not a single thing in that regard [she was referring to politics]."

More and more, Vict., I'm horrified by the tropical and nontropical misery of
our countries. At least nineteen of them. And by now this is a kind of obsession

in me. And I feel that almost all we creoles are condemned now and for all time because of that: because of what we see day by day and let run and run like the water of our rivers, but a water that was filthy. [G.70]

In reality, this allowing things we cannot condone or accept to run on and on is very familiar to us here, and Gabriela, seized with panic by the gravity of this attitude that she called *criolla*, was in despair over it. I call this our sin of omission . . . I don't know why, in general, a sin of omission is not considered serious. And those who sin through taking action make the most of it.

In 1945 when the war was winding down, Gabriela wrote me on the day of her birthday, which was also mine. On that date, she tended to send letters that seemed somewhat like a last will or like advice from a deathbed:

Now, Votoya, steady your arm for the feces of war, that is, so that the sewers — or pipes — don't overflow and toss the stopped-up and fermented filth into the streets and plazas. Retain for this . . . your arm, your strong voice, your instinct for deep cleanliness, your brain, your soul, and even more, your spirit. I hug you. God keep you. [G.43]

And so it happened. I was in fact going to need the protection of divine Providence. Gabriela, far away, prayed for me. With that unconscious and involuntary humor of hers, she wrote to me while I was going through disagreeable times (I went from a material jail to another form of jail: that of being locked up in my country for lack of a passport and a certificate of good conduct):

Don't laugh at me, now. I have — in me — an almost childlike devotion, a most ingenuous faith in San Antonio, the Italian, that is, of Padua. I stay away from bothering the saints, but every time that something presses on me, I ask him, my Italian. — It seems that the Spanish saints have never protected me. [G.76]

In fact, I did laugh and I asked her why, given that she was so American and so linguistically partial to Golden Age Spain, she didn't pray to St. Theresa de Cepeda or to Santa Rosa de Lima. What was the meaning of becoming Italian in her communications with heaven, where most certainly she would experience a much more extended residency than in her terrestrial consulates or her valley of tears in Elqui? What sense did that infidelity make in the extraterrestrial zone that borders on death? Death which, as a faithful old Basque maid of my mother's used to say, was lifelong. Gabriela may have turned to Saint Anthony of Padua for her personal and terrestrial problems, but in doing so, she was entering an impersonal, supraterrestrial zone that was infinitely more important than our own. And upon entering that zone, what was she doing? Abandoning America and Spain, but without any intention of celestial internationalization. For after all, she was proclaiming the superiority of Italy in regard to saints and declaring herself partial to an Italian saint.

I would say these kinds of things to her to defuse the drama of the moment, especially vis-à-vis my own situation, which she considered more tragic than I did. I understood that my confinement was only one of the many injustices (and one of the least serious) in the flood of injustices that was inundating the whole world, not just Argentina. But Gabriela grieved for me as if she were my mother or my sister. She followed the developments step by step and begged me to come live and work with her. When she learned that one night I found crosses painted on the entrance to my house, she wrote me:

That thing about the doors being marked — copied from the age-old persecution of the Jews — sent chills down my spine. That was publicized in Europe, despite the Argentine money that circulates among the journalists. . . . Come live with me, I beg you.[3] [G.52]

She despaired when she didn't receive letters with regularity, when, for whatever reasons, letters had been lost:

When I read these and other things to Doris, I lose all hope and am more and more taken with the idea that we're rolling, like stones in the cordillera, toward an end, a place that exists and that we don't know and where we're all going to end up, just like that, not knowing where and when.

I've always been a pessimist, Vict., so you can imagine the point I've come to. I'm writing you from that condition but at the same time with a seemingly brave desire to see someone who's confronting the calamity . . . [G.60]

During my imprisonment and the years I spent without a passport and thus unable to leave the country unless I tried to escape — and I never believed I should do that — Gabriela wrote or telegraphed the then president Perón, who apparently didn't answer her. Gabriela was the third [*sic*: first] Latin American to win a Nobel Prize, but evidently that wasn't sufficient recommendation to merit a response.

When I got out of Buen Pastor prison, I received a cable from Gabriela saying: "Finally, I can breathe." She wanted me to come right away to her house on Long Island to help her — or so she maintained — finish her famous poem about the plants of America. She made up the story that I knew the names of plants better than she did. But her wish was never fulfilled. I couldn't get a passport. After the coup, for personal reasons, several months passed before I could leave for the

United States. When I got to her great friend Doris Dana's house, Gabriela was already in another world. The dike of time had been broken for her, and she would mix up the past with the present. Her physical presence only seemed to underscore her absence. We would never again really see each other on this bourgeois earth, as she called it, even though I held her hands in mine.

I now prefer to remember her in the happy times that we spent in Mar del Plata. Those days when our little notes without any literary value would go from one floor to the other of my wooden house, notes that referred to meals, to our sleeping habits, to the temperature, the good or bad weather, and our desire to go look at the sea. For example:

I slept, not soundly all in a block, but I slept. And I awoke without knowing where I was, until the face of Victoria came to me, and the peaches and the figs arrived. [G.12]

The peaches and figs of that year! I see them now, chosen especially for her each morning and placed in a little basket between hydrangea leaves. Those earth-bound mornings, those sea-filled mornings that I'll never again share with Gabriela.

June 28, 1957

[*Testimonios VI*, 59–82; trans. Doris Meyer.]

1. A reference to Cuban author-in-exile and revolutionary José Martí's famous essay "Nuestra América" (Mexico, 1891), a manifesto for all American republics to learn to know themselves, not imitate foreign ways, and show their essential worth to the world in order to be duly recognized.
2. VO twice uses the word "raza" in this paragraph, which can be translated equally as "race" or "people." In Spanish, this word does not necessarily have the same connotation as in English. Rather, it refers to an ethnic group or cultural affiliation, much in the way the Chicanos refer to *"mi raza"* as "my people."
3. This last sentence is not in G.52. However, similar sentiments are repeated in many of GM's letters at the time.

ꙮ

[The following are Ocampo's responses to interview questions that were found on typed pages among her papers and carry no date. Ocampo did not like giving interviews, but she would often respond to written queries. This interview, the source of which has not been found, took place some time after Mistral's death.]

"VICTORIA OCAMPO ON HER FRIENDSHIP
WITH GABRIELA MISTRAL"

1. In 1925, we tried but didn't manage to meet. She had written me. I answered. I met her in person during a visit to Madrid [in 1934] when she was the Chilean consul in Spain. María de Maeztu took me to her house. I've written elsewhere about the three reproaches she greeted me with: First: Why had I been born in Buenos Aires? (For her, with the exception of certain northern provinces, Argentina wasn't *her* America). Second: Why was I such a Francophile? Third: Why hadn't I become friends with Alfonsina Storni?

Astonished, I looked at that woman who had a special kind of beauty — the beauty of a quiet statue with the gift of speech. Her sacerdotal quality struck me right away. She would say surprising, sometimes irrational things (like those three reproaches) without blinking an eye, with great assurance and a mask that seemed to be her face. Then suddenly, a smile would humanize her. But she would smile at curious times, often when the moment had passed in which a smile should have appeared to respond to something. I noticed this habit of the delayed smile right from the beginning, but to myself, without articulating it. It was a sensation, not an observation. Later I thought about it and began to look for an explanation, which I haven't found yet.

That day I was petrified, not knowing how to respond to that type of offensive. But the sympathy Gabriela felt for me was so evident that she could have reproached me for Alfonsina's suicide and the disastrous results of the first founding of Buenos Aires and I wouldn't have been irritated. What mattered to me more was what I sensed behind the words without connection to reality: reproaches that clearly weren't justified, as I wasn't responsible for my birth or the education I received. Insofar as Alfonsina was concerned, I saw her once and knew nothing about her life. Alfonsina was a writer, and I was a nobody.

Gabriela seduced and disconcerted me. I saw that she saw what she imagined, not so-called reality. And what she imagined she took as gospel. Made up.

Was she difficult? Perhaps haughty, in her way. Timid, without being so. She wasn't easy to define.

2. Our friendship began in earnest when she came to Buenos Aires and I invited her to spend a while in Mar del Plata. I found out that she had arrived there when her secretary telephoned me from the station to announce (without prior notice) that they were waiting there for someone to come and get them. It was pouring, and there was no

taxi around, and they didn't know for sure where I lived. Of course, I sent a car right away. I was in bed with a bad cold at the time. How those two women managed to make their way around and land in Mar del Plata with such vague ideas of where they and I were is something I've never figured out. But Gabriela had an angel on her shoulder, as they say, and she would find a secretary of one sort or another wherever she set foot.

A half hour after I sent the car, Gabriela was sitting next to my bed. She talked to me not only about the rain, but about the earth, heaven, and the human condition. My fever went up, and the next day Gabriela wrote me that she felt responsible for my being worse and she would punish herself that day by not coming into my room.

3. I think she felt at home right away. She was never distant with me. She would talk to me about everything, except that episode of neuralgia in her youth: the suicide of the man she loved. Since I didn't like to force anyone's hand, I never asked her anything about it. I let her tell me what she really wanted to. One day, however, I wrote her:[1] "Lucía [sic] Godoy, we're losing time. I want to write something about your history. To do it, I need information and facts. Why don't you talk to me chronologically about your past life?" She replied (I have the letter, but don't have the time to look for it) that I should stop this foolishness because there would be time enough to write about her when her bones were bleaching. I answered that she was crazy, and that when her bones were bleaching, she wouldn't be able to tell me anything and I didn't like secondhand versions. That's the way it went. I didn't want to insist because it seemed to me that she feared reawakening tremendous anxieties that she was never able to digest; with the suicide of Yin Yin, they would become more acute. She later wrote to me about this suicide and talked to me about it at length, mixing concrete facts with things she imagined.

4. I especially remember a night in Washington. Gabriela was returning after having received the Nobel Prize in Sweden. I was arriving in New York from Buenos Aires, very tired. An urgent telegram was waiting for me at the hotel. Gabriela wanted me to go immediately to Washington. I left the next day, grumbling about how Gabriela was spoiled. She came to meet me at the station, but we missed each other. It had to do with rhythms: Gabriela lived in andante and I in presto, or allegro vivace (although I may not always be vivacious). I got to the appointed house before she did, and I waited for her. When she arrived, she announced that that very night there was a big dinner in her honor and I was invited. "Invited, but not consulted, Lucía Godoy," I said. "I would do anything for you but go to a dinner tonight." She tried to convince me that this would be bad form, and I

to convince her that she was a despot. We agreed that after eating, she would come to my hotel at eleven. She was punctual, and she stayed until four or five in the morning talking about Yin Yin. She assured me that she conversed daily with him and that Yin Yin was with her. . . . She said this to me with that tranquil face that didn't jibe with the frightful words she was pronouncing with the edges of her mouth turned down. Her tale was so convincing and dramatic that it made me live what she was living. Gabriela spoke admirably and with absolute naturalness. Her language (because she had her own language) was always expressive. I listened to her in silence.

That night I was so struck by the depth of her despair, her obsession, her not wanting to let go of her beloved Yin Yin, that I was trembling. I was filled with superstitious fear, very unlike me. I looked inside the closets, under the bed, lit all the lamps, and didn't sleep. I don't know how I got into such a state of contagion. Gabriela had created a ghost and had left it with me for a few hours.

5. I don't know. I believe she preferred, as I did, to talk *tête-à-tête*.

Gabriela spent a happy time at my house in Mar del Plata (and then in Buenos Aires). In those years, a lot of children would visit my house, and they entertained her. Two children of my Japanese chauffeur, two that belonged to my housekeeper, one of my maid's, another of my sister's butler, and the daughter of a bath attendant, a darling creature whom I took to live with me. They were all happy and lovely. Also, Gabriela was surrounded by trees, flowers, birds. The ocean was nearby and affection everywhere.

Early on the seventh of April of that year, I went to say good morning to her before she got up. It was our birthday. I found her sitting on the bed writing with a pencil, as was her custom. She was writing the *"Recado"* [Message to VO in Argentina] that she published in *Tala*. There was nothing she needed to thank me for. She loved me, I think, as much as I did her. That was more than enough to repay me for what little I could do for her when the occasion arose.

I don't ascribe any literary position to anyone. The enchantment of certain of Gabriela's poems is always, for me, what it was then. To read them is to hear her. Her entire being was impregnated with that indescribable atmosphere that poetry creates, which is poetry, not only in the pages of a book but in a living person.

V.O.

[Translated by Doris Meyer]

---

1. It was Victoria's custom, which Gabriela also practiced while in VO's house, to write spontaneous notes from room to room when she wasn't with her guests. I experienced this myself when staying with Victoria on several occasions in the 1970s [DM].

Chronology

1889: April 7. Lucila de María del Perpetuo Socorro Godoy Alcayaga born in Vicuña, Chile. Her parents are Petronila Alcayaga Rojas, age forty-five, seamstress and singer, and Jerónimo Godoy Villanueva, age thirty-one, ex-seminarian, unemployed schoolteacher, and singer-poet-songwriter. She has a half-sister, Emelina, sixteen years older than herself, a schoolteacher who supports the family after Jerónimo Godoy leaves, in 1892, to seek his fortune elsewhere.

1890: April 7. Ramona Victoria Epifanía Rufina Ocampo born in Buenos Aires. Her parents are Ramona Máxima Aguirre, age twenty-three, and Manuel Silvio Cecilio Ocampo Regueira, age thirty, architectural engineer. The oldest of six girls, Victoria is named for her great-aunt and great-grandmother. Because she is the oldest and there are no male children, Victoria eventually inherits much of the family fortune.

1896–1897: VO makes her first trip to Europe with family, where she encounters the languages and cultures of France and of England, the study of which would be continued under governesses in Argentina.

1901: VO and sister Angélica (one year younger) together produce a magazine in French, which lasts for three issues. Angélica would continue to be a helpmate to Victoria in later years but never took an official role in any publishing ventures.

1904–1909: Provincial newspapers publish writing by Lucila Godoy under the pseudonym "Gabriela Mistral." Her writings are attacked as "incoherent ravings." The normal school in the local provincial city of La Serena bars the young woman's entrance. Although her formal schooling has ended, Lucila Godoy finds work as an aide and schoolteacher in various rural schools. In 1908, her work is included in an anthology of local poets.

1906: VO begins an intimate correspondence in French with Delfina Bunge, an older Argentine friend, which continues for four years. Letters show VO's concern that patriarchal customs will inhibit her intellectual and spiritual development.

1908–1911: Second extended stay in Europe for the Ocampo family. VO takes classes at the Sorbonne and meets writers and artists. VO's beauty at the time is captured in striking portraits by Paul Helleu and Dagnan Bouveret (See Meyer, *Against the Wind and the Tide*, for illustrations).

Argentina emerges as one of the leading nations of South America due to notable economic and social progress.

1911: Having passed equivalency exams, GM is appointed as a teacher of Hygiene and Drawing in the Girls' High School in the desert mining city of Antofagasta, Chile, where she contributes to the local newspaper, using the pseudonym "Gabriela Mistral" almost exclusively. She joins the local Theosophist Lodge and begins publishing in the Santiago magazine *Sucesos*. Her father, whom she hasn't seen for some years, dies and is buried in an unmarked grave.

The revolt in Mexico leads to the overthrow of the dictatorship of Porfirio Díaz.

1912: GM is appointed teacher of Spanish and History in the Girls' High School in Los Andes, Chile, a half-day trip from Santiago. She publishes her work in various national magazines and initiates correspondences with leading writers and educators, including Pedro Prado, Rubén Darío, Amado Nervo, Eduardo Barrios, and Inés Echeverría. She befriends a local landowner, Pedro Aguirre Cerda, who later became president of Chile.

VO marries Bernardo (Monaco) de Estrada after a short courtship. They honeymoon in Europe; within a year they begin to lead separate lives.

1913: VO meets Julián Martínez in Rome. They become lovers after her return from Europe in 1914. VO seeks spiritual refuge in a wide range of reading.

1914: December. GM wins first prize in a national poetry contest, Juegos Florales, held in Santiago, for her "Sonetos de la muerte" (Sonnets of death). GM engages in what becomes a passionate correspondence with Manuel Magallanes Moure, a poet who is one of the three judges.

Argentina remains neutral in World War I.

1916: VO meets the Spanish philosopher José Ortega y Gasset during his first lecture tour in Buenos Aires. They begin a friendship and correspondence. Through Ortega, VO becomes aware of the expressive power of the Spanish language, but her immersion in French is such that she feels inadequate using Spanish in intellectual contexts.

1917: Substantial selections from GM's verses and poetic prose are printed in the anthology *Selva lírica* and in school textbooks circulating throughout Chile, Mexico, and Argentina. She publishes glosses on the work of the Bengali poet Rabindranath Tagore. The magazine *Sucesos*, formerly friendly to her work, prints two parodies of her poems.

1918: In April, GM becomes director of the Girls' High School in the far southern city of Punta Arenas (Chilean Patagonia). While in Punta Arenas, she founds and contributes to a literary magazine, *Mireya*, and begins corresponding with the Argentine writer Alfonsina Storni.

1920: In March, GM becomes director of the Girls' High school in Temuco, Chile, where she meets and encourages the future poet Pablo Neruda. VO's first article is published in *La Nación*. Entitled "Babel," it is a meditation on the equality and inequality of human beings.

1921: Although GM is appointed director of Girls' High School #6 in Santiago in May, a politically motivated controversy over her qualifications ensues. GM publishes the controversial "Poemas de las madres" in the Costa Rican magazine *El repertorio americano*, edited by Joaquín García Monge.

VO writes a commentary on Dante's *Divine Comedy*, published in 1924 as *De Francesca a Beatrice* by Ortega y Gasset's Revista de Occidente Press in Spain, with a prologue by Ortega.

1922: In June, GM leaves Chile for Mexico to work for the Mexican Ministry of Education under Obregón and Vasconcelos, having received a six-month commission from the Chilean government to study the organization and founding of libraries in postrevolutionary Mexico. Crowds of children and schoolteachers greet her in Mexico City. While working in Mexico, she meets Jaime Torres Bodet, Palma Guillén, Diego Rivera, Daniel Cosío Villegas, Carlos Pellicer, and Alfaro Siqueiros, among others. The commission is extended another eighteen months.

VO makes a definitive break with Monaco Estrada. GM publishes her first volume of poetry, *Desolación*, with the Instituto de las Españas in New York, directed by Federico de Onís.

Benito Mussolini seizes power in Italy.

1923: The Mexican Ministry of Education publishes GM's anthology *Lecturas para mujeres* in an edition of 20,000 copies, for use in the schools. It includes several selections by Alfonso Reyes, Mexican author and diplomat, whose writings on America GM admires and with whom she will correspond for more than fifty years. In Barcelona, the Editorial Cervantes publishes a seventy-five-page selection of her work in the series Las Mejores Poesías (No. 45) with a biographical note and commentary by Manuel de Montoliú. She begins work on a series about St. Francis of Assisi. GM's correspondence from Mexico appears in Santiago's premier newspaper, *El Mercurio*. A second edition of *Desolación*, with a foreword by Pedro Prado, is published in Chile.

1924: In May, GM leaves Mexico with her friend Laura Rodig for Europe. En route, GM makes her first visit to the United States, where she speaks in Washington and New York. GM travels around Europe from June to December, and she has a volume of her children's poetry, *Ternura*, published by Saturnino Calleja in Madrid, after she discovers that a clandestine version has been published in Uruguay.

1925: Mistral returns from Europe to Chile with Laura Rodig in January. In March, GM retires after twenty years of service to the Chilean public schools and begins receiving a pension. Although she initially lives in Santiago, she moves to La Serena in May, where she purchases a house and plans to open a school.

VO publishes an article on Mahatma Gandhi in *La Nación*. Then, from November to January, VO hosts Bengali poet and Nobel laureate Rabindranath Tagore, who has taken sick in Buenos Aires on his way to Peru. She is deeply influenced by Indian poetry and philosophy, and he writes poetry inspired by her.

LETTERS, PART I

1926: Correspondence between GM and VO begins when GM travels to Europe by way of Argentina at the beginning of the year. In Paris, Mistral will work for the Paris-based Institute for Intellectual Cooperation. Other members of the Institute include Paul Valéry, Thornton Wilder, and GM's Mexican friend Palma Guillén. Sometime during this year, perhaps in February, GM meets a young man who claims to be her half brother and who apparently entrusts her with an infant, Juan Miguel Godoy. The third edition of GM's *Desolación* is printed in Santiago, with much of the children's poetry and lullabies removed.

VO meets the Spanish author and educator María de Maeztu, who had studied under Ortega and is in Buenos Aires for a lecture tour. They discuss feminist ideas, education in the Americas, and, undoubtedly, Gabriela Mistral, whom Maeztu had met in Madrid in 1924.

1927: GM attends conferences in Italy on education and the defense of children.

VO meets Alfonso Reyes following his appointment as Mexico's ambassador to Argentina. They have many mutual friends in France, Spain, and the Americas and begin a lifelong correspondence.

1928–1929: GM writes numerous biographical essays on figures such as Thomas Hardy, Augusto Sandino, Pedro Salinas, Napoleon Bonaparte, Saint Vincent de Paul, Camilo Henríquez. She travels extensively, visiting Corsica, Madrid, and Marseilles, but by the end of 1928, she has established a residence in a borrowed house in Avignon.

VO travels to Europe for the first time in fifteen years. She meets many writers and artists, among them Jean Cocteau, Jacques Lacan, Le Corbusier, Pierre Drieu la Rochelle, Paul Valéry, Adrienne Monnier, and Sergei Eisenstein.

1929: In March, GM, working at the Society of Nations in Paris, writes to VO hoping she will visit and mentions their mutual friend María de Maeztu (G.2). GM's mother dies in July while GM is living in southern France with her infant nephew. At the end of the year, GM's pension, her only source of regular income, is suspended as part of an austerity measure by the Ibáñez government. Leaving Juan Miguel Godoy with Palma Guillén in Switzerland, she travels to northern Italy in November, where the Chilean diplomat Carlos Errázuriz and his wife, Carmela Echenique, discover her living in shared rooms, in a pension; they invite her to stay with them and she accepts.

Through Eduardo Mallea, VO meets the U.S. author Waldo Frank, who is in Buenos Aires on a lecture tour of South America espousing a vision of hemispheric spiritual regeneration. She, Mallea, and Frank discuss the possibility of VO's starting a literary review dedicated to promoting a new American spirit.

The last Allied troops leave the Rhineland five years earlier than was established in the Treaty of Versailles timetable. Wall Street crash occurs in October and has worldwide economic and political impact of varying kinds. Sandino leads a popular uprising in Nicaragua. Within a year, military coups take place in Argentina and Brazil, and civil liberties are suppressed. Gandhi begins a civil disobedience campaign to put an end to British rule in India. The dictatorship of Primo de Rivera in Spain comes to an end.

1930: GM is now a regular correspondent for most of the major newspapers of the Spanish-speaking world, including *La Nación* in Buenos Aires, *A.B.C.* in Madrid, *El Tiempo* in Bogotá, *El Universal* in Caracas, and *El Mercurio* in Santiago. Among her many essays published this year are pieces about Domingo Sarmiento and Emily Brontë, both figures important to VO as well. In October, GM travels to the United States, where she gives classes in Latin American literature and pre-Columbian civilization at Barnard College, Columbia University in New York City.

VO is back in Europe testing her idea for a literary journal with friends there (Ortega, Drieu la Rochelle, Ernest Ansermet, and others), and she is encouraged to make the journal a cultural bridge between the Americas and Europe. VO visits Waldo Frank in New York City to continue these discussions. While there she also meets Alfred Stieglitz at his studio, "An American Place," and is inspired by his modernist vision of America.

1931: GM teaches and lectures at Vassar College, Poughkeepsie, NY. She visits the University of Puerto Rico in May, Santo Domingo and Panama in August, and Costa Rica and Guatemala in September, where she receives an honorary doctorate in the latter country and gives a speech, "On the Unity of Culture," about the importance of the university and pedagogy in shaping culture in the Americas. She visits San Salvador in October, then returns to Europe to join Palma Guillén and Juan Miguel Godoy.

VO publishes the first issue of her literary magazine *Sur*, whose editorial board includes authors and artists from Latin America, Europe, and the United States. VO's father dies in January.

For two weeks in Chile, the nation is declared a Socialist republic. In September, the Chilean Education Ministry contacts Mistral, asking her to become director of Primary Education. She declines. Chile's disastrous economy and governmental instability leads the navy to rebel. In Spain, a republic is set up, dominated by liberals and Socialists.

1932: GM is named Chilean consul in Naples, Italy, but resigns in November, after three months, explaining that Mussolini's Fascist government doesn't recognize women as consuls. She publishes articles about Waldo Frank, about Eugenio María de Hostos, about the Curies, and another entitled "The Type of the American Indian." In December, she leaves for another lecture tour of Central America.

VO's friend Pierre Drieu la Rochelle visits Buenos Aires for a lecture tour.

Antonio de Olivera Salazar becomes premier of Portugal, a post he holds for the next thirty-six years.

1933: GM, in Puerto Rico from February through mid-June, gives conferences on Hispanism.

VO founds SUR publishing house and begins bringing out books in Spanish and in translation, eventually including authors such as D. H. Lawrence, Aldous Huxley, C. G. Jung, Virginia Woolf, T. E. Lawrence, Albert Camus, William Faulkner, and Graham Greene.

Hitler, elected Chancellor in Germany, assumes office on January 30 and sets up a Nazi dictatorship. Japan leaves the League of Nations after that body condemns its annexation of Manchuria. In October, Germany leaves the League of Nations. In the United States, Franklin Delano Roosevelt sets up a "New Deal" program of social and economic reforms. In Cuba, an army revolt under General Fulgencio Batista makes him the leading power in the country for the next twenty-five years.

1934: In January, GM is appointed Chilean consul in Spain. The post carries no salary aside from sporadic commissions for bureaucratic work. She continues to make her living from journalism. By late spring, she moves to Madrid with Juan Miguel Godoy and Palma Guillén. In May, Pablo Neruda arrives as Chilean consul in Barcelona.

In the fall, VO and Eduardo Mallea give a series of lectures in Italy sponsored by the Italian Inter-University Institute. VO accepts their invitation to meet Mussolini, with whom she discusses the role of women in the Italian state. That same fall she meets Virginia Woolf in London, introduced by her friend Aldous Huxley. In December, María de Maeztu brings VO to meet GM at GM's house in Madrid.

1935: In January, GM follows up the meeting with VO with a letter full of admiration and advice: "We ask nothing of you, only *a presence*, as complete as possible, within the American movement" (G.3). After another, similar letter, VO and GM exchange photos (G.4). By the middle of the year, a group of European writers, including Miguel de Unamuno, Romain Rolland, Georges Duhamel, and Maurice Maeterlinck, petitions the Chilean government for GM to be given more stable employment. In September, GM is made Chilean consul, with the right to choose her own residence, by a special act of the Chilean legislature. In October, she is forced to leave Madrid, however, after a furor erupts in Santiago following the unauthorized publication of a private letter in which GM is critical of Spain. GM moves to Lisbon, Portugal, and her correspondence with VO and other Latin American writers intensifies.

VO's *Testimonios I* is published in Madrid by Ortega's Revista de Occidente Press. VO's mother dies in December.

Governmental reforms in India again fail to satisfy nationalist demands. Italian forces under Mussolini invade Abyssinia to satisfy Fascist imperialist ambitions. The League of Nations fails to intervene successfully. In September, German Jews are stripped of rights by Nuremberg Race Laws.

1936: Argentine Women's Union is founded by VO and her friends María Rosa Oliver and Susana Larguía. VO is its first president. The union successfully combats a proposed congressional bill intended to restrict women's civil rights. Repeated efforts between 1935 and 1942 to obtain women's suffrage in Argentina are rejected by the legislature. Fascist organizations in Argentina become more active, uniting in a "National Front". The International PEN Club meeting takes place in Buenos Aires. Igor Stravinsky asks VO to do the recitation for "Perséphone" at the Teatro Colon.

The Spanish leader Calvo Sotelo is killed. In July, General Francisco Franco in Spanish Morocco leads the army to rebellion, beginning the Spanish Civil War; intellectuals such as Federico García Lorca and Ramiro de Maeztu are among the first victims (G.6). On October 1, Franco is declared the head of the Spanish state. Hitler remilitarizes the Rhineland, and Mussolini proclaims the Rome-Berlin Axis.

1937: Argentina and Mexico begin accepting refugees from Spain (G.7). GM travels to Paris to take part in a conference of intellectuals in support of the Spanish Republic. Among other people, she meets José Bergamín and Jacques and Raissa Maritain. She asks VO to include her in the women's rights campaign of the Argentine Women's Union (G.8) and expresses her concern about Fascism's possible triumph in the Americas. Later, she asks VO to publish *Tala* on behalf of war orphans in Spain (G.9). By August, GM travels to Brazil (G.10); she urges VO to visit Jacques and Raissa Maritain in Paris.

1938: After visits to Brazil and Uruguay, GM goes on to Argentina, where she spends eight days with VO in Mar del Plata at her home "Villa Victoria" (G.11–13) and then gives several readings in Buenos Aires while also staying in VO's residence there (G.14–17). VO's affair with Eduardo Mallea is drawing to a stormy conclusion. In July, GM's book of poetry *Tala* is published by VO's Editorial SUR, with the proceeds dedicated to aid refugee children of the Spanish Civil War. During the ensuing weeks in Chile, GM is concerned about the explosive political situation and she reports, too, on publishing the book there (G.19–22). GM travels north to the United States, visiting Peru, Ecuador, and Cuba en route (G.24–25). GM visits Pedro Albizu Campos, the Puerto Rican nationalist leader, jailed in Atlanta (G.25). In October, GM's friend Pedro Aguirre Cerda is elected to the presidency at the head of a center-left coalition, the Popular Front. GM turns down appointments to Central America and to Uruguay and, accompanied by Connie Saleva, sails instead to southern France, where she plans to help refugees (G.25).

Austria is annexed by Germany in March. In April the Spanish Republic falls. European powers meet in Munich to discuss German claims in Czechoslovakia, but they fail to restrain Hitler.

1939: VO travels to Europe. With her sister Angélica, VO meets GM's boat in France (G.26). VO and GM travel together to Nice, where GM establishes a consulate. VO brings the French sociologist and writer Roger Caillois to Buenos Aires for a lecture tour in June. He stays in Argentina until 1945 because of the war in Europe. In December, the Ecuadorian writer Adela Velasco writes to Chilean President Pedro Aguirre Cerda to propose GM for the Nobel Prize; he orders the Chilean diplomatic service to see that her works are made available in various languages for the Swedish Academy.

Germans occupy Prague in May, and Japan conquers most of eastern China. Nazi-Soviet nonaggression pact is signed in August. By September, France, Britain, Australia, and New Zealand declare war on Germany. The Soviets invade Poland, and Warsaw surrenders to the Nazis. Soviets attack Finland in November.

LETTERS, PART 2

1940: In June, Germans bomb and enter Paris. Petain becomes French prime minister while Britain recognizes Charles DeGaulle as the leader of the free French. Italy declares war on Britain and France; Norway surrenders to the Nazis. The Battle of Britain begins in July.

VO is a co-founder of Argentine Action, an organization formed to counteract Nazi-Fascist infiltration in Argentina. She is unstinting in her support of and economic aid to refugees of Nazi aggression in Europe.

With Europe engulfed in war, GM moves with her nephew, Yin Yin, and secretary, Connie Saleva, to Brazil, where she lives first in Rio (G.30), then establishes a consulate in Niteroi (G.31), then another in Petrópolis. Throughout this year and the next, GM writes VO expressing concerns about France (G.32–34). She is increasingly preoccupied by the situation of friends stranded in Europe and the prospective influence of Fascism in Latin America.

1941: VO's *Testimonios II* is published by Editorial SUR. In the middle of the year, the magazine *Lettres Françaises*, edited by Roger Caillois, begins publication, financed by VO. It becomes an important voice for free French writers during the war, and a medium for European writers to learn about Latin American writers such as Borges.

In June, Germany attacks the Soviet Union. In December, the Japanese bomb Pearl Harbor and the United States declares war on Japan.

1942: VO's biographical study *338171 T.E. (Lawrence de Arabia)* is published by SUR. Waldo Frank, on another lecture tour, visits GM in Brazil, where she has bought a house (G.35–37). When Waldo Frank visits Fascist-leaning Buenos Aires, he is attacked by anti-Semitic thugs. VO and María Rosa Oliver nurse him back to health when others shun his company. The end of this year, December 23, marks the first extant letter from VO to GM (V.1).

In November, Germany and Italy invade unoccupied Vichy, France. Conservative government in Argentina refuses to break with Axis powers after attack on Pearl Harbor.

1943: In August, GM's teenaged nephew, Juan Miguel Godoy (Yin Yin), commits suicide under mysterious circumstances, and GM suffers a total physical and emotional collapse (G.41).

From May to November, VO travels in the United States on a Guggenheim fellowship (G.44). She returns via Mexico, where she visits Alfonso Reyes (V.1, V.3).

In July, Mussolini falls but returns to power in September. A military coup in Argentina installs a pro-Axis government.

1944: VO sends Roger Caillois to visit GM, in deep mourning, in Brazil (G.42). VO also publishes French translations of GM's poetry and invites GM to visit her in Argentina (V.5–6). In June, the Allies enter Rome. D-Day landings are followed by the liberation of Paris in August.

1945: U.S. President Franklin D. Roosevelt dies in April, and Adolf Hitler commits suicide in Berlin. VO's friend Drieu la Rochelle, who collaborated with the German occupation, commits suicide in Paris (V.7; G.44). May brings V-E Day to Europe. In August, the United States drops atomic bombs on Japan, and Japan surrenders. Juan Domingo Perón becomes head of the Argentine military junta in October, and marries Eva Duarte several days later.

In December, GM becomes the first Nobel laureate in literature from Latin America. In late November, she travels from Brazil to Sweden to accept the prize "as the direct voice of the poets of my race." VO writes a celebratory essay, "GM and the Nobel Prize," in which she says, "to hear Gabriela speak of her continent is to hear a branch blossom — if that entertainment were destined for the ear — when the sun leans on it with all its strength" (Meyer, *Against the Wind and the Tide,* 250).

1946: Traveling from Sweden, GM visits England, France, Italy, and Wash-ing-gton, D.C. VO returns to Europe and attends the Nuremberg trials at the invitation of Great Britain. VO visits GM in Washington and is startled by GM's belief that she can communicate with the spirit of Yin Yin. By September, GM is living in Monrovia, California, outside of Los Angeles (G.45).

1947: VO's *Testimonios III* is published by Editorial Sudamericana. GM suffers a diabetic attack, which lands her in the hospital (G.46); her sister and only surviving family member dies this year (G.49). She relocates to Santa Barbara, California, where she purchases a house.

1948–1949: GM travels to Mexico.

1949: China becomes Communist. NATO is established. Soviet Russia gets the atom bomb.

1950: VO's *Soledad sonora (Testimonios IV)* is published by Editorial Sudamericana. VO writes GM, asking her to contribute to the twentieth-anniversary issue of *Sur* (V.8). In June, President Truman commits U.S. troops to Korea.

1951: GM moves to Italy, living first in Rapallo (G.48–50), then in Naples (G.51). In Argentina, literary awards to VO are coupled with increasing political harassment (V.10). In September, VO and *Sur* are targeted as "national traitors." During a visit to France, VO writes to GM and describes the political persecution in these terms: "The world is out of joint" (V.11), and herself as "heartsick" about Argentina (V.12). Writing from Naples, GM's letters indicate her awareness of the political situation: "Our countries are living a grotesque but nonetheless serious hysteria" and offers to help (G.52–57). Throughout the later part of the year, GM is working on *Poema de Chile* (G.54). In November, VO visits Berlin for the first time since the end of the war (V.13).

1952: In the early part of the year, VO and her sister Angélica travel to France and Italy. GM and VO have a short visit in Rome (G.58). Not long afterward, GM establishes her residence in New York.

LETTERS, PART 3

1953: GM by now is living in New York; signs of ill health are apparent throughout her writings (G.60 onward). In March, VO writes GM, suggesting that her mail is routinely intercepted and read. On April 15, two bombs explode in the Plaza de Mayo. Perón blames radical intellectuals and the oligarchy. From May 8 to June 2, VO is arrested by the Perón government and held in Buen Pastor Prison in Buenos Aires. After VO's release, she is unable to obtain a passport for two years; she tries to comply with GM's request for help with *Poema de Chile* (V.15–17; G.63–64). July 1953 brings a ceasefire in the Korean War. Despite invitations from Turin and the University of Puerto Rico, VO is still denied a passport (V.18–19). At the year's end, GM visits Cuba (G.66) for a conference on Martí.

1954: VO sends GM a copy of a poem in which Neruda mocks her (V.21; G.68). In September, GM makes a month-long official visit to Chile, accompanied by Doris Dana (G.70–72, 74–75). Enormous crowds greet her everywhere. GM invites VO to join her, but the government's refusal to grant VO a passport renders her unable to travel outside of Argentina (G.72; V.25–26).

1955: GM continues working on *Poema de Chile* throughout the spring, although her health is clearly failing (G.73–75). VO asks her to intervene with the Argentine government so that she might be granted a passport, and GM does so, but without success (V.27–28; G.76). The Perón government is overthrown later this year. VO declines to accept the ambassadorship to India (V.31–33). *Sur* ends the year with a substantial economic deficit (V.33).

1956: Twenty-fifth anniversary of *Sur's* publication (V.35). Economic straits keep VO from traveling outside Argentina until the middle of the year (V.34). She goes to Europe first (V.36), then to the United States. In December, VO visits GM, who is near death in a Hempstead, Long Island, hospital.

1957: After GM's death in January, a mass is celebrated in New York's St. Patrick's Cathedral. GM's body is brought in state to Chile for three days of official mourning. A special tomb, paid for by subscription of the Chilean Teachers' and Writers' Unions, is constructed for her in Montegrande, Valley of Elqui.

In March, VO publishes an essay-elegy to GM in *La Nación* (see appendix, "And Lucila Who Spoke Like a River"). In June VO writes a long bio-essay about her friendship with GM, based primarily on their correspondence (see appendix, "GM in Her Letters").

Doris Dana, the poet's executor, publishes Mistral's unfinished *Poema de Chile* ten years after the poet's death. During the 1970s, volumes collecting her hundreds of essays begin to be published. In 1982, microfilms of her unpublished writings are deposited with the Organization of American States, the Library of Congress, and the National Library of Chile. Collections of her poetry and correspondence circulate throughout the Spanish-speaking world.

VO survives another twenty-three years. She will publish six more volumes of *Testimonios*, write her memoirs (six posthumous vols.), and publish numerous other essays. In 1977, she is elected the first woman member of the Argentine Academy of Letters. *Sur* endures past her death as a special issues magazine, a publishing house, and a foundation.

Biographical Dictionary

Acheson, Dean (1893–1971). Lawyer, writer, U.S. diplomat. Prior to and during his service as U.S. secretary of state from 1949 to 1953, Acheson helped create and administer the Marshall Plan for the post–World War II rebuilding of Europe.

Aguirre Cerda, Pedro (1879–1941). Writer, educator, lawyer, and president of Chile (1938–1941), elected by the "Popular Front," a coalition of radicals and moderate leftists. Aguirre Cerda and his wife, Juana, befriended GM during her years in Los Andes, Chile, 1912–1918. He helped GM's career with appointments in Punta Arenas, Temuco, and Santiago, and the campaign to award GM the Nobel Prize began during his presidency. He died in office in 1941.

Alberini, Coriolano (1886–1960). Italian/Argentine professor, philosopher, and director of the *Revista de la Universidad de Buenos Aires*.

Alessandri Palma, Arturo (1868–1950). President of Chile, first in 1920–1924, representing the Radical Party; again in 1925; and for a third term in 1932–1938, this time representing the Conservatives. Known as "El León de Tarapacá" because of his origins in the desert north, he was president in 1933 when the Chilean legislature passed a bill making GM special consul (2nd class), with the right to choose her own residence.

Alvarez Quintero, Joaquín (1873–1944) and Serafín (1871–1938); brothers. Spanish dramatists specializing in comedy of local life in Andalusia.

Arciniegas, Germán (1900–1999). Colombian author and diplomat who wrote extensively about Latin American history and Europe's role in the Americas. Among his more than fifty books are *Este pueblo de América* (1945), *Entre la libertad y el miedo* (1952), *El continente de los siete colores* (1965), and *América en Europa* (1975).

Baeza, Ricardo (1890?–1956). Spanish author, translator, diplomat; Spanish ambassador to Chile in 1930s before the defeat of the Republic. He went to live in Argentina after the Spanish Civil War. A frequent translator of VO's writings in French, he was also on the editorial board of *Sur*.

Belaúnde Terry, Fernando (1912–). President of Peru (1963–1968 and 1980–1985), architect, and university professor.

Benavente, Jacinto (1866–1954). Spanish dramatist and satirist, winner of the Nobel Prize in literature in 1922.

Bergamín, José (1895–1983). Spanish writer, editor, and member of the Spanish Republican delegation to the Institute for Intellectual Cooperation conference. The Spanish Civil War pushed Bergamín into exile.

Bollo, Sarah (1904–1987). Uruguayan poet, literary critic, and literary historian.

Bonnet, Henri (1888–1978). French diplomat who worked with the League of Nations until the outbreak of World War II.

Braga, Dominique (dates not known). French essayist and head of the Institute for Intellectual Cooperation, predecessor of UNESCO. As the holder of a Brazilian passport, he took refuge in Petrópolis, Brazil, during World War II.

Brecht, Bertolt (1898–1956). German playwright and ardent Socialist whose plays include "Mother Courage and Her Children," "Galileo," and "The Caucasian Chalk Circle."

Brunet, Marta (1901–1967). Chilean author of regionalist fiction; designated consul in La Plata, Argentina, in 1939.

Caillois, Roger (1913–1978). French sociologist, intellectual, and writer. Caught in Buenos Aires when war broke out in France, he worked with Ocampo and others to make Buenos Aires an important center for French refugee artists and intellectuals. Following his return to France after the war, he was instrumental in publicizing Latin American literature in Europe.

Cantiló, José María (1877–1953). Argentine diplomat. As minister for foreign relations, he sought to establish closer ties with Chile, and in 1940 he proposed moving Argentina from a "neutral" to a "non-belligerent" status with respect to the war in Europe.

Carril, Delia del (1884–1989). Argentine-born painter, married to poet and diplomat Pablo Neruda from 1934 to 1954, following his separation from his first wife. Delia del Carril had many close friends in common with VO.

Chacel, Rosa (1898–1994). Spanish novelist and frequent contributor to *Sur*. Forced into exile following her service as a nurse to Spanish Republican troops during the civil war, she moved first to France, then to Buenos Aires during World War II. She subsequently lived in Rio de Janeiro, New York, and Madrid.

Claudel, Paul (1868–1955). French poet, playwright, and diplomat; an important leader of the French Catholic Renaissance in the first half of the twentieth century.

Cosío Villegas, Daniel (1990–1976). Mexican historian and politician who, with his wife, Ema, befriended GM during her first residence in Mexico, in 1922–1924, when DCV and GM both worked for José Vasconcelos to reform the Mexican national education system.

Dana, Doris (1923–). U.S. writer who joined Gabriela Mistral as a traveling companion in Mexico in late 1949. They subsequently lived together in Italy and then Rosalyn Harbor, New York, until Mistral's death in January 1957.

Darío, Rubén (1867–1916). Nicaraguan poet, journalist, and diplomat; founder of the "modernismo" movement, which was highly influential in both Latin America and Spain.

Díaz Arrieta, Hernán (pseud. "Alone"; 1891–1984). Chilean writer, lead literary and cultural critic for Santiago's *El Mercurio*, and also a contributor to *La Nación*. His friendship with GM dated from 1915; he later visited her in Italy, in the 1950s.

Díez Canedo, Enrique (1879–1944). Spanish poet, critic, translator, journalist, and diplomat. Through the PEN Club, he arranged for GM to meet leading Spanish intellectuals during her first visit to Europe, in 1924. As an ambassador from Republican Spain to Argentina, he returned to Spain at the start of the civil war. Following the war, he lived in exile in Mexico.

Drieu la Rochelle, Pierre (1893–1945). French novelist, dramatist, and essayist who moved from Dadaism to Communism and, by 1934, aligned with Fascism. Under the German occupation of France, he directed the openly pro-Nazi magazine *Nouvelle Revue Française*. He committed suicide toward the end of the war.

Duhamel, Georges (1884–1966). French novelist, physician, literary critic, playwright, and member of the French Academies of Letters and of Sciences; also active in the Institute for Intellectual Cooperation. *Sur* published his work. His wife, Blanche Albane, was an actress.

Dujovne, León (1899–?). Argentine writer on philosophy and translator from medieval Hebrew, affiliated with *Sur*.

Echeverría Bello de Larraín, Inés (pseud. "Iris"; 1868–1949). Chilean essayist, travel writer, and novelist who helped organize the "Club de Señoras," one of the earliest women's self-improvement groups in Chile, in the early twentieth century. Her friendship with GM began when the poet initiated a correspondence with her in 1913.

Entwistle, William J. (1896–1952). Scots/English scholar of the Spanish Golden Age, succeeded Salvador de Madariaga as Professor and Chair of Spanish literature at Oxford. GM knew him as a colleague from the Institute for Intellectual Cooperation.

Eyzaguirre Gutiérrez, Jaime (1908–1968). Chilean philosopher trained in law who became a leading historian of Chile. He founded and directed the magazine *Estudios* (1932–1957).

Fabra, Pompeu (1868–1948). Catalan mathematician, engineer, and university professor who directed the creation of the first authoritative dictionaries and grammars of the Catalan language.

Fani (short for "Estefanía") (18??–1949). Estefanía Alvarez was a Spanish-born maid who entered the Ocampo household in 1907 or so and was "given" to VO by her parents following her marriage. Fani usually traveled with VO and was with her for forty-two years.

Focillon, Henri (1881–1943). French professor of art history and affiliate of the Institute for Intellectual Cooperation. Exiled by World War II, Focillon was at Yale from late 1940 until his death in 1943.

Frank, Waldo (1889–1967). North American leftist writer and journalist who made several very successful lecture tours of South America and befriended numerous writers there, including Ocampo and Mistral. Eduardo Mallea was his translator during his first lecture tour to Argentina in 1929.

Godoy, Juan Miguel. See "Yin Yin."

González Tuñón, Amparo (dates not known). Argentine friend of VO, from a literary family: her brothers Raúl and Enrique were both poets and novelists.

González Videla, Gabriel (1898–1980). President of Chile (1946–1952), originally elected by a left-wing coalition. One of his first acts as president — under pressure from the United States, which was facing the onset of the Cold War — was to outlaw the Communist Party. This act sent Chilean poet Pablo Neruda, then a Communist Party senator, into exile.

Goyanarte, Juan (1901–1967). Argentine author and editor. He founded a publishing house in his own name in 1956 after being a managing director of SUR. He and VO had a falling out over his preference for sacrificing quality for profit.

Granada, Luis de (1504–1588). Spanish Dominican friar and author of numerous books of spiritual counsel. Pursued by the Inquisition for his unorthodox Catholicism.

Guéhenno, Jean (1890–1978). French writer and educator, largely self-educated, and a member of the French Resistance. His work appeared in *Sur*.

Guillén de Nicolau, Palma (1893–1975). Mexican diplomat, educator, and writer who first met GM during the latter's first residence in Mexico, from

1922 to 1924. The two women subsequently kept in close touch in Europe, sharing the task of caring for GM's nephew, "Yin Yin," from 1925 to 1943.

Güiraldes, Ricardo (1886–1927). Argentine novelist, author of the classic gaucho novel *Don Segundo Sombra*. Güiraldes was a close friend of various members of the Ocampo family, including VO.

"H.D." (Hilda Doolittle; 1886–1961). U.S. poet, one of the best-known exponents of "imagism," and author of the alternative epic *Helen in Egypt*. H.D. lived most of her adult life as an expatriate in Europe, alongside her lover Bryher.

Haya de la Torre, Victor Raúl (1895–1979). Peruvian founder of the anti-imperialist movement known as "Aprismo," from the APRA (Alianza Popular Revolucionaria Americana) Party.

Ibáñez del Campo, Carlos (1877–1960). Military leader and president of Chile (1927–1931 and 1952–1958).

Ibarbourou, Juana de (1895–1979). Uruguayan poet, author of several volumes of poetry as well as books for children. She was elected to the Uruguayan Academy and won the National Prize for Literature. Because of her work's popularity, she was known as "Juana de América." Ibarbourou and Mistral (along with Alfonsina Storni) met and worked together in Montevideo in January of 1938.

Imaz, Eugene (1900–1951). Basque/Spanish writer, secretary of the Junta de la Cultura España, affiliated with the Republicans, and director of the magazine *Cruz y Raya*. Imaz was later exiled to Mexico, where he was a university professor.

Kent, Victoria (1898–1987). First woman lawyer in Spain, representative in Congress, and General Director of Prisons. The Spanish Civil War forced her into exile in 1939, first to France, where she assisted in smuggling out refugees, then to Mexico and ultimately to New York, where she worked for the United Nations.

Keyserling, Hermann (1880–1946). Russo-German author and philosopher who founded the School of Wisdom in Darmstadt. He and VO met in Europe in 1929 and had a stormy literary relationship.

Labarca Hubertson, Amanda (1886–1975). Chilean writer, educator, Radical Party political activist, and co-organizer of women's reading groups. Though Labarca was initially friendly with Gabriela Mistral, the two women parted company in 1915, and GM subsequently regarded her as a rival and enemy.

Larguía, Susana (dates not known). Argentine women's rights activist and friend of VO, co-founder of the Argentine Women's Union in 1936. She petitioned for women's suffrage in 1938 and was imprisoned with VO under Perón in 1953.

Latorre, Mariano (1886–1955). Chilean novelist from Maule, inclined to realism and depiction of the countryside.

Laval, Pierre (1883–1945). French politician who rose to power under the German occupation of France during World War II. In 1942 and 1943, he assisted in rounding up forced labor from France for the German war effort. Extradited from Franco's Spain, he was tried and executed as a collaborator in 1945.

León, Luis de (1527–1591). Spanish Augustinian friar, poet, and professor of Latin and Scripture at the University of Salamanca.

MacLeish, Archibald (1892–1982). U.S. poet, three-time Pulitzer Prize winner, and Librarian of Congress (1939–1944).

Maeztu, María de (1882–1948). Basque/Spanish writer, feminist, founder and director of the Residencia de Señoritas in Madrid, a professional educational institution. She received an honorary degree from Smith College in 1919 for her work in education.

Maeztu, Ramiro de (1874–1936). Basque/Spanish writer, member of Spain's "Generation of 1898," and follower of the monarchists. The brother of María de Maeztu, he was executed in Madrid amid the chaos of the first months of the Spanish Civil War.

Mallea, Eduardo (1903–1982). Argentine novelist and essayist whose works capture the existential malaise of urban Argentine society in the 1930s and 1940s. Close friend of VO; the two traveled together in Europe in the 1930s. He was editor in chief at *Sur* until September 1938.

Mallo, Maruja (1909–1995). Spanish painter and ceramicist. Sent into exile by the Spanish Civil War, she lived in Argentina from 1937 to 1964 and also exhibited her work in Uruguay, Chile, and Bolivia.

Mann, Thomas (1875–1955). German novelist and 1929 Nobel laureate for *Buddenbrooks*. Mann moved to Switzerland in 1933 when the Nazis began campaigning against him. He subsequently became a U.S. citizen in 1940. GM much admired Thomas Mann.

Marañón, Gregorio (1887–1960). Celebrated Spanish physician and writer with monarchist sympathies who went into exile from 1937 to 1943. Because he was neither Socialist, Communist, nor sympathetic to Basque or Catalan nationalists, he was allowed to return to Spain under Franco without penalty.

Maritain, Jacques (1882–1973). French Thomist philosopher and political thinker; a close friend and advisor to GM.

Maritain, Raissa (1883–1960). Russian/French writer and contemplative, married to Jacques Maritain.

Martí, José (1853–1895). Cuban poet, orator, journalist, diplomat, educator, and patriot who fought for Cuban independence from Spain. He was killed in a battle against the Spanish army in 1895.

Merezhkovsky, Dmitri (1865–1941). Russian novelist and biographer.

Mitre y Vedia, Mariano (1881–1958). Argentine historian and translator of English poets.

Molina, Emelina (1875–1947). Half sister to GM, died in La Serena, Chile, 28 March 1947.

Neruda, Pablo (1904–1973). Chilean poet, diplomat, and political figure. Born Neftalí Ricardo Reyes in Parral, he was raised in Temuco, Chile, where he first met then schoolteacher GM. Although they always acknowledged one another as colleagues in poetry and in diplomacy, they were not close friends. Pablo Neruda's books of poetry have been translated into many languages, and he received the Nobel Prize in 1971.

Nicolau d'Olwer, Luis (1888–1961). Catalan classicist, writer, and supporter of the Republic sent into exile by the Spanish Civil War. Following his marriage to Palma Guillén, Nicolau took refuge in Mexico, where he became an authority on pre-Columbian manuscripts.

Núñez del Prado, Marina (1910–1995). Bolivian sculptor, first woman elected to the Bolivian Academy of Art; she worked abroad for many years. Her work is modern, yet inspired by native themes.

Ocampo, Angélica (1891–1980). Argentine, younger sister of VO. Active in numerous charities, she and VO remained close confidantes throughout their lives.

Ocampo, Silvina (1903–1994). Argentine, writer of fiction and poetry; the youngest sister of VO. Married to author Adolfo Bioy Casares.

Oliver, María Rosa (1898–1977). Argentine writer and political activist, a lifelong friend of VO who joined her in starting the Argentine Women's Union in 1936 and as a member of the original *Sur* group. GM met María Rosa Oliver during a visit to VO's house in Mar del Plata. As María Rosa became prominent in the postwar left-wing international peace movement, she had an extended correspondence with GM.

Parra, Teresa de la (1889–1936). Venezuelan novelist born in France and resident there for many years. With her close friend the Cuban writer Lydia Cabrera, de la Parra met GM in France.

Pascoli, Giovanni (1855–1912). Italian poet, classicist, essayist. His subjects are primarily pastoral, with some historical and patriotic poems. Gabriele D'Annunzio called him "the last heir to Virgil."

Peixoto, Afrânio (1876–1947). Brazilian novelist and educator who was also trained in medicine; his many public charges included membership in the Brazilian Academy and in the Institute for Intellectual Cooperation.

Pilsudski, Józef (1867–1935). Polish general and politician who proclaimed an independent Polish republic, with himself as chief of state, in 1918.

Prezzolini, Giuseppe (1882–1982). Italian writer and teacher.

Reyes, Alfonso (1889–1959). Mexican diplomat, author, and philosopher. Lived extensively in Europe and wrote many important essays about the place of the Americas in the larger framework of universal culture. A close literary friend of both GM and VO.

Reyles, Carlitos (dates unknown). Uruguayan writer affiliated with *Sur*; son of the acclaimed Uruguayan novelist, also named Carlos Reyles (1868–1938).

Riefenstahl, Leni (born Helena Berthe Amalie; 1902–2002). German cinematographer known primarily for making Nazi propaganda films such as *The Triumph of the Will* (1935).

St. John of the Cross (1542–1591). Spanish poet and priest who also worked with St. Teresa of Avila in founding the Discalced Carmelites. Wrote lyric poems inspired by his mystical experiences while imprisoned by Calced friars in 1577–1578.

St. Teresa of Avila (1515–1582). Spanish nun, writer, and founder of the Discalced Carmelites. Her best-known works include *Camino de perfección* and *El castillo interior o Las moradas*, which explain her ascetic doctrine and spiritual experience.

Saleva, Consuelo. (19??–1968?). Puerto Rican teacher who accompanied GM on several of her travels, beginning in about 1937 to 1943, when, for reasons unknown, she moved out of the house she shared in Brazil with GM and Juan Miguel Godoy not long before Godoy's death. Connie (also Coni) returned to help nurse GM back to health in California in 1947 (G.46). They subsequently traveled together in Mexico in 1948–1949, after which the friendship apparently fell apart, and Connie seems to have returned to Puerto Rico.

Salinas, Pedro (1891–1951). Spanish poet. He worked at various universities throughout Spain and Europe until the civil war forced him into exile in the United States. He subsequently taught at Wellesley, Johns Hopkins, and the University of Puerto Rico.

Salotti, Marta (1889–1980). Argentine educator and author of children's stories who was a mutual friend of VO and GM.

Sarmiento, Domingo Faustino (1811–1888). President of Argentina (1868–1874); writer, best known for *Facundo o Civilización y barbarie*; and educational reformer. A close friend of VO's grandparents, he frequently visited the Ocampo households.

Steiner, Rudolf (1861–1925). Austro-Slovenian founder of anthroposophy, the "science of spirit," which originated among German followers of the theosophist Helena Petrovna Blavatasky.

Storni, Alfonsina (1892–1938). Argentine writer of poetry, drama, and journalism who corresponded with Gabriela Mistral beginning in 1920.

Stravinsky, Igor (1882–1971). Russian-born U.S. composer of operas, ballets, orchestral and instrumental music. VO performed "Perséphone" under his baton on several occasions in South America and Europe and remained friends with him until his death.

Torre, Guillermo de (1900–1971). Spanish-Argentine literary critic, historian, and leading authority of the avant-garde who contributed regularly to *Sur, La Nación*, and *Crítica*.

Torres Bodet, Jaime (1902–1974). Mexican diplomat and writer of poetry and fiction who, with GM, participated in the reform of the Mexican educational system in 1922–1924. From 1948 to 1952, Torres Bodet was the second director general of UNESCO, whose roots can be traced to the Institute for Intellectual Cooperation, founded in 1925.

Unamuno, Miguel de (1864–1936). Basque/Spanish philosopher, writer, and professor of Greek at the Universidad de Salamanca, Spain. He was among the writers who petitioned the Chilean legislature on GM's behalf in 1933, so that she received a consular post that permitted her the income to live outside of Chile.

Valéry, Paul (1871–1945). French poet and essayist. Despite GM's objections, Valéry was paid by the Chilean government to provide a foreword for a book of her poems translated into French. The publication was instrumental in Mistral's being awarded the Nobel Prize in 1945.

Vargas, Getúlio (1883–1954). President of Brazil (1930–1945 and 1950–1954). Trained as a doctor.

Vasconcelos, José (1882–1959). Mexican writer, educator, and statesman. He worked to reform the Mexican national education system under President Alvaro Obregón in 1920–1924, and he was the author of a number of controversial books, including *La raza cósmica* and *Indología*, as well as a four-volume autobiography. He unsuccessfully ran for president of Mexico in 1929.

Vyshinsky, Andrey Yanuaryevich (1883–1954). Soviet foreign minister during the early 1950s who attacked the Marshall Plan as U.S. imperialism.

"Yin Yin," nickname for Juan Miguel Godoy (1925?–1943), nephew of Gabriela Mistral. He is thought to have been born in Barcelona to an Argentine half brother of GM and a Catalan woman, María Mendoza or Mendonza, who died of tuberculosis shortly afterward.

Zaldumbide, Gonzalo (1885–1965). Ecuadorian novelist, literary critic, diplomat, and friend of GM.

Zuloaga, Ignacio (1870–1945). Basque/Spanish avant-garde painter.

Zweig, Stefan (1881–1942). Austrian writer who, together with his second wife, sought refuge in Petrópolis, Brazil, during World War II. A pacifist and a Jew, Zweig was best known as a biographer, but he also wrote novels, poetry, and criticism. Depressed by the state of the German-speaking world, Zweig and his wife committed suicide on 23 February 1942.

Works Cited

GABRIELA MISTRAL: PUBLISHED CORRESPONDENCE

Antología mayor, Gabriela Mistral. Vol. 3: *Cartas,* ed. Luis Vargas Saavedra. Santiago: Lord Cochrane, 1992.

Boletín del Museo-Biblioteca en Vicuña y Epistolario de GM 1912-1918. Vicuña, Chile: Privately printed, 1983.

Cartas a Lydia Cabrera: Correspondencia inédita de Gabriela Mistral y Teresa de la Parra. Ed. Rosario Hiriart. Madrid: Torremozas, 1988.

Cartas de amor de Gabriela Mistral. Ed. Sergio Fernández Larraín. Santiago: Andrés Bello, 1978.

"Cartas de Gabriela Mistral a Amado Nervo." Ed. Juan Loveluck. *Revista iberoamericana* 36 (1970): 495-508.

"Cartas de Gabriela Mistral a Jaime Eyzaguirre." Ed. Luis Vargas Saavedra. *Mapocho* 23 (spring 1970): 19-29.

En batalla de sencillez: Epistolario de Gabriela Mistral a Pedro Prado. Ed. Luis Vargas Saavedra, M. Ester Martínez Sanz, Regina Valdés Bowen. Santiago: Dolmen/ Universitaria, 1993.

Epistolario: Cartas a Eugenio Labarca (1915-1916). Introduction and notes by Raúl Silva Castro. Santiago: Anales de la Universidad de Chile, 1957.

Epistolario de Gabriela Mistral y Eduardo Barrios. Ed. Luis Vargas Saavedra. Santiago: Centro de Estudios de Literatura Chilena, 1988.

Gabriela anda La Habana . . . a medio caminar el olvido y la memoria. Ed. Jorge Benítez G. Santiago: LOM, 1998.

Gabriela Mistral and Joaquín García Monge: Una correspondencia inédita. Ed. Magda Arce with Eugenio García Carrillo. Santiago: Andrés Bello, 1989.

Memorias (1911-1934) y correspondencias con Gabriela Mistral y Jacques Maritain. Eduardo Frei Montalva. Santiago: Planeta, 1989.

El otro suicida de Gabriela Mistral. Ed. Luis Vargas Saavedra. Santiago: Universidad Católica de Chile, 1985.

Tan de usted: Epistolario de Gabriela Mistral con Alfonso Reyes. Ed. Luis Vargas Saavedra. Santiago: Universidad Católica de Chile, 1991.

Vuestra Gabriela: Cartas inéditas de Gabriela Mistral a los Errázuriz Echenique y Tomic Errázuriz. Ed., preface, and notes by Luis Vargas Saavedra. Santiago: Zig-Zag, 1995.

GABRIELA MISTRAL: POETRY

Desolación: Poemas. New York: Instituto de las Españas, 1922.

Lagar. Santiago: Editorial del Pacífico, 1954.

Poema de Chile. Barcelona: Pomaire, 1967.

Poesías completas. Ed. Margaret Bates; intro. by Esther de Cáceres. Madrid: Aguilar, 1958.

Tala. Buenos Aires: SUR, 1938. Reprint, Santiago: Andrés Bello, 1979.

Ternura. Madrid: Saturnino Calleja, 1925; rev. Buenos Aires: Espasa-Calpe, 1945.

GABRIELA MISTRAL: ESSAYS

"Alfonsina Storni" (1953). In *Recados para hoy y mañana: Textos inéditos.* Vol. 1, ed. Luis Vargas Saavedra, 204-206. Santiago: Sudamericana, 1999.

"Algo sobre Eduardo Mallea" (1940). In *Recados para hoy y mañana: Textos inéditos.* Vol. 1, ed. Luis Vargas Saavedra, 132-137. Santiago: Sudamericana, 1999." Algunos semblantes: Alfonsina Storni." In *Gabriela piensa en . . . ,* ed. Roque Esteban Scarpa, 37-39. Santiago: Andrés Bello, 1978.

"Castilla." In *Gabriela Mistral anda por el mundo,* ed. Roque Esteban Scarpa, 203-213. Santiago: Andrés Bello, 1978.

"Centenario por el nacimiento de José Martí." In *Gabriela anda La Habana,* ed. Jorge Benítez G., 111-116. Santiago: LOM, 1998.

"Cinco años de destierro de Don Miguel Unamuno." In *Gabriela piensa en . . . ,* ed. Roque Esteban Scarpa, 245-249. Santiago: Andrés Bello, 1978.

"Colofón con cara de excusa." In *Ternura,* 165-172. Argentina: Espasa-Calpe, 1945.

"Como escribo." In *Páginas en prosa,* ed. Jose Pereira Rodríguez, 1-3. Buenos Aires: Kapelusz, 1962, 1965.

"El divorcio lingüístico de nuestra América." *Sur* 46 (July 1938): 85-88.

"Emilia Brontë: La familia del Reverendo Brontë." In *Gabriela piensa en . . . ,* ed. Roque Esteban Scarpa, 25-36. Santiago: Andrés Bello, 1978.

"Enrique Díez Canedo." In *Gabriela piensa en . . . ,* ed. Roque Esteban Scarpa, 260-263. Santiago: Andrés Bello, 1978.

"Gente americana: Teresa de la Parra." In *Gabriela piensa en . . . ,* ed. Roque Esteban Scarpa, 40-48. Santiago: Andrés Bello, 1978.

"La lengua de Martí" (1934). In *Gabriela anda La Habana,* ed. Jorge Benítez G., 65-82. Santiago: LOM, 1998.

"Marina Núñez del Prado." In *Gabriela Mistral. La tierra tiene la actitud de una mujer,* ed. Pedro Pablo Zegers, 280-285. Santiago: Red Internacional del Libro, 1998.

"Mi estimado compañero José Miguel Ferrer" (1940). In *Recados para hoy y mañana: Textos inéditos.* Vol. 1, ed. Luis Vargas Saavedra, 142-147. Santiago: Sudamericana, 1999.

"Mi experiencia con la Biblia" (1938). In *Prosa religiosa de Gabriela Mistral,* ed. Luis Vargas Saavedra, 49-56. Santiago: Andrés Bello, 1978.

"Página para Pedro Salinas" (1928). In *Gabriela piensa en . . . ,* ed. Roque Esteban Scarpa, 254-257. Santiago: Andrés Bello, 1978.

"La palabra maldita." *Repertorio americano* 48 (January 1951): 2. Reprinted in *Gabriela Mistral, escritos políticos,* ed. Jaime Quezada, 159-161. Santiago: Fondo de Cultura, 1994.

"Sarmiento en Aconcagua." In *Gabriela piensa en . . .* , ed. Roque Esteban Scarpa, 177-183. Santiago: Andrés Bello, 1978.

"Los 'Versos sencillos' de José Martí." In *Gabriela anda La Habana*, ed. Jorge Benítez G., 83-96. Santiago: LOM, 1998.

"Victoria Kent." *Sur* (May 1936). Reprinted in *Gabriela piensa en . . .* , ed. Roque Esteban Scarpa, 75-83. Santiago: Andrés Bello, 1978.

"Victoria Ocampo." In *Gabriela piensa en . . .* , ed. Roque Esteban Scarpa, 49-56. Santiago: Andrés Bello, 1978.

GABRIELA MISTRAL: COLLECTIONS

Gabriela anda por el mundo. Ed. Roque Esteban Scarpa. Santiago: Andrés Bello, 1978.

Gabriela Mistral, escritos políticos. Ed. Jaime Quesada. Mexico City: Fondo de Cultura Económica, 1994.

Gabriela piensa en . . . Ed. Roque Esteban Scarpa. Santiago: Andrés Bello, 1978.

Lecturas para mujeres. Mexico City: Ministerio de Educación, 1924. Reprint, Mexico City: Porrúa, 1977.

Páginas en prosa. Buenos Aires: Kapelusz, 1962, 1965.

Prosa religiosa de GM. Ed. Luis Vargas Saavedra. Santiago: Andrés Bello, 1978.

Recados para hoy y mañana: Textos inéditos. Vol. 1, ed. Luis Vargas Saavedra. Santiago: Sudamericana, 1999.

La tierra tiene la actitud de una mujer. Ed. Pedro Pablo Zegers. Santiago: Red Internacional del Libro, 1998.

VICTORIA OCAMPO: PUBLISHED CORRESPONDENCE

Cartas a Angélica y otros. Buenos Aires: Sudamericana, 1997.

Cartas echadas: Correspondencia, 1927-1959, Alfonso Reyes, Victoria Ocampo. Ed. Héctor Perea. Mexico City: Universidad Autónoma Metropolitana, Dirección de Difusión Cultural, Departamento Editorial, 1983.

Correspondencia (1939-1978): Victoria Ocampo/Roger Caillois. Ed. Odile Felgine, Laura Ayerza de Castilho, and Juan Alvarez Márquez; trans. Federico Vilegas. Buenos Aires: Sudamericana, 1999.

Obieta, Alfonso de. *Victoria Ocampo.* Buenos Aires: Corregidor, 2000. [Contains VO-Obieta correspondence, Chapter 5, 121-177]

VICTORIA OCAMPO: ESSAYS

"Albert Camus." In *Testimonios VI*, 183-188. Buenos Aires: SUR, 1963.

"Alfonso Reyes." In *Testimonios VI*, 180-183. Buenos Aires: SUR, 1963.

"El capítulo de la correspondencia." *Clarín* (Buenos Aires), 22 April 1971: N.p.

"Carta a Waldo Frank." *Sur* 1 (summer 1931): 7-10.

"Cartas abiertas: De Victoria Ocampo a José Bergamín." *Sur* 32 (May 1937): 67-74.

"Fani." *Vogue*, 1 March 1953, 184-185.

"Gabriela Mistral en sus cartas." In *Testimonios VI*, 59-82. Buenos Aires: SUR, 1963.

"Gabriela Mistral y el premio Nobel." In *Testimonios III*, 171-181. Buenos Aires: Sudamericana, 1946. Translated by Doris Meyer in *Victoria Ocampo: Against the Wind
and the Tide*, 246-251. New York: George Braziller, 1979. Reprint, Austin: University of Texas Press, 1990.

"Gandhiji." *Sur* 336-337 (January-December 1975). [Special issue]

"Huxley en Centroamérica." In *Testimonios I*, 359-384. Madrid: Revista de Occidente,
1935. Translated into English by VO in *Aldous Huxley (1894-1963), A Memorial Volume*, ed. Julian Huxley, 73-85. London: Chatto and Windus, 1965.

"Malandanzas de una autodidacta." In *Testimonios V*, 15-26. Buenos Aires: SUR, 1957.
Translated into English by Doris Meyer in *Contemporary Women Authors of Latin
America: New Translations*, ed. Doris Meyer and Margarite Fernández Olmos,
217-225. Brooklyn, NY: Brooklyn College Press, 1983.

"María de Maeztu." Trans. Doris Meyer. In Doris Meyer, *Victoria Ocampo: Against the
Wind and the Tide*, 212-216. New York: George Braziller, 1979. Reprint, Austin:
University of Texas Press, 1990.

"Las memorias de Victoria Ocampo." *Life en español*, 17 September 1962, 62-76; 1 October 1962, 45-53.

"Memories of Virginia Woolf." *Vogue*, 1 September 1946, 202, 250-256.

"Palabras francesas." In *Testimonios I*, 19-41. Madrid: Revista de Occidente, 1935.

"Pierre Drieu la Rochelle: Enero de 1893-marzo 1945." In *Testimonios III*, 153-158.
Buenos Aires: Sudamericana, 1946.

"Problemas de la traducción." *Sur* (January-December 1976): 338-339.

"Roger Caillois." In *Testimonios II*, 406-414. Buenos Aires: SUR, 1941.

"South America: Merecemos la ignorancia de Europa?" In *Domingos en Hyde Park*,
27-48. Buenos Aires: SUR, 1936.

"Vísperas de guerra." *Sur* 61 (October 1939): 7-19.

VICTORIA OCAMPO: BOOKS

338171 T.E.(Lawrence of Arabia). Trans. David Garnett. New York: E. P. Dutton, 1963.

Autobiografía (I-VI). Buenos Aires: SUR, 1979-1984.

De Francesca a Beatrice. Madrid: Revista de Occidente, 1924.

Diálogo con Mallea. Buenos Aires: SUR, 1969.

Domingos en Hyde Park. Buenos Aires: SUR, 1936.

Emily Brontë (terra incognita). Buenos Aires: SUR, 1938.

Lawrence de Arabia y otros ensayos. Madrid: Aguilar, 1951.

San Isidro, con un poema de Silvina Ocampo. Buenos Aires: SUR, 1941.

Soledad sonora. Buenos Aires: Sudamericana, 1950.

Tagore en las barrancas de San Isidro. Buenos Aires: SUR, 1961.

Testimonios I. Madrid: Revista de Occidente, 1935.

Testimonios II. Buenos Aires: SUR, 1941.

Testimonios III. Buenos Aires: Sudamericana, 1946.

Testimonios V. Buenos Aires: SUR, 1957.

Testimonios VI. Buenos Aires: SUR, 1963.
Testimonios VIII. Buenos Aires: SUR, 1971.
Le vert paradis. Buenos Aires: SUR, 1944.
El viajero y una de sus sombras: Keyserling en mis memorias. Buenos Aires: Sudamericana, 1951.
Virginia Woolf en su diario. Buenos Aires: SUR, 1954.

ADDITIONAL BOOKS AND ARTICLES

Alegría, Ciro. *Gabriela Mistral íntima.* Ed. Dora Varona, vda. de Alegría. Lima: Universo, 1968.
Alegría, Fernando. *Genio y figura de Gabriela Mistral.* Buenos Aires: Universitaria, 1966.
"Alone" [Hernán Díaz Arrieta]. *Cuatro grandes de la literatura chilena durante el Siglo XX.* Santiago: Zig-Zag, 1963.
———. *Pretérito imperfecto (Memorias).* Ed. Alfonso Calderón. Santiago: Nascimento, 1976.
Alvarez Gómez, Oriel. *Jerónimo Godoy V., padre de Gabriela.* N.p., n.d., 20 pages.
Arce, Magda, and Gaston von demme Bussche, eds. *Proyecto preservación y difusión del legado literario de Gabriela Mistral.* Santiago: Zig-Zag, Organization of American States, 1993.
Arce de Vázquez, Margot. *Gabriela Mistral: The Poet and Her Work.* Trans. Helene Masslo Anderson. New York: NYU Press, 1964.
Auden, Wystan Hugh. "In Memory of W. B. Yeats." *New Republic,* 8 March 1939, 123.
Ayala, Francisco. *Recuerdos y olvidos. 2. El exilio.* Madrid: Alianza, 1982.
Ayerza de Castilho, Laura, and Odile Felgine. *Victoria Ocampo: Intimidades de una visionaria.* Buenos Aires: Sudamericana, 1992.
Bernardete, M. J., ed. *Waldo Frank en América Hispana.* New York: Instituto de las Españas en los Estados Unidos, 1930.
Blanco, José Joaquín. *Se llamaba Vasconcelos: Una evocación crítica.* Mexico City: Fondo de Cultura Económica, 1977, 1993.
Brunet, Marta. *Obras completas de Marta Brunet.* Santiago: Zig-Zag, 1962.
Callan, Edward. *Auden: A Carnival of Intellect.* New York: Oxford University Press, 1983.
Concha, Jaime. *Gabriela Mistral.* Madrid: Júcar, 1986.
Délano, Luis Enrique. *Sobre todo Madrid.* Santiago: Universitaria, 1970.
Desanti, Dominique. *Drieu la Rochelle ou le séducteur mystifié.* Paris: Flammarion, 1978.
Figueroa, Virgilio. *La divina Gabriela.* Santiago: Impreso El Esfuerzo, 1933.
Fiol-Matta, Licia. "Gabriela Mistral: Maestra de América." In *Entiendes: Queer Readings, Hispanic Writings,* ed. Emilie L. Bergmann and Paul Julian Smith, 201-227. Durham: Duke University Press, 1995.
———. *A Queer Mother for the Nation: The State and Gabriela Mistral.* Minneapolis: University of Minnesota Press, 2002.
———. "'Race Woman': Reproducing the Nation in Gabriela Mistral." *GLQ, A Journal of Gay and Lesbian Studies* 6, no. 4 (2000): 491-527.

Franco, Jean. *Critical Passions.* Ed. Mary Louise Pratt and Kathleen Newman. Durham: Duke University Press, 2001.

Frank, Waldo D. *The Rediscovery of America.* New York: Charles Scribner's, 1929.

Frei Montalva, Eduardo. *Memorias (1911-1934) y correspondencias con Gabriela Mistral y Jacques Maritain.* Santiago: Planeta, 1989.

The Gabriela Mistral Collection, Barnard College Library. New York: Barnard College, 1978.

Gascón-Vera, Elena. "Gabriela Mistral y España: Colonialismo y esencialismo." *Taller de letras,* Número especial (Universidad Católica de Chile, 1996): 11-23.

Gazarian-Gautier, Marie-Lise. *Gabriela Mistral, the Teacher from the Valley of Elqui.* Chicago: Franciscan World Herald Press, 1975. Originally published as *GM, La maestra de Elqui,* Buenos Aires: Crespillo, n.d.

Gracián, Baltasar. *Pocket Mirror for Heroes* [El héroe y el discreto]. Trans. Christopher Maurer. New York: Doubleday, 1996.

Granada, Luis de. *Maravilla del mundo.* Ed. Pedro Salinas. Mexico City: Séneca, 1940.

Guillén de Nicolau, Palma. "Introducción." In *Lecturas para mujeres,* ed. Gabriela Mistral, vii-xii. Mexico City: Porrúa, 1977.

Horan, Elizabeth. "Las canciones de cuna de Federico García Lorca y Gabriela Mistral: Tradición literaria e historia cultural." With Ana Brenes García. *Letras peninsulares* 9, no. 2 (1996/1997): 219-237.

———. *Gabriela Mistral: An Artist and Her People.* Washington, D.C.: Organization of American States, 1994.

———. "Gabriela Mistral: Language Is the Only Homeland." In *A Dream of Light and Shadow: Portraits of Latin American Women Writers,* ed. Marjorie Agosín, 119-142. Albuquerque: University of New Mexico Press, 1995.

———. "Gabriel(a) Mistral's Alternative Identities 1906-1920." In *Reading and Writing the Ambiente: Queer Sexualities in Latino, Latin American, and Spanish Culture,* ed. Susana Chávez Silverman and Librada Hernández, 147-177. Madison: University of Wisconsin Press, 2000.

———. "Matrilineage, Matrilanguage: Gabriela Mistral's Intimate Audience." *Revista canadiense de estudios hispánicos* 14, no. 3 (1990): 447-457. Reprinted in *Twentieth-Century Spanish American Literature to 1960,* ed. David William Foster and Daniel Altamiranda, 85-95. New York: Garland, 1997.

———. "Santa Maestra Muerta: Body and Nation in Portraits of Gabriela Mistral." *Taller de Letras* (Universidad Católica de Chile) 25 (1997): 21-43.

———. "Sor Juana and Gabriela Mistral: Locations and Locutions of the Saintly Woman." *Chasqui: Revista de literatura latinoamericana* 25, no. 2 (1997): 89-103.

Index to Gabriela Mistral Papers on Microfilm (1912-1957). Washington, D.C.: Organization of American States, 1982.

Indice general de la revista Sur [Argentina] 1931-1954. Bibliographic Series No. 46. Washington, D.C.: Unión Panamericana, 1955.

Jrade, Cathy. *Modernismo, Modernity, and the Development of Spanish American Literature.* Austin: University of Texas Press, 1998.

Jurado, Alicia. "La amistad entre Gabriela Mistral y Victoria Ocampo." *Boletín de la Academia Argentina de Letras* 54, nos. 213-214 (July-December 1989): 523-561.

Kaminsky, Amy. "Essay, Gender, and Mestizaje: Victoria Ocampo and Gabriela Mistral." In *The Politics of the Essay: Feminist Perspectives*, ed. Ruth Ellen Boetcher Joeres and Elizabeth Mittman, 113-130. Bloomington: Indiana University Press, 1993.

Kent, Victoria. *Cuatro años en París (1940-1944).* Málaga: University of Málaga, 1997.

Keyserling, Hermann. *The Travel Diary of a Philosopher.* Vol. 1. Trans. J. Holroyd Reece. London: Jonathan Cape, 1925.

———. *The World in the Making.* New York: Harcourt, 1927.

King, John. *Sur: A Study of the Argentina Literary Journal and Its Role in the Development of a Culture, 1931-1970.* Cambridge: Cambridge University Press, 1986.

Klingenberg, Patricia. *Silvina Ocampo: Fantasies of the Feminine.* Lewisburg: Bucknell University Press, 1999.

Labara Hubertson, Amanda. "Letters to Gabriela Mistral." *Boletín Museo Gabriela Mistral de Vicuña* 5 (May 1984): 30-39.

Lawrence, T. E. *The Seven Pillars of Wisdom, a Triumph.* Garden City, N.Y.: Doubleday, Doran, 1935.

Lillo, Gastón, and J. Guillermo Renart, with Naín Nómez, eds. *Re-leer hoy a Gabriela Mistral: Mujer, historia y sociedad en América Latina.* Ottawa: University of Ottawa and Editorial Universidad de Santiago, 1997.

Loveluck, Juan. "Cartas de Gabriela Mistral a Amado Nervo." *Revista iberoamericana* 36 (1970): 495-508.

Loveman, Brian. *Chile: The Legacy of Hispanic Capitalism.* 2d ed. New York: Oxford University Press, 1988.

Lugones, Leopoldo. *Poemas solariegos.* Buenos Aires: Biblioteca Argentina de Buenas Ediciones Literarias, 1928.

Mallea, Eduardo. *Historia de una pasión argentina.* Buenos Aires: SUR, 1937.

Marchant, Elizabeth. *Critical Acts: Latin American Women and Cultural Criticism.* Gainesville: University Press of Florida, 1999.

Martí, José. *Nuestra América* (1891). Ed. José Antonio Michelena. Havana: Extramuros, 1991.

Masiello, Francine. *Beyond Civilization and Barbarism.* Lincoln: University of Nebraska Press, 1990.

Matamoros, Blas. *Genio y figura de Victoria Ocampo.* Buenos Aires: EUDEBA, 1986.

Mendes, Murilo. *Poemas escogidos.* Rosario, Argentina: La Ventana, 1976.

Meyer, Doris. "The Correspondence of Gabriela Mistral and Victoria Ocampo: Reflections on American Identity." *Journal of the Institute of Romance Studies* 4 (1996): 269-279. [In Spanish: "La correspondencia entre GM y VO: Reflexiones sobre la identidad americana." *Taller de letras* 24 (November 1996) (Revista de Literatura del Instituto de Letras, Universidad Católica de Chile).]

———. "The Early (Feminist) Essays of Victoria Ocampo." *Studies in Twentieth-Century Literature* 20 (winter 1996): 37-59.

————. "Letters and Lines of Correspondence in the Essays of Victoria Ocampo." *Inter-American Review of Bibliography* 17 (August 1992): 233-240.

————. "The Multiple Myths of Victoria Ocampo." *Revista/Review interamericana* (fall 1982): 385-392.

————. "Reciprocal Reflections: Specular Discourse and the Self-Authorizing Venture." In *Reinterpreting the Spanish American Essay: Women Writers of the 19th and 20th Centuries*, ed. Doris Meyer, 102-114. Austin: University of Texas Press, 1995.

————. *Victoria Ocampo: Against the Wind and the Tide.* New York: George Braziller, 1979. Reprint, Austin: University of Texas Press, 1990.

————. "Victoria Ocampo and Alfonso Reyes: Ulysses's Malady." *Studies in Twentieth-Century Literature* 24, no. 2 (summer 2000): 307-324.

————. "Victoria Ocampo and Spiritual Energy." In *A Dream of Light and Shadow*, ed. Marjorie Agosín, 55-73. Albuquerque: University of New Mexico Press, 1995.

————. "Victoria Ocampo, Argentine Identity, and the Landscape of the Essay." *Review: Latin American Literature and Arts* 48 (spring 1994): 58-64.

————, ed. *Rereading the Spanish American Essay: Translations of 19th and 20th Century Women's Essays.* Austin: University of Texas Press, 1995.

Neruda, Pablo. *Confieso que he vivido: Memorias.* Barcelona: Círculo de Lectores, 1974.

————. *España en el corazón: Himno a la gloria del pueblo en la guerra (1936-1937).* Santiago: Ercilla, 1937.

————. *Las uvas y el viento.* Santiago: Nascimento, 1954.

Ocampo, Silvina. *San Isidro, un poema de Silvina Ocampo y fotografías de Gustav Thorlicher.* Buenos Aires: SUR, 1941.

Oliver, María Rosa. Letter to Gabriela Mistral, 19 March 1947, Houghton Library Collection, Harvard University.

————. *Mundo, mi casa.* Buenos Aires: Sudamericana, 1970.

————. *La vida cotidiana.* Buenos Aires: Sudamericana, 1969.

Parra, Teresa de la. *Las memorias de Mamá Blanca.* Buenos Aires: Editorial Universidad de Buenos Aires, 1966.

Pratt, Mary Louise. *Imperial Eyes.* New York: Routledge, 1992.

————. "Women, Literature, and National Brotherhood." In *Women, Culture, and Politics in Latin America*, ed. Emilie Bergmann et al., 48-73. Berkeley: University of California Press, 1990.

Reyes, Alfonso. "Notas sobre la inteligencia de América." *Sur* 6 (September 1936): 7-15.

————. "Un paso de América." *Sur* 1 (summer 1931): 149-158.

————. "Utopías americanas." *Sur* 8 (January 1938): 7-16.

Rodig, Laura. "Presencia de Gabriela Mistral: Notas para un cuaderno de memorias." In *Homenaje a Gabriela Mistral*, 282-292. Santiago: Anales de la Universidad de Chile, 1957.

Rojo, Grinor. *Dirán que está en la Gloria (Mistral).* Santiago: Fondo de Cultura, 1997.

Rubio, Patricia. *Gabriela Mistral ante la crítica: Bibliografía anotada.* Santiago: Universitaria/Dirección de Bibliotecas, Archivos y Museos, 1995.

———. "Sobre el indigenismo y el mestizaje en la prosa de Gabriela Mistral" *Taller de letras* (Universidad Católica de Chile) 24 (1996): 25-40.

Samatán, Marta. *Gabriela Mistral, campesina del Valle de Elqui.* Buenos Aires: Instituto de Amigos del Libro Argentino, 1969.

Scarpa, Roque Esteban. *La desterrada en su patria: Gabriela Mistral en Magallanes 1918-1920.* Santiago: Nascimento, 1977.

Schneider, Luis Mario. *Gabriela Mistral: Itinerarios veracruzanos.* Xalapa: Universidad Veracruzana, 1991.

———. "Gabriela Mistral en México: Una devota del misionerismo vasconcelista." In *Re-leer hoy a Gabriela Mistral: Mujer, historia y sociedad en América Latina,* ed. Gastón Lillo and J. Guillermo Renart with Naín Nómez, 147-158. Ottawa: University of Ottawa and Editorial Universidad de Santiago, 1997.

Silva Castro, Raúl. *Producción de Gabriela Mistral de 1912 a 1918.* Santiago: Anales de la Universidad de Chile, 1957.

Spinola, Magdalena. *Gabriela Mistral: Huéspeda de honor de su patria.* Guatemala: Tipografía Nacional, 1968.

Stabb, Martin S. *In Quest of Identity: Patterns in the Spanish American Essay of Ideas (1890-1960).* Chapel Hill: University of North Carolina Press, 1967.

Steinman, Lisa Malinowski. *Made in America: Science, Technology, and American Modernist Poets.* New Haven: Yale University Press, 1987.

Torre, Guillermo de. *Tres conceptos de la literatura hispanoamericana.* Buenos Aires: Losada, 1963.

Torres Rioseco, Arturo. *Gabriela Mistral. Una profunda amistad; un dulce recuerdo.* Valencia: Castalia, 1962.

Vargas Saavedra, Luis. *Castilla, tajeada de sed como mi lengua.* Santiago: Universidad Católica de Chile, 2002.

———. "Hispanismo y antihispanismo en Gabriela Mistral." *Mapocho* 22 (winter 1970): 5-24.

———. "Once cartas a Jaime Eyzaguirre 1940-1946." *Mapocho* 23 (spring 1970): 19-29.

Vásquez, María Esther. *Victoria Ocampo.* Buenos Aires: Planeta, 1991.

Woodall, James. *Borges: A Life.* New York: Basic Books, 1997.

Woolf, Virginia. *A Room of One's Own.* London: Hogarth Press, 1929.

Writers Alliance. "Una declaración de la 'Alianza de Intelectuales de Chile para la Defensa de la Cultura' y su respuesta." *Sur* 8, no. 41 (February 1938): 79-85.

Zegers B., Pedro Pablo, ed. *Alone y los Premios Nacionales de Chile.* Santiago: Dirección Bibliotecas y Museos, 1992.

Zemborain, Lila. "Las resonancias de un nombre: Gabriela Mistral." *Revista iberoamericana* 66, no. 190 (January-March 2000): 147-161.

Index